"Strad" as a nickname based on the name of Stradivarius the maker of the most expensive and valuable violins in the world.

7 █ July 2014

VERSE BY VERSE

THE OLD
TESTAMENT

VOLUME TWO

Other volumes in the Verse by Verse series
by D. Kelly Ogden and Andrew C. Skinner

The Old Testament, volume 1: Genesis through 2 Samuel, Psalms

The Four Gospels
Acts through Revelation

The Book of Mormon, volume 1: 1 Nephi through Alma 29
The Book of Mormon, volume 2: Alma 30 through Moroni 10

VERSE BY VERSE

THE OLD TESTAMENT

VOLUME TWO
1 KINGS THROUGH MALACHI

D. KELLY OGDEN
ANDREW C. SKINNER

DESERET
BOOK

SALT LAKE CITY, UTAH

Library of Congress Cataloging-in-Publication Data

Ogden, D. Kelly (Daniel Kelly), 1947– author.
  Verse by verse : the Old Testament /D. Kelly Ogden and Andrew C. Skinner.
    volumes cm
  Includes bibliographical references and index.
  ISBN 978-1-60907-591-0 (hardbound : alk. paper; v. 1)
  ISBN 978-1-60907-592-7 (hardbound : alk. paper; v. 2)
  1. Bible. Old Testament—Commentaries. I. Skinner, Andrew C., 1951– author.
II. Title.
  BS1151.52.O33 2013
  221.7—dc23   2013022790

Printed in the United States of America
R.R. Donnelley, Crawfordsville, IN

10   9   8   7   6   5   4   3   2   1

he was our neighbor in the old 73th ward. we prove that he was given to BYU students awards.

Ellis T. Rasmussen
Old Testament scholar, mentor, and friend
1915–2011

Ellis T. Rasmussen was one of the great Old Testament scholars of The Church of Jesus Christ of Latter-day Saints. For thirty years Dr. Rasmussen taught Old Testament and other scripture at Brigham Young University, where he also served as chairman of the department of Ancient Scripture and as dean of Religious Instruction. He wrote numerous books and articles, guided study tours to the Holy Land and other lands of the Near East, and served with his wife, Oda Fonnesbeck Rasmussen, as special representatives of the Church and Brigham Young University in the Holy Land. Perhaps his greatest contribution to the Church, however, came through his role from 1972 to 1981 in supervising, under the direction of apostles Thomas S. Monson, Boyd K. Packer, and Bruce R. McConkie, the preparation of the Latter-day Saint edition of the Bible published in 1979 and the 1981 editions of the three other standard works of the Church.

We pay tribute to Dr. Ellis T. Rasmussen and express our gratitude for his life's work.

CONTENTS

CONTENTS

PREFACE

The series Verse by Verse, which began with *The Four Gospels,* *Acts through Revelation,* and *The Book of Mormon,* continues here with *The Old Testament,* a commentary that is one book in two volumes.

This is the second of those two volumes. The division between them reflects the way in which courses on the Old Testament are structured in the institutes of religion of The Church of Jesus Christ of Latter-day Saints and on the campuses of Brigham Young University: Genesis through 2 Samuel, together with Psalms; and 1 Kings through Malachi. The introduction to the commentary appears in the first volume. Each volume contains its own table of contents, preface, list of sources, and index. Occasionally, cross-references between the two volumes appear in the text.

The unique and central aspect of our commentary is its focus on seeing Jesus Christ in the verses of the Old Testament. Special feature sections describe the lives of Joseph, Moses, Joshua, Ruth, Job, Elijah, Elisha, Jeremiah, and Esther as types and foreshadowings of Jesus Christ.

Because the Old Testament is as long as all the other standard works combined, we have been selective in treating the subjects addressed in the thousand-year span of sacred scripture. We have provided a clear, concise explanation of significant events and doctrines recorded by the ancient patriarchs, prophets, historians, and poets, and we have attempted to clarify and resolve significant textual problems and inconsistencies—passages that appear to have been transmitted to us incorrectly. This commentary is thus at the same time both comprehensive and easily understood. We are certain that students of the Old Testament will find much in it to nurture their passion for intellectual and spiritual growth, learning, and understanding.

Several features of this commentary are especially helpful to Latter-day Saints. Passages of scripture from the Pearl of Great Price, the Book of Mormon, and the Doctrine and Covenants that directly correlate with Old Testament passages are included in the text. Photos, paintings, drawings, maps, and charts illustrate scriptural content, and important archaeological discoveries are discussed. Certain topics, such as the names of God, the concept of perfection, prophecies of the Messiah, how to understand Isaiah, the two prophets in Jerusalem in the last days, and others, are treated in more depth.

A glance at the table of contents of this volume shows that we have not followed exactly the order of the books in the Old Testament as found in either the King James Bible or the ancient Hebrew Bible. Rather, we discuss the individual books chronologically, according to our understanding of the historical period to which they belong, and to avoid duplication, we correlate the books of Samuel and Kings with the parallel accounts in Chronicles. Thus, the first volume of our commentary addresses the Pentateuch, or the five books of Moses, and then the historical and prophetic books in chronological order through 2 Samuel (and 1 Chronicles); the literary work Psalms is inserted between the two books of Samuel, according to its place in the chronology. This concluding volume of our commentary begins with 1 Kings (including parallel accounts in 1 and 2 Chronicles) and treats the historical and prophetic books in chronological order; literary works whose chronology can be determined, such as Proverbs, Ecclesiastes, Song of Solomon, and Lamentations, are placed within that chronology; and such literary works as Job, which have no apparent time frame, are grouped with other literary works.

We have used the following terms in precise ways in this commentary:

- Except in quotations from other works, *Temple* is capitalized when referring to a sanctuary of God approved by God and his prophets, which occasionally requires a judgment on our part; *temple* is not capitalized when it refers to pagan structures and shrines. Similarly, *Church* is capitalized when identifying the Church of Jesus Christ, which he established; the apostate church, contrariwise, is indicated by lowercase *church.*

- The designation *Near East* is preferred to *Middle East.*
- The name *Palestine* is used for that time in history when it designated the former land of Canaan, or Israel, beginning in the second century after Christ, in the days of the Roman emperor Hadrian, and continuing into the twenty-first century. In Old Testament times, the country was first called Canaan, then Israel, and then—when divided into two kingdoms—Israel and Judah. After the return of the Jews from exile during the period of Persian rule, the land was called Yehud (Judah), or, in the later Greek form, Judea.
- The abbreviations B.C. ("before Christ") and A.D. (*anno domini,* "the year of our Lord," meaning "after the birth of Christ") are used instead of terms that avoid the name of Christ: B.C.E. ("before the common era") and C.E. ("of the common era").
- The abbreviation *ca.,* for the Latin *circa* ("about"), indicates an approximate date.
- The abbreviation *ff* means "and following," referring to the verse or page cited plus the following verses or pages.
- Bible Dictionary refers to the dictionary at the end of the Latter-day Saint edition of the King James Version of the Bible.
- Bible Map refers to the maps at the end of the Latter-day Saint edition of the King James Version of the Bible. The maps in printings dated 2013 and later are particularly helpful; they are also available online at lds .org.
- Topical Guide refers to the topical guide at the end of

the Latter-day Saint edition of the King James Version of the Bible.

• // designates parallel scriptures as, for example, Isaiah 29 // 2 Nephi 27.

We extend appreciation to a number of individuals who have made this commentary possible. Foremost is Dr. Ellis T. Rasmussen, whose work on the Old Testament commentary he wrote in the early 1990s for use in Brigham Young University Independent Study courses was essential to our writing this commentary. Approximately one-third of the material in our volumes is drawn from those original writings of Dr. Rasmussen and is used by permission of BYU, Division of Continuing Education.

We likewise acknowledge with appreciation other colleagues and students at Brigham Young University for their helpful suggestions during the many years we have been preparing this commentary. We thank Connie Lankford Brace for her assistance in typing and proofreading and for her patience with innumerable corrections and additions; Jillian Mather for meticulously checking for accuracy every scripture reference throughout these volumes; and professors Jeffrey R. Chadwick, David B. Galbraith, Shon D. Hopkin, and our legal scholar and friend, Jay Deverich, for reading the entire manuscript and giving us valuable feedback. We thank Tricia von Bose for her insight into Isaiah 55:8–9, David Meidell for his recollection of an anecdote related to Jeremiah 1:4–5, Paul Hanks for his reflections on Jeremiah 19, and Cynthia Litchko for her thoughts on Malachi 3:5–12. We also extend heartfelt appreciation to Deseret Book Company, particularly Cory Maxwell, director of publishing; Lisa Roper, product manager; Suzanne Brady, managing editor; Shauna Gibby, designer; and Malina Grigg, typographer.

FIRST KINGS

First Kings is a continuation of the historical narrative begun in 1 and 2 Samuel. Together the four books of Samuel and Kings recount the whole history of monarchy in ancient Israel from the rise of Saul under the prophet Samuel to the fall of Zedekiah at the hands of the Babylonian empire. Like 1 and 2 Samuel, 1 and 2 Kings were originally one book, called simply Kings. The division of Kings was made by the translators of the Septuagint, sometime between 250 and 100 B.C.

We do not know with any degree of certainty who wrote 1 and 2 Kings. Jewish tradition ascribes authorship to Jeremiah, though this is doubted by some scholars. One thing seems clear; the author or authors used various sources to prepare the Hebrew version of Kings from which the King James translators did their work. We know that one source was "the book of the acts of Solomon" (1 Kings 11:41), another was "the book of the chronicles of the kings of Israel" (14:19), and still another was "the book of the chronicles of the kings of Judah" (14:29). The "chronicles" mentioned in 1 Kings 14 are different from 1 and 2 Chronicles in our Old Testament. The word *chronicles* could better be translated as "annals."

Undoubtedly, other sources were also used in the compilation of Kings. Some of these were also used by the author or compiler of 1 and 2 Chronicles and are mentioned therein. The author or authors of 1 and 2 Kings were very familiar with the book of Deuteronomy, the summary of the law of Moses that undergirds several passages in Kings.

A note on the books of 1 and 2 Chronicles. The books of 1 and 2 Samuel and 1 and 2 Kings have some parallel material in 1 and 2 Chronicles. Two separate records were kept in the northern and in the southern kingdoms of the covenant people: records of the kings of Israel and of Judah, and the chronicles of the kings, dealing predominantly with the southern kingdom of Judah. The first nine chapters of 1 Chronicles review the genealogy from Adam to David, and then the rest of 1 Chronicles and all of 2 Chronicles parallels the books of Samuel and Kings, in many places duplicating them virtually word for word. In this commentary we have interwoven the various records; there is thus no separate commentary on 1 and 2 Chronicles. Instead, 1 and 2 Chronicles are cross-referenced to their parallel material in the records of Samuel and Kings and commented on there. The unique material in Chronicles is also noted in the commentary on the books of Samuel and Kings.

1 Kings 1:1–10

Chapter 1 of 1 Kings picks up the historical sequence from 2 Samuel 20:22. It records Solomon's struggles and rise to the throne.

David had grown old. The description of his condition in verses 1–3 is picturesque enough, although to us it may seem a bit crass.

Adonijah may quite logically have assumed that he should prepare to be his father's successor, but no one in Israel could properly make himself king; recall how Saul and David were prophetically selected and inaugurated. According to 2 Samuel 3:2–4, Adonijah was the fourth son of David; but two of his older brothers, Amnon and Absalom, were already dead, and a third (called Chileab in 2 Samuel 3:3 and Daniel in 1 Chronicles 3:1) is not mentioned in the text after the account of his birth.

Though Adonijah had the support of Joab and Abiathar in his attempted coup, there were other important persons he did not have on his side. He seemed aware that Solomon was the heir apparent to the throne because he did not invite him to his inauguration. Later Adonijah admitted that he knew that the kingship was Solomon's "from the Lord" (1 Kings 2:15).

1 Kings 1:11–27

Because the installation of Solomon as king was initiated by the prophet Nathan, it must have had the approval of the Lord. The promise that Solomon should be king as mentioned by Nathan in his advice to Bathsheba is not found in the books of Samuel but is recorded in 1 Chronicles 22:9. The prophet and Bathsheba took steps to ensure that Solomon's appointment was secure.

According to plan, Solomon's mother, Bathsheba, gave David several facts to influence his action in favor of Solomon as his successor. Nathan's confirmation of what Bathsheba had said, combined with additional information making Adonijah's usurpation apparent, and a bit of sarcastic innuendo were all well calculated to stimulate action by David favorable to Solomon.

1 Kings 1:28–40

The prophet, the chief priest, and the military leader, with the royal bodyguard of loyal mercenaries, were instructed where to go to anoint and proclaim Solomon as king. The place specified was the Gihon spring, a central gathering place for Jerusalem just below the City of David, in the Kidron Valley (the spring still flows there today). The anointing, the announcement, the fanfare, the cheering, the riding on the king's own mule, and the presence of some six hundred well-organized and dependable troops frustrated Adonijah's earlier self-installation as king. In ancient Israel the mule or ass was a symbol of peace and royalty. On the other hand, the horse was a symbol of warfare and destruction. During his first coming, Jesus entered Jerusalem to be hailed as the great king riding upon an ass (Matthew 21:1–9). At his second coming, a time of war and destruction, he will come riding a white horse and subdue all enemies under his feet (Revelation 19:11; see also 6:2, 4, 5, 8). Solomon's act of riding on a mule, the great symbol of peace and royalty, to the Gihon spring sent a powerful, two-pronged message to all Israel. He was the legitimate king, and his focus was peace. Solomon's name in Hebrew, *Shlomo,* literally means "his peace." Such an act forestalled the possibility of Adonijah's attempt to claim the throne and thereby plunge the kingdom into tumult.

The anointing was done using the "horn of oil" from the Tabernacle. Note the symbolism involved. The "horn" represented power anciently (see 1 Samuel 2:1, footnote *a*), and the symbolism of transferring power and protection by means of the anointing is well known. Pure olive oil was used in the holiest place on earth to anoint the sacred vessels of the Tabernacle, where heavenly power

Brigham Young University students reenact Solomon's anointing at the Gihon Spring. "Zadok the priest, and Nathan the prophet . . . went down, and caused Solomon to ride upon king David's mule, and brought him to Gihon. And Zadok the priest took an horn of oil out of the tabernacle, and anointed Solomon. And they blew the trumpet" (1 Kings 1:38–39)

resided (Leviticus 8:10–11). Three classes of people in ancient Israel were anointed to perform their functions: prophets, priests, and kings (Exodus 40:15; 1 Samuel 10:1; 16:13; 1 Kings 1:39; 19:16.). This anointing foreshadowed the role of *the* Anointed One, Jesus Christ, our "Prophet, Priest, and King" (*Hymns,* no. 136). Anointing oil (pure olive oil) represents the Atonement of Jesus Christ in many ways (see Skinner, *Gethsemane,* 83–89).

1 Kings 1:41–53

Adonijah and his supporters soon realized that their cause was lost and that their status in the new regime was precarious. Adonijah took refuge in the sanctuary, at the horns of the altar (symbolic of protection), to safeguard his life until he could get assurance from the king that he would be spared the expected death penalty for such an attempted coup. Solomon's response sounds judicious and tolerant. See Exodus 21:13–14 concerning the sanctuary as a refuge. The word *sanctuary* is still used similarly today; that is, one seeking a place of security and protection is still said to be seeking sanctuary.

4

1 Kings 2:1–9

As David prepared to die, we see the peaceful transition of power from one leader to another, something David had not experienced. Included here is a short version of David's charge to Solomon (see also Psalm 72). The Lord's promise that this dynasty should continue is found in 2 Samuel 7:12.

David passed on to Solomon at least three duties that he (David) had either avoided or neglected: Joab was to be punished, specifically for his assassination of Abner and Amasa; no mention is made of his dispatch of Absalom nor his affiliation with Adonijah's coup; Shimei, whose curses had once been tolerated philosophically by David, was at last to be punished; Barzillai's sons were to be fed at the royal table for the good done by their father to David when he fled from Absalom years before; Barzillai himself had refused such rewards.

1 Kings 2:10–12 (1 Chronicles 29:22–30)

David's burial was in the City of David (see also Nehemiah 3:16). Usually Israelite burials were outside the cities, not within residential areas. Various sites for the burial of David and his successors have been suggested, but the lack of conclusive evidence leaves the actual location in doubt.

1 Kings 2:13–46

Adonijah asked Solomon's mother, Bathsheba, to lobby her son to grant Adonijah's request: David's wife Abishag to become Adonijah's wife. Adonijah knew that anyone who received any of the king's wives was supposed to be an heir of the deceased king. Whatever Adonijah's motives, Solomon was particularly sensitive about the significance of Adonijah's request and, with autocratic swiftness, decreed his half-brother's death.

In fact, in this chapter we see Solomon "clean house" as three men are sentenced to death: Adonijah, Joab, and Shimei. David's former priestly friend Abiathar, survivor of Saul's purge at Nob, lived on but was not permitted to continue to perform priestly duties because he had affiliated with Absalom.

Joab found temporary sanctuary beside the altar in the tent set up by David to house the Ark. He insisted that if they would kill him, they would have to kill him there. Indeed, his execution was ordered to be done there. No doubt justice demanded that he be punished, but it is unfortunate that the execution was performed in violation of the sanctuary.

The quarantine of Shimei led inevitably to an event for which he could be put to death. David had promised that Shimei would not be killed for cursing him.

1 Kings 3:1–4 (2 Chronicles 1:1–6)

Throughout history, alliances between one country and another were often cemented through marriages. These alliances were a way to secure peaceful borders between nations, to placate each other, and to receive certain benefits. That Egypt participated at this time in this arrangement suggests the growing importance of Israel on the international scene. Few other kingdoms in ancient history boasted the honor of a marriage between a king and a royal princess of Egypt. The decision to align himself politically and familially with Pharaoh was not a wise decision, as shown by verse 1 in the Joseph Smith Translation: "And the Lord was not pleased with Solomon, for he made affinity with Pharaoh king of Egypt."

A few chapters later, we learn that Pharaoh had conquered the Canaanite city of Gezer and given it to his daughter after she became Solomon's wife. It then became Solomon's property, which he rebuilt and made into an important administrative center (1 Kings 9:16–17). Thus it may be that Solomon thought the marriage alliance was necessary because he wanted Gezer. The name of the pharaoh who gave his daughter to Solomon as a wife is not known.

The need of royal housing for such an important wife as the daughter of the Egyptian pharaoh is evident. The account of Solomon's royal residences and other establishments will follow later.

The rationale for building a Temple was to combat the tendency of the people to sacrifice on the old pagan "high places." Additional reasons were given in 2 Samuel 7, and still other possible reasons will be discussed in this commentary.

Solomon's devotion and magnificence in sacrifices and worship are depicted. The so-called "high places" were ordinarily the hilltop shrines where all religious people have seemed inclined to worship, perhaps because of their nearness to heaven. Later, sacrificing to the Lord at such places was banned in Israel because the Israelites were too often inclined to worship the old gods there or to worship Jehovah as if he were the Canaanite Baal.

1 Kings 3:5–15 (2 Chronicles 1:7–13)

The quest of mortals to enter the presence of God is a significant theme in the Old Testament, a theme that is illustrated by this story, in which Solomon may be seen at his best. In Gibeon the Lord appeared to Solomon and gave him the opportunity to ask the Lord for whatever he desired. Solomon humbly asked for "an understanding heart" for the sole purpose of governing and blessing the Lord's people. He had no selfish requests: his heart was pure. In response, the Lord promised him wisdom and all other things that are good. This revelation was in a dream, according to verse 15.

The commendation of David in verse 14 may be surprising in view of the record of his life from the time he committed adultery and murder. The emphasis here and elsewhere seems to be on his loyalty to the Lord in never turning to other gods. Some of the later writers specify that his behavior was right in the eyes of the Lord except for the sins against Uriah and Uriah's wife, Bathsheba.

1 Kings 3:16–28

In this well-known story illustrating Solomon's wisdom, you may think he was simply fortunate. Ordinarily no woman who really wanted a child would agree to such a shocking and unsatisfying solution as Solomon proposed. Perhaps his wisdom lay in his perceiving that the false claimant would be brazen or selfish enough to agree to the dividing of the child. Naturally, the true mother gave in rather than consent to the child's death.

1 Kings 4:1–6

Solomon's cabinet officers, as well as his twelve procurement officials, are listed, making an impressive retinue—and a huge bureaucracy. It is surprising that Abiathar is listed; he served only until "banished" to the ancestral priestly city of Anathoth.

Some of David's old officers apparently had remained, and some sons of old officers were put into posts their fathers had held. It would be interesting to know if the sons of Nathan mentioned were sons of Nathan the prophet. The one who is called "the principal officer and the king's friend" is really called in Hebrew "a priest, the king's friend." It would also be interesting to know what the various titles and positions actually were.

1 Kings 4:7–28

Solomon reorganized his nation into twelve administrative districts, preserving some of the old tribal units but altering others. One of his twelve procurement officials, the one over Mount Ephraim, was named Ben-Hur, and two others were sons-in-law. The duty of these twelve officers was to receive the people's contributions of food for the royal household. The daily ration was 330 bushels of fine flour; 660 bushels of meal; ten fat oxen and one hundred sheep; plus gazelles, roebucks, harts, fowl, barley, straw, etc. Some have estimated that that amount of food would have been sufficient for thirty-five thousand persons. Such a number would include officials, servants, military personnel, and others, even outside Jerusalem, because Jerusalem itself was not that densely populated in those days. Add to this the annual payment to Hiram of Tyre when the building projects were contracted, amounting to 220,000 bushels of wheat and 180,000 gallons of olive oil. These demands on the agricultural economy of Solomon's nation were incredibly high.

The twelve districts assigned to meet the royal needs excluded Judah. The exemption of Judah from certain taxes must have been a source of irritation to the rest of Israel. In fact, we find during the very next generation that the northern tribes rebelled against the unfair economic policies and favoritism of Solomon. That rebellion would result in the most wrenching split in Israel's history, and mark, for all intents and purposes, the beginning of the nation's decline.

Solomon reigned from the Euphrates to the border of Egypt (2 Chronicles 9:26; see Bible Map 4). Details are given of the population and prosperity of Judah and Israel. Apparently, since the beginning of David's reign, the two regions of the nation remained somewhat distinct. Recall the friction between northern Israel and David upon his return to the throne after Absalom's usurpation. Solomon's throne-name (Hebrew, *Shlomo*) means "his peace," but there are periodic hints in these scriptural records that all was not peaceful during his reign.

1 Kings 4:29–34

Another allusion to the extraordinary wisdom of Solomon is seen in the assertion that he wrote three thousand proverbs and a thousand and five songs, or psalms. The present book of Proverbs contains teachings and counsel that would logically come from the life experience of Solomon. Our best impression of his wisdom may come from a study of those proverbs. By stating that his wisdom exceeded that of the Egyptians, the writer seems to be invoking the highest standard in the ancient Near East. Solomon used nature as a significant, meaningful and sublime theme for his instruction.

1 Kings 5 (2 Chronicles 2)

Hiram, king of Tyre, "ever a lover of David," began a long and favorable commercial relationship with Solomon as he prepared to build the Temple. "Sidonians" is the usual biblical term for any of the people of the Phoenician city-states. At other times when Tyre happened to be in the ascendancy, they were called the people of Tyre. In the period under consideration, the Tyrians dominated, but the biblical scribes continued to use the old term "Sidonians." Sidon and Tyre were indeed the two chief cities of the Phoenician peoples. Iron Age invasions and displacements of various peoples left the ancient Near East weakened and thus created a window of opportunity for smaller nations, like the Phoenicians and the Israelites, to become powerful. The Phoenicians were sea-going Canaanites who carried on a vast maritime trade centering on two products—cedar wood and purple dye. A century or so after Solomon's reign they established Carthage in North Africa. In fact, the very term *Phoenician* derives from the Greek word *phoenix*, which means red-purple dye.

The laborers who cut the timber for the buildings which Hiram contracted to build for Solomon were mostly people of other lands, while the Israelites, according to their record, functioned chiefly as foremen (see 2 Chronicles 2:17; 8:9; 1 Kings 9:20–23; and our corresponding commentary).

Verse 13 mentions that Solomon raised a "levy" of thousands of Israelite men. This was a *corvee*, or conscription. Solomon did not want to deplete the national treasury by purchasing slaves, so he mandated that as a civic duty male citizens devote part of their time and energy to constructing a Temple, a palace, and other public building projects. Solomon's part of the exchange with King Hiram included some "twenty thousand measures of wheat" (v. 11), or 125,000 bushels, according to some measurements. Israel truly was a breadbasket at this time. Could it be that the Lord blessed Israel with prosperity and peace precisely so they could build him a holy House?

1 Kings 6 (compare 2 Chronicles 3:1–14)

The date given for beginning the Temple construction, 480 years after the Exodus, is an important one for correlating biblical chronology. The period of the wilderness wandering was 40 years long, and the reigns of Saul and of David were each 40 years. This would leave 360 years for events in the books of Joshua, Judges, Ruth, and Samuel. In this case, the terms of service of the various judges in different parts of Israel cannot be added end to end, because they add up to more than the available total. It is apparent that some of the judges were contemporaries serving in different parts of the land during terms that overlapped.

Attempting to create an absolute chronology using the date given here, some scholars put the Exodus around 1446 B.C., during the rule of Pharaoh Amenhotep II, and the commencement of the Temple's construction around 966 B.C. However, others maintain, for a variety of reasons, that the Exodus could not have occurred before the rule of Pharaoh Ramses II of the nineteenth dynasty (ca. 1290–1226 B.C.). The matter remains unresolved, and a relative chronology continues as our best measure of time.

To get a sense of the size of Solomon's Temple, reckon a cubit at about 18 inches. The dimensions of the Temple proper would be about 90 x 30 x 45 feet. The Salt Lake Temple, by comparison, measures 186 x 118 x 210 feet.

The adornment of Solomon's Temple must have been beautiful. Many biblical commentaries, dictionaries, and handbooks show reconstructions or drawings of the structure as specified

Model of Solomon's Temple

here. The materials were all prefabricated before reaching the Temple site so that reverent quietness could be preserved there during construction.

A brief, reassuring revelation (vv. 11–13) came to Solomon from the Lord during the course of construction. A similar promise has been given by the Lord in our dispensation: "And inasmuch as my people build a house unto me in the name of the Lord, and do not suffer any unclean thing to come into it, that it be not defiled, my glory shall rest upon it; yea, and my presence shall be there, for I will come into it, and all the pure in heart that shall come into it shall see God" (D&C 97:15–16; 124:24, 27). Temples of the Lord are the most holy and important structures in mortality. Each is literally the House of the Lord, the place where heaven and earth intersect, the representation of the environment of heaven in this fallen world. The Prophet Joseph Smith taught that we need the Temple more than anything else (*History of the Church*, 6:230).

Solomon continued the building project for seven years. The most holy place was evidently the most ornate, and the finishing work must have required much time. The details are interesting. The cherubs were about fifteen feet high and fifteen feet wide

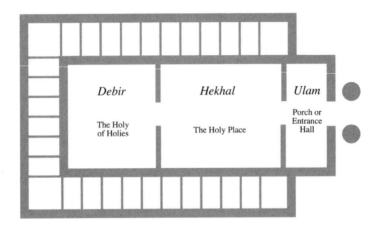

Diagram of Solomon's Temple

from wingtip to wingtip. They were made of olivewood overlaid with gold. The Ark was placed under the arch of the wings and had its own smaller cherubs on top of it. Recall that these carved objects were not in violation of the second of the Ten Commandments, because that is a ban upon making images to be *worshiped*. The Hebrew word *pesel*, translated "image" in the King James Bible, means "idol," which was the thing forbidden in Exodus 20:4.

1 Kings 7:1–12

The king's palace and other buildings for government functions, the housing for his foreign wives, the reception hall, and so on, required some thirteen years to build. Compare that number to the seven years it took to build the Temple, and compare the dimensions of the two structures: the Lord's House was 90 x 30 x 45 feet, but Solomon's house was 150 x 75 x 45 feet. What would be the general reaction if a president of The Church of Jesus Christ of Latter-day Saints built himself a home next to the Salt Lake Temple but almost twice as big?

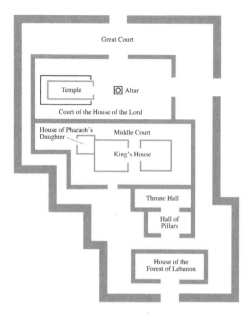

Solomon's royal buildings

1 Kings 7:13–51 (2 Chronicles 3:15–5:1)

Solomon's Temple was built according to the Lord's specifications by Phoenician artisans. One craftsman of Tyre named Hiram was important to the building projects. This Hiram was not the king of the same name but the son of a woman of Naphtali and a Tyrian father (see 2 Chronicles 2:11–14). His amazing productions in cast metal included two colossal bronze pillars to stand at the entrance to the Temple proper. These twin pillars were ornamental, not structural. They were given names with messianic and covenantal overtones: Jachin (Hebrew, "He will establish"), and Boaz (Hebrew, "In Him is strength/splendor"). In the Temple, important covenants with the Lord were made and renewed.

The font of bronze, or "molten sea," was placed on the backs of twelve oxen grouped in four sets of three, oriented toward the cardinal points of the compass. The number twelve represented the twelve tribes of Israel. The font was a hand breadth in thickness and has been calculated by various Old Testament scholars to have a possible capacity of between eleven and sixteen thousand gallons. This capacity is immense by any standard. By comparison, modern Latter-day Saint Temples, which are of varying sizes, contain baptismal fonts holding anywhere from five hundred to two thousand gallons. Perhaps the Lord was trying to teach ancient Israel something symbolically about the significance of ordinances and ritual washings. According to 2 Chronicles 4:2–6, it was for the ceremonial "washing of priests." Temples of other religions customarily had such basins for the storage of water for ceremonial ablutions. No record of baptisms or ritual immersions in this basin has been found, though the book of Moses and the Joseph Smith Translation mention baptism from Adam's time to that of Enoch. Joseph Smith's translation of Genesis 17:5 says that proper baptism had ceased among the apostate peoples at Abraham's time, and no further mention of it is made. Christians in general, and Latter-day Saints in particular, have wondered about the likelihood of baptism in Solomon's Temple. As was observed in connection with the laws in Exodus and Leviticus, various forms of washing the outward body to symbolize inner, spiritual cleansing were common. The Tractate of the Mishnah, which gives specifications for the ceremonies of *Yom Kippur* (Day of Atonement), indicates that the priest officiating in the slaughter of the sacrificial animal was repeatedly "baptized" (the Hebrew word used means "immersed"), and clean garments were placed upon him after each immersion, before each successive step in offering the sacrifice. Doctrine and Covenants 124:36–39 appears to indicate that baptisms were performed in the ancient Temple, although they would have been only for the living because baptisms for the dead would not be performed until after the Savior's initiation of missionary work in the spirit world.

Elder Bruce R. McConkie explained: "It must be remembered that all direct and plain references to baptism have been deleted from the Old Testament (1 Ne. 13) and that the word *baptize* is of Greek origin. Some equivalent word, such as *wash,* would have been used by the Hebrew peoples. In describing the molten sea the Old Testament record says, *'The sea was for the priests to wash in.'* (2 Chron. 4:2–6.) This is tantamount to saying that the priests performed baptisms in it.

"In this temple building dispensation the Brethren have been

14

led by the spirit of inspiration to pattern the baptismal fonts placed in temples after the one in Solomon's Temple" (*Mormon Doctrine*, 104).

To make so much bronze work possible, the famous "King Solomon's mines" (just north of modern-day Eilat at the northern end of the eastern branch of the Red Sea) might have been working to capacity. Copper deposits are still found there. Note also the record of the silver, gold, and vessels previously gathered and dedicated by David for the Temple, which his son would build (v. 51).

1 Kings 8:1–53 (2 Chronicles 5:2–6:42)

With an appropriate entourage of priests, elders, and tribal leaders, the Ark of the Covenant was brought up from the tent which David had pitched for it in his citadel called Zion. With the Holy Ark placed in the Temple, the northern mount (formerly called Moriah) began to be known as Zion.

At this point in history there was nothing in the Ark but the tablets of stone received by Moses at Sinai, or Horeb. Where the writings of Moses, Joshua, and others were at this time is not mentioned, unfortunately. After the Ark was placed in the most holy place—the Holy of Holies—the cloud indicating that the presence of God filled his House.

Solomon expressed his thanks to God and his acknowledgment of the blessings that made it possible for him to accomplish the building of the Temple anticipated for so long by his father, David.

Solomon in his dedicatory prayer proposed seven typical situations wherein the people might supplicate the Lord in the Temple, or facing toward the Temple (compare Daniel 6:10), and he asked that God would hear them in such cases if they worthily approached him. His mention of strangers (non-Israelites) in verses 41–43 hints that some conversions to the God of Israel were taking place. A later verse (60) echoes Moses' prayer that the people might so live that others would be impressed with the evidences of the presence of God with them. These are hints of an awareness of the mission of Israel. Verses 46–50 teach that every individual sins and needs to repent (see Romans 3:23) and also foreshadow the yet future captivities of the kingdom of Israel at the hands of the Assyrians (721 B.C.) and the kingdom of Judah by the Babylonians (586 B.C.).

Unfortunately, more of the dedicatory prayer has not been transmitted to us through the ages. What we do have bears some resemblance to specific points in the dedicatory prayer of the Kirtland Temple (see D&C 109). The period of Solomon's reign should have been a golden age for such sacred Temple activities. What happened to him later, however, was quite the opposite of what should have happened in his royal house.

1 Kings 8:54–66 (2 Chronicles 7:1–10)

The dedicatory observances concluded with another blessing upon the people by the king and a seven-day program of sacrifice. It appears that this was a festival "peace offering" in which some of the fat was burned upon the altar, the priests received a portion for food, and the remainder was eaten by the families on whose behalf the animals were sacrificed (Leviticus 3; 7:11–21). It doesn't seem likely that the "continual burnt offering" was involved in this celebration (Exodus 29:38–42; Leviticus 6:8–13; 8:18–21; Numbers 28:3–8). After the seven days' dedication feast, another feast was celebrated. This was most likely the festival of *Sukkot,* based on the time of the year indicated in verse 2 of this chapter. It is still a joyful festival throughout Judaism. In English it is referred to as the Feast of Tabernacles. Anciently, it also emphasized the theme of Israel's obligation to be a light to the rest of the world, to gather the gentiles to God's true religion. In Jesus' day huge menorahs, burning brightly, were set up in the Temple courtyard to symbolize Israel's mission to the world. They provided the backdrop for Jesus' discourse on the "light of the world" (John 8:12).

Verse 65 identifies the territorial limits of Solomon's empire at the time: from the "entering in of Hamath," that is, from *Lebo-Hamath* (footnote 65*b* is a correct translation, but the phrase designates a specific place name) to the river of Egypt, likely the Wadi El-Arish in northern Sinai.

1 Kings 9:1–9 (2 Chronicles 7:11–22)

The Lord responded with another revelation, appearing to Solomon and repeating certain promises regarding the blessings that follow faithfulness. He assured the king that his "eyes and

© D. Kelly Ogden

Solomonic gates at strategic fortified cities

heart shall be there perpetually" at the Temple to be in communication with his people (see commentary at 1 Kings 6:1–38). The Lord also added a dire warning about what would happen if the king and the people ever turned and utterly forsook him and his commandments and served other gods.

1 Kings 9:10–28 (2 Chronicles 8:1–18)

It appears that Solomon could not pay all of his construction costs and was obliged to give King Hiram twenty cities situated along the coastland of western Galilee from the present location of the Arab village of Kabul (east of modern Haifa and Acco) northward and adjoining Phoenician lands south of Tyre. The cities apparently didn't please Hiram, as you can see by his epithet, the meaning of which is given in footnote 13*a*.

It would seem that the six score (120) talents of gold referred to in verse 14 may be the sum of the gold mentioned in verse 11. Six score talents could weigh nearly 13,000 pounds!

A survey is given of Solomon's fortified cities on major routes of travel beyond Jerusalem, especially along the international highway through the Jezreel Valley and along the coast. What archaeologists describe as "Solomonic Gates," constructed from the same architectural plan, featuring six inner chambers, three on each side, and nearly identical in dimension, have been uncovered at Hazor, Megiddo, and Gezer—just as verse 15 implies, thus corroborating the biblical text.

Again it is indicated that the non-Israelite peoples of the land, descendants of those left there in the days of Joshua and the judges, were made slaves of the state to do the menial labor. The Israelite drafted laborers were not slaves but supplied the supervisory personnel, the military, and the royal service (compare 1 Kings 5).

Solomon's navy, based at Ezion-geber (modern-day Eilat) on the shore of the Red Sea, traded with Ophir. The abundant source of gold at Ophir apparently corresponds to someplace in the Arabian Peninsula, possibly the land of Punt, with which the Egyptians had a rich trade. Experts in seamanship, the Phoenicians aided Solomon in this project also.

1 Kings 10:1–13 (2 Chronicles 9:1–12)

The story of the visit of the queen of Sheba illustrates the fame and reputation of Solomon and his kingdom. (Sheba was in southwestern Arabia or in east Africa—or both.) The "hard questions" mentioned in verse 1 were riddles; the same word was used for Samson's riddle in the book of Judges. Since both Sheba and Ophir are mentioned in Genesis 10:28–29 among the descendants of Joktan, brother of Peleg, both of whom were sons of Eber, it would seem plausible that the trade with Ophir mentioned earlier was with peoples of the Arabian peninsula and that the visiting queen came from the same peoples. Still, there is the persistent claim of the Ethiopians that for centuries their rulers have been direct descendants of a child born of the union between the Queen of Sheba and Solomon. It was written in the 1955 revised constitution of Ethiopia that the royal line "descends without interruption from the dynasty of Menelik I, son of the Queen of Ethiopia, the queen of Sheba, and King Solomon of Jerusalem." The tradition is possible, given the historian's remark in verse 13: "And king Solomon gave unto the queen of Sheba all her desire, whatsoever she asked." It should be noted, however, that there is no positive evidence to support this tradition.

When the queen saw Solomon's palace with all its pomp and glitter, his court officials, and "all" his wisdom, meaning perhaps all the trappings of his style of monarchy, "there was no more spirit in her," meaning she was overwhelmed (v. 5). Solomon's greatness did have a positive effect on the queen, for she blessed and praised the God of Israel. There is a lesson in this—outward appearances are noticed by others. Solomon sent the queen home with a rich trove of gifts.

1 Kings 10:14–29 (2 Chronicles 9:13–28; 1:14–17)

This impressive description of gold and precious things may represent Solomon's income, his imports of precious metal, and that which he received in taxes, duties, and tribute. During the time that his kingdom was famous and powerful, such munificence was possible; however, watch to see what happens to it within a few years after the kingdom is divided. The heavy costs of Solomon's reign and the resultant demands in taxation and labor levies brought his country to the breaking point economically and politically by the end of his life. Though Solomon was a legend in his own day, and his name and historical reports of his reign suggest peace, all was not well in Solomon's kingdom.

Solomon's imports of horses and chariots from Egypt, both to supply his military needs and to sell to his neighbors to the north, must have constituted a major commercial operation in his time (see footnote 28*a*).

1 Kings 11:1–8

The fall of Solomon resulted from his marrying royal women from all the countries round about—which may have been for economic and political reasons as well as for his "love" of "strange [foreign] women" (v. 2). Nevertheless, marriage outside the covenant brought grave consequences. Since he not only tolerated their religions but caused shrines and sacrificial high places to be built for them and "went after" their gods and goddesses himself, it seems that he was seeking power from every imaginable source. Solomon directly violated the will of the Lord as given in the warnings of Moses and Samuel (Deuteronomy 7:1–4; 1 Samuel 8:10–18). The king built idolatrous shrines, temples to other gods, on "the hill that is before [east of] Jerusalem," later known as "the mount of offense" or "the mount of corruption" (2 Kings 23:13). David drove out the Canaanites and their gods; Solomon brought them back in.

Chemosh and Molech (also called Milcom; v. 5) were worshiped with human sacrifices, a most reprehensible and devilish practice. Worshipers of Molech, believed to be the god of fire, burned children alive to gain his supposed favor (see Deuteronomy 18:10; 2 Kings 3:27; 2 Chronicles 28:3). How could Solomon have fallen so low?

The favorable evaluation of David as compared to Solomon is based simply on David's fidelity to God in resisting idolatrous practices. This was the quality for which many later writers in the Bible praise him. In some cases, David's moral and ethical breach and his sins in connection with Bathsheba and Uriah are not mentioned; in other cases, it is mentioned that he did that which was right in the sight of the Lord in all except that case. Joseph Smith's translation of verse 6 rearranges the phrases to present quite a different comparison of David and Solomon. Solomon's violation of the marriage law (v. 2) led to his breaking the first and second of the Ten Commandments; David's breach of the Tenth Commandment led to his breaking the seventh and then the sixth of the Ten Commandments.

1 Kings 11:9–13

In view of Solomon's faults in this matter, it may be difficult to see why he was allowed to continue to enjoy his kingdom because of the merits of his father. In our own dispensation, a person who turned from the Church and from the Lord and participated in strange worship practices to the extent that Solomon did would be excommunicated, his eternal destiny considered seriously impaired, and his hopes of exaltation forfeited.

There was undoubtedly more to consider during Solomon's later reign than just punishing a wicked king, however. There was the political and military stability of Jerusalem to think about, not only because the Temple (the only legitimate House of the Lord on the earth at that time that we know of) had just been built but also because of the righteous people living in Jerusalem and Israel during this period. All through time, there have been political leaders who have acted immorally but have, through political skill, kept their country stable. To wrench the kingdom from Solomon at that moment might have led to consequences that only God could foresee and wanted kept at bay. In fact, the Lord did declare that the kingdom would be torn apart after Solomon's death and one tribe would be given to Solomon's son. But notice the reason why: "for David my servant's sake, *and for Jerusalem's sake which I have chosen*" (v. 13; emphasis added).

Perhaps a more important point to focus on is how the Lord's hand is directly involved in history so many times. He said that *he* would "rend the kingdom" from Solomon and give it to his servant. Indeed, that is what came to pass.

1 Kings 11:14–40

Adversaries from some of the oppressed peoples who had been conquered by David and made to pay tribute by Solomon quite naturally began to arise as soon as the conditions in Solomon's kingdom allowed.

One notable adversary arose in Solomon's own realm— Jeroboam the Ephrathite (or Ephraimite, in this case). His capacity and ambition to rule were factors in his rebellion, but the prediction by Ahijah the prophet that he would be king over ten of the tribes was apparently the chief stimulus. Though he had been a trusted foreman over the laborers of the tribes of Joseph in Solomon's building projects, his life was sought when his anticipated future became known. Just like Saul and David before him, now Solomon desired to murder someone in the way of his own rule and influence.

It is understandable that in spite of peaceful relations between Solomon and Egypt, the pharaohs there were not averse to harboring potential adversaries to such a rival.

1 Kings 11:41–43 (2 Chronicles 9:29–31)

A rather terse note, with the barest hint of eulogy, tells of Solomon's death. Later writers of scripture refrain from recalling Solomon's name with the aura of idealism they associate with David. David united the kingdom of Israel; Solomon, through his policies, divided it.

It may be that David was perpetually honored because of his

historic achievement in establishing a firmly united kingdom in his best days, or he may have been chiefly honored because of the prophetic destiny of the kingdom to come under the rule of a descendant of David, the promised Messiah (Isaiah 9:7; Jeremiah 23:5; 33:15–17; Zechariah 12:7–12).

During the tenth century before Christ, united Israel was divided into two nations: the northern kingdom, called Israel, and the southern kingdom, called Judah.

Long-standing jealousies, antagonisms, and tensions between the tribes of Israel erupted violently after Solomon's death, causing a rebellion against Rehoboam, Solomon's only known child and successor. However, the biblical record wants the reader to see that the split was really brought about by the Lord, just as he had promised (1 Kings 11:31). Furthermore, the Joseph Smith Translation makes clear that a principal reason for the division of the Davidic kingdom in the Lord's eyes was "the transgression of David" (JST 1 Kings 11:39).

The message is subtle but profound. God is not outside the historical process. He is the principal agent in history. He has a plan for Israel and intervenes through his prophets in the affairs of men to bring about his work and purposes. The division of the Davidic kingdom, or house of Israel, was a step preparatory to the scattering of Israel, in which God also took a personal role (Jeremiah 16:13; Ezekiel 5:10; Jacob 5:8).

While the northern tribes had greater numbers and better land, Judah had the political prestige and religious power of the great city of Jerusalem, including the Temple; they also had a stable line of kings. The beginning of the end was approaching for the northern tribes.

You may want to read the following entries in the Bible Dictionary: "Rehoboam"; "Jeroboam"; "Israel, Kingdom of"; "Judah, Kingdom of"; "Ahab"; "Elijah"; "Moab"; "Elisha"; and "Molech." In the *Encyclopedia of Mormonism*, see "Elijah," "Prophecy," and "Prophecy in Biblical Times."

1 Kings 12:1–15 (2 Chronicles 10:1–15)

After Solomon's death, forty-one-year-old Rehoboam, Solomon's son, traveled to Shechem to be installed as the new king. It was important for Rehoboam to go to Shechem to be formally recognized as king because Shechem was among the most ancient of the sacred towns of the northern Holy Land and, thus, a chief city of the northern tribes of Israel (see Bible Map 10). It was at Shechem that Abraham camped when he first arrived in Canaan (Genesis 12:6). It was at Shechem that the Israelites buried the bones of Joseph when they came out of Egypt (Joshua 24:32). It was at Shechem that Joshua gathered together all the tribes of Israel to give them instructions and establish a special covenant between God and the people. Undoubtedly, the heir apparent to Solomon recognized the need to be confirmed at this important place in order to cement northern allegiance to a united kingdom. At Shechem Rehoboam met Jeroboam, the Ephraimite adversary of Solomon, who had returned from exile in Egypt at the request of the northern tribes of Israel.

The people who had gathered at Shechem from all the tribes of Israel, after the death of Solomon, yearned for increased rights and respect. Their proposal was simple: if Rehoboam would concede reductions in the burdens of taxes and labor-conscription, they would accept him and serve him. But Rehoboam was not ready to accept what his grandfather, David, would have encouraged at the beginning of his reign. David had worked hard to win over and to unite the people under his government.

The older counselors to the young king recommended a government with mutual responsibilities and benefits: let the king be a servant to the people, and the people would be servants to the king (compare King Benjamin in Mosiah 2). But the younger counselors advised that the king make no such covenant and instead rule by despotic proclamations and threats. Rehoboam chose to follow the latter advice. (The "scorpions" mentioned were a type of whip with barbed, multiple lashes.) That action marked the beginning of the end of the united nation of Israel.

1 Kings 12:16–24 (2 Chronicles 10:16–11:4)

So the northern tribes, with Jeroboam at their head, revolted. Recall the origin of this Ephraimite leader (1 Kings 11:26–40); remember also that the northern tribes were a separate unit in the first seven years of David's reign and perhaps even in the days of Joshua.

The people in the northern tribes rebelled and declared their independence from the Judah-based monarchy. The division of united Israel must have pleased the Egyptian government, as the pharaoh there was planning some imperialistic moves of his own. Things might have proceeded differently had the northern tribes understood the wisdom later embodied in the teaching of Jesus: "Every kingdom divided against itself is brought to desolation; and every city or house divided against itself shall not stand" (Matthew 12:25).

Rehoboam sent his supervisor of the forced-labor corps, Adoram, into the camp of Israel, presumably to carry on business as usual. The supervisor was stoned to death, and Rehoboam fled, knowing the northerners were deadly earnest in rejecting him. He then reacted to the northern secession by mobilizing an army from Judah and Benjamin to quell the rebellion, force the return of the errant northern territories, and preserve political unity. But the Lord, through the prophet Shemaiah, forbade him to carry out a war. When war did come a short time later, it proved to be a futile and lengthy enterprise. We are told simply that "there was war between Rehoboam and Jeroboam all their days" (1 Kings 14:30). The division between their two kingdoms created two separate nations with separate histories from that time on. The author of this section of the biblical narrative puts it succinctly: "So Israel rebelled against the house of David unto this day" (v. 19). It will only be in Christ's millennial kingdom that the two kingdoms will become one again (Ezekiel 37:22). The phrase "unto this day" is interesting because it tells us that the text was composed after the kingdom was divided but before the northern kingdom was conquered and its inhabitants deported by the Assyrians in 721 B.C.

Judah and Benjamin showed loyalty to Rehoboam at the assembly in Shechem. The Septuagint (the Greek translation of the Old Testament) note at 20b explains that Judah and Benjamin stood together in the southern nation; Simeon had also been assimilated into Judah, as well as some Levites and others from the various northern tribes who had fled the religious corruptions in their own tribal lands.

1 Kings 12:25–33

Jeroboam, son of Nebat, was made king over the Israelites in the north, with their first capital city at Shechem. Later, Omri made Samaria their capital (see Bible Map 10).

The most significant aspect of Jeroboam's reign (ca. 922–901 B.C.) was his immediate idolatry. Rather than slowly drifting away from proper religious practices, northern Israel quickly adopted idolatrous religion, and Jeroboam provided them with a non-Levitical, apostate priesthood taken from the dregs of society. The king's innovation and manipulation of golden-calf idols and of feasts and incense-burning were willful perversions for political reasons. Jeroboam had seen the Egyptians use the apis bull in their cultic practices. He used this perversion of true worship to further secure the loyalty of his Israelite subjects by diverting the religious traffic from Jerusalem, the rival capital, to apostate shrines established in Dan and Bethel on the northern and southern frontiers of his new northern kingdom of Israel. To do that, he put forward an almost verbatim quotation of the people's proclamation at the golden calf incident during the Exodus (Exodus 32:4). Remember, the Exodus was an event central to the very identity of Israelites. Jeroboam's cheap but clever imitation of true religion included a non-Levitical priesthood, sacrifices, and holy days.

In imitation of the Feast of Tabernacles, which was also related to the Exodus, Jeroboam instituted in the north his own perverted feast and made unauthorized sacrifices. In all this he sinned greatly. Yet in his view these innovations gave the Israelites everything they could want: the god of Joseph, the god of the Exodus, their own holy days, their own priests, and their own sympathetic king. In short, what he hoped the people would believe he was providing was not a new, perverted religious order but rather a new royal administration legitimized by old religious rites that were now being given renewed attention in a new day and age.

The huge cultic high place, the "house of high places [Hebrew, *bet bamot*]" (v. 31) has been discovered at the site of ancient Dan, corroborating the biblical text. Jeroboam's cultic aberrations would be known for centuries thereafter in the writings of historians and prophets as "the sin of Jeroboam."

Second Chronicles 11:13–15 mentions that false priests were

The high place at Dan. "And this thing became a sin: for the people went to worship . . . even unto Dan" (1 Kings 12:30)

appointed for the high places, as well as goat and calf idols that Jeroboam made. In the King James text, the goat idols are called "devils." These idols were *se'irim*, sometimes translated "satyrs," believed anciently to be goat-legged beings living in the deserts that made travel dangerous (see 2 Chronicles 11:15 note *b*.)

The 2 Chronicles account (11:13–14) indicates that all the legitimate priests fled from northern Israel and lived thereafter only in Judah.

1 Kings 13

There are some problems in this story of a man of God who came from Judah to warn the king of northern Israel and lost his life in the mission. Some help is available in Joseph Smith's translation of verse 18, which indicates that the old prophet said, "Bring him back . . . that I may prove him; and he lied not unto him." Also there is a change in verse 26, in which the last part reads: "therefore the Lord hath delivered him unto the lion, which hath torn him, and slain him, according to the word of the Lord, which he spake unto me." These make the account more understandable (the young prophet should have obeyed God), but still the interpretation is tentative. In verse 24 the facts that the donkey did not run away after the lion had attacked the man of God and that the lion did not attack the donkey seem to be a sign of divine judgment. There actually were lions in the Holy Land during biblical times; for example, young David killed a lion and a bear in the shepherds' fields around Bethlehem (1 Samuel 17:34–36). Lions continued in the land until the time of the Crusaders, around the twelfth century after Christ.

As for wicked King Jeroboam, verse 33 confirms that he continued to elevate the dregs of society to leadership positions, and verse 34 makes it clear that his idolatry yielded dire results for him and his family. Fulfillment of the prophecy about the destruction of his idolatrous altar is related in 2 Kings 23:15–18.

1 Kings 14:1–20

Because of the sins of Jeroboam and his people, the Lord foretold the scattering of the northern tribes—two hundred years before its occurrence. He said he would "cut off from Jeroboam him that pisseth against the wall" (v. 10). To modern ears this phrase may seem vulgar, even offensive. It is, however, a superb illustration of the down-to-earth figures of speech used by the ancient Hebrew writers, who were literary artists, painters of powerful mental pictures that conjured up lasting images and impressions. The phrase "him that pisseth against the wall" equates with the concept of exterminating a family. The same idiom (but without the offensive term) occurs, with the same meaning, in modern scripture: "And not many years hence, that they and their posterity shall be swept from under heaven, saith God, that not one of them is left to stand by the wall" (D&C 121:15).

In verse 15, Israel's destruction is directly tied to their making of "groves." The Hebrew reads 'asherim, meaning wooden poles dedicated to the goddess Asherah, the consort of the Canaanite deity 'El ('el is the general Semitic term for "god"). Around these poles Israelites carried out their idolatrous and abhorrent practices. The fulfillment of this prophecy of the destruction of the northern kingdom of Israel is seen in 2 Kings 17:5–6.

1 Kings 14:21–31 (2 Chronicles 12:1–16)

It is evident that some proper religious practices were perverted in Judah as well. Worship under "green trees" and the "sodomites" (the word in Hebrew designates men dedicated to cultic prostitution) indicate that a fertility cult stole away the hearts of the people from the proper ways of the Lord. Such sexual perversions were a troubling feature of Canaanite religion. As a consequence of the moral, emotional, and physical weakness that accompanies such behavior among an unfit people, the still-lively foreign power to the south, Egypt, was able to enter the Holy Land and wreak havoc.

The Egyptian pharaoh who had harbored malcontents against Judah during Solomon's reign was ready and anxious to try to plunder the riches of the Israelites. In 918 B.C. the Libyan-Egyptian Shishak (Sheshonk in extrabiblical texts) invaded Israel and Judah with twelve hundred chariots, sixty thousand cavalry, and "innumerable" foot soldiers. He ravaged the Temple in Jerusalem and took away as booty all "the treasures of the house of the Lord" (vv. 25–26). Although the Bible mentions only Judah, evidence indicates that Shishak invaded the northern kingdom as well. A fragment of Pharaoh Shishak's inscription has been found at Megiddo, and a list of cities attacked during his campaign in Israel and Judah is found at the Temple of Karnak in Egypt. He inscribed the names of many northern cities on his victory relief at Karnak. Thus, both Israel in the north and Judah in the south were greatly weakened by Shishak during and after the reigns of their respective evil kings, Jeroboam and Rehoboam. Shishak's campaign in Canaan was the basis for the film *Raiders of the Lost Ark,* which supposes that if the pharaoh took away the treasures of the House of the Lord, then the Ark of the Covenant was also taken to Egypt, though there is no historical evidence that the Ark was removed from Jerusalem at that time.

1 Kings 15:1–8 (compare 2 Chronicles 13:1–14:1)

From this point in the historical narrative to the account of the actual fall and deportation of the kingdom of Israel (2 Kings 17:6), the writers of Kings skillfully weave back and forth from one kingdom to the other to report contemporaneous occurrences in both. They used sources no longer in existence today (1 Kings 14:19). Those missing official records, kept by the kings of both Judah and Israel, are one more bit of evidence for the actuality of lost scripture and the importance that was placed on record keeping in ancient times, even during the reigns of wicked rulers.

Another generation in the Davidic dynasty is quickly accounted for in the story of Abijam, son of Rehoboam, who reigned only three years. His name honored Yam, the Canaanite god of the sea—certainly an apostate name for David's great-grandson. Abijam kept up the tradition of his father's evils. Mention is made (as it will be many times) that David, the father of the line of Judah's kings, was right in the eyes of the Lord most of his life, except in the matter of Uriah and Bathsheba.

"And there was war between Rehoboam and Jeroboam all the days of his life" (v. 6). "And there were wars between Rehoboam and Jeroboam continually" (2 Chronicles 12:15). These two succinct statements by biblical historians describe the border disputes that developed between the first two kings of the divided nation. These disputes would persist for generations after them.

1 Kings 15:9–24 (compare 2 Chronicles 14:2–17:1)

Of the long and noteworthy reign of Asa (41 years), next in the Davidic lineage of the southern kingdom, only three major projects are mentioned in Kings: (1) his religious reforms, which included even the removal of the idolatrous queen mother, (2) his war with Israel and his subsequent alliance with Syria, and (3) his construction for defense. The chronicler (2 Chronicles 15), on the other hand, uses a whole chapter to tell of Asa's religious reforms through a man of God named Azariah. This account mentions the migration of northern Israelites to Judah; in particular, people from Ephraim and Manasseh (we don't know why Simeon is also mentioned in 2 Chronicles 15:9, since Simeon was already a part of the southern kingdom of Judah). This could account for the presence of people from Ephraim and Manasseh in Jerusalem three hundred years later, when Lehi departed.

Good kings such as Asa in Judah made the difference between the unstable condition of Israel and the relatively stable condition of Judah. During the two hundred years that the kingdoms existed side by side, the northern kingdom of Israel had nineteen rulers from nine dynasties, eight of which began with violence, seven of these by assassination. Meanwhile Judah had twelve rulers, with only one coming to the throne by violence—the daughter of Ahab and Jezebel. Judah survived 130 years longer than Israel and still had only twenty rulers, only one more than Israel, and all from one dynasty. David was promised a royal lineage, and he believed the promise. Jeroboam of the northern kingdom was promised the same, but because he was disloyal to the Lord, the promise was not fulfilled. There were no righteous kings in the northern kingdom of Israel.

Verses 16–22 refer to border feuds between Baasha of Israel and Asa of Judah. Both kingdoms, dominated by the leadership tribes of Joseph and Judah, viewed control of their border region as vital to their own interests. This political and religious enmity would be perpetuated for millennia, though Isaiah did prophesy that the enmity between them would someday disappear: "The envy also of Ephraim shall depart, and the adversaries of Judah shall be cut off: Ephraim shall not envy Judah, and Judah shall not vex Ephraim" (Isaiah 11:13).

Regarding the seemingly curious, human-interest detail of Asa's diseased feet (v. 23), 2 Chronicles 16:7–12 indicates that there is a thematic reason for including it. The ailment came upon him in the thirty-ninth year of his reign because he did not rely upon the Lord in the matter of the escape of Aram's army and then put a seer named Hanani in prison for reproving him (Asa) for his lack of faith. Though the disease was severe, he made things worse—he failed to seek help from the Lord and instead relied only upon physicians. His lack of trust in God turned into belligerence once he was chastised for his foolishness. This is a powerful lesson for us.

1 Kings 15:25–34

Jeroboam's would-be dynasty lasted only two years after his death, when his son Nadab fell by the conspiracy of Baasha, who took it upon himself to exterminate the first royal house of northern Israel. Although Baasha is credited with fulfilling the warning prophecies against Jeroboam, his was not a positive contribution to Israel. It is mentioned only that he fought Judah and "did evil" all his days.

1 Kings 16:1–20

Though Baasha did as had been prophesied and utterly destroyed the house of Jeroboam, we should not suppose that he was ordained of the Lord to do so. Enter a prophet named Jehu, the son of the seer Hanani. Jehu was just like his father (2 Chronicles 16:7–10) in that he brought word to a king regarding the Lord's condemnation. In addition, like the prophet Amos later on, Jehu was sent from the south to a northern king. Jehu's prophetic ministry would last about fifty years, until the reign of King Jehoshaphat of Judah (see 2 Chronicles 19:2; 20:34).

So it was that the recorder of the sacred history tells us that by the hand of Jehu, the word of the Lord came against Baasha and against his house for all the evil he had done—not only for acting like the house of Jeroboam but for killing him as well. The house of Baasha was then exterminated by Zimri. Prophets can prophesy what men will bring upon themselves without the Lord's direct involvement. Jesus said, "All they that take the sword shall perish with the sword" (Matthew 26:52).

The captain Zimri, who slew his king, reigned for seven days; but some of the people made Omri, another captain, king. When Omri besieged Zimri, Zimri turned first to arson and then to suicide.

1 Kings 16:21–28

Israel was divided, and violence and bloodshed were rampant. Part of the people chose yet another man, Tibni, to be king; the civil war that ensued ultimately established Omri. He reigned first in Tirzah, then in the new capital, Samaria. Nonbiblical sources tell us more about Omri's eleven years as king than does the Bible. In addition to securing Samaria and building it into a well-fortified capital city for northern Israel, Omri conquered Moab and exacted tribute from them all his days, according to the stone inscription of Mesha, king of Moab. This stone is often called the Moabite Stone (see commentary at 2 Kings 1:1ff; Bible Dictionary, "Moabite Stone"). Later inscriptions, such as the annals of the Assyrian king Shalmanezer III, designate Israel as the "land of the house of Omri," and its kings were called in that text "sons of Omri," even after his dynasty had been long replaced by another ruling family. Ben Hadad of Syria said his father took certain cities from Omri and forced him to allow free trade in Samaria. Omri made an alliance with Ethbaal, king of Tyre (in Phoenicia), and took the Phoenician princess Jezebel for his son Ahab to marry. That alliance had deep and serious results in the religious and political life of Israel and Judah for the next fifty years.

1 Kings 16:29–34

This passage marks the beginning of the era of Ahab and Jezebel. The writer said that this king did more to provoke the Lord God of Israel to anger than all the kings of Israel that preceded him. That is saying something, considering who preceded him. He not only considered it trivial that he committed all the sins of Jeroboam, son of Nebat, but worst of all he married Jezebel, daughter of Ethbaal, king of the Sidonians (ancient Phoenicia) and openly promoted Baal worship by building an altar and temple dedicated to him. The word *Baal* literally translates as "lord" and was the Canaanite rival of Jehovah (the Phoenicians were sea-going Canaanites).

Recall the prophecy of Joshua concerning the doom of any who would try to rebuild Jericho (Joshua 6:26). The man who rebuilt Jericho, Hiel the Bethelite, suffered for his attempt.

1 Kings 17:1–7

Here is the abrupt introduction of the man who tried to counteract the influence of Ahab and Jezebel. Some have claimed that after Moses, Elijah was the greatest man in Israel's religious life. Some regard him as the best-known person in Hebrew history. Even today questions about Judaism and Jewish living that resist solutions are ultimately answered by the rabbis with the phrase, "when Elijah comes," meaning the returning prophet will have to solve this problem. Although Elijah left no extant writings himself, historians have preserved his story in 1 Kings 17 through 2 Kings 2. In 1 Kings 17:1 we learn that Elijah was a Tishbite, an inhabitant of Gilead. Tishbe was in Israelite Gilead, in Transjordan (east of the Jordan River). Elijah's name in Hebrew means "my God is Jehovah." All true prophets testify of Christ. Elijah held the keys of the sealing power and the fulness of the priesthood in his day (see Smith, *History of the Church*, 4:211; 6:251–52).

Elder Bruce R. McConkie wrote about Elijah: "For dramatic manifestations and the visible exhibition of divine power, the ministry of Elijah the prophet scarcely has an equal. He sealed the heavens, was fed by the ravens, extended the widow's barrel of meal and cruse of oil, raised the dead, destroyed the priests of Baal, called down fire from heaven on at least three occasions, fasted 40 days and nights, was attended frequently by angelic ministrants, and finally was translated and taken up into heaven without tasting death. (1 Kings 17; 18; 2 Kings 1; 2.)

"Centuries later Malachi prophesied that Elijah would return before the great and dreadful day of the Lord. (Mal. 4:5–6.) With Moses, another translated being, he appeared to Peter, James, and John on the Mount of Transfiguration to give those apostolic ministers the keys of the kingdom. (Matt. 17:1–13; *Teachings*, p. 158.) During the night of September 21st–22nd, 1823, Moroni told Joseph Smith that the Lord would soon reveal unto him the priesthood by the hand of Elijah the Prophet [Joseph Smith–History 1:29–39]; and on April 3, 1836, Elijah came (in fulfilment of the promises of Malachi and Moroni) to Joseph Smith and Oliver Cowdery, in the Kirtland Temple, and conferred upon them the keys of the sealing power. (D. & C. 110:13–16.)" (*Mormon Doctrine*, 222–23).

Elijah's first recorded use of the sealing power was to shut up the heavens, causing a dearth of rain for three and a half years. His purpose in stopping the rains was the same as expressed later by Nephi in the Book of Mormon:

"O Lord, do not suffer that this people shall be destroyed by the sword; but . . . rather let there be a famine in the land, to stir them up in remembrance of the Lord their God, and perhaps they will repent and turn unto thee" (Helaman 11:4; compare this humbling technique also found in Amos 4:6–11).

Because of the severe famine that resulted, Elijah fled to the brook Cherith to find drinking water and be fed by ravens. Traditionally Cherith has been equated with Wadi Qilt, along which the Roman-period Jericho was later built, although the biblical text itself says that the brook was "before Jordan," meaning *east* of Jordan. If Cherith was indeed east of Jordan, the site has not been discovered.

1 Kings 17:8–24

When the drought and famine forced Elijah to go elsewhere, the Lord directed him to the sea coast city of Zarephath, between Tyre and Sidon, some fifty miles north of Mount Carmel, to a widow whom the Lord had commanded to sustain him. The woman recognized Jehovah, the God of Elijah. Jesus pointed to this as an example of blessings going to others because those closest at hand will not accept them (Luke 4:25–26). The faith of the woman is noteworthy: she willingly responded to Elijah's request to give him first of the cake made with her last bit of flour and oil on the promise that the oil and meal would continue to be available. Faith precedes the miracle.

Thus at Zarephath one of the greatest recorded Old Testament miracles took place when Elijah raised the widow's son from death by the power of God, perhaps using some form of artificial resuscitation (v. 21; see also 2 Kings 4:34; commentary at 2 Kings 2:23–25, including "Elijah, Elisha, and Christ"). The widow sacrificed all she had for the Lord's prophet and, by extension, the Lord's kingdom. Are we willing to do the same?

1 Kings 18:1–18

At length it was time for a confrontation between Ahab and Elijah, representative of a confrontation between Israel and the Lord—between evil and good. Not all, but apparently almost all, of Israel had departed from the covenant of the Lord and from all trust in the Lord's promises. Ironically, Ahab's own chief steward, Obadiah, was still faithful enough to harbor and hide a hundred refugee prophets of the Lord under those wicked conditions. It is also ironic that Ahab would accuse Elijah of "troubling Israel," whereas Elijah knew that Ahab and his foreign, Baal-worshiping wife were the real troublemakers. So the confrontation was to be resolved in a contest between a false god and the true God.

34

1 Kings 18:19–40

When all the people were assembled at Mount Carmel, the geographic meeting point between Israel's Jehovah and Phoenicia's Baal, the issues were pronounced tersely: whichever of the deities was truly God, the people should serve him. On Baalism, see commentary at Judges 2:11–23 in volume 1 of this commentary; see also Bible Dictionary: "Baal," "Grove," "High Places," and "Idol."

This was to be one of Elijah's major dramatic efforts to turn the hearts of the children back to the true and living God, and to the divine promises and covenants of their fathers. The name of the location where this contest occurred is particularly poignant, for Carmel (Hebrew, *Kerem-el*) means "vineyard of God." Mount Carmel was a place where true worship had previously taken place; Elijah "repaired the altar of the Lord that was broken down" (v. 30). The priests of Baal and Elijah each prepared sacrifices for their god. The true God was to signify his acceptance of the sacrifice by sending down fire to burn up the wood and the sacrifice, and the people watched with approval. After the prophets of Baal had prayed all day and had made their final frenzied attempts to get response from their idol, Elijah taunted them that their god must be talking, busy, on a journey, or sleeping, because he did not respond. They even cut themselves, perhaps owing to a perverted notion of a genuine truth—the shedding of sacrificial blood brings divine favor. Elijah then uttered a simple, significant prayer that gained the Lord's immediate and dramatic response. Even though every advantage was given to Baal, Jehovah triumphed. The people, who had been "halting between two opinions" (literally, vacillating back and forth concerning the two possibilities) momentarily prostrated themselves before the Lord and confessed, "The Lord, he is God!" A powerful lesson can be drawn for us in our day: you can't hedge your bets when it comes to the kingdom of God; you can't keep one foot in the kingdom and the other in the world; you can't please the world and expect God to approve.

With the forces of public opinion temporarily on his side, Elijah was able to have the prophets of the vanquished "god" executed (see Deuteronomy 17:1–7). The site of the execution was at the Kishon River, which still flows along the northern foot of Mount Carmel.

1 Kings 18:41–46

These verses recount Elijah's further attempt to drive home the point that Jehovah is the true and living God, and the only One concerned for Israel's welfare. Elijah had sealed up the heavens for three and a half years. This new contest was actually to see whose deity could bring rain and fertility back to the land. Baal was supposed to be the preeminent rain god, a fertility god. But Jehovah is shown by irrefutable evidence to be the only true and living God who can send forth both fire and rain, who watches over storms and the fertility of the land. Jeremiah later wrote:

"Are there any among the vanities [idols] of the Gentiles that can cause rain? or can the heavens give showers? art not thou he, O Lord our God? therefore we will wait upon thee: for thou hast made all these things" (Jeremiah 14:22).

What the fertility god Baal could not do, Jehovah did. His mighty control of the elements was evidenced by the ensuing fierce winds and pounding rain, in which Elijah ran ahead of Ahab's chariot almost twenty miles to the entrance of Jezreel (see Bible Map 10 for the location of Mount Carmel and Jezreel).

1 Kings 19:1–18

The strength and popularity (or fear) of Jezebel in the hearts of the people must have been greater than the power of the Lord in their hearts, else they would have arisen to free the country from her influences. When she threatened the prophet Elijah's life, he seems to have had no hope that the people would save him or that there was any real conviction on their part that "the Lord is God." Thus his bitter outcry in his feeling of failure: "It is enough; now, O Lord, take away my life. . . . I have been very jealous for the Lord God of hosts: for the children of Israel have forsaken thy covenant, thrown down thine altars, and slain thy prophets with the sword; and I, even I only, am left; and they seek my life, to take it away" (vv. 4, 10). Here we catch a glimpse of mortal feelings being displayed by one of the greatest of godly souls—the truth that even prophets get discouraged. We also see another example of Elijah's role as a type of Christ in suffering because of the wickedness of others. Many prophets have likewise suffered, as Jesus taught (Matthew 5:12; 23:37).

When Jezebel threatened to kill him, as she had killed many other prophets, Elijah fled south more than a hundred miles to Beersheba and then continued on to Mount Sinai (also called Mount Horeb). The discouraged prophet needed encouragement. At Mount Sinai, the Lord spoke to Elijah, not through the dramatic forces of nature but through "a still small voice" and told him that he had work to do. Elijah was to get a companion and be assured that there were still many other righteous souls who had not endorsed Baal worship. Elijah was not alone.

It is noteworthy that Elijah did not flee to Jerusalem, to the House of the Lord. Because Melchizedek Priesthood holders were generally not functioning in the Temple at Jerusalem, perhaps Elijah chose to flee to the earlier holy place, Mount Sinai, because that is where the God of Israel had made his last known appearance to a prophet—to Moses, more than half a millennium earlier.

Elijah then journeyed over five hundred miles to the wilderness of Damascus (v. 15) to anoint two men as future kings: Hazael to be king in Syria and Jehu to be king in Israel. Elijah's ministry was stunningly arduous, both physically and spiritually. His next assignment was to anoint Elisha to serve as his companion and later to succeed him as prophet.

1 Kings 19:19–21

When Elijah found Elisha, he symbolically placed his mantle on Elisha. Observe that Elisha, like the followers of Jesus in New Testament times, was required to leave all and follow him (compare Matthew 4:18–22; Luke 9:59–62). The Lord's principles are constant through every dispensation.

1 Kings 20:1–34

A league of kings under the command of Ben-hadad of Aram-Damascus (modern-day Syria) attempted to besiege and extort treasures from Ahab in his capital city of Samaria. Ahab's forces were able to repulse them. Ben-hadad is the name-title for several kings in Damascus; it means "son of [the storm god] Hadad."

Within a year Ben-hadad was back, ready to attack Israel again. This time the battlefield was on the Golan, the high plateau just east of the Sea of Galilee. This second battle with the Syrians ended in humiliating defeat for the king of Damascus, who had promised to return disputed lands to Israel. Such campaigns gained a respectful reputation abroad for Ahab. Nevertheless, his accomplishments were not much honored by Bible writers. The Lord's help seems to have been given him for Israel's sake, not for any worthiness of his own.

Verse 28—The man of God is apparently the same prophet mentioned in verses 13 and 22. This reminds us of Father Lehi's observation offered centuries later that many prophets can serve the Lord at the same time (1 Nephi 1:4).

Verse 30—The collapsed wall reminds us that Jehovah directed Israel's armies and engineered other events to help his people.

Verse 31—Obviously, rumors had circulated throughout the Near East that Israel's kings operated by a social code different from those of their ruthless counterparts in other countries. It is unfortunate that these Israelite kings were lacking in what should have been the main difference—loyalty to Jehovah.

1 Kings 20:35–43

At this point a curious group known as "the sons of the prophets" became more prominent in events of the northern kingdom of Israel. The word "sons" here is not used in the sense of a male child or descendant. It refers to followers or disciples of the prophets. Because another man was disobedient to a command from one of these sons of the prophets, he was penalized in a fashion reminiscent of what happened to the man of God from Judah (1 Kings 13:23–24), and likewise, something seems to be missing from the story. It does, however, set the stage for a prophetic curse leveled against Ahab. He allowed the captured king to live and thus incurred prophetic wrath for disobedience: Ahab himself would die.

1 Kings 21:1–13

Here is the account of a petulant and covetous king and his violent wife involved in an old, unscrupulous game. Israel had been forewarned that kings take land: "And he will take your fields, and your vineyards, and your oliveyards, even the best of them" (1 Samuel 8:14). No legal way existed to seize or purchase a man's ancestral land if he did not wish to part with it. The king wanted the additional real estate to satisfy his palatial landscaping whims, and so he pouted and threw a tantrum (v. 4) because he could not get *that* vineyard. But Jezebel, his ambitious wife, was from a different land with different laws, and she thought it silly for a king not to "rule" over what he wanted. Might equals right, in her mind. She easily devised a way to circumvent the law and the moral code in the name of piety, so no one in Israel could object. She arranged for the owner of the vineyard to be charged with blasphemy by the false witnesses of two "sons of Belial" ("worthless ones"; verses 10–13). Would anyone have believed that Jezebel cared if anyone blasphemed the Lord? She did it, of course, in the name of the king. After she had the owner of the vineyard stoned to death, the king simply took over the land.

1 Kings 21:14–29

If this ruse shielded Ahab and Jezebel from anyone, or even from everyone, it didn't shield them from the Lord and his prophet. The terrible message of doom the prophet delivered was both appropriate and deserved: "Thus saith the Lord, Hast thou killed, and also taken possession?" Recall that David did the same thing.

Then the prophet pronounced the verdict and sentence: Where Ahab had spilled the blood of Naboth, dogs would lick up the king's blood, and dogs would eat the flesh of Jezebel. All of that happened at the city of Jezreel, where the winter palace of Ahab and Jezebel was located. There seems to be almost a note of awareness of his guilt in Ahab's query: "Hast thou found me, O mine enemy?" (v. 20).

If it seems that justice is abrogated in verse 29, realize that the reprieve referred only to the loss of the kingdom by Ahab's descendants; he was still to suffer personally the fate indicated, which is disclosed in the next chapter of 1 Kings.

1 Kings 22:1–40 (2 Chronicles 18:1–34)

We note at this point an important historical development. While involved in their own petty local conflicts, kings of the several eastern Mediterranean states began to notice a powerful

Erich Lessing/Art Resource, NY

Ivory plaque found at the palace of Ahab in Samaria. 1 Kings 22:39 mentions
"the acts of Ahab, and all that he did, and the ivory house which he made"

Assyrian military machine rising in the east. They declared a temporary truce in order to join forces to stop the advancing Assyrians: "They continued three years without war between Syria and Israel" (1 Kings 22:1).

Twelve kings stood against Shalmaneser III at Qarqar on the Orontes River in northwestern Syria. Ahab of Israel commanded a substantial part of the coalition army against Assyria.

After the battle of Qarqar, Ahab asked for and received the assistance of the pious Jehoshaphat of Judah to retake from the Syrians the city of Ramoth in Gilead, in the central transjordan territory of Gad. What Jehoshaphat's motivation was is not clear, although his son had married a daughter of Ahab and Jezebel. It is possible that he hoped to promote the reunion of all Israel, or perhaps it was upon Ahab's initiative (or that of Jezebel) out of the hope or intent to subjugate Judah. Quite possibly, Israel had enough power at the time to compel Judah to lend assistance. Since the writers usually gave credit when credit was due Judah, it seems likely that had the initiative been Judah's, the scribes would have given proper credit for it.

One difference between Ahab's religion and Jehoshaphat's more reverent faith is that Ahab sought and received guidance from his four hundred court prophets, all of whom reassured him. Jehoshaphat stood by and judiciously inquired, "Is there not here a *prophet* of the Lord besides, that we might enquire of him?" (v. 7; emphasis added).

The true prophet Micaiah sarcastically repeated the other prophets' message, followed by the true message of doom to Ahab. His explanation of the Lord's sending a "lying spirit" (v. 23), causing the other prophets to mislead Ahab so that he would go to his doom, is strange theology (compare Numbers 23:19; 1 Samuel 15:29; Enos 1:6; Ether 3:12). It is apparently either sarcasm spoken in disdain or the words have been transmitted to us incorrectly.

So Ahab and Jehoshaphat went into battle, the former disguising himself while telling the latter to be sure to wear his royal robes. By attempting to deflect attention from himself and hoping the enemy would focus on Jehoshaphat, Ahab demonstrated his cunning cowardice. He hoped he could minimize any chance that Micaiah's prophecy would be fulfilled. But the word of the Lord caught up to Ahab at the point of an arrow. Someone randomly shot at him, hitting him between the sections of his armor and killing him. Ahab was taken back to his summer palace in Samaria for burial. As his chariot was being washed out, the dogs licked up his blood, just as the Lord declared would happen.

It must have been by reason of his own worthiness and the influence of the Lord that Jehoshaphat was spared in battle, for it is strange that the enemy would spare any opponent, especially a royal one. Notice that the king of Syria had told those who were looking for Ahab to fight against no one else. Recall again how the writer describes Ahab at the beginning of this account; namely, that he did more evil than all who were before him (1 Kings 16:30).

Verse 39 makes particular note of the ivory house that Ahab had made in Samaria. Early in the twentieth century, Harvard University excavators corroborated the biblical text by discovering hundreds of plaques and ornamental pieces of ivory that had decorated the furniture in the royal palace of Ahab at Samaria during the ninth to eighth centuries before Christ. Many of the pieces feature Egyptian and Mesopotamian artistic motifs. They attest to the luxury living so rigorously condemned by the prophets at the time (compare Amos 3:15).

1 Kings 22:41–50 (2 Chronicles 20:31–21:1)

Jehoshaphat's contributions in religious and social reform, and in international relations, are commended by the writers. He did fail, however, to halt the worship of the Lord at inappropriate shrines called "high places" that were originally to worship Jehovah but had been perverted to other uses. The people tended to revert to making offerings to fertility deities there, or to worship the Lord in the same manner as they worshiped Baal, just as some systems of worship today preserve practices borrowed from pagan religions. The unfortunate fact that Jehoshaphat's son and heir was married to Athaliah, daughter of Ahab and Jezebel, is not mentioned until later (2 Kings 8:18).

1 Kings 22:51–53

The reign of Ahaziah, son of Ahab of Israel, is tragically similar to those of the other kings of northern Israel.

SECOND KINGS

2 Kings 1:1

On Ahab's death, the Moabites seized the opportunity to rebel against Israel and free themselves (see commentary at 1 Kings 16:21–28). A translation of King Mesha's description of this event on the Moabite Stone, the record written by Mesha and discovered in the ruins of Dibon in 1868 (see 2 Kings 3), sounds as if it were the record of the final fall of Israel!

2 Kings 1:2–18

King Ahaziah, son of Ahab, fell from his upper chamber in the capital city of Samaria and sent messengers to inquire of the god Baal-zebub in Ekron, a Philistine city, whether he would recover. Elijah stopped the messengers and sent them back with a chastisement of the king for not inquiring of the true God of the land. The king received his answer from the Lord: he would not recover but would surely die. And so he did, according to the word of the Lord. The king sent soldiers to apprehend Elijah, but the prophet called down fire from heaven to consume them.

Verse 8 describes Elijah's appearance, which recalls the image of John the Baptist (Matthew 3:4), who was closely associated with Elijah by the Jews (John 1:19–25; Matthew 11:14; Malachi 4:5).

Baal-zebub, written Beelzebub in the New Testament (Matthew 12:24), where it is used almost as a cognomen for Satan, was a Philistine god whose name means "lord of the flies." His domain in the false religious beliefs of the day paradoxically included both disease and healing.

2 Kings 2:1–15

This passage recounts the miraculous departure of Elijah. In verses 2, 4, 6, and so on, notice the loyalty of Elisha. In verses 3, 5, and 15, the "sons of the prophets" are seen in a somewhat subordinate relation to Elijah and Elisha, but their nature and function as an institution in Israel are not clear. In verse 9, Elisha's request for a "double portion" of Elijah's spiritual gift is to be understood in connection with the law of inheritances (Deuteronomy 21:17). The law specifies that an heir, or birthright son, receives a larger portion of the inheritance than the other children. It is as if Elisha asked to be made Elijah's official heir, spiritually speaking. The mantle of Elijah that was earlier placed symbolically on Elisha (1 Kings 19:19) was now transferred to him. This significant garment has become proverbial in our references to "the mantle of the prophet" falling upon someone.

The Lord or his messenger apparently came to take up Elijah with a "chariot of fire, and horses of fire." These terms are symbolic, as with "wings" on angelic messengers (see D&C 77:4), representing the glory that surrounds his presence. Since prophets are types of Christ, it is not surprising that the Lord will come again the same way, with chariots of fire (see Isaiah 66:15).

The two great prophets Moses and Elijah were taken into heaven without tasting death at the same location, east of the Jordan River. Later, they returned to earth together at the Mount of Transfiguration in Christ's day and again in our own dispensation.

The scriptures contain several allusions to Elijah's translation into heaven and to his mission in both the meridian of time and the fulness of times. See, for instance, the inquiry about him by Jesus' apostles (Matthew 17:10–11). In Jesus' reply it is evident not only that the prophet was still expected to help usher in the messianic age but also that others, such as John the Baptist, could serve as forerunners of important dispensations.

The Hebrew name "Elijah" in the English Old Testament becomes, through Greek transliteration, "Elias" in the New Testament; only by context can one tell whether the reference is to Elijah, to any "forerunner," or to a prophet named Elias.

Elijah's coming to "plant in the hearts of the children the promises made to the fathers" is spoken of in Joseph

Smith–History 1:38–39. This wording is slightly different from the Old Testament version of Malachi 4:5–6 or that alluded to by the apostles in Matthew 17:10–11. Besides some discussion of his future mission by the Prophet Joseph Smith, there are numerous references to Elijah in the Doctrine and Covenants; note especially his appearance in the Kirtland Temple on April 3, 1836, as recorded in Doctrine and Covenants 110:13–16.

Moses and Elijah were translated to fulfill a later assignment on this earth. Only beings who have belonged to this earth may minister here (D&C 130:5). Moses and Elijah were translated in order to have tangible bodies to confer priesthood keys on the three apostle-leaders on the Mount of Transfiguration (Smith, *Doctrines of Salvation*, 2:110–11). Keys are the power and authority to direct the use of the priesthood. A translated being is of the *terrestrial* order, the same condition the earth will enjoy during the Millennium (Dahl and Cannon, *Encyclopedia of Joseph Smith's Teachings*, 674).

Elijah was the Old Testament prophet commissioned to confer the keys of the sealing powers of the priesthood. "The spirit, power, and calling of Elijah is, that ye have power to hold the key of the revelation, ordinances, oracles, powers and endowments of the fullness of the Melchizedek Priesthood and of the kingdom of God on the earth; and to receive, obtain, and perform all the ordinances belonging to the kingdom of God, even unto the turning of the hearts of the fathers unto the children, and the hearts of the children unto the fathers, even those who are in heaven. . . . I wish you to understand this subject, for it is important" (*Joseph Smith* [manual], 311–12).

For many centuries, Jewish people have honored Elijah with a vacant place for him at every Passover table; Elijah is the anticipated herald of the messianic kingdom as they understand it from the promise of the prophet Malachi (see Malachi 4:5–6).

THE SONS OF THE PROPHETS

As the time of Elijah's departure approached, a curious group of men known as the "sons of the prophets" (and also called "prophets") became more prominent in the events surrounding the transition of authority from one prophet to another. Perhaps they are best understood as a group of disciples who followed the prophets, preserved their words, and spread their messages. Since "the testimony of Jesus is the spirit of prophecy" (Revelation 19:10), perhaps we should look upon these individuals as the devoted disciples of the Lord in their day. In a time of general apostasy in the kingdom of Israel, it may be that these men and their families were the few who had the light of the gospel, which was largely absent in their generation because of unworthiness. People who live by the Spirit are "prophets" in their own right, and these, who looked on Elijah and then Elisha as their teachers and leaders, were called, symbolically, the sons of their masters. In this regard, Elisha cried out to Elijah, "My father, my father," when he saw the fiery chariot (2 Kings 2:12).

How the sons of the prophets were organized is not known. During the time of Elijah and Elisha, they were found at various places, including Gilgal, Bethel, and Jericho. We know that some of them had families and that they were not exempt from working for their livelihood. Their families were not unfamiliar with economic misfortune (2 Kings 4:1).

The sons of the prophets were spiritually mature and perceptive, as is evident in their recognition that the promised mantle of authority actually rested on Elisha at the time of Elijah's departure (2 Kings 2:15). They also assisted the great prophets in their duties and even officiated when called to perform in the prophetic office themselves, as was the case when Elisha sent one of them to Ramoth-gilead to anoint Jehu king over Israel (2 Kings 9:1–10). That young prophet was specifically commanded to use the prophetic formula "Thus saith the Lord" in fulfilling his appointed task (2 Kings 9:3).

2 Kings 2:16–22

Elisha returned to the west side of the Jordan and parted the waters once again with Elijah's mantle. He remained in Jericho for several days, and the men of the city pleaded with him to do something about their water supply. In response, Elisha miraculously healed the spring water. This spring at the eastern foot of the mound of old Jericho is still called Elisha's Spring.

Elisha's healing the spring may have been a cause of great amazement because the spring, only a few miles north of the Dead Sea—the saltiest body of water on earth—was becoming polluted and turning brackish, and yet *salt* was the prophetically prescribed cure.

Salt is such a significant element and symbol that it is mentioned in the Old and New Testaments, the Book of Mormon, and the Doctrine and Covenants. Anciently salt was a vital part of daily life as well as religious practice. It was a condiment or seasoning agent, a preservative, a purgative, a medicine, and a crucial element in the sacrificial system of Mosaic law. Job asked, "Can that which is unsavoury [tasteless] be eaten without salt?" (Job 6:6). It was customary to rub newborn babies with salt for medicinal as well as religious reasons (Ezekiel 16:4). Knowledge of the symbolism of salt and its curative powers seems to have prompted Elisha to use it to purify the spring at Jericho. "And he went forth unto the spring of the waters, and cast the salt in there, and said, Thus saith the Lord, I have healed these waters; there shall not be from thence any more death or barren land" (2 Kings 2:21).

Scholars have argued that the declared cure of barrenness applied not to the land but rather to persons and animals: "Neither death nor miscarriage shall come from it [the waters]" (Buttrick, *Interpreter's Dictionary of the Bible*, 4:167). That the word *land* in 2 Kings 2:21 is in italics in the King James Version, which indicates that it is not in the original Hebrew text, makes the latter reading plausible.

2 Kings 2:23–25

Most stories of Elisha are about his "good turn" miracles for people, but this one is different. On his way from Jericho to Bethel, the same route on which the Israelites had first conquered their way into the land, a gang of youths (Hebrew, *na'arim,* "youths," not "little children") challenged Elisha to ascend (as they had perhaps heard that Elijah had ascended), and taunted and mocked him repeatedly with the disrespectful epithet "bald head." Elisha turned, looked at them, and called down on them a curse in the name of the Lord (compare Leviticus 26:21–22). The curse became a symbol of the judgment that befell the entire nation for mocking and disobeying the Lord's anointed (see 2 Chronicles 36:16). This early action in Elisha's ministry may be seen symbolically as something of a pattern for what would follow in Israel and Judah: those who mocked, arrogantly taunted, or rebuffed the prophetic voice would be cursed, while the obedient would be blessed.

The rest of the account does not say the bears ate the youths, nor even that they killed them, but *tore* them. The Hebrew word *baqa*, translated here as to "tear," also means to "lacerate."

ELIJAH, ELISHA, AND CHRIST

Though of course there were specific differences between Elijah and Elisha, the latter's ministry greatly resembled and paralleled that of his master, Elijah. That was due in part to Elisha's request that he be endowed with a double portion of Elijah's spirit, which he was (2 Kings 2:9). More importantly, the similar lives and ministries of both men foreshadowed and typified the life of Jesus Christ, who would be the heavenly Jehovah come to earth. Consider the following:

- Elisha's first miracle—smiting the waters of the Jordan with Elijah's mantle—was also the last miracle performed by his master (2 Kings 2:8, 14).
- Elisha, like Elijah and Christ, had control over the elements, especially water (2 Kings 3:17; Mark 4:41).
- Elisha, again much like Elijah, multiplied a widow's oil to sustain her family (1 Kings 17:10–16; 2 Kings 4:1–7).
- In an episode foreshadowing one of Christ's great miracles, Elisha fed one hundred men with only twenty loaves and some grain and had food left over (2 Kings 4:42–44; Mark 6:33–44).
- Like Christ, Elisha healed the sick, as in the example of the Syrian general, Naaman (2 Kings 5).
- Elisha raised a woman's son from the dead in much the same way as Elijah had done (1 Kings 17:21–22; 2 Kings 4:32–35). Raising the dead, especially a widow's son (Luke 7:11–15), was also graphic testimony of Christ's divine power (Mark 5:41–42; John 11:41–44).

- Elisha, like both his masters, Elijah and Christ, prophesied the future and constantly inveighed against the idolatry of Israel.
- Elijah, Elisha, and Christ suffered at the hands of wicked men.

The resemblances of the ministries of Elijah, Elisha, and Christ are attested in the New Testament, especially in those passages that show that Jesus was mistaken for the returning Elijah (see Matthew 16:14). The New Testament also indicates that Christ was keenly aware of Elijah's and Elisha's missions and even identified with them (Luke 4:24–27). Truly, the lives and activities of Elijah and Elisha were similitudes of the God whom they served.

2 Kings 3:1–5

When Ahaziah, son of Ahab, died without an heir, his brother Jehoram (not to be confused with the son of Jehoshaphat by the same name, who became king of Judah) reigned in his stead.

As you will recall, the Moabites broke away from the political and tributary impositions of Israel when Ahab, the northern kingdom's most powerful king, was killed in battle. Second Kings 3 describes the alliance formed between Israel, Judah, and Edom to arrest the rebellion. Despite the victorious efforts of the three kings, Moab successfully threw off the yoke of Israel and reconquered lands east of the Dead Sea.

Often called the Moabite Stone, the Victory Stele of Mesha, king of Moab, was discovered in 1868 in the town of Dibon, which lies astride the King's Highway in Transjordan, now known as the Hashemite Kingdom of Jordan. The inscription dates to the ninth century before Christ (about 830 B.C.) and augments the biblical account of the Moabite rebellion against Israel, from the point of view of the Moabite king, Mesha.

Most of the inscription, as translated by W. F. Albright, is presented below. Known place names are italicized. Chemosh was the idol god worshiped by the Moabites. Israelite kings Omri and Ahab are referred to in the inscription. This inscription is one of the best of the archaeological discoveries that authenticate and corroborate the biblical record:

"I (am) Mesha, son of Chemosh-[. . .], king of Moab, the Dibonite—my father (had) reigned over Moab thirty years, and

Erich Lessing/Art Resource, NY

The Victory Stele of Mesha, king of Moab.
Often called the Moabite Stone, it is
displayed in the Louvre, Paris. "Mesha king
of Moab was a sheepmaster . . . but it came
to pass, when Ahab was dead, that the
king of Moab rebelled against the
king of Israel" (2 Kings 3:4–5)

I reigned after my father, (who) made this high place for Chemosh in Qarhoh [. . .] because he saved me from all the kings and caused me to triumph over all my adversaries. As for Omri, king of Israel, he humbled Moab many years (lit., days), for Chemosh was angry at his land. And his son followed him and he also said, 'I will humble Moab.' In my time he spoke (thus), but I have triumphed over him and over his house, while Israel hath perished for ever! (Now) Omri had occupied the land of Medeba, and (Israel) had dwelt there in his time and half the time of his son (Ahab), forty years; but Chemosh dwelt there in my time.

"And I built *Baal-meon*, making a reservoir in it, and I built Qaryaten *[Kiriathaim?]*. Now the men of Gad had always dwelt in the land of Ataroth, and the king of Israel had built Ataroth for them; but I fought against the town and took it and slew all the people of the town as satiation (intoxication) for Chemosh and Moab. . . . And Chemosh said to me, 'Go, take *Nebo* from Israel!' So I went by night and fought against it from the break of dawn until noon, taking it and slaying all, seven thousand men, boys, women, girls and maid-servants, for I had devoted them to destruction for (the god) Ashtar-Chemosh. And I took from there the [. . .] of Yahweh, dragging them before Chemosh. And the king of Israel had built *Jahaz*, and he dwelt there while he was fighting against me, but Chemosh drove him out before me. And I took from Moab two hundred men, all first class (warriors), and set them against Jahaz and took it in order to attach it to (the district of) *Dibon*. . . .

"I cut beams for Qarhoh with Israelite captives. I built Aroer, and I made the highway in the Arnon (valley); I built Beth-bamoth, for it had been destroyed; I built *Bezer*—for it lay in ruins—with fifty men of Dibon, for all Dibon is (my) loyal dependency.

"And I reigned [in peace] over the hundred towns which I had added to the land. And I built [. . .] *Medeba* and *Beth-diblathen* and *Beth-baal-meon,* and I set there the [. . .] of the land. And as for Hauronen [Horonaim], there dwelt in it. [. . . And] Chemosh said to me, 'Go down, fight against Hauronen.' And I went down [and I fought against the town and I took it], and Chemosh dwelt there in my time" (*Ancient Near East,* 1:209–10).

2 Kings 3:6–20

As in the days of Ahab, Jehoram (king of Israel) sought and received the collaboration of Jehoshaphat (king of Judah). They joined forces against Moab. The avenging armies of Israel and Judah and their allies from Edom found they needed water. Because of the presence of the righteous Jehoshaphat, Elisha supplicated the Lord for a miracle in their behalf, that they might have water and see that it was "but a little thing in the sight of the Lord" to be able to deliver them. The next morning, water flowed from the distant mountains of Edom.

2 Kings 3:21–27

The Moabites erred and walked into the Israelite camp, and the Israelites smote them all the way back to their fortified city. At length, the Moabites were able to withstand the siege. The Moabite king sacrificed his son and heir as a burnt offering. Then followed "great indignation against Israel," and the Israelites departed. The Hebrew suggests that God's wrath descended upon Israel, but the text does not say why. This was apparently the victory of which king Mesha boasted in his inscription on the stone.

2 Kings 4:1–7

These verses present one of several stories about Elisha's kind deeds. In this one, he aided the widow of one of the "sons of the prophets." Elisha blessed her oil that it would increase enough to give her sufficient income that she could pay her debts and save her sons from slavery. In its creative nature and compassionate purpose, this miracle resembles some of Jesus' deeds.

2 Kings 4:8–37

This is one of the most beautiful and heartwarming stories in the Bible. A barren Shunammite woman had provided for the prophet in his journeys through the Jezreel Valley. Because of her care, she was promised a son. Years later, the boy suffered some kind of ailment and died. The grieving mother sent for Elisha, who was then at Mount Carmel, begging him to return quickly. The prophet hurried to Shunem and used some form of artificial resuscitation, along with priesthood power, to raise the boy from the dead. This is the second case of the rarest type of miracle told in the Old Testament—the raising of the dead (recall the other from 1 Kings 17:17–24). Jesus later performed a similar miracle in raising a boy from the dead in the little village of Nain, which is on the opposite side of the same mountain, the Hill of Moreh (Luke 7:11–15; see Bible Maps 10, 11). The miracles performed by Elisha, Elijah, and Jesus also parallel one performed by the apostle Paul when he raised a young man back to life by embracing him (Acts 20:10).

2 Kings 4:38–44

When all of the sons of the prophets ate a stew with a noxious gourd in it, they became very ill. Elisha miraculously healed them.

In another good turn, Elisha multiplied some loaves of bread and some grain to feed a hundred. This was also similar to miracles later performed by Jesus (see footnote 44*a*).

2 Kings 5:1–18

Leprosy is one of the most feared diseases throughout the Bible. Elder James E. Talmage wrote: "In Biblical usage [leprosy] applied to several diseases, all, however having some symptoms in common, at least in the earlier stages of the malady. The real leprosy is a scourge and a plague in many oriental lands today. . . . Deems, *Light of the Nations,* p. 185, summing up the conditions incident to the advanced stages of the dread disease, writes: 'The symptoms and the effects of this disease are very loathsome. There comes a white swelling or scab, with a change of the color of the hair on the part from its natural hue to yellow; then the appearance of a taint going deeper than the skin, or raw flesh appearing in the swelling. Then it spreads and attacks the cartilaginous portions of the body. The nails loosen and drop off, the gums are absorbed, and the teeth decay and fall out; the breath is a stench, the nose decays; fingers, hands, feet, may be lost, or the eyes eaten out. The human beauty has gone into corruption, and the patient feels that he is being eaten as by a fiend, who consumes him slowly in a long remorseless meal that will not end until he be destroyed'" (*Jesus the Christ,* 186).

A high-ranking Syrian army officer called Naaman had contracted the dreaded disease of leprosy. A faithful young Israelite girl was working as a maid (a captured slave) in his house and had apparently shared her testimony of a living prophet in Israel who had power to cure the disease. Upon her suggestion Naaman headed for Israel. He eventually ended up at Elisha's house, and the prophet instructed him, through his servant, to go and wash seven times in the Jordan River. Naaman was insulted and enraged, because he had expected the prophet to come out and instantly cure him. He further argued that the two rivers in Damascus were better than the muddy ditch called Jordan. He dismissed Elisha's counsel, but his servants finally convinced him to heed Elisha's instructions.

Naaman's pride almost prevented him from receiving the Lord's blessings, because he was thinking, in a sense, "I'm too great a man to be treated this way." Do we sometimes deprive ourselves of experiences because of pride, experiences that could otherwise be great blessings in our lives? We also need to remember Mosiah 3:19: "For the natural man is an enemy to God, and has been from the fall of Adam, and will be, forever and ever, unless he yields to the enticings of the Holy Spirit, and putteth off the natural man and becometh a saint through the atonement of Christ the Lord, and becometh as a child, submissive, meek, humble, patient, full of love, willing to submit to all things which the Lord seeth fit to inflict upon him, even as a child doth submit to his father."

When Naaman "dipped" (Hebrew, *immersed*) himself seven times, his skin was cleansed and became as the skin of a little child. Notice how he felt when he realized he had been healed. During his mortal ministry, Jesus spoke of this great miracle of Elisha, as recorded in Luke 4:23–27.

Did the Jordan River's water heal Naaman? Was it the clay or the Pool of Siloam's water that healed the blind man sent there by Jesus? Is it consecrated olive oil that heals us? We learn from these and other scriptures that water and clay and oil do not heal; healing comes through the priesthood power of God and people's faith.

It should be understood that Naaman's religious background would allow him also to worship Israel's Jehovah without giving up his national gods. Since Jehovah was thought to be a god of Israel only, he took some of Israel's dirt back to Syria that he might appropriately build an altar there on Israel's soil! He really was sorry that he would still have to acknowledge other gods.

2 Kings 5:19–27

In a tragic sequel, Elisha's servant, Gehazi, couldn't quite resist the gifts Naaman offered to Elisha for the Lord's blessing and which Elisha rejected. When he deceitfully obtained some of the offered goods for himself, Gehazi's punishment, pronounced by the prophet, was appropriate but terrible. Obviously that incident would end Gehazi's services with Elisha. When his name appears again in chapter 8, we understand that either he had been forgiven and cleansed or that the story is out of chronological sequence.

After reading this sad story we might ask, "Can you lie to a prophet?" When Elisha asked Gehazi, essentially, "Where have you been?" the servant responded, in essence, "Oh, I didn't go anywhere . . ." to which the prophet asked with some pathos, "Went not mine heart with thee?" We grieve as we note that the servant's heart was set so much on the things of this world—the tragedy of the world overcoming testimony. After all, Gehazi was like a personal secretary to the prophet. He had seen with his own eyes a boy raised from the dead and many other miracles. He had been faithful, but faithfulness must endure.

2 Kings 6:1–7

This story is another good-turn miracle, also occurring at the Jordan River. A man was distressed over the loss of his neighbor's axe head, and Elisha miraculously made it float in order to recover it. At that time an iron axe head was a valuable and costly tool which one of the sons of the prophets probably could not afford to purchase anew. Some have tried to explain the floating axe head by means of natural phenomena. It was a miracle!

2 Kings 6:8–23

Syria (the Arameans) and Israel again went to war, and Elisha told the king of Israel where to find the main camp of Syria's king. Syrian spies sent to find Elisha learned that he was in Dothan. The Syrian king dispatched a great host of horses, chariots, and soldiers, who surrounded the city of Dothan. When Elisha's servant saw that they were trapped and, he thought, about to be slaughtered, the prophet calmly taught him a lesson: "Fear not: for they that be with us are more than they that be with them" (v. 16). The spiritual eyes of the young man opened, and he could see the innumerable host of heavenly forces standing poised to protect the Lord's anointed. For everyone today who tries to keep his covenants, it may be said spiritually, if not physically, that the hosts of heaven that be with us are more than they that are against us.

Elisha temporarily blinded the Syrian army and led them to the capital city of Samaria, where they were well treated and sent back home. Note the code of military conduct that Elisha lived by. The king of Israel would have killed the Syrians. Elisha said not to and then taught an impressive lesson: "Would you really kill men you have captured without giving them a fair chance? Instead, give them food and water." Significantly, Aram then stopped raiding Israel. In effect, one enemy of Israel was destroyed, at least for a time, but through kindness and honorable behavior instead of slaughter.

2 Kings 6:24–7:20

This account preserves the record of another Syrian infiltration into the kingdom of Israel during another time period. Benhadad of Syria (Aram-Damascus) besieged Samaria, cutting it off from food supplies. During the vicious famine that followed, Samarians resorted to cannibalism. Notwithstanding the despicable and hopeless conditions, Elisha prophesied incredible plenty in Samaria. The prophecy was literally fulfilled when the Lord caused the Syrians to hear the noise of a great host approaching them. Thinking the Israelites had hired Hittites and Egyptians, they fled in the twilight, leaving tents, animals, and valuable commodities for the citizens of Samaria to loot. In verses 16–20 we see how, through a series of phrases, Israel was reminded that things do happen as God promises and that the word of the Lord's prophets is sure: "according to the word of the Lord," "as the man of God had said," and "as the man of God had spoken."

2 Kings 8:1–6

These verses are a sequel to the earlier story of the noble-woman who provided a room for Elisha and whose son Elisha raised from death (2 Kings 4:32–35). The woman had now been further blessed by having her house, lands, and trees restored to her. She overheard Gehazi telling the king about Elisha's deeds, and the king granted her the restoration of her properties after a famine. Whether Gehazi was still functioning as Elisha's servant and the story is out of order chronologically, or whether he was telling of his former master's qualities, is not evident.

2 Kings 8:7–15

It is not known why, but the prophet of Israel foretold who Syria's next king would be. Elisha journeyed to Damascus and found Ben-hadad sick. When the king heard that the prophet was near, he sent forty camels loaded with the best goods of Damascus. Hazael, the messenger sent to Elisha, was told that his king's disease was not fatal, but that he would die by other means.

"And he settled his countenance stedfastly, until he was ashamed: and the man of God wept.

"And Hazael said, Why weepeth my lord? And he answered, Because I know the evil that thou wilt do unto the children of Israel: their strong holds wilt thou set on fire, and their young men wilt thou slay with the sword, and wilt dash their children, and rip up their women with child.

"And Hazael said, But what, is thy servant a dog, that he should do this great thing? And Elisha answered, The Lord hath shewed me that thou shalt be king over Syria" (vv. 11–13).

Ben-hadad's death soon afterwards resulted in Hazael's rise to the Syrian throne, as Elisha had prophesied. Indeed, as had also been foreseen, Hazael afflicted and oppressed Israel, Judah, and

Philistia, all the days of Jehoahaz (2 Kings 10:32; 13:22), successor king in the kingdom of Israel to Jehu, whom we have not yet encountered. Hazael turned out to be one of the most ruthless of Syrian kings.

2 Kings 8:16–24 (compare 2 Chronicles 21:1–20)

This brief review of the reign of Jehoram, Jehoshaphat's son and successor in Judah, picks up the narrative again from the point where it left off in 1 Kings 22:50, except for the nonchronological insertion in 2 Kings 3:4–27 of another episode from Jehoshaphat's day. The names Joram and Jehoram are interchangeable. For a time Israel and Judah had kings of the same name. Joram of Judah was a brother-in-law to Joram of Israel, having married Athaliah, daughter of Ahab and Jezebel. Through that marriage the worship of Baal was introduced into the royal house of Judah. Yet, the Lord would not destroy Judah for the sake of David; that was a promise he had made to David. Under Joram of Judah the kingdom of Edom revolted, as did Libnah, and gained freedom.

2 Kings 8:25–29 (2 Chronicles 22:1–6)

More of the evils of Ahab and Jezebel were felt in Judah as Ahab's grandson, Ahaziah, son of Jehoram and Athaliah, continued in the idolatry of his father and mother. Athaliah is called "daughter of Omri" (v. 26), although she was actually his granddaughter. And Ahaziah is called the "son-in-law" of the house of Ahab, although technically he was the son of the "son-in-law," Jehoram. That there was a Jehoram followed by an Ahaziah in Judah, contemporary with an Ahaziah followed by a Jehoram in Israel, adds to the confusion (see Bible Appendix, "Chronology").

Jehoram (or Joram) of Israel was an ally to Ahaziah of Judah during a war against Hazael of Syria. After Joram was wounded and lay ill in Jezreel, Ahaziah visited him. This visit led to the death of both of them.

2 Kings 9 (compare verses 14–29 with 2 Chronicles 22:7, 9)

Here is another case of a military commander overthrowing a king. Elisha appointed a young prophet to go and anoint Jehu king over Israel, with specific instructions regarding his reign. Anointing with oil by a prophet was performed on prophets, priests, and kings in order to inaugurate their tenures. Elisha's associate went and declared that the purpose of Jehu's reign was to obliterate the house of Ahab to avenge the blood of all the prophets that Jezebel had executed (1 Kings 18:13). Note again the phrase in verse 8 used to refer to mature males.

As Jehu was acclaimed king, garments were placed under him at the top of the stairs in the palace, and trumpets were blown. The use of garments in this way symbolized the peoples' recognition of his kingship and their pledge of loyalty. A similar act was performed for Jesus at his triumphal entry (Luke 19:36). For other episodes involving clothing used as a symbol for witnessing an act see Acts 7:58 or Alma 46:12–24.

The zealous Jehu began at once to implement his charge "to smite the house of Ahab" as he understood it, undertaking a purge. The king of Judah, who was related to Ahab and Jezebel through his mother, Athaliah, also suffered the fate of the house of Ahab in Israel—he was slain by Jehu. Recall the prophecy of the fate of Ahab and Jezebel, given at the time when they connived to steal the vineyard of Naboth (1 Kings 21:20–24). Jehu recalled the prophecy and set about to bring it to full fruition in that very vineyard. How ironic and filled with poetic justice!

Jezebel knew the history of the overthrows of Israel's dynasties before and scathingly compared Jehu to Zimri (1 Kings 16:8–12) as she greeted him. When Jezebel was readying herself to meet Jehu, she painted her face, coiffed her hair, and, looking out the window, tried to use feminine charms to manipulate the situation, even in her old age. Anciently, women typically painted their eyelids by daubing them with kohl, a soot-like compound, to draw attention to their eyes.

Undaunted, Jehu proceeded with his bloody executions. He commanded two or three eunuchs (chamberlains) to throw Jezebel out the window. In graphic detail the Hebrew text says her blood "spattered" on the wall and on horses, which trampled her body. All they found to bury were her skull, feet, and palms of her hands. The Lord fulfills his prophecies with thoroughness. Verse 37 makes it clear that, unlike many other renowned persons, Jezebel would

This Phoenician ivory plaque, on display in the British Museum, London, is reminiscent of Jezebel in her final mortal moments. "Jezebel . . . painted her face, and [adorned] her head, and looked out at a window" (2 Kings 9:30)

have no great monument dedicated to her fame.

As you read the actions of Jehu and wonder about his motivation and justification, see the evaluation (Hosea 1:4–5) of him by Hosea, who lived in the century after Jehu. Of course it is quite possible for one to zealously do what he supposes is the will of the Lord when the motivation is really from within himself.

Some people erroneously think prophets have no business involving themselves in politics. Such people must have never read the Old Testament. Elijah and Elisha were very involved in the politics of their times. Later, we will see that Isaiah, Amos, Jeremiah, Daniel, and others were also very involved in the politics of their day. The Lord does not have a limited sphere of influence.

President Ezra Taft Benson outlined fourteen powerful principles for understanding and following the Lord's prophet, including this one: "The prophet tells us what we need to know, not always what we want to know. . . ." Said President Harold B. Lee: "'You may not like what comes from the authority of the Church. It may conflict with your political views. It may contradict your social views. It may interfere with some of your social life . . . Your safety and ours depends upon whether or not we follow . . . Let's keep our eye on the President of the Church.' (Conference Report, October 1970, p. 152–153.)" Indeed, President Benson continued: "The prophet may well advise on civic matters. When a people are righteous, they want the best to lead them in government. Alma was the head of the Church and of the government in the Book of Mormon; Joseph Smith was mayor of Nauvoo and Brigham Young was governor of Utah. Isaiah was deeply involved in giving counsel on political matters and of his words the Lord himself said, 'Great are the words of Isaiah.' (3 Ne. 23:1.)" (*Liahona*, June 1981; paragraphing altered).

President Benson's classic address has been referred to by more recent general conference speakers (see Costa, *Ensign*, Nov. 2010, 11–13; and Duncan, *Ensign*, Nov. 2010, 35–36). President Benson's address and the principles he articulated are well worth our attention in modern times, and they certainly help to illustrate the relationship anciently between the Lord's prophet and the Lord's covenant people.

2 Kings 10:1–11

Most pathetic among the bloody actions of Jehu in this revolution was the beheading of the unfortunate sons and grandsons of Ahab. Because the guardians and teachers of these were required to do the deed and deliver their heads in baskets—in the same manner as tyrants have done other lands—the account is even more ghastly.

2 Kings 10:12–14 (2 Chronicles 22:8)

Joram (or Jehoram) of Israel, grandson of Ahab and Jezebel through their son Ahaziah, met death at the hands of the violent Jehu, as did Ahaziah of Judah, grandson of Ahab and Jezebel through their daughter Athaliah. Next, forty-two brethren of the former king of Judah who chanced to visit northern Israel were slain.

2 Kings 10:15–28

Verse 16 points to Jehu's problem. He boasted of his "zeal" for the Lord, but as we know, strengths can become weaknesses, and they certainly had in Jehu's case (see Oaks, *Ensign*, Oct. 1994, 11). His unchecked slaughter of human beings was abhorrent, but it continued. The priests of Baal worship in Israel who gullibly assembled at Jehu's call for a great sacrifice to Baal became the sacrificial victims themselves at Jehu's command.

Just what the role was of Jehonadab, the son of Rechab, is unclear. He was a member of a distinguished family and tribe, the

The basalt Black Obelisk of Shalmaneser, displayed in the British Museum in London, shows Israel's King Jehu prostrating himself before the Assyrian king

Kenites (Judges 1:16; 4:11). Evidently, they were descendants of Moses' brother-in-law (see commentary at Judges 1:16–21).

As indicated in verse 22, special clothing was required of all worshipers in the temple of the false god Baal. This was a perversion of a true principle.

2 Kings 10:29–31

The commendation given Jehu in verse 30 does not accord with the condemnation of him spoken later by the prophet Hosea (chapter 1). Nor does it seem consistent with the characterization of his lack of religious integrity in verse 31.

The Black Obelisk of Shalmaneser III, an extrabiblical source dating to the last half of the ninth century before Christ, corroborates the existence of two Old Testament–period kings. Discovered at Nimrud in Mesopotamia, the obelisk depicts Jehu, king of Israel, prostrate before the Assyrian king, with an identifying inscription reading "Jehu of the house of Omri." It is the only pictorial rendition ever found of an Israelite monarch. It also illustrates Israelite attire.

2 Kings 10:32–36

Hazael of Syria began the war against Israel that Elisha anticipated (recall 2 Kings 8:7–15). During the century from 830 to 730 B.C. there was an incessant parade of internal conflicts and overthrowing of kings, military threats and invasions of foreign powers, and general apostate conditions. The people with whom God had established his covenant and to whom he had promised his divine protection had, as a people, abandoned him. Politically they were trusting in the arm of flesh, and spiritually they were gone "a whoring after other gods" (Judges 2:17).

It appears that the Lord could no longer continue to give Israel every chance to repent. So, "In those days the Lord began to cut Israel short." He allowed Hazael to smite them in "all the coasts of Israel; from Jordan eastward, all the land of Gilead, the Gadites, and the Reubenites, and the Manassites, from Aroer, which is by the river Arnon, even Gilead and Bashan" (2 Kings 10:32–33; see Bible Map 10).

Before long, however, the two small nations, Syria and Israel, had a common enemy to worry about—Assyria.

2 Kings 11:1–20 (2 Chronicles 22:10–23:21)

More bloodshed occurred in the branch of Ahab's house which existed in the southern kingdom of Judah. After Jehu killed the king of Judah, Athaliah, mother of the king of Judah, seized the opportunity to kill all others of the royal house so that she herself might rule alone in Judah. One grandson of Athaliah was saved, along with a nurse, by his aunt who was the wife of the high priest, Jehoiada. The terrible Athaliah reigned for six years. Remember, Athaliah was just like her mother, Jezebel. As the wife of Jehoram, king of Judah (2 Kings 8:18, 26; 2 Chronicles 18:1; 21:6), Athaliah introduced Baal worship into the southern kingdom, just as her mother had introduced it into the northern kingdom (2 Chronicles 22:3–4; 24:7).

In due time, Jehoiada allied with military leaders and engineered a coup, and Jehoash (or Joash) was proclaimed king in his seventh year. Fortunately there were still enough faithful people in Judah to rally behind the high priest, break the power of Athaliah, and begin a reform movement. The pillar where the newly proclaimed king stood as Athaliah tore her clothes and cried treason was probably one of the two pillars of the Temple set up by Solomon, which he had named Jachin and Boaz (1 Kings 7:21). Thus came the caution from the priest that Athaliah not "be slain in the house of the Lord" (2 Kings 11:15).

Important religious and political retrenchment was achieved when Jehoash reigned in Judah under the covenant relationship of people, king, and God. The moving force behind the reform was a righteous and capable high priest, Jehoiada.

2 Kings 11:21–12:16 (2 Chronicles 24:1–14)

Apparently the most persistent institution and thus the most difficult reform to accomplish was the removal of false worship in the "high places" (the old hilltop shrines) where the people continued to burn incense and offer sacrifices, sometimes to the Lord and sometimes to idols.

Jehoash revised the system for channeling the money offerings of the Temple into the proper uses, for it was evident that the priests were not repairing and maintaining the Temple as they should. According to verse 4, the money consisted of sacred offerings brought to the Temple, money collected in the census, money received from personal vows, and money brought voluntarily. This had not been used properly, and, as the chronicler tells us, Athaliah had vandalized the Temple (2 Chronicles 24:7). Additionally, no accounting was required from the foreman over Temple repairs, to whom was given money to pay the workmen (v. 15).

2 Kings 12:17–21 (2 Chronicles 24:23–27)

About this time, Judah also felt the rampaging power of Hazael of Syria. Amazingly, the plunderers were willing to go away and relinquish their siege when given a sufficient offering. They must have thought they would come again for additional tribute if the people were left to accumulate more wealth. This occasion was another in a long series of repeated plunderings of the Temple throughout the centuries.

After the death of Jehoiada, Joash drifted away from his fidelity to the Lord. The story of his breach of the covenant is not related in 2 Kings but is told in 2 Chronicles 24. The worst deed recorded was the stoning of Zechariah, son of his old high priest

advisor, in the court of the Temple (see 2 Chronicles 24:20–22).
Jesus cited this as a typical deed of wickedness of the stiff-necked
people of old in Matthew 23:35 and Luke 11:51. It seems that it
was because of such breaches of propriety and morality that palace
servants slew Joash.

2 Kings 13:1–13

Apparently Jehoahaz was one of the relatively less wicked
kings of northern Israel, as the only thing here recorded against
him was that the worship in Dan and Bethel at Jeroboam's
shrines was not terminated. Still, the northern kingdom was
wicked enough that the Lord's anger "burned hot," and he again
used a foreign power as the instrument of divine chastisement
(2 Kings 10:32). When the people were suffering under Syria's
Hazael, however, they were given some respite by the approaching Assyrians. Thus, the Lord, in his infinite mercy, "gave Israel
a saviour" (Hebrew, "a delivering one"). This was probably
King Adad-nirari III (811–783 B.C.), who defeated Damascus in
802 B.C. But Israel's respite would only be temporary because
they would not abandon their idolatry, the worship of the goddess Asherah, headquartered in Samaria.

2 Kings 13:14–25

Here is the account of the prophet Elisha's death. It is noteworthy that Jehoash spoke respectfully and appreciatively to the
old prophet, who was lying on his deathbed. Ironically, Jehoash
said to Elisha exactly what Elisha had said to Elijah when the latter
was taken, "O my father, my father, the chariot of Israel, and the
horsemen thereof" (compare verse 14 and 2 Kings 2:12). Perhaps
this was a recognized formula anciently used to extol prophets
in the mold of the great Elijah. Certainly, prophets were more
important to Israel's success militarily, economically, and spiritually than the sword or anything else (see Alma 31:5). Yet, Israel
refused to recognize this. The symbolic acts done with arrows by
the king and interpreted by the prophet as harbingers of freedom
from Syria were not done with exact obedience nor sufficient zeal
to indicate faith in Jehovah's promises. Thus the prophet was
disturbed. Also unusual is the account of a miracle wrought by
Elisha's bones sometime after his death.

Apparently Jehoash was able to recover some territory, liberating a few Israelite cities from Syrian rule after the death of King Hazael of Syria.

2 Kings 14:1–20 (2 Chronicles 25:1–28)

The righteous king, Amaziah of Judah, followed the example of his father. However, he did not remove the high places where false worship continued. He showed admirable awareness of the law of justice found in Deuteronomy 24:16. He practiced it properly in handling those guilty of assassinating his father. But he did not slay the children of the assassins.

Judah successfully conquered Edom in the Rift Valley south of the Dead Sea (the Arabah) and in the rock-hewn city of Selah (possibly Petra in the modern country of Jordan). The account in 2 Chronicles 25 gives an additional bit of information about the hiring and subsequent dismissal of a large army from Israel before the war began. This resulted in some bad feelings between Judah and Israel.

Judah's subsequent aggressive exploit against Israel seems to have had no good purpose and resulted in disaster for Judah. This was the only time when Israelites actually plundered their own holy house, the Temple of the Lord.

Again, assassination of the reigning king in Judah, Amaziah, differed from similar deeds in Israel, where the assassins always became king. Judahite forces preserved the royal seed of the Davidic dynasty and perpetuated them on the throne. The sixteen-year-old Azariah succeeded his father, Amaziah, as king.

It appears that two religious and political factions vied constantly with each other in positioning and patronizing the kings; as a result, orthodox and apostate religions alternated, parallel to the political changes.

2 Kings 14:21–22 (2 Chronicles 26:1–2)

As the youthful successor to the assassinated king, Azariah began his reign in Judah. This account describes only his recovery of the Red Sea port of Elath. Elath was also called Ezion-geber, which had been used by Solomon as home port for his Red Sea fleet that sailed to Ophir and Arabia (1 Kings 9:26). Accounts in 2 Kings 15:1–7 and in 2 Chronicles 26 indicate that Azariah was righteous for a number of years but then usurped priestly authority and functions and was smitten with leprosy. Azariah is called Uzziah in 2 Chronicles and in 2 Kings 15:13. The two names of the king, Azariah and Uzziah, could be translated "Help of the Lord" and "Strength of the Lord," respectively; they are closely related in meaning.

2 Kings 14:23–29

This passage switches back to northern kingdom history. Jeroboam II, the son of Joash of Israel, must have been a capable leader. He reigned longer than most and recovered the territories taken from the kings of Israel. It is actually indicated that the Lord saved Israel through Jeroboam from further distress. Also, Jeroboam is not condemned for anything except the usual reference to worshiping at the shrines of Dan and Bethel, where the first Jeroboam, the son of Nebat, had set up the golden calves.

The mention of prophetic guidance in Jeroboam II's day by Jonah, the son of Amittai, is also of interest. The prophetic book of Jonah does not tell anything of his mission at home but only of his foreign mission to Nineveh. It is evident here that he served at home first and that the record of his teachings is missing.

The prophet Amos ministered in the days of both Azariah/ Uzziah of Judah and Jeroboam of Israel (Amos 1:1; 7:10–13). Chronologically, the beginnings of the books of Jonah and Amos fit at the end of verse 27.

2 Kings 15:1–7 (2 Chronicles 26:3–23)

Here is the remainder of the account of the reign of Azariah, also known as Uzziah. His son Jotham was coregent during the time of his exclusion from public life after he contracted leprosy.

Note that 2 Chronicles 26:22 indicates that the prophet Isaiah wrote a more complete account of history in his days; this function of the prophets in recording history as well as their prophecies is significant.

2 Kings 15:8–15

The last king of the house of Jehu was assassinated after six months' reign. As the fourth generation of kings of the line of Jehu, Zachariah, son of Jeroboam II, fulfilled a prophetic promise given to Jehu (see 2 Kings 10:30), but just why the promise was made and what good he did in fulfilling it is not apparent. The "rest of the acts of Zachariah, behold they are written in the book of the chronicles of the kings of Israel" but we do not have that book. In the modern Bible, Chronicles is not the same as the "chronicles of the kings of Israel"; it says nothing at all about many of Israel's kings.

Shallum, assassin of King Zachariah, reigned only one month before he in turn was assassinated by Menahem, whose brutality is recorded in verse 16. The prophet Hosea said of Israel, "By swearing, and lying, and killing, and stealing, and committing adultery, they break out, and blood toucheth blood" (Hosea 4:2). The last phrase suggests a condition of violence on top of violence.

2 Kings 15:16–26

The next assassin-king in the kingdom of Israel, Menahem, remained in power for ten years, being strengthened in his hold on power by Tiglath-pileser III of Assyria (here called "Pul"; see Bible Dictionary, "Tiglath-pileser"). Menahem paid for that support with immense tribute exacted from the "mighty men of wealth" of the land of Israel. An Assyrian inscription relates the following boast of Tiglath-pileser's military successes in the land of Israel:

"As for Menachem I overwhelmed him like a snowstorm and he . . . fled like a bird, alone, and bowed to my feet. I returned him to his place and imposed tribute upon him. . . . Israel (lit.: 'Omri-Land') . . . all its inhabitants and their possessions I led to Assyria. They overthrew their king Pekah and I placed Hoshea as king over them. I received from them 10 talents of gold, 1,000 talents of silver as their tribute and brought them to Assyria" (*Ancient Near East*, 1:194). This inscription corroborates the biblical record. One thousand talents of silver is about thirty-seven tons of that precious metal.

After Menahem died, his son Pekahiah reigned two years before being overthrown by another military leader. The northern kingdom was descending into a condition of thorough political weakness just as her greatest threat was looming on the horizon.

2 Kings 15:27–31

Just before this time Assyria had captured Damascus, allowing Israel (under Jeroboam II) and Judah (under Uzziah) their greatest expansion in the history of the divided kingdoms. Uzziah, king of Judah, had already conquered Edom, rebuilt Elath, and subjugated much of Philistia. Now, while Assyria and their northern and western antagonists, Urartu and the Aramean states, were involved in their own local conflicts and internal revolts, Israel and Judah united to produce a strong front and won back all of the transjordan area and expanded to the size of the former Davidic kingdom.

Many years of military victories and territorial expansion resulted in prosperity, pride, and a sense of security. Prophets were sent to condemn the moral and spiritual failings of the Israelites. The warning voices of Amos, Isaiah, Micah, and Hosea were heard in the land of Israel. They pronounced with emphatic clarity that Assyria was the greatest political threat to Israelite existence (Isaiah 7:17; 8:4, 7; Hosea 8:9; compare Amos 5:27). Their warnings to Israel and their pleas for repentance, along with their promises of future fulfillment of God's purposes, have come down to us in the prophetic books of the Bible. Hosea pleaded with northern Israel to return to Jehovah. Amos, a shepherd from Judah, told in the court of Jeroboam about the injustices done to the poor by political and religious leaders. Micah proclaimed his warnings and visions of the future. The dean of all these prophets was Isaiah, who prophesied at Jerusalem in the court of the king there but spoke to all Judah and Israel.

In the political arena, the army captain Pekah, who took the kingdom from Pekahiah, reigned a little longer as external threats grew more intense and Assyria conquered several Israelite regions.

The great expansionist, Tiglath-pileser III (reigned 745–727 B.C.), often referred to as the father of the Assyrian Empire, began the systematic, permanent absorption of foreign territories as provinces of greater Assyria. To exercise greater control over subdued peoples, he initiated a policy of exiling people from one part of the empire to other parts. The course of his campaigns in Israelite-held lands is detailed in verse 29. His first campaign into the territory he called Philistia, of which he considered Israel a part, took place in 734 B.C. Later on, Tiglath-pileser's successor, Shalmaneser V (727–722 B.C.), would lay siege to Samaria for three years. He died before Israel was fully conquered and the subjugated Israelites deported. Sargon II (722–705 B.C.) would deport the ten tribes, but all that was still in the future.

2 Kings 15:32–38 (2 Chronicles 27:1–9)

Again Jotham is mentioned (see vv. 1–7). This is apparently the beginning of his reign proper after the death of his incapacitated father. The beginning of Israel's alliance with Syria is introduced here (see also Isaiah 7).

2 Kings 16:1–5 (2 Chronicles 28:1–7)

Ahaz, king of Judah, was religiously one of the worst of his lineage. The phrase "made his sons to pass through the fire" means that he sacrificed children to the dread, fire-belching idol, Molech. Ahaz knew of Jehovah and had Isaiah available as a prophetic advisor, but he apparently preferred other gods for his "security."

Around 735 B.C. Syria and Israel wanted to form a coalition of nations to stand against Assyria, which they saw as their only chance for national survival ("united we stand, divided we fall," as they thought). They wanted Judah to join them, but Judah refused, so Syria and Israel planned to invade Jerusalem and replace the Davidic king Ahaz with a man who would support them. Again, the chief players in this political drama are as follows: Pekah, king of Israel; Rezin, king of Syria; and Ahaz, king of Judah.

The great prophet Isaiah met with King Ahaz at the Gihon Spring in Jerusalem to warn him not to fear the "two tails of these smoking firebrands" and not to join their losing effort and, in addition, not to form any kind of alliance with Assyria, whom Isaiah saw as an infinitely greater danger (see Isaiah 7).

2 Kings 16:6–20 (2 Chronicles 28:16–27)

Yet Ahaz turned to Assyria for help, against Isaiah's advice. He took treasures out of the Temple, which also served as the kingdom's economic center, as well as the king's house, and sent them to Tiglath-pileser with a request that the Assyrian king rid him of his adversaries to the north. Tiglath-pileser was more than pleased to accommodate Ahaz, of course. Tiglath-pileser's forceful action included the subjugation of Philistia in 734 B.C., the conquest and deportation of people in the northern and eastern lands of Israel in 733 (see 2 Kings 15:29 above), and Damascus in 732. Ahaz then replaced Jehovah's altar in the Temple with a strange Assyrian one. Urijah the priest was a coconspirator. The construction of the Assyrian altar was probably intended as a sign of submission to the Assyrians. When Ahaz returned to Jerusalem he offered, basically, the same sacrifices on the unauthorized altar that had been offered at the dedication of the Temple many decades before (1 Kings 8:64). Ahaz also made other changes to the Temple in deference to the king of Assyria.

2 Kings 17:1–6

After a nine-year reign in Samaria, Hoshea, the last king of Israel, a vassal king, decided to ally himself with Egypt in an attempt to throw off the Assyrian yoke. Assyria's response was rapid and terminal. Shalmaneser V (reigned 724–722 B.C.) besieged Samaria, the capital city of the northern kingdom of Israel, for three years. The greatest achievement during his short reign was the capture of Samaria.

"In the ninth year of Hoshea the king of Assyria took Samaria, and carried Israel away into Assyria, and placed them in Halah and in Habor by the river of Gozan, and in the cities of the Medes" (2 Kings 17:5–6).

To be read correctly, that first verse needs a comma after Hoshea: "In the ninth year of Hoshea, the king of Assyria took Samaria . . ." The next phrase, "and carried Israel away into Assyria," would seem to refer to the same king, but that is not the case. Shalmaneser besieged Samaria from 724 to 722 B.C., and in September of 722 he finally captured the city. He apparently died in December of the same year.

Sargon II (reigned 721–705 B.C.) succeeded Shalmaneser on the throne of Assyria. Sargon carried away the northern tribes and made Samaria a province of Assyria. He took full credit for the conquest and deportation of the northern Israelites in one of his annalistic inscriptions: "I besieged and conquered Samaria, [and] led away as booty 27,290 inhabitants of it" (*Ancient Near*

East, 1:195). Sargon had reliefs carved on his palace walls showing Israelite men driving grain-loaded carts pulled by oxen, and women and girls carrying sacks while plodding along wearily on foot to their places of exile. Verse 6 says he placed them in Halah (modern location not known) and in Habor by the river of Gozan, and in the cities of the Medes. Gozan was west of Nineveh in Upper Mesopotamia. A river flowing beside Gozan is called the Habor. Note that in the King James Bible the word *by* in verse 6 is italicized. That means the word does not appear in the original Hebrew text, and it has been supplied to give the passage more sense in English (a process called ellipsis). Sometimes italicized words have been incorrectly supplied, however, as is the case here. The phrase should actually read that Sargon deported them and placed them along the Habor, the river of Gozan, and in the cities of the Medes, in the northern part of what is called Iran today. Thus the initial locations of the "lost tribes" are known.

The tribes of Israel carried away by Assyria are generally referred to in scripture (D&C 110:11, etc.) as ten tribes, though by this point in history there was no strict delineation such as ten tribes in the north and two in the south. Families from various tribes lived in Jerusalem (see 1 Chronicles 9:3). Simeon had assimilated into Judah; Benjamin was aligned with Judah; and because of apostasy and idolatry in the northern kingdom, many of the tribe of Levi resided in the south. There is no point, then, in indicating that exactly "ten" tribes were carried away.

2 Kings 17:7–23

Here is Israel's epitaph. The historian sadly began, "For so it was [a phrase like "and thus we see" in the Book of Mormon] that the children of Israel had sinned against the Lord." Had they been a different, peculiar, special people as they had been called to be? Had the people accomplished what they were chosen to do? Read Leviticus 18:26–28 and Deuteronomy 4:25–26. After an independent existence of some 215 years, the northern tribes of Father Jacob's once great and powerful family ceased to be part of Israel in their promised land.

2 Kings 17:24–41

Sargon followed Tiglath-pileser's policy of population deportation, doing as his famous predecessor had done to transjordanian and northern Israelites ten years earlier. Removing peoples from their native lands tended to inhibit rebellion. But Sargon took it a step further. He initiated a policy of transpopulation, or a repopulation method of subjugating conquered peoples. He deported Israelites and then imported foreigners from other conquered lands to take their place. Sargon brought to Samaria foreigners from Babylon, from Cuthah (southern Mesopotamia), from Hamath (north of Damascus), and from Arabia. These foreigners, by intermarriage with the few Israelites who remained in the land produced a people that came to be known as Samaritans. The Samaritans' motivation to learn of the God of Israel and their worship of him were peculiar. The resultant mixed religion, like their mixed blood, elicited only scorn from observant Jews and their prophets.

Sargon made Samaria a province of the Assyrian Empire. The kingdom of Judah submitted to Assyria, becoming a vassal kingdom of the empire, and was spared destruction.

2 Kings 18:1–8 (2 Chronicles 29:1–31:1)

The contrast between Hezekiah of Judah and Hoshea of Israel, who were contemporaries, is striking. Hoshea sought to free his land from the burden of paying tribute to Assyria and instead brought about the total destruction of his nation. In contrast, Hezekiah tried in a very different way to strengthen and defend his land after discontinuing tribute to Assyria. With the help of Isaiah, he succeeded.

Hezekiah kept the commandments and trusted in the Lord. He ordered the Temple to be cleansed and sanctified, appointed the proper courses of priests and Levites, and commanded that Israelites from Dan to Beersheba join in a grand Passover celebration once again, and that they pay their tithes (2 Chronicles 29–31). Hezekiah removed the idolatrous high places and altars, broke down the images, and cut down the groves where idolatrous practices had taken place. He then destroyed the bronze serpent that Moses had made in Sinai because Judahites had been burning incense to it, thus perverting a symbol of the Messiah (v. 4; also 2 Chronicles 31:1). The name "Nehushtan" may derive either from the Hebrew word for "serpent" or from the Hebrew word for "bronze." The alloy used by the ancients for making cast objects can more properly be called bronze than brass.

Hezekiah not only freed his nation from the Assyrian oppression but drove the old Philistine foe out of the land.

"And the Lord was with [Hezekiah]; and he prospered whithersoever he went forth: and he rebelled against the king of Assyria, and served him not" (2 Kings 18:7; see also 2 Chronicles 31:21).

Bible Map 5 shows the extent of the mighty Assyrian Empire and the tiny tributary kingdom of Judah. What a daring move it was to rebel against Assyria! The map doesn't tell the whole story, however. With the death of Sargon in 705 B.C., cities all up and down the coasts of Phoenicia and Canaan revolted against Assyria. Babylon also had a new, aggressive and ambitious king. Egypt was ready to make a stand against Assyrian penetration there. Hezekiah knew the time was right to break away from the Assyrian overlords, but he also realized that it was only a matter of time before the brutal armies of the empire returned to the land of Israel intending to crush any rebellion.

To prepare Jerusalem for the retaliatory invasion, Hezekiah began refortifying the city walls. A two-hundred-foot section of Hezekiah's wall has been uncovered in recent decades in today's Jewish Quarter of the Old City. The Broad Wall, as it is called later in Nehemiah 3:8 and 12:38, is nearly twenty-three feet wide and likely over twenty-five feet high—testimony of the serious fortification works of Judah's king. As archaeologists cleared away the debris of centuries, they found houses that were destroyed along the course Hezekiah laid out for the protective wall, indicating that the wall was erected in a time of crisis. That some homes had to be displaced is just as Isaiah noted:

"Ye have seen also the breaches of the city of David, that they are many: and ye gathered together the waters of the lower pool. And ye have numbered the houses of Jerusalem, and the houses have ye broken down to fortify the wall" (Isaiah 22:9–10).

Hezekiah also cut an underground tunnel eighteen hundred feet long (about one-third of a mile) to ensure the constant supply

Hezekiah's Broad Wall (looking northeast). "And they fortified Jerusalem unto the broad wall" (Nehemiah 3:8)

of water from the Gihon Spring into the city. It is one of the largest and most impressive hydrotechnical projects in the history of the Holy Land. Hezekiah's Tunnel is mentioned in 2 Chronicles 32:30, which says, "This same Hezekiah also stopped the upper watercourse of Gihon, and brought it straight down to the west side of the city of David" (see also 2 Kings 20:20). An inscription, often called the Siloam Inscription, was discovered in 1880; it relates the meeting of the two underground teams of workers who had been digging from opposite ends to meet in the middle (see Bible Dictionary, "Hezekiah's Tunnel"). The Siloam Inscription is the longest biblical Hebrew inscription ever found in the Near East.

The Broad Wall and Hezekiah's Tunnel provide direct and dramatic corroboration of the biblical record.

Inscription found in Hezekiah's Tunnel. 2 Kings 20:20 notes "the acts of Hezekiah, and all his might, and how he made a pool, and a conduit, and brought water into the city"

With fortifications in place, Hezekiah and Judah awaited the Assyrian onslaught.

2 Kings 18:9–12

Here is another statement about the fall of northern Israel and the dispersion of the ten tribes among the nations named (see 2 Kings 17:5–6). The reason for the collapse of the nation of Israel was that "they obeyed not the voice of the Lord their God, but transgressed his covenant."

2 Kings 18:13–37 (2 Chronicles 32:1–19; Isaiah 36:1–22)

Another of the archaeological discoveries that help corroborate the Bible is King Sennacherib's record of the invasion called the Sennacherib Prism, a six-sided prism of baked clay in cuneiform script, of which three copies have been found (see photo, page 80). The Prism confirms that indeed the Assyrians under Sennacherib began their planned conquest of the kingdom of Judah by conquering forty-six of the territory's walled cities (what v. 13 calls "fenced" cities). Sennacherib saved the two greatest cities for last: Lachish and Jerusalem. Lachish fell, leaving only Jerusalem.

The Sennacherib Prism also indicates that Hezekiah did try to buy off the Assyrians, and the tribute imposed was eight hundred

Erich Lessing/Art Resource, NY

Lachish siege panels from the palace of Sennacherib showing Assyrian warriors impaling Jewish prisoners

talents of silver and thirty of gold—which would amount to millions of dollars. According to verses 15–16, Hezekiah gathered together all the silver and gold in the Temple and in the king's house, even stripping gold from Temple doors and pillars.

A contingent of Assyrians was sent to Jerusalem from Lachish (see Bible Map 10, A6), where Sennacherib was besieging Judah's strongest fortified position in the Shephelah (the region between the coastal plains and the hill country). Of all the conquered cities and fortifications, Sennacherib must have been particularly proud of his siege of Lachish. When he returned to his palace in Nineveh, he had his artisans carve thirteen panels—a magnificent battle panorama—showing details of the siege ramp constructed for the battering rams to ascend and penetrate the strong and heavily guarded walls of Lachish. The battle panorama also shows the fighting gear and apparel of Assyrians and Judahites and the barbaric methods employed to kill captives (see also commentary at Jonah 1:1–10).

Sennacherib's palace wall reliefs were discovered in excavations in the mid-1800s in Nineveh and are now in the British Museum. Excavations at Lachish also reveal intense destruction, thick layers of ash—Sennacherib's calling card at Lachish. Archaeologists working there have claimed that "there is no other archaeological site in the Holy Land whose archaeological remains illustrate so accurately the records of the Old Testament" (*Excavations at Lachish,* 12).

Though archaeologists have found several layers, or levels, of occupation that document the history of Lachish, the Bible records three great destructions of the city: during Joshua's day (Joshua 10:3, 23, 26), during Hezekiah's day (2 Kings 18:13; 2 Chronicles 32:9), and during Zedekiah's day (Jeremiah 34:6–7).

Reconstruction of Lachish from the perspective of the Assyrians during the battle

In other words, the Israelites, the Assyrians, and the Babylonians all conquered Lachish, making it one of the most fascinating and important cities of the Old Testament to study.

Sennacherib sent officers to Jerusalem to harass and threaten King Hezekiah and his people. The names Rabsaris and Rab-shakeh are anglicized forms of position titles: Rabsaris from *rav-shares*, "army commander," and Rab-shakeh from *rav-shaqeh*, "chief chamberlain [of the king]." The Assyrians came up and "stood by the conduit of the upper pool, which is in the highway of the fuller's field" (v. 17), in other words, across from the Gihon Spring. The Assyrians taunted the citizens of Jerusalem in their own Hebrew language and warned them not to trust in the bruised reed of Egypt. Egypt's power and glory had long dissipated by this time. The Egyptian New Kingdom period, the apex of the country's might, had ended by 1090 B.C., and Egypt had begun a steady decline.

The Assyrian leaders asserted that the Lord would not help them because they had torn down his altars on the "high places," that the Lord had told Sennacherib to destroy Judah, and that the Lord could not defend it against the might of Assyria even if

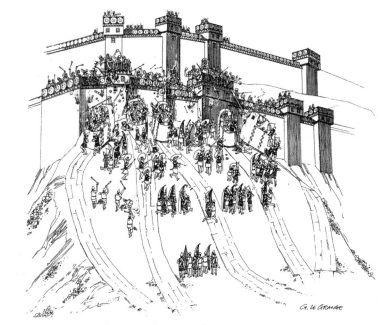

Drawing by Gert le Grange, from *The Conquest of Lachish by Sennacherib*, by Dr. David Ussishkin (1982), 122–23; courtesy Institute of Archaeology of Tel Aviv University

*Reconstruction of assault on main siege ramp
at Lachish from the perspective of the Assyrians*

he wanted to do so—any more than the gods of other lands had defended them! All of these assertions were half-truths or bold assumptions or both. Verse 26 references the "Syrian language," which probably means Aramaic, because by the eighth century before Christ, Aramaic had become the international language of politics and diplomacy. Verse 28 makes reference to the "Jews' language," or Hebrew. That the term "Jews" is being used probably indicates that by this time all surviving Israelites were now recognized as residents of Judah. Its first use is found in 2 Kings 16:6.

2 Kings 19:1–34 (2 Chronicles 32:20; Isaiah 37:1–35)

Sennacherib's plan was to systematically remove all opposition at Judah's western approaches and then advance on Jerusalem, the political eagle nesting in the tops of the hills. After heavy losses in the Shephelah, Jerusalem had no hope of standing up to Sennacherib's war machine. Any further resistance was futile. Judah's doom was sealed (in Sennacherib's mind).

78

In that very hour one lone voice, the voice of a man speaking for God—the great Isaiah—was heard in the city, assuring the king and his subjects that the place God had chosen was still in His hands. The Assyrian blasphemers, the prophet warned, would find only death and destruction for themselves if they came to Jerusalem.

When Rab-shakeh went to report the resistance at Jerusalem and found the Assyrian armies still battering away at another fortified position near Lachish, messengers were sent back to make another try at frightening the people of Jerusalem into submission, this time by means of a letter filled with reviews of what the Assyrians had done to other lands—and to their gods.

Faithful Hezekiah literally spread out the letter before the Lord and humbly supplicated him to defend the city and his own holy name.

The answer to Hezekiah's prayer came through Isaiah the prophet. Note the eloquent contrast of the catalog of what the Lord had done as compared to the list of the things the Assyrian king boasted of having done. The promise was made that the Assyrian host would be restrained and sent out of the country of Judah to their own land.

2 Kings 19:35–37 (2 Chronicles 32:21–23; Isaiah 37:36–38)

In the fateful year of 701 B.C., Sennacherib was poised to strike at Jerusalem with his full military might and force the rebels into humiliating submission.

From the Sennacherib Prism come the following excerpts of his view of the campaign:

"As to Hezekiah, the Jew, he did not submit to my yoke, I laid siege to 46 of his strong cities, walled forts and to the countless small villages in their vicinity, and conquered (them) by means of well-stamped (earth-)ramps, and battering-rams brought (thus) near (to the walls) (combined with) the attack by foot soldiers, (using) mines, breeches as well as sapper work. I drove out (of them) 200,150 people, young and old, male and female, horses, mules, donkeys, camels, big and small cattle beyond counting, and considered (them) booty. Himself I made a prisoner in Jerusalem, his royal residence, like a bird in a cage. I surrounded him with earthwork in

*The Sennacherib Prism,
from Nineveh, dated to 691 B.C.*

order to molest those who were leaving his city's gate" (*Ancient Near East,* 1:200).

Sennacherib's final statement is a boast that is historically untrue, as we learn from the biblical account. Isaiah had prophesied that he would "not come into this city, nor shoot an arrow there, nor come before it with shield, nor cast a bank [a siege ramp] against it" (v. 32).

Verses 35–37 describe what actually did happen to Sennacherib and his hosts. The Greek historian Herodotus (fifth century before Christ) suggested that mice were the cause of the Assyrians' withdrawal when some kind of plague swept through their camp (*Persian Wars,* 2:141).

One of our pre-med students at Brigham Young University commented: "The hypothesis that the 'angel of the Lord,' which wiped out 185,000 Assyrians in their sleep, was actually a plague is certainly credible. But a more potent pathogen than *Yersinia pestis,* the causative agent of bubonic plague, could account for such rapid mortality. The bacteria *Clostridia botulinum* grows in alkaline foods, such as vegetables, and releases a toxin that causes paralysis when it is ingested. The victim will die in less than twenty-four hours from an inability to breathe. Small amounts of the toxin are lethal, and its effects can be widespread if many among a given population, such as an army, eat the same infected food. On the other hand, plague is transmitted more slowly by fleas on rats and may not be fatal for a few days. The description the Old Testament gives is not conclusive, but it may be that the 'angel of the Lord' who 'went forth' did so by conveying botulism food poisoning."

That Sennacherib did abandon his siege of Jerusalem, return, and dwell at Nineveh is confirmed in Assyrian annals, and the fact that his sons later murdered him (twenty years later, in 681 B.C.) is also confirmed in Assyrian documents. Thus were prophecies of Isaiah fulfilled.

The confrontation between Hezekiah and Sennacherib and the miraculous deliverance of Jerusalem made an indelible impression on the citizens of Judah. The episode received further attention and fame in modern day through the splendid poetry of Lord Byron in "The Destruction of Sennacherib" (1815):

The Assyrian came down like the wolf on the fold,
And his cohorts were gleaming in purple and gold;
And the sheen of their spears was like stars on the sea,
When the blue wave rolls nightly on deep Galilee.

Like the leaves of the forest when Summer is green,
That host with their banners at sunset were seen:
Like the leaves of the forest when Autumn hath blown,
That host on the morrow lay wither'd and strown.

For the Angel of Death spread his wings on the blast,
And breathed in the face of the foe as he pass'd;
And the eyes of the sleepers wax'd deadly and chill,
And their hearts but once heaved, and for ever grew still!

And there lay the steed with his nostril all wide,
But through it there roll'd not the breath of his pride;
And the foam of his gasping lay white on the turf,
And cold as the spray of the rock-beating surf.

And there lay the rider distorted and pale,
With the dew on his brow, and the rust on his mail:
And the tents were all silent, the banners alone,
The lances unlifted, the trumpet unblown.

And the widows of Ashur are loud in their wail,
And the idols are broke in the temple of Baal;
And the might of the Gentile, unsmote by the sword,
Hath melted like snow in the glance of the Lord!
(Poetical Works of Lord Byron, 82)

The Lord can protect those who have faith and trust in him. During the American Revolutionary War, for example, it is amazing how often the Lord helped by freezing the ground so American revolutionaries could transport cannons or providing clouds to hide the soldiers' escape. Consider also the protection given to Zion's Camp led by Joseph Smith in 1834. The Lord sent a fierce storm of wind, rain, thunder, lightning, and hail to protect them from their enemies (Smith, *History of the Church*, 2:104–5).

2 Kings 20:1–11 (2 Chronicles 32:24–26; Isaiah 38:1–8, 21–22)

Sometime after the Assyrian siege of Jerusalem, Hezekiah suffered some sort of abscess, which, had it been allowed to run its course, would have caused his death. But he prayed humbly and sincerely to be healed. He received the answer through the prophet Isaiah and was assured that he could live for fifteen more years.

Why the ailment needed a healing poultice and why Hezekiah also wanted a reassuring sign would be difficult to guess without further information. However, this is not all that different from our own day. We ask the Lord for help, for reassurance of his help, and we also employ the best remedies available to us. The sign given to assure Hezekiah that God indeed confirmed the promise spoken through the prophet was most unusual.

"Forward" is eastward, and "backward" is westward; the sun's shadow would go backward, that is, westward, and therefore the sun would go back eastward. Scientific logic tells us that if the earth were suddenly stopped and turned backward, everything on its surface might be smashed flat by the immense rotational inertia that would have to be overcome. We do not know how the Lord accomplished this, but dare we suppose that anything is impossible for the Creator of the world?

2 Kings 20:12–19 (2 Chronicles 32:31; Isaiah 39:1–8)

The seemingly compassionate mission from Babylon to Hezekiah as recorded in this passage may have had strategic and political motivations. Merodach-baladan (Isaiah 39:1) tried twice to take the rule of Babylon away from the Assyrians, and a rebellion in Judah might have distracted Assyria, thus helping Babylon.

It seems incredibly benevolent of the Babylonian prince to send messengers simply on a mission of mercy. Nevertheless, the occasion provided the context for an important prophecy. Sennacherib subdued Merodach-baladan in 704 B.C.

Isaiah's prophecy about the future Babylonian conquest of Judah doubtless was intended to serve as a warning to Judah a century later when Babylon invaded.

2 Kings 20:20–21 (2 Chronicles 32:32–33)

The eulogy of Hezekiah mentions the amazing engineering feat of bringing the waters of Gihon to the new Pool of Siloam (see also 2 Chronicles 32:30). The earlier conduit and pool where Hezekiah's father, Ahaz, and Isaiah had met (Isaiah 7:3) has also been excavated in modern times.

2 Kings 21:1–18 (2 Chronicles 33:1–20)

Despite all of Hezekiah's goodness and his religious reforms (more fully detailed in 2 Chronicles 29–32), an apostate reaction set in with a vengeance as soon as he was dead. His son and successor, Manasseh, only twelve years old, was undoubtedly controlled by political factions that had smarted under the righteousness of Hezekiah and liked better the lax moral life, the dramatic nature worship, and the arousing fertility rites of the common Baal religions that always attracted the less dedicated people. "Asherah" (rendered "grove" in vv. 3, 7) was not a grove of trees but a fertility goddess represented by a tree, a sort of tree of life in a crass manifestation. She was normally considered a wife or consort of Baal.

The terrible worship of Molech was also resumed, where infants were cast into or onto a fire-belching idol. It has been said that Manasseh did more abominations than even the Canaanites had done. Moses had forewarned Israel about such aberrations (see Leviticus 18:26–28).

The prophets were out warning the people. The Lord was going to bring such disaster upon Jerusalem because of their wickedness that the city would be wiped clean as a dish is wiped clean. The metaphor here also speaks of a "line" and a "plummet," which are carpentry terms. It appears that Manasseh must have purged some of the opposition party. His shedding of "much blood" in

Jerusalem would refer to such purges and not merely to sacrifices, which would have been offered in shrines and in the corrupted Temple grounds. Tradition says that Manasseh even killed the great prophet Isaiah (see commentary at the introduction to Isaiah).

Second Chronicles 33:11–19 has the strange story of Manasseh being taken away into "Assyria" where he repented until the Lord could restore him. Neither prophets nor traditions confirm an account of a righteous Manasseh. Assyrian records indicate that he was an Assyrian vassal and often gone from Judah.

2 Kings 21:19–26 (2 Chronicles 33:21–25)

The accounts in the books of Kings and Chronicles agree that Amon, son of Manasseh, was as bad or worse than his father. He aroused an opposing party strong enough to assassinate him, but still his young son, Josiah, of the royal lineage, succeeded him, for the people refused to have anyone other than a member of the royal line of David on the throne. It is remarkable that a righteous father (Hezekiah) could produce such a thoroughly wicked son (Manasseh) and grandson (Amon), only to have them succeeded by a righteous great-grandson (Josiah). A powerful lesson for each of us is that family trends or behavioral tendencies do not have to determine our response to sacred things.

2 Kings 22:1–20 (2 Chronicles 34:1–3, 8–28)

The counterrevolutionaries behind Josiah's installation helped the boy king to be as upright as young David had been.

Josiah instigated some rigorous religious reforms, as his great-grandfather Hezekiah had done. He made repairs to the Temple, during which a copy of the book of the law was found. No direct record identifies the book, but many of the king's reforms parallel Deuteronomy 16:2; 18:10–11; 23:2–4, 7, 17–18, 21, 24; 31:11.

The king and priests read in the book of the law some terrible curses that would follow the kind of spiritual rebellion and apostasy that had persisted during the previous two generations. They knew that the Lord was angry with the nation of Judah. They approached a prophetess named Huldah and inquired of her whether or not all those curses would be forthcoming. Her response was specific and foreboding.

It is important to understand that while Huldah did not

possess priesthood authority or keys, as we nowadays equate with "prophets," we see in her a manifestation of the principle articulated in Alma 32:23, that the gift of revelation is not limited to male leaders, and priesthood authority does not prevent others from possessing spiritual power: "And now, he imparteth his word by angels unto men, yea, not only men but women also. Now this is not all; little children do have words given unto them many times, which confound the wise and the learned" (Alma 32:23). In the Bible we read of women called prophetesses (see commentary at Exodus 15:20–27).

Other prophets who influenced Josiah and his reforms include Zephaniah and Jeremiah, who began his ministry during Josiah's reign (see Jeremiah 22:15–16). There may also have been others (see Bright, *History of Israel,* 309, 319–23).

2 Kings 23:1–20 (2 Chronicles 34:4–7, 29–33)

Josiah called a solemn assembly with priesthood leaders, prophets, and all the inhabitants of Jerusalem listening while he read the book of the covenant that had been found in the Temple.

President Spencer W. Kimball wrote profoundly of King Josiah's experience because, said President Kimball, it is "most profitable" for us to liken unto ourselves (see 1 Nephi 19:24):

"I am convinced that each of us, at some time in our lives, must discover the scriptures for ourselves—and not just discover them once, but rediscover them again and again. . . .

"Josiah was only eight years old when he began to reign in Judah, and although his immediate progenitors were extremely wicked, the scriptures tell us that 'he did that which was right in the sight of the Lord, and walked in all the way of David his father, and turned not aside to the right hand or to the left.' (2 Kings 22:2.) This is all the more surprising when we learn that by that time . . . the written law of Moses had been lost and was virtually unknown, even among the priests of the temple! [When Josiah was in his twenties, he ordered that repairs be made to the temple. At that time Hilkiah, the high priest, found the book of the law that Moses had placed in the Ark of the Covenant, and the high priest delivered the book to the king.]

"When the book of the law was read to Josiah, he 'rent his clothes' and wept before the Lord. . . .

"The king then read the book before all the people, and at that time they all made a covenant to obey all the Lord's commandments 'with all their heart and all their soul.' (2 Kings 23:3.) Then Josiah proceeded to clean up the kingdom of Judah. . . .

"I feel strongly that we must all of us return to the scriptures just as King Josiah did and let them work mightily within us, impelling us to an unwavering determination to serve the Lord" (*Ensign*, Sept. 1976, 4–5).

King Josiah and all the people covenanted to keep the Lord's commandments. The king and priests burned all objects of Baal worship in the Kidron, the valley between the Temple Mount and the Mount of Olives. An idol representing the fertility goddess Asherah, which had been in the House of the Lord, was ground to powder in the Kidron. Josiah ousted all idolatrous priests and destroyed all shrines from Geba to Beersheba, which were the borders at that time. He ordered the destruction of all "the high places that were before Jerusalem, which were on the right hand of the mount of corruption, which Solomon the king of Israel had builded for Ashtoreth" and other idol gods. He also ordered a team of wreckers to break down and burn the altar and high place that were still at Bethel from the days of Jeroboam.

The prophecy made by an unknown prophet hundreds of years earlier about the destruction of Jeroboam's altar finally came to pass (see 1 Kings 13:2).

Verse 20 contains the Lord's prophecy of Josiah's death. Its declaration that Josiah would be buried in peace refers to his being laid to rest in a Jerusalem that was still relatively peaceful—at a time before it was totally destroyed and the population deported. We say this because the actual cause of Josiah's death may not seem very peaceful, in a battle with Pharaoh Necho of Egypt.

2 Kings 23:21–27 (2 Chronicles 35:1–19)

Josiah's reforms earned him a reputation for righteousness above and beyond that of any before or after him. But the seeds of degradation were not totally destroyed; they could not be in a single generation, and Josiah's generation was too short. The writer of the record explained that the imminence of Judah's destruction in spite of all of Josiah's good work was the result of the Lord's lingering anger. If the Lord continued to be angry with Judah, there was continuing cause. Had everyone truly repented, the teachings of prophets indicate that grace would have been forthcoming.

During these years the Assyrian Empire was rapidly disintegrating. Judah was able temporarily to expand—its last period of "greatness."

2 Kings 23:28–30 (2 Chronicles 35:20–27)

Josiah's life ended tragically at Megiddo. He went there to stop the Egyptian advance under Pharaoh Nechoh II (also spelled Necho, 610–594 B.C.), who was marching towards the Euphrates to help the last Assyrian king make a stand against the new Babylonian Empire. Josiah apparently wanted to keep Egypt from acquiring any control over Canaan, which Pharaoh Necho did upon Josiah's death, for about four years (609–605 B.C.) prior to Babylonian invasions. Josiah's death marked the beginning of the end for the kingdom of Judah. Perhaps in Josiah's death we see an example of the adage that sometimes our mistakes or errors in judgment have greater immediate consequences than our sins. Josiah was righteous, but he miscalculated.

The prophet Jeremiah, first introduced in Chronicles as a mourner of Josiah's death, finds more to mourn in Judah's decline and demise as a nation in the next two decades (612–586 B.C.), for there were no righteous kings after Josiah.

2 Kings 23:31–37 (2 Chronicles 36:1–5)

Josiah's first son, Jehoahaz, was an unacceptable successor to the throne in the eyes of the Egyptian Pharaoh Necho, who had conquered Judah and made her a tributary; perhaps the very fact that the people of Judah had made Jehoahaz king was grounds enough for Necho to remove him and put another man of his own choosing on the throne who would do his will.

Note that Jeremiah of Libnah, mentioned here as the father of the mother of King Jehoahaz, should not be confused with Jeremiah of Anathoth, who was the prophet.

Necho renamed Josiah's second son, who replaced Jehoahaz,

when he placed him on the throne. Eliakim means "El [God] shall raise up"; Jehoiakim means "Jehovah shall raise up." The name change reflected no change in the king's unfaithfulness, however.

2 Kings 24:1–7 (2 Chronicles 36:6–8)

The history of the Holy Land is essentially an account of the struggles between Mesopotamia and Egypt to control the land bridge of the Near East. The contest between Babylon and Egypt at the end of the seventh century before Christ is a classic illustration of this historical axiom. During this struggle Judah was eventually annihilated. Egyptian domination of Judah ended when King Nebuchadnezzar of Babylon defeated Pharaoh Necho at Carchemish in 605 B.C., and in 604 Jehoiakim was forced to submit to the Babylonian ruler. By that time Nebuchadnezzar of Babylon (v. 7) ruled the entire Levant, the eastern Mediterranean coastal lands. Jehoiakim's death perhaps occurred in 598 B.C. We wonder if he was assassinated. Certainly he was not honored at the time of his death (Jeremiah 22:18–19; 36:30).

2 Kings 24:8–16 (2 Chronicles 36:9–10)

A very young Jehoiachin became king but only for three months. He was besieged by his Babylonian overlord and removed. Nebuchadnezzar's first siege of Jerusalem probably began early in 597 B.C. The so-called Babylonian exile technically began at this point in history. Young king Jehoiachin was taken captive to Babylon along with all the eminent people of the realm, including craftsmen, metal workers, and other trained and educated citizens. Only the poorest of society were left to cultivate the land to assure ongoing tribute. This group of exiles apparently included Ezekiel. Daniel had been taken to Babylon in an earlier wave of exiles.

2 Kings 24:17–20 (2 Chronicles 36:11–21; Jeremiah 52:1–3)

Jehoiachin's uncle, Zedekiah, who was next on the throne, became the kingdom of Judah's last king of the Davidic line. According to the Book of Mormon (1 Nephi 1:4), he began to reign sometime around 600 B.C. Although he may have had some good intentions (Jeremiah 37:17–21; 38:7–28) he was neither righteous nor competent. Though he was placed in power by Babylon to cooperate and pay his tribute dutifully, he rebelled and tried with Egypt's help to throw off the Babylonian yoke. Though Jeremiah tried to advise Zedekiah's three predecessors, most of his work came in the reign of this last king. So hopeless was the nation's moral condition and religious inclination that the Lord could not be expected to help them; nevertheless, Jeremiah continually told his people that they could not free themselves without the Lord. Jeremiah recommended that they submit to the oppressive condition that their way of life had brought upon them (see Jeremiah 27:8ff). But because of such advice he was maligned and mistrusted.

Yet another prophet was in the city at the time, teaching similar things. Lehi warned of the impending destruction of Jerusalem also, and he testified of the people's wickedness and of the coming of a messiah. "And when the Jews heard these things they were angry . . . and they also sought his life" (1 Nephi 1:20).

The Book of Mormon says, "There came many prophets, prophesying unto the people that they must repent, or the great city Jerusalem must be destroyed" (1 Nephi 1:4). Amos had earlier taught that God would do nothing without first revealing it to his prophets (Amos 3:7). The Lord always gives plenty of warning. The Book of Mormon's mention of "many prophets" is true: Jeremiah, Lehi, Huldah, Zephaniah, Habakkuk, Daniel, Ezekiel, and Urijah were all contemporaries.

Lehi's sons Laman and Lemuel did not believe that Jerusalem could be destroyed. Actually, there was no historical precedent for such a tragic prophecy—Jerusalem had never been destroyed in all of Israelite history. Undoubtedly, in many people's minds the safety of Jerusalem was confirmed by the psalmist who had commented on Jerusalem's enduring, secure status: "They that trust in the Lord shall be as mount Zion, which *cannot be removed, but abideth for ever.* As the mountains are round about Jerusalem, so the Lord is round about his people from henceforth even for ever" (Psalm 125:1–2; emphasis added). God had been patient and long-suffering, and had given ample warning and ample time to repent. Even after Lehi fled Jerusalem to escape its imminent destruction, fourteen years passed before Nebuchadnezzar's armies leveled the city and the Temple.

2 Kings 25:1–7 (Jeremiah 39:1–7)

In spite of the prophetic warnings (such as those found in Jeremiah 38:14–28), Zedekiah tried to free himself, and the Babylonian punitive siege of eighteen months was terrible. The tragic fate of Zedekiah and his sons is tersely told. His sons were slaughtered before his very eyes; he was blinded and taken to Babylon in shackles. His daughters, however, were not taken to Babylon (Jeremiah 43:5–7). Also, the Book of Mormon tells us that a young son of Zedekiah named Mulek escaped by sea and fled to a new land in the western hemisphere (Omni 1:14–19; Helaman 6:10; 8:21).

We know from Jeremiah 34:7 that two fortified positions were the last to hold out against the armies of Babylon:

"When the king of Babylon's army fought against Jerusalem, and against all the cities of Judah that were left, against Lachish, and against Azekah: for these defenced cities remained of the cities of Judah."

Archaeological discoveries corroborate the biblical record of the Babylonian siege and destruction of Jerusalem. Three specific discoveries will be mentioned here.

The Lachish Ostraca were found by J. L. Starkey in the Israelite gateway guardroom at Tel ed Duweir, biblical Lachish, in 1935 (ostraca are potsherds with writing on them; *ostracon* is the singular). They are letters, or drafts of letters, communicating important information between military commanders and/or government officials during the Judeo-Babylonian war prior to the fall of Jerusalem about 587 B.C. The Lachish Ostraca are some of the greatest archaeological evidences of the Old Testament. Harry Torczyner, who published one of the definitive commentaries on the subject, wrote: "In these letters we have the most valuable discovery yet made in the biblical archaeology of [ancient Israel] and the most intimate corroboration of the Bible to this day" (*Lachish I*, 18, as cited in Reynolds and Tate, *Book of Mormon Authorship*, 104).

Lachish Letter No. 4 paints the same woeful picture as Jeremiah 34:7. One line from the letter reads:

"And let (my lord) know that we are watching [over] the signals of Lachish, according to all the indications which my lord hath given, for we cannot see [the signals of] Azekah" (*Ancient*

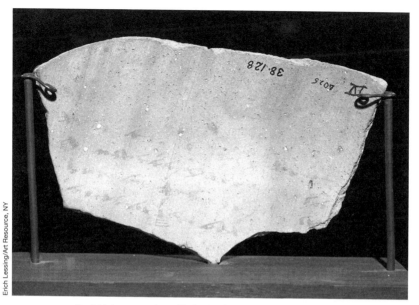

Lachish letter no. 4, on display in the Israel Museum, Jerusalem

Near East, 1:213). This line means that Azekah had fallen to the enemy. Only Lachish was left, and when it fell, the Babylonians marched on Jerusalem.

One particular BYU Israel Study Abroad group in the mid-1980s made the usual field trip into the Shephelah (the low hills that were the battlefield buffer zone between the ancient kingdom of Judah and enemies trying to attack from the western coast). On this occasion, however, the field trip lasted four hours longer than normal, for the following reason described in Brother Ogden's journal: "After eating supper on top of Azekah we left part of the group there and others of us returned to Lachish, to climb it for the second time in one day. Three fellows at each site donned Israelite soldiers' outfits (specially made by female students in the group following ancient reliefs); we then lighted fires at precisely 7 pm to 'signal' to each other. We at Lachish could see very well the signal fire at Azekah. At about 7:20 Azekah's fire went out and we remembered that sad moment in history as recorded on Lachish Ostracon no. 4 and in Jeremiah 34:6–7. We paused on the Iron Age palace for some moments of silence to gaze out

© D. Kelly Ogden

Brigham Young University students reenact the Israelite soldiers' sending signals between Lachish and Azekah. "The king of Babylon's army fought against Jerusalem, and against all the cities of Judah that were left, against Lachish, and against Azekah: for these defenced cities remained of the cities of Judah" (Jeremiah 34:7)

over the countryside under the rising full moon, reflecting on a poignant moment in biblical history."

The Chronicle of Nebuchadnezzar II, part of a series of tablets known as the Babylonian Chronicle, is a cuneiform inscription that cites the displacement of Jehoiachin as king of Judah and the appointment of Zedekiah to the throne in Jerusalem. It also records the Babylonian invasion and destruction of Jerusalem after Zedekiah's revolt.

The Babylonian armies camped on the hills overlooking Jerusalem. One principal camp was on the northern end of the Mount of Olives, also called Mount Scopus (which now includes the site of Brigham Young University's Jerusalem Center for Near Eastern Studies). By surrounding the city, the Babylonians blocked efforts to resupply its citizens. The situation became extremely desperate when food storage was used up and starvation set in.

Nebuchadnezzar's army broke down the walls of Jerusalem,

The Chronicle of Nebuchadnezzar,
part of the Babylonian Chronicle.
"Nebuchadnezzar king of Babylon came,
he, and all his host, against Jerusalem,
and pitched against it; and they built forts
against it round about. . . . And he burnt
the house of the Lord, and the king's
house, and all the houses of
Jerusalem" (2 Kings 25:1, 9)

and his captain "burnt the house of the Lord, and the king's house, and all the houses of Jerusalem, and every great man's house burnt he with fire" (2 Kings 25:9). The Temple of God, nearly four centuries old, was utterly razed and left in ruin. Excavations in the City of David and in today's Jewish Quarter attest to the burning of houses in the siege of Jerusalem from 587 to 586 B.C. The war atmosphere is evidenced by many arrowheads, a destroyed four-room house, a burnt room, and clay *bullae* (letter seals) baked by a great conflagration that swept over the whole city. Inscribed on bullae were fifty-one different names of scribes, court officials, and ministers, a high percentage of them with the theophoric suffix *yahu* (Jehovah). Most of the names are known from the Bible and other inscriptions. One such name is Gemariah son of Shaphan, likely the same as mentioned in Jeremiah 36, a sort of secretary of state in the court of Jehoiakim, king of Judah from 608 to 597 B.C. Another seal, of uncertain provenance, mentions the scribe and friend of the prophet Jeremiah, Berechiah son of Neriah. Berechiah is the long form of Baruch. This same Baruch ben Neriah served as scribe for Jeremiah and recorded his teachings, including

Seal of Gemaryahu ben Shaphan

93

© Zev Radovan/Bible Land Pictures

Clay seals from the City of David

predictions of the downfall of Judah and Jerusalem (see Jeremiah 36:10–25).

As late as 1962 the most widely used textbook on biblical archaeology lamented that "from Jerusalem no archaeological evidence of the Babylonian destruction has been recovered" (Wright, *Biblical Archeology*, 126). The excavations of recent decades make such a statement no longer true. Now there is considerable physical evidence of the fulfillment of Lehi's and Jeremiah's prophecies concerning the destruction of Jerusalem! As we have seen numerous times, the Bible knows what it's talking about.

Other inscriptions found in excavations in the City of David are of interest in light of the Book of Mormon. Archaeologist Yigal Shiloh reported finding three different sherds of local pottery inscribed with South Arabian names in the South Arabian script of ca. 600 B.C. According to Shiloh, "The discovery of such objects, in Jerusalem on the eve of its destruction, is of particular importance in connection with the cultural ties between Judah and the Red Sea and South Arabia in this period" ("Excavations at the City of David," 19). Such finds support the authenticity of the story of Lehi's trek, for he, too, seems to have been acquainted with travel routes between Judah and the Red Sea, and South Arabia is the area to which he led his family, probably following the Frankincense Trail along the western edge of the Arabian peninsula.

2 Kings 25:8–12 (Jeremiah 39:8–10; 52:4–16)

Though Babylonians did carry out mass deportations, they did not follow the Assyrians' policy of transpopulation. Jews were forced away from their land, but no one was brought in to resettle it. The few remaining Jews or Israelites, mostly poor, would eke out a bare existence and produce what tribute they could for the benefit of their conqueror.

2 Kings 25:13–21 (Jeremiah 52:17–27)

The bronze pillars and the font from the front of the Temple must have had considerable value to make them worth transporting as scrap metal hundreds of miles to Babylon. The vessels of the Temple mentioned here appear later, in the books of Daniel and Ezra. Many fine vessels were eventually returned to the Second Temple, which was built on the same site some seventy years later (Ezra 1:7–11; 7:19; 8:24–36).

Certain leaders who had somehow been left were also taken and slain. It should be mentioned, however, that Jeremiah was permitted to do whatever he desired, possibly because of his having encouraged his compatriots to acquiesce to Babylon (Jeremiah 39:11–14).

In one of the greatest understatements in ancient history, verse 21 summarizes one of the most poignant tragedies to have befallen the Jewish people: "So Judah was carried away out of their land." This event (in association with the destruction of the Jerusalem Temple) is regarded by some Jews today as only less catastrophic than the Holocaust of modern times and the destruction of the Second Temple and dispersion of the Jewish people in A.D. 70. The destruction of both the first and the second Temples in Jerusalem (586 B.C. and A.D. 70, respectively) are remembered on the Jewish fast of *Tisha B'Av*, the ninth day of the month of Av of the Jewish calendar. It is a day of mourning to commemorate many tragedies that have befallen the Jewish people but especially the two destructions of God's House, both supposedly on Tisha B'Av, which corresponds to sometime in July or August of the Gregorian calendar. In synagogues all over the world and at the Western, or "Wailing," Wall in Jerusalem, the book of Lamentations is read.

The ancient rabbis asked themselves why the Jerusalem Temple had been destroyed. Stunningly, they said the First Temple was destroyed because three things had occurred among the people: idolatry, unseemly sexual behavior, and bloodshed. And then the rabbis gave an even more arresting reason for the destruction of the Second Temple in A.D. 70—because of *sinat chinam*, "baseless hatred." The Talmud says that baseless hatred is equated with three sins: idolatry, unseemly sexual behavior, and bloodshed (Talmud Yoma 9b). These are the things that destroy a nation and a people. This gives us pause to consider our own day.

2 Kings 25:22–26 (Jeremiah 52:28–30)

The new administrative center of the Babylonians was about seven miles north of Jerusalem at Mizpah, near the modern Palestinian city of Ramallah. The Babylonian-appointed governor, Gedaliah, seems to have been a good man, according to Jeremiah's account (Jeremiah 40). However, one Ishmael, a descendant of the house of David, conspired against Gedaliah, and to the regret of most of the remnant of Judah left in the land, Ishmael slew Gedaliah and others. He himself was attacked and barely escaped to the Ammonites, but remnants of the Judahites were so afraid of repercussions from Babylon that they fled to Egypt. Jeremiah advised against it but to no avail. The history of those who went to Egypt is worth reading (Jeremiah 43–44). Some people believe that Jeremiah and the king's daughters (mentioned in Jeremiah 43:6) eventually fled Egypt and went to present-day Britain, where the royal daughters intermarried with the ancient peoples of that land. However, nothing of that is found in the Bible.

2 Kings 25:27–30 (Jeremiah 52:31–34)

The favor later shown to young king Jehoiachin in the Babylonian captivity is unexplained, unless the new Babylonian king made of him a sort of "government in exile" to help control the Jews there. He would have been very young according to the account in 2 Chronicles 36:9, which asserts that he was eight (rather than eighteen, as in 2 Kings 24:8) and that he was taken captive after three months' reign. The release from prison in Babylon came about thirty-seven years later. Jehoiachin may have been divinely preserved to perpetuate the Davidic line into which the Messiah himself would eventually be born.

It is evident from the book of Ezekiel that the Jews in Babylon were kept in a unit and not scattered, as were the ten tribes who were taken into captivity and relocated to various places by the Assyrians. Both Daniel and Ezekiel functioned as prophets in the captivity—Ezekiel among the people and Daniel in the royal court—but very little is told about their personal lives there (see for example, Ezekiel 1:1–3; 33:21–29; Daniel 1:1–2; 1:7–21).

Jeremiah predicted the Babylonian captivity would be of seventy years' duration (see Jeremiah 25:8–11, and a citation of it in Daniel 9:2). Seventy years did pass from the time the first captives were taken until the first company returned. Also, it was seventy years from the date of the destruction of the first Temple in Jerusalem to the date of the dedication of the second.

With the overthrowing of two Israelite kingdoms and their banishment from the land of promise, a concluding statement is in order. The great Jehovah had desired from the days of Abraham and the days of Moses that his people would seek his face and live, keep his statutes, stay long upon the land, and truly become his peculiar treasure.

"And the Lord God of their fathers sent to them by his messengers, rising up betimes, and sending; because he had compassion on his people, and on his dwelling place: But they mocked the messengers of God, and despised his words, and misused his prophets, until the wrath of the Lord arose against his people, till *there was no remedy*" (2 Chronicles 36:15–16; emphasis added).

The feelings of the exiles far away in the strange land of Babylon are powerfully expressed in Psalm 137:

"By the rivers of Babylon, there we sat down, yea, we wept, when we remembered Zion.

"We hanged our harps upon the willows in the midst thereof.

"For there they that carried us away captive required of us a song; and they that wasted us required of us mirth, saying, Sing us one of the songs of Zion.

"How shall we sing the Lord's song in a strange land?

"If I forget thee, O Jerusalem, let my right hand forget her cunning.

"If I do not remember thee, let my tongue cleave to the roof of my mouth; if I prefer not Jerusalem above my chief joy."

The exiles' feelings are hauntingly paralleled by the medieval Jewish poet Yehuda Halevi, living in Spain, who in a famous couplet expressed his longing for the national homeland:

$$\text{לִבִּי בְמִזְרָח וְאָנֹכִי בְּסוֹף מַעֲרָב־}$$

"My heart is in the east, but I am at the farthest west."

Displaced Jews of the Babylonian captivity must have experienced similar heart-wrenching yearning for their homeland.

An Israelite psalmist summarized the history of his people, describing them as a vine that the Lord planted in the vineyard of Israel which flourished and expanded for a time and was then uprooted, and adding a plea to the Lord of the vineyard to visit his vine and have mercy on them:

"Thou hast brought a vine out of Egypt: thou hast cast out the heathen, and planted it.

"Thou preparedst room before it, and didst cause it to take deep root, and it filled the land.

"The hills were covered with the shadow of it, and the boughs thereof were like the goodly cedars.

"She sent out her boughs unto the sea [the Mediterranean], and her branches unto the river [the Jordan].

"Why hast thou then broken down her hedges, so that all they which pass by the way do pluck her?

"The boar out of the wood doth waste it, and the wild beast of the field doth devour it.

"Return, we beseech thee, O God of hosts: look down from heaven, and behold, and visit this vine;

"And the vineyard which thy right hand hath planted, and the branch that thou madest strong for thyself" (Psalm 80:8–15).

Happily, the books of Kings end on a hopeful note. Though the Lord's chosen people were exiled, they were not abandoned. The Lord would seek after them and return them to their land and freedom after a sojourn in Babylon of some fifty years

(586–538 B.C.). This return is symbolized in Jehoiachin's release from prison while in Babylon and his being given a seat at the king's table and a regular allowance as long as he lived. God's promises concerning the continuation of the house of David would be fulfilled.

PROVERBS

Our English word *proverb* is used to translate the Hebrew *mashal* (plural, *mashalim*). The primary meaning of the root is "ruled, had power over, had power to do," as in ruling or having power over one's life, or possessing the wisdom to rightly govern one's life. Hence the book of Proverbs begins by describing its purpose as helping one to gain wisdom: "To know wisdom and instruction; to perceive the words of understanding; to receive the instruction of wisdom, justice, and judgment, and equity; to give subtilty to the simple, to the young man knowledge and discretion. A wise man will hear, and will increase learning; and a man of understanding shall attain unto wise counsels" (Proverbs 1:2–5). The book itself declares that the source of all wisdom, understanding, and good judgment is the Lord: "For the Lord giveth wisdom: out of his mouth cometh knowledge and understanding" (2:6).

"Wisdom" is the equivalent of the Hebrew *hokhmah,* which probably derives from an ancient root that originally meant "firm" or "fixed." The attainment of wisdom, personified as a female, was described as the principal object of life: "Wisdom is the principal thing; therefore get wisdom: and with all thy getting get understanding. Exalt her, and she shall promote thee: she shall bring thee to honour, when thou dost embrace her. She shall give to thine head an ornament of grace: a crown of glory shall she deliver to thee" (Proverbs 4:7–9). It was by wisdom that the Lord "founded the earth; by understanding . . . he established the heavens" (3:19).

Proverbs is a good example of Hebrew wisdom literature, derived apparently from the experiences of mortals and epitomized as rules of wise behavior. Proverbs contains some divinely inspired material, but more is attributed to human observation, presenting universal and timeless principles for righteous living.

The book of Proverbs contains much that is attributed to King Solomon. As to Solomon's authorship of proverbs, 1 Kings 4:32 credits him with speaking thousands of them, covering all facets of the relationships of nature, man, and God. Whether the proverbs in the Bible include all of Solomon's proverbs, and indeed whether all that are attributed to him are really his, is difficult to tell now. Later transmitters of the Bible copied and disseminated some of Solomon's proverbs in different collections, as we are told: "These are also proverbs of Solomon, which the men of Hezekiah king of Judah copied out" (Proverbs 25:1).

Chapters 1–9 of Proverbs are entitled Proverbs of Solomon. They are largely in the form of advice from a father to his son but also include some long poems about wisdom. In chapter 8, for instance, wisdom is personified and seems to be not an abstraction but a person. Chapters 10–22:16 are also appropriately entitled Proverbs of Solomon and contain only the formal, pithy poetic couplets that are proverbs by definition. From 22:17 to the end of chapter 24 is a variety of longer admonitions and maxims on moral and social matters. Chapters 25–29 also constitute a unit called Proverbs of Solomon. Chapter 30 is called The Words of Agur and chapter 31 The Words of King Lemuel.

The Hebrew *mashal* covers a broader category of literary forms than does our word *proverbs*; it can also mean "to be like, to represent, to compare." Indeed, many proverbs contain comparisons or contrasts of things that are alike or not alike.

The most common type of proverb is called "antithetic" or "opposite" and usually employs the contrasting word "but." Consider the following excellent and well-known examples:

"The fear [reverence] of the Lord is the beginning of knowledge: but fools despise wisdom and instruction" (1:7).

"A wise son maketh a glad father: but a foolish son is the heaviness of his mother" (10:1).

"A virtuous woman is a crown to her husband: but she that maketh ashamed is as rottenness in his bones" (12:4).

"The way of a fool is right in his own eyes: but he that hearkeneth unto counsel is wise" (12:15).

"He that spareth his rod hateth his son: but he that loveth him chasteneth him betimes" (13:24).

"Righteousness exalteth a nation: but sin is a reproach to any people" (14:34).

"A soft answer turneth away wrath: but grievous words stir up anger" (15:1).

"A merry heart doeth good like a medicine: but a broken spirit drieth the bones" (17:22).

"Faithful are the wounds of a friend; but the kisses of an enemy are deceitful" (27:6).

"The wicked flee when no man pursueth: but the righteous are bold as a lion" (28:1).

"He that covereth his sins shall not prosper: but whoso confesseth and forsaketh them shall have mercy" (28:13).

Other proverbs are called "comparative" or "synthetic," where the second phrase complements or adds to the thought of the first phrase. The following are some examples:

"My son, despise not the chastening of the Lord; neither be weary of his correction: For whom the Lord loveth he correcteth; even as a father the son in whom he delighteth" (3:11–12).

"Reprove not a scorner, lest he hate thee: rebuke a wise man, and he will love thee" (9:8).

"As a jewel of gold in a swine's snout, so is a fair woman which is without discretion" (11:22).

"The liberal soul shall be made fat: and he that watereth shall be watered also himself" (11:25).

"Pride goeth before destruction, and an haughty spirit before a fall" (16:18).

"He that is slow to anger is better than the mighty; and he that ruleth his spirit than he that taketh a city" (16:32).

"Train up a child in the way he should go: and when he is old, he will not depart from it" (22:6).

"As cold waters to a thirsty soul, so is good news from a far country" (25:25).

"As a dog returneth to his vomit, so a fool returneth to his folly" (26:11).

"Where no wood is, there the fire goeth out: so where there is no talebearer, the strife ceaseth" (26:20).

In addition to proverbs, there are other succinct, usually single-idea statements of truth or insights into human behavior: aphorisms, maxims, axioms, or adages. The following are a few examples from the book of Proverbs:

"By pride cometh contention" (13:10).
"The way of the transgressors is hard" (13:15).
"Before honour is humility" (15:33).
"Wealth maketh many friends" (19:4).
"The borrower is servant to the lender" (22:7).
"As he thinketh in his heart, so is he" (23:7).
"Let another man praise thee, and not thine own mouth" (27:2).
"Where there is no vision, the people perish" (29:18).

The book of Proverbs has no particular unity of theme but could be studied by topics. For instance, one of the prominent subjects is the ways and dangers of immoral women (see 2:15–19; 5:3–5, 15–20; 6:23–29, 32; 7:5–23, 26). President Spencer W. Kimball wrote that young people would often plead with him that "we are not taught frankly enough. . . . We need warnings—frank warnings" (*Miracle of Forgiveness*, 231). Numerous passages of Proverbs do contain frank warnings.

Probably the best known and most beautiful of the quotable passages in Proverbs is 3:5–6. That counsel can change your life.

Proverbs 6:16–19 identifies seven things that the Lord hates. This passage exemplifies the kind of numerical patterns that we sometimes find in Proverbs and other bodies of wisdom literature in the ancient Near East. Here the formula (note the number seven) symbolizes all of the kinds of things abhorrent to the Lord.

Proverbs 17:27–28 advises us of the wisdom of speaking sparingly.

Proverbs 23:29–32 vividly describes in metaphors and similes the tragic and destructive powers of intoxicating wine.

Proverbs 31:10–31 uses a perfect alphabetical acrostic (that is, each of the twenty-two verses begins with the succeeding letter of the twenty-two letters of the Hebrew alphabet) to describe the ideal woman.

ECCLESIASTES

The Hebrew title of Ecclesiastes is *koheleth*, derived from the root *kahal*, meaning "to gather, assemble, or call together." By extension, this title refers to the person who addresses those who are gathered—"the preacher."

Ecclesiastes is another type of biblical wisdom literature. It is like a report of a man's search for that which is enduring among the world's transitory things. You will doubtless agree with some of his observations about what is vain and what is valuable. You will find some genuine gems in this book. But you will also find the author lacks some knowledge of the gospel as we know it, and errs sometimes as a result. You will likely gain appreciation of the gospel's philosophy of life as you go through Ecclesiastes.

In chapters 1 and 2, the Preacher introduces himself and his problem and gives a preliminary report of what is transitory and what is of enduring worth. In chapters 3 and 4, he observes that though there is a time for everything, many things are done out of time and place, and much injustice exists. Chapters 5 and 6 continue in much the same vein after a few proverb-like admonitions; most of this segment concerns some common frustrations. After a few more proverbs—most in a pessimistic tone—the next three chapters present further observations on the frustrations and inequities of life. Chapter 10 and part of 11 are on the subject of wisdom; the rest of chapter 11 and all of chapter 12 contain the author's parting advice and his summation of the duty of man. See also Bible Dictionary, "Ecclesiastes."

Ecclesiastes 1:1

Exactly why the reporter of these cogitations designates himself as the Preacher is unknown. Neither is it known whether he really was David's son, King Solomon, or whether the writer means to sum up the experiences and learnings derived from a life like Solomon's. But who he was really doesn't matter; he is any man, he is mankind, and he lives in the world; and the world, in some ways, is still very much the same today as then.

Ecclesiastes 1:2–18

The introductory statement presents the author's observation that all things tend to be cyclically transient and repetitive. The word "vanity" means basically "emptiness" and "uselessness" combined with the idea of transitoriness; it translates here the Hebrew word *hevel,* which is a mere breath, a puff, a whiff that is here and then gone. The meaning seems always to be (in the context of this book) that which is ephemeral and generally not enduring.

The Preacher presents a further introduction of himself and a description of his findings in his initial quest for wisdom. "Vexation of spirit" renders Hebrew words which mean literally "feeding on wind" or "consumption of spirit," and in context the phrase here seems to categorize things that are frustrating or exasperating. It is used again in 2:11 and 6:9.

Ecclesiastes 2

This is the report of the Preacher's adventure in seeking satisfaction from wealth, beauty, and sensual gratification. After all were tried, these too were found to have been vanity—empty gain, futile—like "striving after wind." The phrase "under the sun" means "on earth."

Evaluating his efforts, he further concluded that in spite of wisdom and great labor to produce wealth, he would eventually die just as the foolish man dies, and neither wisdom nor wealth would be of any final worth.

The Preacher was able to report *one* positive finding: one who labors can eat and drink and have enjoyment in his toil, and if he pleases God, God will give him wisdom and knowledge and joy. On the other hand, a sinner only works and gathers to give his gain to others who survive him, which is also vanity.

Ecclesiastes 3

It is not certain whether his concept of "a time to every purpose under the heaven" embraces the idea of a fixed, determined, set time predestined for everything, a proper and propitious time, or simply a sequence of cause and effect. However, it is true that in mortality there are appropriate times to do certain things in life: a time for schooling and spiritual preparation, a time for missionary service, a time for marriage and family life, a time for hard work, a time to contribute to society, and so forth. In the Lord's economy and kingdom timing is everything. In this passage the writer is also describing a sort of cyclical alternation in all things— birth and death, hurting and healing, breaking down and building up, weeping and laughing, etc. Perhaps this is his way of saying there is opposition (or opposites) in all things. There can be no sweetness without the bitter, no good without evil, and so forth (see 2 Nephi 2:13, 22).

The author continues by asserting that ordinary man cannot understand the purposes and processes of all these actions and reactions unless he partakes of "the eternal" which only God can set in his heart. The word rendered "world" in the King James English text (v. 11) is the Hebrew *'olam;* but this word is, in all other biblical contexts except one, translated "eternal" or "eternity" (only in later Mishnaic Hebrew does the word come to be used for "world"). Read footnote 11*b.* The Hebrew text gives the impression that we *can* know the things of God.

The author also espouses a philosophy of life that encourages hard work, doing good, and enjoying the fruits of one's labor. These things are gifts of God.

The Preacher observes further that there is much injustice done on earth. In the end there is no difference between man and beast; all must die and go back to dust.

Ecclesiastes 4

The author again touches on the oppressions of life, which are part of the human condition that brings tears. He lists various other frustrations and concludes in a seeming moment of pessimism that the dead are better off than the living, and the unborn are better off still!

He concedes, however, that two together in life can make things more tolerable for each other than one alone can make for himself. There is strength and power, emotional and spiritual power, in numbers. He allows a glimmer of optimism to show in his evaluation of a poor and wise youth above an old and foolish king. But still all must come and go, and there will be nothing lasting left.

Ecclesiastes 5

The theme of the first part of this chapter is the worthlessness of superficial religious observances. The Preacher admonishes reverence for God and fidelity in keeping covenants with him, apparently regardless of the outcome—for it is better not to have God angry with you.

There is some value in governments, but he warns against anyone being surprised if injustices are done under them, in spite of all the chain of "watchers" over each other.

The gaining of goods is ultimately useless; the laborer who enjoys his sleep after work is better off than the rich man who has accumulated many goods from his labor. The Preacher contrasts the futility of gathering riches to the satisfaction of enjoying one's work and making food and drink available.

Ecclesiastes 6

And again, if a man lives long and gains much wealth but does not enjoy life's good things along the way and goes down into the insignificant grave, what use was it all? Sometimes the Preacher seems oriented only to the values of this life, expressing little of the eternal values of wisdom or experience. However, he hints that to live righteously is advisable and comes to that conclusion at the end of the book.

For the time being though, all of life, or at least a good deal of it, is vain, or transitory, and no one can tell what will come to pass after him on this earth. Thus, we might conclude as well that we should live each moment to the fullest, enjoying God's blessings.

Ecclesiastes 7

The Preacher leaves the general impression in this collection of proverbs that soberness is better than levity, wisdom than foolishness, patience than anxiety. These are, in fact, valuable truths. He seems to recommend that one take things as they come—prosperity and adversity—with thoughtfulness and tolerance.

The Preacher admonishes wisdom, moderation, and balance, along with reverence for God and contentment to leave things as God has made them. The word "inventions" is from a word in Hebrew which means "thoughts, reckonings, devices," and is better understood if rendered thus at the close of verse 29. His warning against an enticing woman is like many in the book of Proverbs.

Ecclesiastes 8

Again, he recommends reverence for God and respect for a king's command. He seems to sense some likelihood that sometime, somewhere, those who so behave will be better off than the cynical and rebellious.

Ecclesiastes 9

Death, so far as the Preacher knew, is not to be desired, in spite of his earlier observations on the vicissitudes of life (chapter 4). Since there is nothing more "under the sun" (meaning "on this earth") for the dead, a "living dog is better than a dead lion." So, live joyfully with loved ones while you may.

Ecclesiastes 10

He leaves a few proverbs regarding folly—even a little of it can be disastrous, whether in social acts, in relaxing restraints, in talking too much, or in being slothful. To act with restraint but to enjoy life is his most common admonition.

Ecclesiastes 11

Faith is more dominant than pessimism and cynicism in this chapter. Do what is right no matter what. Be obedient come what may. The Preacher recommends faith in certain good principles and processes even if man does not fully understand the rationale behind them all, for some of the greatest things happening nearest to man (such as the miracle of birth, verse 5) are subtly done by

God, who makes everything. Enjoy youth, do your heart's desire, but remember that God holds you accountable.

Ecclesiastes 12:1–8

Finally, the author once more admonishes recognition of God's overruling hand and the doing of that which is good before the dust which mortal man is made of goes back to dust, and the spirit to God who gave it. Here at last he expresses what was elsewhere implied—that there is a duality to the human soul and that something goes elsewhere when the body goes to the tomb. He may not have known what we know (such as we read in 1 Peter 3:18–22; 4:6 or in Alma 40–42), but he seems at this point to have embraced the concept of an ongoing, living spirit of man after the body's death.

The Preacher's comment that "the spirit shall return unto God who gave it" parallels the teaching in Alma 40:11 that "the spirits of all men . . . are taken home to that God who gave them life." Of that teaching President George Q. Cannon wrote: "He does not intend to convey the idea that they are immediately ushered into the personal presence of God." (*Gospel Truth*, 58). And President Joseph Fielding Smith added: "'Taken home to God' simply means that their mortal existence has come to an end, and they have returned to the world of spirits, where they are assigned to a place according to their works with the just or with the unjust, there to await the resurrection" (*Answers to Gospel Questions*, 2:85). On this point, the Savior is our best, most important witness. We know that not even he was taken immediately into the presence of his Father after his death. He went to the world of spirits (D&C 138), and even after his own Resurrection, being "the firstfruits of them that slept" (1 Corinthians 15:20), he said to the first mortal to see his resurrected body, "Touch me not; for I am not yet ascended to my Father" (John 20:17).

Ecclesiastes 12:9–12

An editorial insert commends the Preacher's words and compares his wise admonitions to goads that stimulate action and to nails that firmly fix truths.

Ecclesiastes 12:13–14

Another summation, like those throughout, to heed God's teachings and keep the commandments, ends the dissertation—with one added statement of faith that triumphs over the pessimism he expressed earlier about all going down to death; here he observes that after death every deed shall be judged whether it was good or evil.

This book of Ecclesiastes may well be the most misunderstood book in the Bible. It indeed might appear pessimistic and out of harmony with the rest of the Old Testament if it didn't conclude with the final lines: *"Fear God, and keep his commandments: for this is the whole duty of man."* The word "duty" is in italics in the King James Version because it is not there in the Hebrew. It has been supplied by the translators to give more sense to the passage; however, the original teaching is that as we reverence God and keep his commandments, we become *the whole man*—that is, the complete or perfect man. See explanation of the word *perfect* in the commentary at Genesis 17:1–8.

Ecclesiastes presents a quest to find meaning in life; it describes the dead ends we often pursue and offers the only true alternative to the vanity and futility we may experience: a God-centered life.

SONG OF SOLOMON

The Song of Solomon is a short book that appears in our King James Bible between Ecclesiastes and Isaiah. The eight chapters of pastoral love poetry constitute love songs attributed to Solomon; in the Hebrew Bible, the work is entitled *Shir haShirim*, the very first words of the first verse, which mean "Song of Songs." The Joseph Smith Translation manuscript indicates that "The Songs of Solomon are not inspired writings." Some may understandably question why are they then retained in the LDS edition of the Bible? Our answer is that if we can find *any* writings from the ancient biblical world, we want to preserve them. The songs of Solomon contain some of the most beautiful love poetry in the world. And it is good that among all the writings of "the people of the book" who wrote volumes on the laws of God, religious history, wisdom literature, and prophecy, this one small opus on love was preserved. Romantic love is a vital facet of life. These chapters' identification as "not inspired writings" may negate their role as inspired symbolism representing the love of the Lord for Israel, or for the Church, but it does not negate or depreciate their value as romantic prose and poetry from a highly literate people. It is interesting to note that some of the world's great religions use the language of physical love to present their teaching regarding an individual's personal, intimate communion with the Divine or the Infinite.

JOB

"Job is one of the greatest masterpieces of the human mind. It is, perhaps, the greatest masterpiece. And to-morrow, if all literature was to be destroyed, and it was left to me to retain one work only, I should save Job."—Victor Hugo (Uzanne, "Conversations and Opinions of Victor Hugo," 570).

"[Job is] the greatest poem of ancient or modern times."—Alfred, Lord Tennyson (as cited in Anderson, "The Book of Job," 238).

"I call [the book of Job], apart from all theories about it, one of the grandest things ever written with pen. . . . There is nothing written, I think, in the Bible or out of it, of equal literary merit."—Thomas Carlyle (*On Heroes*, 65–66).

"The Book of Job . . . taken as a mere work of literary genius, [is] one of the most wonderful productions of any age or in any language."—Daniel Webster (*Boston Atlas*, 2).

Although some consider Job merely a fictitious character in this literary masterpiece set in the form of a dramatic play, Latter-day Saints believe he was a real person. Not only do the Old and New Testaments attest the historicity of Job (see Ezekiel 14:14; James 5:11) but modern revelation also mentions him (D&C 121:7–10). The time period in which Job lived is unknown; he is variously placed between Abraham and Malachi. Job 19:24 mentions "iron," and the Iron Age in the land of Israel begins about 1200 B.C. Yet, other passages find a better fit within the late patriarchal age, just before the Iron Age. For example, Job lives 140 years *after* his great trial (42:16), which is characteristic of the long lives of the patriarchs. Also, Job's wealth is measured in livestock (Job 1:3), characteristic of the period from Abraham through Moses. Job functioned as did the pre-Aaronic patriarchs,

112

serving as his own priest and offering sacrifices. The raids of the Sabeans and Chaldeans better fit the second millennium B.C. (Job 1:15, 17 and footnote *a*). The universal message of the book of Job could, of course, apply to any time period.

The location of Job's residence is also unknown, though some hints are given in the first chapter: he lived in the land of Uz, which could be in the land of Edom (compare Lamentations 4:21); Job was "the greatest of all the men of the east" (1:3); "the Sabeans" fell upon his livestock (1:15; an Arab tribe, according to the Bible Dictionary); "the Chaldeans," another group from the east, also carried away some of Job's possessions (1:17); and there came "a great wind from the wilderness," resulting in the death of some of his children (1:19). These cumulative hints suggest that Job lived in one of the eastern desert lands of the Bible.

The book of Job is situated in the third division of the Hebrew Bible, the Writings (remember we have the Law, the Prophets, and the Writings). It consists mainly of the words of Job and his associates, with at least two profound declarations by Jehovah. Job's name in Hebrew (*'yov*) means "miserable" or "misery," which is the essence of this great man's condition as well as the pivotal point of the story.

Job does not answer the question of how evil and suffering can exist in a world created by a perfectly just and loving God. Some theologians call this the problem of theodicy—how to make sense of the justice of God in light of unjust human suffering. Rather, it tries to explore and highlight how profound faith can and does bless a person in the depths of their suffering. Job challenges the simplistic beliefs that the righteous will always be blessed, or that suffering is a sign of divine displeasure (see Deuteronomy 7:11–16; 28:1, 4, 58, 59; Psalm 1:6). The story of Job forces us to think in terms of eternity—and is, in fact, an allegory on one of Jesus Christ's foundational principles: "in the world ye shall have tribulation: but be of good cheer; I have overcome the world [and so may you]" (John 16:33).

Job 1 and 2 contain the "prologue"—a prose, narrative background for the great poetic drama that follows. Chapter 3 records Job's first utterance of complaint about his grief, and chapters 4–31 record the threefold arguments of his friends, with each followed by Job's replies, reasonings, and further supplications. Chapters 32–37 present the somewhat different speeches of another "friend," Elihu. Chapters 38–41 record the Lord's speech to Job, and in 42:1–6 Job humbly submits to the Lord. In 42:7–17 a prose "epilogue" tells of a restoration and actual increase of such earthly status and possession as he had before his trial.

Because the book of Job is long and complicated, our commentary is something of a paraphrase-synopsis, intended to assist in reading and appreciating the text. Since the paraphrase is in itself an interpretation, only a little additional explanation is added. Verse numbers in parentheses are provided within the commentary to help readers follow the synopsis along with the biblical text; only the verse number that begins each summarized segment is indicated. Chapters 1–3, 6–7, 10, 19, 30, 32–34, 38, 42, plus 5:17; 14:14; and 23:10 contain the essence of the book of Job.

Job 1

(1) Job is a circumspect, God-fearing, law-abiding man; he is portrayed as rich, whole-hearted, upright, reverent to God and quite immune to evil. He is the model of piety and righteousness. (6) But the adversary (as *satan* should properly be translated, for it is used here in Hebrew as a common noun, not a proper name) challenges the essence of Job's righteousness, and (12) God is willing to let him be tested. But even when his possessions are taken, his children smitten, and all of his blessings apparently lost, he still faithfully trusts in God and dutifully praises him. (20) He mourns in the traditional Hebraic manner but does not get angry or attribute unfairness to God. Job turns out to be a powerful reminder of what Jesus of Nazareth experienced as the mortal Messiah.

JOB AND JESUS CHRIST: PARALLEL EXPERIENCES

1. Job is described as "perfect" (1:1); Jesus was perfect (Hebrews 5:9; 3 Nephi 12:48).
2. Job once held a position of great honor but was brought low (Job 29:25; 30:1). Likewise, Jesus held a high position of honor

in premortality but condescended to come to earth and was held in great derision (Mark 5:40).

3. The adversary was allowed to tempt Job (Job 2:6), just as Satan was allowed to tempt Jesus (Matthew 4:3–11; Hebrews 4:15).

4. Job was rejected by his own, and at one point, felt he was a stranger in his own house (Job 19:14–15). Likewise, Jesus was rejected by his own (John 1:11; Luke 4:24; Isaiah 53:2–4).

5. Job's physical suffering and anguish caused him to wish he had died from the womb (Job 3:11). Jesus' suffering caused him to tremble because of pain and shrink from unimaginable suffering and anguish (D&C 19:18).

6. Job's cry was "God hath delivered me to the ungodly, and turned me over into the hands of the wicked" (Job 16:11). This was exactly Jesus' experience, as Peter testified (Acts 2:23).

7. Job said of his associates, "They abhor me, they flee far from me, and spare not to spit in my face" (Job 30:10). This also was Jesus' experience (Matthew 26:67).

8. Both Job and Jesus suffered alone (Job 19:19; D&C 76:107; 121:10; 133:50).

9. Neither Job nor Jesus got what they "deserved" but endured tremendous contradiction (see *Lectures on Faith,* 59).

10. One of Job's statements even prefigures the burial of Jesus. The King James Version of Job 21:32 says, "Yet shall he be brought to the grave, and shall remain in the tomb." But the Hebrew text (as other English versions attest) says: "He is carried to the grave, *and a watch is kept over his tomb*" (compare Matthew 27:65).

Job 2

(1) "The satan" (the adversary) does not concede that Job's righteousness has really been proven until his person has been smitten; he claims a man will give up even life for physical relief. So physical misery is also tried. (9) Job's wife, outraged, asks him to curse that God who would permit him to experience such suffering, so that then he could die to be free of it; but Job rebukes her for speaking "as one of the foolish women," and refuses to do so. (11) Three friends come to comfort him; they

sit in astonishment for seven days without saying anything. This mourning practice is called "sitting shiva" ("seven") and is still practiced in Judaism today upon the death of a loved one. Family and close friends come and sit on the floor of the home of those who are grieving. Then Job's composure breaks down, and he utters his first outcry of complaint.

Chapters 1 and 2 are prose, but Job's outcry in reaction to his excruciating misery is in Hebrew poetry of excellent quality. Watch for all types of parallelism; often the meaning of a difficult line is enhanced by its companion-line, whether that line is synonymous or antithetical to it. Versions of the Bibles that print the poetry in its proper stichs and strophes (lines and stanzas) make it easier to read and understand these passages.

The exact nature of Job's physical affliction, hinted at in 2:7 but never named, is elsewhere described by horrible symptoms: deteriorated appearance (2:12; 19:19); sores with worms (7:5); nightmares (7:14); weight loss to the point of emaciation (17:7; 19:20); bad breath (19:17); tremendous fever (30:27, 30); skin turning black (30:30); and constant pain (30:17). We know that physical health is interwoven with spiritual well-being; Job's affliction was truly a debilitating trial physically, emotionally, and spiritually.

Job 3

(3) Here begins the long poetic section. In this first utterance Job does not blame God but simply wishes he (Job) were nonexistent; that is, unborn, stillborn, or dead in infancy. His expressions are poignant. Sometimes great lessons come out of tough experiences: (20) "Wherefore is light given to him that is in misery" (compare D&C 122:7).

Job 4

Eliphaz, the oldest of Job's friends, makes the first diagnosis: (2) He feels that Job, who had often given advice, should now receive it. Job had acted as *all* righteous people are commanded to act: he had instructed many and "strengthened the weak hands" (D&C 81:5). (7) He asserts that there is a cause for every effect; therefore, wickedness is behind this suffering. Who has ever perished of suffering while innocent? (17) No man is perfect, or just.

Job 5

(1) Eliphaz continues, recommending that Job should not be angry or foolish but accept his trouble, as all must do. (7) Seek God, and commit your cause to him, and (17) accept correction and (19) God will deliver you and prosper you again.

Job 6

In chapter 6 Job rebuffs Eliphaz's optimistic speech, that is, "repent and things will get better," and pleads his cause as right. He says he has not sinned and that Eliphaz is not only unkind but a bit hypocritical.

Job's first reply: (2) My misery has not been weighed. Does anything happen without a cause? (4) Job gives us some idea of the depth of his spiritual misery. (8) Would that I could die! Why wait or hope? (14) I need friends, but they have all melted away, even you three. (24) Tell me wherein I am in the wrong. Is there any injustice in my tongue? My cause is righteous.

Job 7

In chapter 7 Job presents a response to the Lord. He confesses that he is a sinner but doesn't know why God is not forgiving him. (1) Can I not at least hope for the end of my term of misery? As I am, I exist without hope. (7) My life is transitory, and by and by I shall be seen no more; therefore, I will speak while I can. (12) (To God) Why dost thou watch me? Why must I be visited every day with sore affliction from thee? What have I done to thee? How have I burdened thee, even if I have sinned? Why not forgive me and relieve me? When I lie in the earth thou shalt no longer find me to afflict me.

Job 8

Bildad gives his first diagnosis: (2) Why speak thus, as if God perverted justice? (5) If you were worthy you would be heard—if you would but seek him. (8) Inquire into the experience of the past; it will tell you that (11) there is a cause for every phenomenon; they who are cut down are they who have forgotten God. (20) God doesn't cast away the innocent, nor will God uphold evildoers.

Job 9

Job offers his second reply: (2) I know that those things are true about God, but who can interrogate or contend with God? He manages all things in the universe; the forces of chaos and all the created universe bow to him. (9) Job even knows the names of the great stellar constellations. (11) How could I answer him or contend with him? He is both my judge and my accuser. (17) But he makes all to suffer. Though I am innocent in fact, how can I prove my innocence with words? (23) He neither cares about the calamity of the innocent nor the prosperity of the wicked. (33) There is no arbiter between us, and I am afraid to plead my cause. His hand is already too heavy upon me, and I know not the reason.

Job 10

Job continues his reply: (1) Since I loathe my life, which cannot be any worse, I will approach God directly and bid him not to contend and ask him why he oppresses what his own hands have made. (2) "Shew me wherefore thou contendest with me." *Why is all this happening to me?* (4) Hast thou the eyes of man, that thou must test me so? (7) God, you know that I am not wicked. (8) Thy hands have made me as I am, but whether innocent or guilty, I cannot find relief. (15) If I am wicked woe unto me; but if I am righteous I am full of confusion over the things I am suffering. Therefore, God, please see my affliction. (18) Why indeed was I made? Let me but have a little comfort ere I come to oblivion.

Job 11

Zophar, the youngest of the friends, gives his first diagnosis (he is more direct and less patient than the others): (2) You boast in your own judgment and declare yourself pure, and should we not answer such perversion? Would that God might instruct you in wisdom. He punishes you less than you deserve. (7) Can you find out God's infinite ways and purposes? (13) Repent; put away iniquity and all will be well, for only the wicked fall.

Job 12

Job's third response: (2) What you know, I know; my wisdom isn't inferior to yours. Who doesn't know such things? (4) But it doesn't apply here: I was prayerful, just, innocent—and now I am a laughingstock, (6) while robbers prosper. (7) The beasts, the fowls, and all things show that they are God's work. (13) He is greater than all and makes judges as fools before him, and he overrules princes, nations, chiefs. God has power over the elements; he can make the strong become weak; he controls the destiny of nations.

Job 13

(1) I know all the precepts you know. But I would rather reason with God; you plaster me with lies. I am not guilty. Would you discover my faults for God? You look to your own ways. (13) Leave me alone; I will put all up to him, and *though he slay me, yet will I trust him* (v. 15; compare Habakkuk 3:17–19). I am no hypocrite before him; I know that I shall be justified. (2) Two requests I have: withdraw thy hand of punishment, and speak thou unto me. Tell me what my sins are. Why should I be further persecuted?

Ultimately, verse 15 gives us one of the meanings and purposes of suffering in God's grand design. Suffering, especially undeserved suffering, tests our loyalty to him, and eternal life hangs in the balance. Joseph Smith said that when the Lord has "thoroughly proved" a person and finds that the person is determined to serve God "at all hazards," the person will find his or her exaltation guaranteed or made sure (see the entire quote in commentary at Numbers 20:2–13).

Job 14

(1) Few are the days of man, and what is there left for me? Only look away from me and let me rest until the end; (7) for a felled tree sprouts again, but if a man die what is left? Let me die and hide in Sheol until thy wrath be past. (14) *If a man die shall he live again?* If so, I would gladly die and wait, and when thou callest I would answer. (16) But now there is ever more and more suffering, and my charge is still hidden from me; all this wears me down and destroys hope. So man passes on—there is nothing but pain and mourning.

Job 15

Eliphaz's second attempt to reason with Job: (1) Why should one reason with such as you? Your own mouth condemns you. (7) Are you older and wiser than all? (12) Why be carried away to say such things? (17) I will tell you there isn't much to man when he opposes God; such men are wicked and shall perish.

Job 16

Job's fourth reply: (2) I have heard enough of such things. Sorry comforters are you all. If you were in my place, I could also criticize you, but I would say words to assuage your suffering. (6) Yet if I speak of myself am I eased? Or if I keep silence, am I relieved? God persecutes me; my friends gape at me. He destroys me although there is not violence in my hands and my prayer is pure. (18) Let not my suffering be hidden; let my cry be heard. For I know *my witness and my record are in Heaven* even now. I appeal to God even though I contend with God. There is but little time now for me to live.

Job 17

(1) Soon my grave will be ready for me. Those around me are mockers, (3) but give thou a promise to be my surety! Who else will covenant with me? All others are unjust judges. (6) God has made me despised among all people, they who judge me turn night into day. My hope and I go down soon together to rest in the dust.

Job 18

Bildad's second attempt to reason with Job: (2) Why do you so angrily reject us? Should the laws of nature be altered to justify you? (5) The wicked must suffer, and perish; his strength and his confidence shall fail, and he shall have no descendants. (21) This is the destiny of him who does not know God.

Job 19

Chapter 19 is a masterpiece. There is no more important doctrine than the atoning sacrifice of the Savior, including the resurrection, which Job testifies of in a powerful way, and there are not many testimonies of the resurrection in the Old Testament

(vv. 25–27; compare Isaiah 25:8; 26:19; Daniel 12:2; Ezekiel 37:1–14).

Job's fifth reply: (2) How long will you vex and crush me with words? Ten times you have reproached me and are not ashamed. (It was really five.) (4) If I have erred it is hidden from me, and God has overwhelmed me. (7) There is no justice in this. (9) God has stripped me of all I had (13) and all friends and kin have forsaken me. (20) I am nothing but skin and bones; I am staying alive only by the skin of my teeth! (21) Have pity on me! Why persecute me further? I hope that my case is recorded. (25) Still *I know that my Redeemer lives* and *I shall eventually see him.* (The Book of Mormon expresses the same concept: "In our bodies we shall see God"; 2 Nephi 9:4.) (28) Beware, oh friends, lest punishment come to you, and you shall know there is a judgment at last.

One of the more pitiable declarations of Job is recorded in verse 19: "All my inward friends abhorred me: and they whom I loved are turned against me." It is not hard to understand how the Lord could say essentially to Joseph Smith during one of his great trials that he should cheer up because things were not as bad for him as they had been for Job: "Thy friends do stand by thee, and they shall hail thee again with warm hearts and friendly hands. Thou art not yet as Job; thy friends do not contend against thee, neither charge thee with transgression, as they did Job" (D&C 121:9–10).

When we sit in judgment of others we make their burdens greater. Only when we have been given stewardship for others, and thus are entitled to the inspiration of heaven, do we have the right and expectation to offer analysis of others.

Job 20

Zophar's second attempt: (1) My thoughts still constrain me to speak, though I have heard reproof that makes me ashamed. (4) The triumph of the wicked is short-lived, and he shall eventually suffer, and his children will have to make up for all that he has taken unrighteously, and he shall have no peace in it. (27) The heavens shall reveal his iniquity, and the earth shall rise up against him. His portion will not be good forever.

Job 21

Job's sixth reply: (2) Suffer me to speak again, and then mock on. (4) My complaint is not against man (therefore not really against you friends). Look at what has happened to me, whereas (7) the wicked prosper and suffer no such things. Their families, homes, flocks are all prosperous. (11) They enjoy life and reject God. (17) And how often do you find them suffering?

It is said that they are as stubble and that God lays up their iniquity against them and visits it upon their children; but I say, let the wicked feel the results of it themselves. (22) Surely God must know that both rich and poor, wicked and righteous go down to death in the same way, and the grave is sweet to them both. (34) You try in vain to comfort me with your reassurance that justice is done here in this earth.

Job 22

Eliphaz's third attempt: (2) Have you done anything that is helpful or profitable to God? Would he punish you for righteousness? (5) Is not your wickedness great? (6) You have done all manner of unrighteous things. (Here Eliphaz lists every sort of trumped-up charge that could be imagined and assumes Job must have done them all, since he is being "punished" so severely.) (12) Yet you say that God does not know what is going on in this earth! (15) Will you therefore refuse to repent as other wicked ones have done and perished in their sins? (21) Acquaint yourself with God and be at peace. Return to him. (29) He saves the humble and innocent.

Job 23

Job's seventh reply: (2) My condition is worse really than my complaint. (3) Oh that I knew where I might find God, that I might come before his seat and plead; he would hear, and I would be delivered. (8) But I cannot find him. (10) And as things are, he knows the course I will take; when he finishes with me, I shall be proved as gold (that's a comment on the foreknowledge of God; compare Zechariah 13:9; 1 Peter 1:7). I have been obedient to him but he does whatever he desires to me, and his will cannot be changed. (15) Therefore I am terrified at his presence, because I am hemmed in by darkness (that is, I don't know what is coming).

As Job reminds us (v. 10) trial and adversity are a refiner's fire. They refine and purify us and actually make us more fit to dwell with our Heavenly Parents. Elder Orson F. Whitney provided this insight:

"No pain that we suffer, no trial that we experience is wasted. It ministers to our education, to the development of such qualities as patience, faith, fortitude and humility. All that we suffer and all that we endure, especially when we endure it patiently, builds up our characters, purifies our hearts, expands our souls, and makes us more tender and charitable, more worthy to be called the children of God . . . and it is through sorrow and suffering, toil and tribulation, that we gain the education that we come here to acquire and which will make us more like our Father and Mother in heaven" (in Kimball, *Tragedy or Destiny?*, 4).

Job 24–25

Bildad's third attempt: All dominion and glory are with God; the shining of the moon and stars cannot compare with him. How then can man be pure in his sight? Mortal man and the descendants of men are but worms compared to him. (The phrase "son of man" as used in 25:6 is a common idiom in Hebrew for "human"; it is also used in Ezekiel; see commentary at Ezekiel 2:1–7.)

Job 26

Job's eighth reply: (2) (Sarcastically to Bildad:) How have you helped me, or anyone—poor, needy, or weak? (5) By contrast, how mighty and terrible is God; he ordains all things and controls all; (10) he was the Creator, and smote chaos and organized the heavens. (14) Who can understand even a portion of his ways?

Job 27

(2) (Evidently reacting to what Bildad had said:) I cannot and will not say that you are right in saying that no man can be pure, for until I die I will hold to my own integrity and my righteousness. (7) May my enemies have the fate of the wicked, (13) for whom there is no hope, no answer from God, no blessing of offspring, no permanent treasure, and no security.

Job 28

(1) Man can find ores in the deepest earth by taking light into mines or hanging from cliffs, in places no other creature can touch, but (12) where can wisdom be found, and the place of understanding? It cannot be found like precious ores; it cannot be bought, nor can it be compared to material things. (20) Whence then does it come? Neither creature nor death can say, but God understands the way to it and used it as he ordered all creation; therefore (28) the fear of the Lord is wisdom, and to depart from evil is understanding.

Job 29

(1) Job continues his discourse (begun in chapter 27): (2) Oh, that I were as in former times—blessed, respected, a man of charity, a man of justice, a man of means, a man of counsel.

Job's own testimony of his righteousness in this chapter (vv. 12–17) is not just admirable but enviable. He describes a kind of care for others that became a hallmark of Christian discipleship hundreds of years after him. Job "delivered the poor that cried . . . caused the widow's heart to sing for joy . . . put on righteousness [that clothed him] . . . was eyes to the blind, and feet . . . to the lame . . . father to the poor . . . brake the jaws of the wicked." One cannot find a more Christ-like example in all of the Old Testament than this. Perhaps we could adopt the creed that if the Lord needs an errand to be run, we will run it for him.

Job 30

(1) Now the immature make sport of me; the lowest deride and scorn me. (16) I have no rest, no relief, no answer from God. (24) Although I hearkened to the cry of the suffering and had compassion, (26) when I cry out, no one helps, but more evils come until (30) I am in abject misery.

Job described more graphic symptoms of his wretched physical afflictions (vv. 26–30). But, again, he did not understand their cause or purpose.

Job 31

(1) I have made a covenant; how would I even look lustfully? Let me be justly weighed that God may know my integrity,

and if I have sinned let me be destroyed. If I have been (9) lustful, or (13) inconsiderate, (16) uncharitable, (24) materialistic, (29) or spiteful, or (33) if I have hidden any sins, (35) then let the Almighty hear me; and let my adversary write my indictment; if it be sins against the earth itself, I would accept my recompense. *The end of the words of Job, and of his "comforters."*

Job 32

(1) When Job ceased, along with the other three, a young man, Elihu, felt dissatisfied and angered that Job should be so self-righteous and that the three could find no solutions. The brashness and abundant confidence of youth is manifest when he speaks: (6) Though I waited for the older and wiser to give good answers, they disappointed me; but (8) there is a spirit in man to which the Almighty gives understanding; therefore hearken and I will give my opinion. (11) I waited, but none of you answered Job (22), so I will answer, but neither with words like yours nor with flattery or prejudice.

Job 33

Elihu continued: (1) Hearken, O Job: I speak out of uprightness and sincerity. (4) The Spirit of God made me and gave me life, and I am toward God as you are. (9) (First charge) You have said you are clean and without transgression, and yet God punishes you. (12) In this you are not right, nor in saying that God will not answer. He answers in many ways to chasten and correct man and save him from perishing. (19) Man indeed may suffer, but (23) if an intercessor can vouch for his ransom, then God will be gracious to him and will refresh and renew him, and he can realize God's grace and salvation, for the repentant can be restored and renewed. (29) God has done these things many, many times. (31) Now listen, Job, and if you have any answer, speak; but otherwise, be silent.

Job 34

(1) Listen, all of you (second charge): (5) Job has said "I am righteous, but God has taken away my right, and I am counted a liar and wounded by him!" (9) He has said it profits nothing to be in accord with God. (10) God does no wickedness; he is over all, and created all. If he took away breath and spirit, the flesh of

earth would perish and turn again into dust. (17) Shall one who hates right condemn the Mighty One who is greater than kings, just and impartial to all, all being the work of His hands? (21) He is aware of all and imposes upon no one that which is not right. (31) It is proper to say to God, "I have borne chastisement and will sin no more; teach me what I should do, and I will do it." (33) Should he requite you to suit your request according to your desire? (35) Job has spoken without knowledge or insight, like a wicked man, and has added rebellion to his sins.

Job 35

More comments from Elihu: (1) Is it right to say (third charge): "My righteousness is more than God's! What advantage is there to righteousness; or what profit is there more than to sin?" (4) I will answer Job and his friends. Look to heaven. Is it any help to God that you are righteous, or any harm to him if you sin? (7) Your wickedness and your righteousness are done unto man. (9) How much less will he hear one who doubts or is impatient? (15) Is it for naught that he punishes? Does he not know of arrogance, such as Job has shown?

Job 36

Ongoing commentary from Elihu: (1) I would like to say more in God's behalf; I will speak truth out of perfection of knowledge. (5) God is mighty (as Job said; 9:1ff). He despises not anyone, and he preserves not the wicked, nor does he ignore the righteous. (8) If you are oppressed, he shows you why and admonishes your return. (12) If you repent not, you perish. (15) He delivers the humble and afflicted and opens their ears by tribulations, (16) even you, Job. (17) But you are full of vindictive feelings; beware lest your wrath void your ransom and (20) do not long for the night of death. (22) God is a teacher. (24) Evaluate his work truly, for he is great. (29) Can you indeed understand his works? (33) He cannot tolerate iniquity.

Job 37

Continuation of Elihu's poetic description of God's power and greatness: (1) He is the Mighty One who controls and causes lightning, thunder, snow, and rain, and (7) he seals with his own seal the hand of every man so that man may see God's work and know of his majesty. (8) All beasts, all nature respond to him whether for correction or for love, for he communicates with all. (14) Job, do you know the greatness of God? Should a man counsel him? He is great in power and justice and righteousness, therefore men fear him.

Job 38

The Lord finally speaks to Job out of the whirlwind as recorded in the next four chapters. Elihu had foreshadowed the event when he described the passing wind cleansing men and God coming in terrible majesty (37:21–22). God asked if Job really thought he was smart enough to counsel Deity.

(1) *The Lord speaks to Job:* (2) Who is this that speaks without knowledge? (He is referring to Job, not to Elihu.) (4) What do you know about creation, (7) or the joy of the stars and the sons of God when its foundations were laid? (8) Do you know who controls the sea, (13) or the light of morning, (16) the springs of the sea, (17) the gates of death, (18) the expanse of earth or the sources of light? (21) You should know, for you were born then, and the number of your days is great! (22) Do you know whence the snow or the hail or the source of light or wind, or what causes the rain? (31) Can you order the constellations, (34) or indeed even the weather? (39) Can you provide that the lions have food, or the ravens?

Verses 1–7 teach the doctrine of our premortal existence. Our Father in Heaven's children shouted for joy over his plan and the opportunity to progress to their second estate (see Moses 4:1–4; Abraham 3:23–28). Job was among them. God doesn't give specific answers to Job's complaints but he gives him unparalleled perspective.

Job 39

(1) Do you know how the wild goats (ibex) or the deer multiply, or order the bringing forth of their young and make the young independent? (5) Who sent forth and set free the animals—the wild ass, the wild ox? Can you catch or bind them to serve you? (13) The proud and swift ostrich leaves eggs and young, and who takes care of them? (19) The horse (which man rides), who gives

him strength and courage? (26) Do you know how to make the hawk soar, or the eagle to make its nest and provide for its young?

Job 40

(1) *The Lord challenges Job to answer him,* but (3) Job feels of such small status that though he had spoken once or twice, he declines to speak any more. (6) Then out of the whirlwind again the Lord asks Job (8) whether he would void God's judgment or condemn him to justify himself. (10) Also the Lord challenges Job to assume the status of God and do what God can do and show that he deserves victory in his controversy with the Lord. (15) Again God calls Job's attention to the marvels of creation and of nature controlled by the Lord, such as the great *behemoth* (Hebrew, "beast" or "hippopotamus").

Job 41

(1) The Lord asks if man can control such creatures as the crocodile (Hebrew, *leviathan,* "crocodile") or play with him or tame him. In later verses (for example, 18–20), the beast like a dragon seems to symbolize all the powers of nature and the created things controlled by the Creator, things impossible for man to presume to control.

Job 42

Then Job answers (2) that he knew that the Lord can do all things, and no purpose of his could be thwarted. Job recalls (3) the Lord's challenging questions as to who dared counsel without knowledge and confessed that it was he who had uttered things he does not understand. He recalls the Lord's charge that he hear and be questioned and declares that he now feels he could perceive God as he is and is most humbled by the experience.

In short, Job repents for what he sees as a presumptuous attitude. (5) He now knows for himself things he took on faith before.

The Lord tells Eliphaz and company they have not spoken that which is true, as Job had, and admonishes them to offer an offering in repentance, and have Job pray for them!

Job's friends and brethren all return to him and bring condolences and gifts, and he is restored with twice as many livestock and an equal number of children as before—and he lives one hundred forty years, unto the fourth generation of his descendants. Not only was Job blessed with more than he had before, but his understanding of God and His work had greatly expanded and intensified. His sense of nothingness and humility and his testimony of God had grown immensely through the heaven-sent trials and afflictions.

Conclusion

We cannot possibly understand all the experiences of this life. The Lord never intended us to understand all our earthly experiences while in mortality. It is our response to tragedy and suffering that increases or limits our wisdom and understanding. True greatness can best be measured by how well we respond to events in our lives that seem to us unfair, unreasonable, and undeserved. How did Job feel about himself and his standing with God? He felt confused, as many of us feel at times, as he attempted to explain the unexplainable. He had kept the commandments, so he couldn't understand why God didn't give him immediate answers. A man or woman can know that he or she has lived a life of reasonable righteousness and so is acceptable to God. It was this knowledge that made Job feel his position was unreasonable.

At the end of this study of Job's life story, read carefully and prayerfully the following thoughts and quotations, keeping in mind your own life experience:

From *Lectures on Faith:* "An actual knowledge to any person, that the course of life which he pursues is according to the will of God, is essentially necessary to enable him to have that confidence in God without which no person can obtain eternal life. It was this that enabled the ancient saints to endure all their afflictions and persecutions, and to take joyfully the spoiling of their goods, knowing (not believing merely) that they had a more enduring substance. (Heb. 10:34.)

"Such was, and always will be, the situation of the saints of God, that unless they have an actual knowledge that the course they are pursuing is according to the will of God they will grow weary in their minds, and faint . . . For a man to lay down his all, his character and reputation, his honor, and applause, his good name among men, his houses, his lands, his brothers and sisters, his wife and children, and even his own life also—counting all things but filth and dross for the excellency of the knowledge of Jesus Christ—requires more than mere belief or supposition that he is doing the will of God; but actual knowledge, realizing that, when these sufferings are ended, he will enter into eternal rest, and be a partaker of the glory of God.

"Let us here observe, that a religion that does not require the sacrifice of all things never has power sufficient to produce the faith necessary unto life and salvation . . .

"Those, then, who make the sacrifice, will have the testimony that their course is pleasing in the sight of God; and those who have this testimony will have faith to lay hold on eternal life, and will be enabled, through faith, to endure unto the end, and receive the crown that is laid up for them . . .

"All the saints of whom we have account, in all the revelations of God which are extant, obtained the knowledge which they had of their acceptance in his sight through the sacrifice which they offered unto him" (*Lectures on Faith*, 67–70).

From the Prophet Joseph Smith:

"It is a false idea that the Saints will escape all the judgments, whilst the wicked suffer; for all flesh is subject to suffer, and 'the righteous shall hardly escape'" (*History of the Church*, 4:11).

"Inasmuch as God hath said that He would have a tried people, that He would purge them as gold, now we think that this time He has chosen His own crucible, wherein we have been tried; and we think if we get through with any degree of safety, and shall have kept the faith, that it will be a sign to this generation, altogether sufficient to leave them without excuse; and we think also, it will be a trial of our faith equal to that of Abraham, and that the ancients will not have whereof to boast over us in the day of judgment, as being called to pass through heavier afflictions; that we may hold an even weight in the balance with them" (*History of the Church*, 3:294).

From President Brigham Young and others:

"All intelligent beings who are crowned with crowns of glory, immortality, and eternal lives must pass through every ordeal appointed for intelligent beings to pass through, to gain their glory and exaltation. Every calamity that can come upon mortal beings will be suffered to come upon the few, to prepare them to enjoy the presence of the Lord. If we obtain the glory that Abraham obtained, we must do so by the same means that he did. If we are ever prepared to enjoy the society of Enoch, Noah, Melchizedek, Abraham, Isaac, and Jacob, or of their faithful children, and of the faithful Prophets and Apostles, we must pass through the same experience, and gain the knowledge, intelligence, and endowments that will prepare us to enter into the celestial kingdom of our Father and God. How many of the Latter-day Saints will endure all these things, and be prepared to enjoy the presence of the Father and the Son? You can answer that question at your leisure. Every trial and experience you have passed through is necessary for your salvation" (*Discourses of Brigham Young*, 345).

"It is recorded that Jesus was made perfect through suffering. If he was made perfect through suffering, why should we imagine for one moment that we can be prepared to enter into the kingdom of rest with him and the Father, without passing through similar ordeals?" (*Discourses of Brigham Young*, 346).

"You will have all kinds of trials to pass through. And it is quite as necessary for you to be tried as it was for Abraham and other men of God, and . . . God will feel after you, and he will take hold of you and wrench your very heart strings, and if you cannot stand it you will not be fit for an inheritance in the Celestial Kingdom of God" (Taylor, *Journal of Discourses*, 24:197).

"Every Latter-day Saint who gains a celestial glory will be tried to the very uttermost. If there is a point in our character that is weak and tender, you may depend upon it that the Lord will reach after that, and we will be tried at that spot for the Lord will test us to the utmost before we can get through and receive that glory and exaltation which He has in store for us as a people" (Cannon, *Gospel Truth*, 81).

"If ever you are brought into the presence of God, and exalted to a seat in His celestial kingdom, it will be by virtue of the Holy Priesthood, therefore you have got to be proved, not only by being tempted by the devil, but the Priesthood will try you—it will try you to the core. If one thing won't try you, something else will be adopted, until you are like the passive clay in the hands of the Potter. If the Lord our God does not see fit to let the devil loose upon you, and mob you, He will employ some other means to try you as in a crucible, to prove you as gold is tried seven times in the furnace" (Grant, *Journal of Discourses,* 2:14).

"You may search all the ages for [a person who has had no problems] . . . you may look through the . . . streets of heaven, asking each [one] how he came there, and you will look in vain everywhere for a man morally and spiritually strong, whose strength did not come to him in a struggle. . . . Do [not] suppose that [there is any man who] has never wrestled with his own success and happiness. . . . There is no exception anywhere. Every true strength is gained in a struggle" (Evans, *Improvement Era,* Apr. 1964, 306, paraphrasing Brooks, "Sea of Glass Mingled with Fire").

"As a result of his many experiences with suffering, that great humanitarian Dr. Albert Schweitzer gave this advice: 'Don't vex your mind by trying to explain the suffering you have to endure in this life. Don't think that God is punishing you or disciplining you or that he has rejected you. Even in the midst of your suffering, you are in his kingdom. You are always his child, and he has his protecting arms around you'" (Lee, *Teachings of Harold B. Lee,* 188).

"Being human, we would expel from our lives physical pain and mental anguish and assure ourselves of continual ease and comfort, but if we were to close the doors upon sorrow and distress, we might be excluding our greatest friends and benefactors. Suffering can make saints of people as they learn patience, long-suffering, and self-mastery" (Kimball, *Faith Precedes the Miracle,* 98).

"The greatest trials of life are reserved for the saints" (McConkie, *Doctrinal New Testament Commentary,* 3:318).

"Just when all seems to be going right, challenges often come in multiple doses applied simultaneously. When those trials are not consequences of your disobedience, they are evidence that the Lord feels you are prepared to grow more (see Prov. 3:11–12). He therefore gives you experiences that stimulate growth, understanding, and compassion which polish you for your everlasting benefit" (Scott, *Ensign,* Nov. 1995, 16).

The last and best words on the meaning of suffering have been given to us by the Lord himself: "My son [or daughter], peace be unto thy soul; thine adversity and thine afflictions shall be but a small moment; and then, if thou endure it well, God shall exalt thee on high; thou shalt triumph over all thy foes" (D&C 121:7–8).

JONAH

At this point we begin our study of the prophets who left us some of their writings, following as best we can a chronological order of their ministries.

Jonah, whose Hebrew name means "dove," was a prophet from Gath-hepher, a small village west of the Sea of Galilee (Sea of Chinnereth; see Bible Map 10). He probably lived around 800 to 790 B.C. (see Bible Appendix, "Chronology"). He apparently had a mission to the court of Jeroboam II in Samaria, as noted in 2 Kings 14:25. But something else was also happening. During the reign of Jeroboam II, the kingdom of Israel was able to take advantage of Assyria's defeat of Syria (Damascus) and complete its recovery of territory previously lost to the king of Damascus (2 Kings 13:25). Assyria was also having internal troubles, and Israel thought about garnering an even greater advantage on the international political stage. The Lord's prophets were speaking to Israel about these international political affairs. Elisha had earlier discussed Israel's future triumphs over Damascus (2 Kings 13:14–19). Jonah himself then prophesied of Jeroboam II's success (2 Kings 14:25). In response, Israel became haughty over perceived favored status with the Lord, expecting that he would continue to elevate them over their enemies, no matter what. At that very time, however, the Lord sent the prophets Amos and Hosea to the kingdom of Israel to declare to them that the Lord would no longer support them or spare them (Amos 7:8, 8:2). Their pride and iniquity had brought them down, and they would be exiled by the very Assyrians they had hoped to take advantage of. At the same time that Israel was being made aware of divine condemnation, the Lord sent Jonah to the great Assyrian capital of Nineveh to warn the people there of divine judgment from the true and living God.

The book of Jonah does not identify its author, nor does it claim to be written by Jonah—only about him. In fact, it focuses solely on him and his prophetic mission, unlike several other prophetic narratives in the Old Testament. The book is really a story about repentance, and how God desires all of his children to repent. Because of this theme, in our day the book of Jonah is read in synagogues on the holiest day of the year for the Jewish people—the Day of Atonement, or Yom Kippur—which also centers on repentance and forgiveness.

The God of Israel is concerned about nations other than Israel, even an enemy nation. All are children of our Heavenly Father.

Some biblical scholars have questioned whether Jonah ever really lived and have discounted the book as ancient fiction. On three occasions that we know about, however, the story of Jonah was validated by our Lord when, during his mortal ministry, he was asked to display a sign from heaven. He boldly referred his listeners to the "sign of the prophet Jonah," which was a symbol and foreshadowing of his own atoning death and resurrection (Matthew 12:39–41; 16:4; Luke 11:29–30). In this way, Jonah is a symbol of Jesus Christ, even though he lacked other qualities so evident in the Savior.

Jonah 1:1–10

The book opens by reciting a common prophetic credential: "The word of the Lord came . . ." But Jonah did not want to deliver it.

Jonah undoubtedly knew that no one can actually flee "from the presence of the Lord," so what did Jonah probably fear that motivated him to flee from this Assyrian mission?

Assyrians were infamous for their barbarous methods of conquest and their treatment of captured enemies. They were known to make captives parade through the streets of Nineveh with decapitated heads of other captives around their necks. The Assyrians were masters of torture, cutting off noses and ears and yanking out tongues of live enemies. They flayed prisoners—skinned them while they were alive. Reliefs carved on Assyrian kings' palace walls portraying the siege of Lachish (a fortified town of Judah) show Judahites impaled outside the walls of the city. Assyrian soldiers rammed a sharpened pole up through the middle of a living person (see photo at 2 Kings 18:13–37).

No wonder Jonah had no interest in serving a mission to the capital city of Nineveh, the seat of militaristic terror! When the Lord called him to go northeast to his mission field, he fled the exact opposite direction to escape contact with the hated Assyrians. "I'll go where you want me to go, dear Lord, *except . . .*"! (see *Hymns,* no. 270). As with most Israelites, Jonah may have had deep and bitter feelings against Israel's enemy. He may not have wanted the Lord to allow Assyrians a chance to repent, be forgiven, and be spared.

Incidentally, in the story of Jonah, the adverbs "down" and "up" are significant. Jonah went down to Joppa, down into a ship, down into the sea, down into a great fish. Then he went up out of the fish, up onto the beach, and up to Nineveh.

Interestingly, the place called Tarshish—to which he sailed away westward—may have been Tartessus in southwestern Spain, a town with which Tyre had mineral trade. A hint of such a Phoenician colony in Tarshish may be seen in Isaiah 23.

It is ironic that the shipmaster, or captain, called upon Jonah to pray. We wonder what made the sailors think the storm came upon them by reason of some fault of someone on board. Significantly, Jonah's refusal to fulfill his calling not only brought him into peril but also brought unbelievers into peril. Is this not symbolic of us in our day when we refuse to fulfill our member-missionary opportunities and obligations or other assignments?

The "casting of lots" to determine the identity of any guilty person is a curious procedure. Though widely mentioned in the ancient Near East, its precise method of practice is unclear. Notice that Jonah identifies himself as Hebrew. The word "Hebrew" is usually used as an ethnic term by non-Israelites to designate members of Abraham's family (see Genesis 14:13). Jonah's point in verse 9 is that his God was the only one who could control that tempest. It is ironic that pagans would speak a sacred line from Israelite literature: their question (v. 10) in Hebrew reads, "What is this thou hast done?" which is reminiscent of God's question to Eve in Genesis 3:13.

Jonah 1:11–17

The Lord prepares a way for even a reluctant prophet to be saved. In the case of this runaway missionary, the Lord let him confess, repent, and manifest willingness to sacrifice himself to save those whom he had imposed upon. In so doing, Jonah taught those sailors something about the Lord and those who believe in him.

The way prepared for Jonah's rescue was a miracle. A "great fish," as it is called in Hebrew, was prepared by the Lord to save him. But before Jonah was saved, he had to suffer a trauma in the fish "three days and three nights" and learn another lesson. Again, it was that experience that Jesus cited as symbolic of his own death, the entombment of his body, and the initiation of resurrection for all humankind (see references on 17*a*).

Jonah 2

Chapter 2 is Jonah's prayer of thanksgiving for deliverance from death, his miraculous preservation demonstrating God's mercy notwithstanding his servant's weakness. His prayer is presented in vivid Hebrew poetry and parallels many of the psalms in form and content.

"When my soul fainted within me I remembered the Lord." Ah, human nature. "Except the Lord doth chasten his people with many afflictions, yea, except he doth visit them with death and with terror, and with famine and with all manner of pestilence, they will not remember him" (Helaman 12:3). "In the day of their trouble, of necessity they feel after me" (D&C 101:8).

Jonah ultimately promised that what he had committed to do he would perform. Afterward the Lord "spoke" to the fish, and Jonah was vomited out on dry land. The scriptures contain various examples of animals being subject to the will of their Creator.

Jonah 3

Jonah got a second chance. The whole plan of God is one of second chances for all people, as Jonah was to find out. With his mission call extended anew, Jonah went immediately into the city.

"Three days' journey" could be idiomatic, suggesting a very large city. The size may have reference to "greater Nineveh," or the district of Nineveh.

This little book's terse record reports only one essential warning given by Jonah, along with the miraculous response to his message. Jonah's prophetic message is eight words in English and only five words in Hebrew.

Perhaps the greatest miracle of all was the Ninevites' repentance. If not *all* of the people, at least *enough* of the people, including the king, listened to the warning voice and repented to spare the city for the time being. Dressing in sackcloth and sitting in the dust are customary signs of humility and repentance (1 Kings 21:27; Nehemiah 9:1). That the king did so is remarkable, as well as reminiscent of specific kings in the Book of Mormon (see Alma 18–22). Another example of a people repenting is recorded in Jeremiah 26:18ff.

Note important Joseph Smith Translation changes in 3:9, 10, and 4:2.

Verse 10 contains important doctrine. "If that nation, against whom I have pronounced, turn from their evil, I will repent of [JST, "withhold"] the evil that I thought to do unto them" (Jeremiah 18:8).

This would be a good place to end the story, but another valuable lesson is coming.

Jonah 4

Surprisingly, Jonah was "displeased exceedingly," even "very angry" with the way things turned out. Verse 3 suggests that Jonah saw himself and his mission as failures. "It is better for me to die than to live" are the same words spoken by a discouraged Elijah some time before (1 Kings 19:4). Jonah had been given a second chance, so why should the people of Nineveh not be given a second chance?

The Lord used a plant, a worm, a wind, and a certain powerful, pointed, and repeated question to teach his prophet one more lesson. If Jonah saw value in a living plant and lamented its demise, could he not understand God's valuing a city full of people, including thousands of children who could not yet discern left

from right (wrong from right), and even all the animals? Another
way to read verse 10 is that all the Ninevites were like children,
spiritually, who could not discern even the simplest spiritual matters without God's instruction and mentoring. It is like the lesson
from Ezekiel regarding the Lord's perspective on sinners: "Have
I any pleasure at all that the wicked should die . . . and not that
he should return from his ways, and live? . . . I have no pleasure
in the death of him that dieth, saith the Lord God: wherefore
turn yourselves, and live" (Ezekiel 18:23, 32). The Doctrine and
Covenants poignantly adds, "the worth of souls is great in the
sight of God" and "I, the Lord, will forgive whom I will forgive,
but of you it is required to forgive all men" (D&C 18:10; 64:10).

The prophet himself learned valued lessons from his missionary experiences. If Jonah wrote his own story, he was big enough
to record his personal lessons for all of us.

A final observation: Considering how the Lord often teaches
us through types and symbols, could it be that Jonah represented,
in a sense, the whole Israelite people, who were trying to flee from
their appointed mission? As Jonah was swallowed by a great fish,
so Israel would be swallowed by disaster and exile, but some were
brought back and allowed once again to be tried and proved in
fulfilling their role as a covenant people.

AMOS

During the century from 830 to 730 B.C., an incessant parade of internal conflicts and overthrowing of kings, military threats and invasions of foreign powers, and general apostate conditions prevailed in Israel. God's chosen people, to whom he had promised his divine protection had, as a people, abandoned him. Politically they trusted in the arm of flesh and spiritually they had gone "a whoring after other gods" (Judges 2:17).

In the midst of Israelite military victories, territorial expansion, and the people's resultant pride and sense of security, prophets were raised up to condemn the people's moral and spiritual failings. Amos, from Tekoa in Judah (Amos 1:1), was one of the first of the warning voices. Though he lived in the southern kingdom of Judah during the reign of Uzziah, he was called to minister to, prophesy about, and warn the northern kingdom of Israel during the reign of Jeroboam II. By his own admission, Amos was not a court prophet, like Isaiah, not a priest like Jeremiah, not one of the sons of the prophets like those already encountered, and not mentored and groomed to become a prophet like Elisha. Rather he, like prophets and apostles in modern times, had a regular profession—he was a rural tender of flocks and sycamore groves. What made him a prophet was the Lord's call and the Lord's authority (Amos 7:14–15).

The book of Amos is a well-organized, edited collection of the prophet's words. The dominant theme of his teachings is summed up in Amos 5:14: "Seek good, and not evil, that ye may live: and so the Lord, the God of hosts, shall be with you, as ye have spoken." But the kingdom of Israel did not—would not—listen and the Lord was soon to bring about its destruction in 721 B.C.

When Amos's ministry began, it had been two hundred years

since the Davidic kingdom was divided; the northern and southern kingdoms had often been at odds with each other but sometimes had united to withstand a common enemy. In Amos's day the people of Israel enjoyed considerable stability and prosperity (due, of course, to the fact that there was no great power such as Assyria or Egypt pressing at their borders). Removal of the threat of Ben-hadad III of Damascus allowed Israel at least partial control of territory as far as Lebo-Hamath, sixty miles north of Damascus. Jeroboam and Uzziah both carried on vigorous campaigns of expansion and extended their southern and eastern frontiers to equal the former kingdom of David and Solomon. Assyria was becoming an increasing political threat, and Tiglath-pileser III was on the horizon. Israel, Judah, Syria, and Egypt were all united in their opposition to Assyrian advances westward.

The material prosperity of Israel showed no signs of waning. But it was a hollow prosperity at best; the nation could not long conceal the injustices of their society and the moral corruptions of their lifestyle. Baalism had worn the moral fabric of the people threadbare. When Amos had finished with his summary treatment of the sins of Israel's neighbors, the northern Israelites discovered that his prophecy against them was not to be "for three transgressions and for four" (Amos 1:3, 6, 9, 11, 13; 2:1, 4, 6) but an extensive enumeration of the social and religious ills of the people to whom Jehovah had sent him. The dark list of sins began: sale of innocent people to slavery, mistreatment of the poor, cultic prostitution (sexual abuse of young women, which profaned God's name), exaction of unjust fines, corruption of the court and legal processes, enticement of Nazarites to break their vows, and prohibiting prophets from delivering their prophecies (Amos 2:6–8,12). The charges continue throughout Amos's writings: violence and robbery (3:10; 6:3), oppression of the needy, greed, and drunkenness (4:1; 8:4), hypocrisy in sacred ordinances (4:4–5; 5:21–23), disdain of honest judges (5:10), cheating the poor (5:11), bribery (5:12), idolatry (5:26; 8:14), gluttony and revelry (6:4–7), pride, vainglory, and false sense of security (6:8, 13), deceitful business practices and desecration of the spirit of the Sabbath (8:5–6). All in all, not a flattering picture of God's people. They needed to listen to a prophet's voice.

Amos 1:1–2

The prophet Amos was, before his call to be a prophet, "among the herdmen of Tekoa." His hometown lies about six miles southeast of Bethlehem and twelve from Jerusalem. In addition to his work as a "herdman" or sheep-breeder, Amos was a cultivator or dresser of sycomore figs (7:14). The biblical sycomore doesn't grow in the Near East above one thousand feet above sea level. It does not grow near Tekoa, since Tekoa is much more than twice that elevation, so Amos's work would have also taken him into the lowland (the Shephelah) of Judah.

The mention of "Uzziah king of Judah" and "Jeroboam the son of Joash king of Israel" clearly places the prophet Amos in the mid-eighth century before Christ. His preaching is also dated (beginning) at "two years before the earthquake." Though seismic disturbances are anything but rare in the land of Amos, this very earthquake is the only one *explicitly* mentioned in the Old Testament. It was apparently so severe that it was used for some time to date historical events. It was of such unusual intensity and inflicted such devastation that the memory of it survived for over two and a half centuries, and in Zechariah 14:5, this earthquake in the days of Uzziah served as a pattern of extremely intense and destructive earthquakes: "And you shall flee as you fled from the earthquake in the days of Uzziah, king of Judah." This earthquake in the days of Amos caused damage over a wide area; evidence of it has been discovered in archaeological excavations from one end of the country to the other, particularly at Hazor in the north, Deir-Alla in the Rift Valley, and Beersheba in the south. Professor Yigael Yadin dated the earthquake to approximately 760 B.C. (Yadin, *Hazor*, 113, 181).

"Saw" in the opening clause translates Hebrew *khazah*, which refers to "prophetic vision." It is the same word used of Isaiah in the opening verse of his book. Amos might therefore be justifiably referred to as a seer.

The Lord would "roar from Zion" and "utter his voice from Jerusalem" because the Temple was there, and it was the center of proper religious leadership in all the land of Israel.

Amos 1:3–2:3

These verses constitute a series of prophetic pronouncements against various nations of the region. A repeated formula is seen in 1:3, 6, 9, 11, 13 and 2:1, 4, and 6, stating: "For three transgressions . . . and for four, I will not turn away the punishment." It is a way of saying that those nations were full to overflowing with sin. Three symbolizes fulness, and four, excess.

These specific prophecies against the various nations were all fulfilled. Amos's prophecies of captivity were realized soon afterward by the Assyrians and some later by other conquerors. Damascus (Amos 1:5) was taken by Tiglath-pileser III in 732 B.C. He did exactly what Amos prophesied: he sent military fire upon and destroyed the house of Hazael and the strongholds of Ben-hadad (Amos 1:4), broke the security bar of Damascus (1:5), and cut off inhabitants from the Valley of Aven and officials from Beth-eden by exiling the Syrians (2 Kings 16:9). The chief Philistine cities (Amos 1:6–8) were also besieged by Tiglath-pileser two years earlier in 734 B.C.

Amos's promise of punishment of Tyre was gradually fulfilled. Tiglath-pileser was successfully bought off, but Tyre was later attacked by Shalmaneser during a five-year siege and then by the Babylonian Nebuchadnezzar in a thirteen-year siege. Alexander the Great later built a causeway, connecting the island city with the mainland, and marched his armies to destroy it, selling 30,000 of its inhabitants into slavery, which was the very charge for which Amos had condemned the Tyrians (1:9–10).

Jerusalem was miraculously spared destruction by the Assyrians under Sennacherib in 701 B.C. but was burned by Nebuchadnezzar in 586 B.C., giving literal fulfillment to Amos's prophecy: "I will send a fire upon Judah, and it shall devour the palaces of Jerusalem" (2:5). The northern kingdom of Israel was destroyed and taken captive within a few years after Amos warned them clearly that such would happen. They were exiled "beyond Damascus," as he said (5:27).

Amos 2:4–16

After condemning Israel's neighbors, which Israel applauded, Amos turned the tables and condemned the Lord's people—Israel and Judah. There were significant differences between the condemnations of the other five nations and the condemnation of Israel and Judah. The Israelite nations were worse off because they knew the law of the Lord and his commandments but failed to keep them. The sin of ingratitude to God was particularly grievous because of all Israel's God had done for them. Their abandonment of God and their fulness of iniquity warranted punishment.

Amos 3:1–7

Amos tried to remind Israelites of vital principles by means of rhetorical questions. God always gives plenty of reminders; in fact, he will do nothing without first revealing his will through his servants the prophets. This axiom was well-established anciently and Book of Mormon prophets knew it applied to their own people as well. "Never hath any of them been destroyed save it were foretold them by the prophets of the Lord" (2 Nephi 25:9).

Amos 3:8

The prophet was apparently trying to get the people to apply the principle taught in verses 2–7 by asking two more questions found in verse 8. Compare Amos's anxiety to respond to the prophetic task to that of Jeremiah (recorded in Jeremiah 20:9).

Amos 3:9–15

With irony, the prophet invited the peoples from Ashdod (Philistines) and Egypt to assemble upon the mountains of Samaria, the capital of the northern kingdom of Israel, to see the tumult and oppression among the Lord's people. Consider that Philistines and Egyptians had always been enemies threatening Israel; now these enemies would be allowed to enter the land and plunder it.

The simile in verses 12–15 implies that the shepherd's saving a few pieces of a slain sheep from the lion is like the Lord's saving a remnant of Israel.

Amos 4

It is a lesson of history that when the women of any culture become as corrupt as the men, all is lost, for there is no one then to raise the children as a proper society. Chapter 4 opens with the prophet comparing the upper class, high-society women to "kine [cows] of Bashan," the best-bred cattle of the whole region. Bashan was the plateau of fine pastureland and agricultural land now known as the Golan Heights, east of the Sea of Galilee, where cattle ate their fill and grew fat. The metaphor was a way of reprimanding women's self-indulgences. They and their husbands would be taken away as captives with "hooks" and "fishhooks." Ancient bas-reliefs show Israelite prisoners of war tethered in long, pitiful queues.

Amos pointed out evidences of hypocrisy in worship, as well as recalcitrance in learning godly lessons, and he uttered his message with illustrations from nature. He called on locusts, lions, bird traps, fishhooks, cedars, oaks, wormwood, blight, mildew, kings' mowings, fruit baskets, threshing sledges, siroccos, drought, storms, eclipses, and earthquakes to prophesy vividly and poignantly to warn the people. He saw what was happening to Israelite society, and he saw what God was about to do to it by way of chastisement and punishment. Amos saw upheaval and disruption in nature as a direct result of upheaval and disruption in society.

The prophet sarcastically invited Israelites to go ahead and continue worshiping at idolatrous altars such as those at Bethel and Gilgal. Their reward would be famine: "cleanness of teeth" and "want of bread." He warned, "Prepare to meet thy God, O Israel."

Amos 5

Amos lamented the fall of "the virgin of Israel" as though it had already happened. The prophet and the Lord never gave up hope of saving some. They repeatedly entreated Israel to seek the Lord, their Creator; seek good and not evil; hate the evil and love the good, and establish justice—the only way to eventually see the day of the Lord as a day of joy and light and not of gloom and darkness, and the only way to avoid going into captivity northward, beyond Damascus.

Notice in verse 8 the prophet's familiarity with the constellations in the night sky and the role of the Creator in their ongoing

144

existence. Such imagery is reminiscent of Father Abraham's panoramic vision (Abraham 3). Verse 18 refers to the future time when the Lord will subdue all enemies under his feet and appear in his glory to reign upon the earth (for references to the concept of subduing enemies under the feet, see Joshua 10:24; 1 Kings 5:3; Psalms 18:37–40; 44:5; 45:5; 66:3; 1 Corinthians 15:25, 27; Ephesians 1:22; Hebrews 2:8; 1 Nephi 19:7; D&C 35:14; 49:6; 58:22; 76:61, 106). Amos, however, warned that the day of the Lord would be a day of darkness, not light, for the wicked.

Amos 6

Chapter 6 opens with an ancient principle: "Woe to them that are at ease in Zion" (literally, "woe to those who feel secure in Zion"). But it is a warning that applies directly to God's covenant people in modern times, too. This is exactly what the Book of Mormon declared (2 Nephi 28:24). Nephi went on to lay out a fuller expression of this warning, stating that the "all is well in Zion" mentality is a precept of men and ultimately leads to a denial of the power of the Holy Ghost (2 Nephi 28:25–31). The prophet Amos condemned the typical indulgences among the rich and powerful leaders of Israel, and he showed Israel's lack of logic in confiding in the military and material security they thought they enjoyed in Samaria, and in boasting in their own strength. The only true security and strength is in the God of heaven, the Lord of hosts. In verse 5 we see how David was still extolled as the model of ancient poet-musicians.

Amos 7:1–9

Amos's reaction to his first three visions shows he hoped Israel could be spared. After the first and second vision, the prophet learned that the Lord could possibly overlook and forgive but not after the third vision. The plumb line metaphorically determined the uprightness of Israel. Since they were measured and found wanting, destruction was inevitable.

Amos 7:10–17

We learn here about the nature of Amos's call. The prophet frankly condemned the king and the court priest and was consequently told to go back to his homeland of Judah to prophesy and make his living. Amaziah's implication that Amos was a prophet like those of northern Israel with their priestcrafts aroused the anger of the true prophet. He stated emphatically that his work, his calling, and his authority were from the Lord, not a profession. Instead of seeing Amos's cowering acquiescence, Amaziah received a dire prophecy about himself and his family (compare the fate of the chief Temple official who later condemned Jeremiah in Jeremiah 20:4; 28:15–17).

Amos 8:1–10

In a brilliant demonstration of word play, Amos symbolized with a "basket of summer fruit" (Hebrew, *qayits*) the coming of the end, or fall (also *qayits*), of the nation of Israel. Like ripe fruit, Israel, ripe with iniquity, was ready to be plucked. When that happened, the once joyous songs of the Temple would become dirges, reminders of the national tragedy. Religious feasts would become times of mourning.

Astronomers have long known that a total eclipse of the sun occurred on June 15, 763 B.C. It is possible that Amos used this phenomenon to symbolize the spiritual darkness and doom coming upon Israel.

Amos 8:11–14

Israel did experience a "famine" of hearing the words of the Lord after the time of Amos and the prophets who lived and taught through the end of the Old Testament era. With the exception of the brief mortal ministry of the Savior and the ministry of his apostles there has been one continuous famine of divine truth in that part of the world until the latter-day restoration, which now makes it possible for all the world to feast upon the word of the Lord.

Amos 9:1–10

Like many of the great prophets, Amos saw the Lord. His testimony was based on personal knowledge and experience with very sacred matters. His knowledge of Israel's downfall, therefore, was certain. Thus, the Lord's powers are portrayed as very destructive, inescapable terrors.

From a biblical point of view, the Cushites, Nubians, and Ethiopians are the same people. Caphtor is the ancient equivalent of modern Crete. Amos perceived that Israel's pride and self-esteem had become somewhat distorted or exaggerated. He humbled them with the cold fact that they were *not* intrinsically more valuable or more important to Jehovah than were the Syrians, or the Philistines, or even the far-off Cushites, and he put the Israelite exodus on the same footing as the migrations of other peoples of antiquity (v. 7). There is no denying that God had entrusted to Israel the precious burden of laws, statutes, and ordinances under which he wanted all people to live. Jehovah had, in a sense, cared for Israel above all the families of the earth (Amos 3:2), but Israel did not have preferential status before God because of especially deserving behavior. In response to Israel's assertion of spiritual superiority, Amos points out that Jehovah is God of all peoples, from "beyond Damascus" to the land of Cush. Amos warns Israel in unmistakably plain language that "the eyes of the Lord God are upon the sinful kingdom" (v. 8).

Amos was very clear in predicting that the Israelites would be "sifted like grain" among the nations.

Amos 9:11–15

These last five verses, the epilogue of the book of Amos, paint a completely different scene of restoration to the land and prosperity in it. Many scholars view these verses as presupposing a different time and situation than that of Amos (mid-eighth century before Christ), and consider them the mini-masterpiece of a later disciple, thus denying their authentic provenance from the age of Amos. They also deny the possibility of prophetic preview and see in the description of prosperous times details which seemingly could have been written only by first-hand experience at a later time.

On the other hand, we maintain that the final verses of the book of Amos are an acceptable and essential climax to his writings. The phrase "in that day" (v. 11) itself indicates that the writer was living in one time period and projecting his thoughts into a future time period. Though some would argue that the epilogue is out of harmony with—and even contradictory to—the whole tenor of Amos's pronouncements of virtually irreparable ruin and inconsistent with his condemning voice, it must not be overlooked that there is a visible pattern in Hebrew literature of pronouncing curses, judgments, and destruction followed by a message of hope.

For instance, after the catalogue of plagues, desolations, and pestilences recorded in Leviticus 26, hope is held out to Israel (Leviticus 26:40–46).

Isaiah's predicted doom and destruction to Israel and Judah are followed by messages of comfort and assuring hope to the remnants in a glorious day of restoration (Isaiah 40–66). Critics of course deny that Isaiah wrote those chapters—the same critics who deny that Amos wrote 9:11–15—but Isaiah 4; 11–12; 27; 30; 32; and 35 all end with promises of restoration and blessing after the discipline of exile.

After Hosea's recitations of Israel's unfaithfulness and consequent punishment and exile, the Lord says he will return them to their homeland: "I will heal their backsliding, I will love them freely . . . I will be as the dew unto Israel. . . . They that dwell under his shadow shall return; they shall revive" (Hosea 14:4, 5, 7).

Micah's forthright statement of the disgraceful ruin of both Samaria and Jerusalem is followed by prediction of future restoration to good fortune (chapters 4 and 5).

After the great devastation caused by the armies of locusts, God promises through Joel: "I will restore to you the years that the locust hath eaten. . . . Ye shall eat in plenty, and be satisfied . . . when I shall bring again the captivity [cause the return] of Judah and Jerusalem" (Joel 2:25, 26; 3:1).

It may be properly suggested, then, that Amos perpetuates a prophetic form as he presents a merciful God who promises hope and restoration after disciplinary punishment and repentance. After the typical doom, desolation, and destruction, Amos is certainly not without peer in foreseeing reinstatement, restoration, and redemption.

HOSEA

Hosea, son of Beeri, lived in the final days of Israel's existence as an independent nation. His ministry is thought to have
begun during or immediately after the ministry of Amos. Hosea
was among the earliest of the writing prophets in the last century
of northern Israel's history, and northern Israelites were his primary audience. But because of numerous references to Judah, it is
believed by some scholars that the book of Hosea was composed
in the southern kingdom. His book is often listed among the first
of the twelve minor ("small") prophetic books. Though they may
be smaller in size, these books are not of minor importance; their
doctrines are as true and their messages as vital as those of the
major ("large") books. *Minor* describes the quantity rather than
quality of prophetic content.

The content of the first three chapters of Hosea is perplex-
ing to some readers because it describes Hosea's unusual family
life. In essence, God commanded Hosea to marry an adulterous
woman, Gomer, who had departed from the ways of the Lord.
Furthermore, Hosea's three children were given names that reflected Hosea's ominous, prophetic message to Israel. The children were commanded to drive Gomer out of the house, but it
was her reform, not her isolation, that was desired. Ultimately,
Hosea was commanded to love Gomer and take her back. As a
symbol, such a story surely represents God's relationship to his
people, Israel. It is a graphic illustration of the doctrine of the
scattering and gathering of Israel, of God's abiding love for his
people, his desire for repentance and righteous behavior, and his
view of the abhorrent nature of idolatry, which was described in
early sections of the Old Testament as spiritual adultery; it was
that serious of a problem.

Hosea 1:1

Several of the prophets, including Hosea, Amos, and Isaiah, prophesied in the days of these kings. The names Hosea, Isaiah, and Yeshua (Jesus), are all forms of the Hebrew words meaning "Jehovah saves," "salvation," or "deliverance." As is the case with other prophets, Hosea's name has something to do with his message.

Hosea 1:2

Notice the first line of the headnote to chapter 1. The marriage and family of Hosea parallel the covenant relationship of wayward Israel with the Lord. In Hosea 12:10 the Lord tells us that he has spoken by the prophets, and multiplied visions, and "*used similitudes,* by the ministry of the prophets" (emphasis added). Just as the great Abrahamic test was a similitude of God and his Only Begotten Son (Jacob 4:5), so Hosea's life may have been a similitude, a living drama, of the Lord's relationship with his bride—his covenant people. As Abraham would have some understanding of the Father's sacrifice of his Son, so Hosea would have some understanding of the Lord's merciful caring for his unfaithful people. We do know that Israel was once faithful to God but later became unfaithful.

Hosea 1:3–11

Hosea's three children were given significant and symbolic names. The name of the first child, *Jezreel,* means "God shall sow"; that is, scatter abroad. The name recalls the valley of former king Jehu's bloody purge and anticipates Israel's overthrow in that strategic valley in northern Israel wherein lies Megiddo (New Testament, "Armageddon"), famed for crucial battles past and future. It doubtless alludes, at least in part, to the scattering of Israel.

The name of the second child, *Lo-ruhamah,* warns that "No mercy" will be shown by God. He will not save northern Israel; the northern tribes would be utterly taken away, and only the south would be spared—not by sword or battle but simply by the Lord.

The name of the third child, *Lo-ammi,* literally "Not my people," is like a lament over the broken covenant relationship. But the prophecy immediately follows that someday Israel and

Judah will again be gathered together and it shall yet be said unto them, "Ye are the sons of the living God."

Hosea 2

A prophetic plea continues the subject of Israel's waywardness. The graphic language of this chapter constitutes a running metaphor depicting Israel's spiritual adultery. Israel is called to repent of her idolatry, which is like unto adultery (*adultery* and *idolatry* derive from the same root word). Ingratitude for God's blessings and the evil enticings of carnal indulgence had led Israel into rampant apostasy. The description of promised curses that would follow lack of repentance also uses images of the agriculture that makes possible Israel's very existence.

After the Lord hedges up the way of Gomer (and Israel), through the discipline of exile, she (Gomer and Israel) concludes, "I will go and return to my first husband; for then was it better with me than now" (v. 7). That is the same sentiment expressed by the prodigal son: "when he came to himself, he said, How many hired servants of my father's have bread enough and to spare, and I perish with hunger! I will arise and go to my father, and will say unto him, Father, I have sinned against heaven, and before thee" (Luke 15:17–18). Such was also the feeling of the prodigal daughter, Gomer (and Israel).

The prophet and the people were urged to remember the covenant of the Lord with his people (*Ammi*); then they could receive his mercy (*Ruhamah*).

In the eventual gathering, the valley of Israel's trouble (*Achor* means trouble) shall become *Petah-tiqvah*, "a door of hope" (v. 15). Interestingly, one of the first settlements in the beginning of the return of the Jews to Palestine in the late 1800s was named Petah-tiqvah.

The Lord will, in the end, become the true Husband of Israel upon renewal of the covenant, and that renewal will last forever. In that day, heaven and earth will respond to each other and good things shall thereby be produced.

Hosea 3

This time, the prophet is commanded to love again the unfaithful woman. It appears that after she had forsaken him and had been away a long time, he "purchased" her for half the price of a slave, required her to prove herself, and then let her return to her status as wife. This teaches the mercy of God, who will take the repentant back. Thus Israel shall return to the Lord and shall be subject to the Messiah (symbolized as "David their king"). Perhaps one reason the Lord can be so patient is that he knows the future and he knows his bride (his covenant people) will eventually return.

Hosea 4:1–14:9

Skim the rest of the chapters for examples of the ways in which Hosea preaches repentance to Israel. A review of the chapter headings is a helpful way to do that. You may recall from the Psalms that one of the favorite devices among ancient Semitic writers was to compare something in the human experience with something in nature. Jesus and the New Testament Gospel writers compared humans to grass, plants, olive trees, fig trees, vines, sheep and goats, fish, wolves, vipers, and more. God is often cast in the role of the Stone or Rock, the Branch, the Sower or Husbandman, the True Vine, the Sheep or the Shepherd or the Lamb, and so forth.

Following are striking examples of figurative language from Hosea, a series of rich images poetically describing an apostate northern kingdom of Israel, often called "Ephraim," after the leading tribe. The order of the passages follows the theme of identifying Israel's folly. "Your goodness is as a morning cloud, and as the early dew it goeth away" (6:4); "Ephraim is a cake not turned" (7:8); "Ephraim also is like a silly dove without heart" (7:11); "they have sown the wind, and they shall reap the whirlwind" (8:7); "Ephraim feedeth on wind, and followeth after the east wind [symbolic of destruction]: he daily increaseth lies and desolation" (12:1); "Israel is an empty vine" (10:1); "Sow to yourselves in righteousness, reap in mercy; break up your fallow ground: for it is time to seek the Lord, till he come and rain righteousness upon you. Ye have plowed wickedness, ye have reaped iniquity; ye have eaten the fruit of lies" (10:12–13); "Therefore will I be unto Ephraim as a moth" (5:12); "I will be unto Ephraim as a lion" (5:14); "As for Ephraim, their glory shall fly away like a bird" (9:11); "Ephraim is smitten, their root is dried up, they shall bear no fruit" (9:16); "According to their pasture, so were they filled; they were filled, and their heart was exalted; therefore have they forgotten me. Therefore I will be unto them as a lion: as a leopard by the way will I observe them: I will meet them as a bear that is bereaved of her whelps" (13:6–8).

The Israelites' lack of knowledge (4:6) was one cause of their apostasy. Isaiah 5:13 says the same thing. Joseph Smith added that "it is impossible for a man to be saved in ignorance" (D&C 131:6). Knowledge, especially of God, is indispensable.

The Israelites' twin sins of adultery and idolatry are pointedly described in Hosea 4:11–14. As we explained in the commentary at Judges 2:11–23, the phenomenon of going "a whoring after other gods" (see Hosea 4:12; 9:1) involves the relationship between God and his people. One of the most sacred of covenant relationships is the marriage covenant, and we find frequent symbolism in the scriptures of God's being married to his people (Jeremiah 3:1–2, 6–8, 14; 4:30; Ezekiel 16—especially vv. 2–15, 28–33). Prophets adopted this symbolic relationship because no covenant known to humans requires more fidelity, love, commitment, sacrifice, and patience than the marriage covenant, and, contrariwise, nothing can be quite so destructive to the relationship than for either partner to be unfaithful. In our relationship with God, any infidelity, of course, will always be our fault. The bride is therefore often depicted as the unfaithful one—the harlot, as Hosea teaches: "Ephraim hath hired lovers. . . . Their heart is divided" (8:9; 10:2). The whole image poignantly portrays the depth of feeling on the part of a jealous God who has lovingly nurtured and protected his people, and shows how repulsive it is for God to watch his bride go "a whoring after other gods."

Though most of Hosea's message is addressed to northern Israel, the Lord expressed through him an occasional word for Judah, as in 4:15 and 5:13–14. After many strikingly vivid statements of Israel's ills and evils, the prophet laments that Ephraim has to be destroyed as the cities of the plain (that is, Sodom and Gomorrah and three others) were destroyed. But Hosea also announced a message of hope, that a remnant would be redeemed in the last days (13:9–14; 14:1–7). Hosea, whose name means "salvation" or "deliverance," ends with a hopeful message. God anciently called his people out of Egypt and, as a loving Father, taught Ephraim how to walk, gently "taking them by their arms; but they knew not that I healed them" (11:1, 3). Now once again God will show his long-suffering and unceasing care: "I will heal their backsliding, I will love them freely. . . . I will be as the dew unto Israel: he shall grow as the lily, and cast forth his roots as Lebanon. His branches shall spread, and his beauty shall be as the olive tree. . . . They that dwell under his shadow shall return" (14:4–7; see also Ezekiel 16:60, 62).

Many of the predictions of the ancient prophets of Israel like Hosea have multiple fulfillment or multiple adaptation. Prophetic utterances are sometimes used in different contexts in different dispensations. For example, Hosea's words, "When Israel was a child, then I loved him, and called my son out of Egypt" (Hosea 11:1), besides applying to the Israelite exodus from Egypt, were adapted by Matthew to another sense: "[Joseph] took the young child and his mother by night, and departed into Egypt: and was there until the death of Herod: that it might be fulfilled which was spoken of the Lord by the prophet, saying, Out of Egypt have I called my son" (Matthew 2:14–15).

One of the most powerful and profound doctrines of the entire book is articulated in 13:4: "Yet I am the Lord thy God from the land of Egypt, and thou shalt know no god but me: for there is no saviour beside me." So important is this doctrine that several other prophets have been inspired to repeat it, including Isaiah (43:11) and the Prophet Joseph Smith: "for the Lord is God, and beside him there is no Savior" (D&C 76:1). Because he had access to a fuller, more explicitly Christ-centered version of the Old Testament, King Benjamin in the New World provides a more complete understanding of the doctrine in Hosea: "And moreover, I say unto you, that there shall be no other name given nor any other way nor means whereby salvation can come unto the children of men, only in and through the name of Christ, the Lord Omnipotent. . . . And this is the means whereby salvation cometh. And there is none other salvation save this which hath been spoken of; neither are there any conditions whereby man can be saved except the conditions which I have told you" (Mosiah 3:17, 4:8).

JOEL

The book of Joel begins with a statement of origin and authority. The prophet's name contains both of the common Hebrew titles for the Lord: *Jo* (pronounced *Yo*) is a contraction of the divine name, Jehovah, and *El* is the common Semitic singular for "God"; therefore, the prophet's name means "Jehovah is God."

Probably no "minor" prophet has been more quoted regarding the restoration of the gospel of Jesus Christ in the latter days than Joel. The rest of the world hardly notices him. It is too bad we don't know more about him. Because of his obvious concern for Judah and Jerusalem some scholars believe he lived in that area.

Joel 1

Joel began by citing the credentials that many other prophets have begun with: "The word of the Lord came . . ." (1:1; see also Jonah 1:1; Hosea 1:1; Micah 1:1; Jeremiah 1:2; Ezekiel 1:3; Zephaniah 1:1; Haggai 1:1; Zechariah 1:1; and Malachi 1:1). He addressed his message to the elders (Hebrew, *zakanim*), probably the recognized officials of the people.

A series of unprecedented cataclysms is symbolized by four future insect plagues. Jepheth ben Ali, an eighth-century Jewish Karaite commentator, proposed that the four plagues of insects symbolized four historic invasions, the Assyrian, the Babylonian, the Macedonian, and the Roman invasions, but could this chapter also represent yet future catastrophes preceding the coming of the Lord? The desolation here depicted would apparently last until "the day of the Lord" (v. 15), which phrase always refers to the Second Coming.

Joel 2

As that "day" approaches, two mighty and highly organized armies are identifiable and characterized in these verses. They are the forces of good and the forces of evil. They are compared to warhorses, chariots, fire, mighty men, and forces of nature. The greater force cannot be stopped; before it the earth quakes, the heavens tremble, and the sun, moon, and stars cease their shining.

For explanation of "the former rain" and "the latter rain" mentioned in verse 23, see commentary at Deuteronomy 11:8–17.

The Lord's people will survive the cataclysms and enjoy the blessings of heaven. Peter repeated Joel's remarkable prophecy (Joel 2:28–32) on the day of Pentecost in Jerusalem (Acts 2:16–21), and it was repeated by Moroni in Joseph Smith's bedroom in 1823 in western New York State (Joseph Smith–History 1:41). Peter said Joel's words were fulfilled on that spiritual occasion, and Moroni said Joel's words were not yet fulfilled but would soon be. Stunningly, President Gordon B. Hinckley declared in October general conference 2001 that the vision of Joel has been fulfilled:

"The era in which we live is the fulness of times spoken of in the scriptures, when God has brought together all of the elements of previous dispensations. From the day that He and His Beloved Son manifested themselves to the boy Joseph, there has been a tremendous cascade of enlightenment poured out upon the world. The hearts of men have turned to their fathers in fulfillment of the words of Malachi. The vision of Joel has been fulfilled wherein he declared:

"'And it shall come to pass afterward, that I will pour out my spirit upon all flesh; and your sons and your daughters shall prophesy, your old men shall dream dreams, your young men shall see visions:

"'And also upon the servants and upon the handmaids in those days will I pour out my spirit.

"'And I will shew wonders in the heavens and in the earth, blood, and fire, and pillars of smoke.

"'The sun shall be turned into darkness, and the moon into blood, before the great and the terrible day of the Lord come.

"'And it shall come to pass, that whosoever shall call on the name of the Lord shall be delivered: for in mount Zion and in Jerusalem shall be deliverance, as the Lord hath said, and in the remnant whom the Lord shall call' (Joel 2:28–32).

"There has been more of scientific discovery during these years than during all of the previous history of mankind. Transportation, communication, medicine, public hygiene, the unlocking of the atom, the miracle of the computer, with all of its ramifications, have blossomed forth, particularly in our own era. During my own lifetime, I have witnessed miracle after wondrous miracle come to pass. We take it for granted" (*Ensign*, Nov. 2001, 5).

Here we have an excellent example of multiple fulfillment of prophecy, a subject we will examine at greater length later (see "Why Should We Study Isaiah?" and commentary at Isaiah 2:3; Jeremiah 31:15; Ezekiel 38–39; Zechariah 12–14).

In regard to the amazing results of the Lord's pouring out his Spirit on all flesh, as recorded in verse 28, President Joseph Fielding Smith many years ago stated specifically that this prophecy was not confined to members of the Church. Rather, "the Lord would pour out his blessings and his Spirit upon all people and use them to accomplish his purposes" (*Doctrines of Salvation*, 1:176). In this regard consider another statement by President Smith:

"I maintain that had there been no restoration of the gospel, and no organization of the Church of Jesus Christ of Latter-day Saints, there would have been no radio; there would have been no airplane, and there would not have been the wonderful discoveries in medicine, chemistry, electricity, and the many other things wherein the world has been benefited by such discoveries. Under such conditions these blessings would have been withheld, for they belong to the Dispensation of the Fulness of Times of which the restoration of the gospel and the organization of the Church constitute the central point, from which radiates the Spirit of the Lord throughout the world. The inspiration of the Lord has gone out and takes hold of the minds of men, though they know it not, and they are directed by the Lord. In this manner he brings them into his service that his purposes and his righteousness, in due time, may be supreme on the earth.

" . . . I do not believe for one moment that these discoveries have come by chance, or that they have come because of superior intelligence possessed by men today over those who lived in ages that are past. They have come and are coming because the time is ripe, because the Lord has willed it, and because he has poured out his Spirit on all flesh" (Conference Report, Oct. 1926, 117).

President Smith clarified that the Lord's Spirit spoken of here was not the gift of the Holy Ghost but rather the Light of Christ. The former is reserved only for those who have been baptized and had that gift conferred upon them by priesthood ordinance.

For the future strange behavior of the sun, moon, and stars (v. 31), see commentary at Isaiah 13:6–18, especially verse 10, and at Isaiah 24:21–23.

Verse 32 clearly suggests that future physical and spiritual deliverance will be found in two holy cities: in Zion (the New Jerusalem), and in Old Jerusalem (see also Joel 3:17). Furthermore, it should be noted that the Lord's Temples are places of security and deliverance. In dedicating the Kirtland Temple the Prophet Joseph Smith prayed that the Saints would be protected and delivered by their association with the Lord's holy house (D&C 109:24–28).

Joel 3

Chapter 3 seems to be an elaboration of the gathering of the Lord's people and of the opposing groups for the confrontation already introduced in chapter 2. This great assembly will be gathered at the "valley of decision," which is really the "valley of Jehovah's judgment" (Hebrew, *Jehoshaphat*). The "valley of decision" is a symbolic name depicting a place where God's ultimate judgment on the nations who have gathered against Jerusalem will be manifest. Tradition associates the location of this valley with the Kidron, the narrow furrow of land situated between East Jerusalem and the Mount of Olives. Verses 9–17 may be a resumé of the war described in chapter 2, what we generally call the battle of Armageddon. The mighty men of the other nations ("Gentiles") are contrasted to the mighty ones of the Lord, meaning all who believe in him. For the wicked it will be a terrible, dark day, but the Lord will be the hope of his people (see "The War of Gog and Magog" in commentary at Ezekiel 38–39).

Verse 15 seems to refer to the same cataclysmic events as did 2:30–31. Verse 17 suggests two holy cities: Zion (the New Jerusalem), and Old Jerusalem (compare Isaiah 64:10). On the fountain coming out of the House of the Lord (v. 18), see further at Ezekiel 47:1 and Zechariah 14:8.

As with many of the other Old Testament prophets, Joel ends with a wonderfully positive conclusion for Jerusalem and Judah. The earth will finally be renewed and become forever productive. Former nations will exist no more, but the righteous, those who are clean, will belong to the kingdom of Zion. And "the Lord dwelleth in Zion" (v. 21). With all the horrendous scenarios that lie ahead for the people of the world in the last days, it is comforting to know that there is something good on which those who trust in the Lord can anchor their souls, something toward which the humble and valiant can look with confidence.

MICAH

The name Micah (Hebrew, *mikah*) is an abbreviated form of Micaiah (Hebrew, *mikayah* or *mikayahu*), meaning "Who is like Jehovah?" Micah was a Morasthite (Micah 1:1; Jeremiah 26:18), one who came from Moresheth-gath, about twenty-five miles southwest of Jerusalem, near the border between Judah and Philistia. His ministry occurred during the reigns of Jotham, Ahaz, and especially Hezekiah, kings of Judah, as corroborated in the book of Jeremiah (26:18–19). Micah was, therefore, a contemporary of the prophets Amos, Isaiah, and Hosea. All of their ministries were set against the same social and political backgrounds, and their messages necessarily depicted the same social ills in the Israelite kingdoms. In fact, Micah's content and style resemble Isaiah's—rich in figures of speech, mention of the mountain of the Lord's house, prophecy about the future Messiah, call for reform to address significant problems in society, and apostasy. Micah sometimes uses wordplay to communicate his message, which may be summarized in a single sentence: the whole duty of humankind is to act justly, to love mercy, and to walk humbly with the Lord (Micah 6:8).

Micah's call was specifically to the capital cities, Samaria (Israel) and Jerusalem (Judah). He prophesied the captivity of northern and southern Israelites, their ultimate restoration to the land, and the coming of the Messiah.

Micah 1:1–7

Micah introduced his prophecies by testifying that the Lord would come down out of his place to take an active part in Israel's history. The Temple was his dwelling place.

Micah declared that peoples throughout the world would hear

and hearken to his words. Interestingly, his ancient words now reverberate through the written and spoken media to the ends of the earth.

Micah's prophecy of doom on Samaria (v. 6), that it would become a heap (Hebrew, "ruin"), and that its foundations would be discovered (Hebrew, "laid bare"), has been literally fulfilled. The foundations of Samaria were laid bare by the ravages of war in generations subsequent to Micah, and today excavations have exposed those same foundations. If idolatry be paralleled with adultery or harlotry, the "hire of an harlot" (v. 7) would represent sacrifices to idol gods.

Micah 1:8–16

Evil influences had come into Samaria and into Judah, and both would experience suffering and destruction. Micah's words imply that each kingdom will get what it deserves. All the places mentioned by name in verses 10–16 are towns in Judah's lowland (Hebrew, *Shephelah*), in the vicinity of Micah's hometown. Verse 12 seems to have been written in the prophetic present tense, Micah having seen things so clearly it was as though they had already taken place. So sure is the word of the Lord that prophecy is history in reverse.

Micah 2

Because Israel lies awake at night thinking of evils to do by day, the Lord will "devise an evil" or plan a disaster against them (v. 3). He will take up a parable, or pronounce a lamentation, against them. Literally rendered, verse 6 says, "Preach ye not, they say; they shall not preach of these things! Reproaches are unending!" The prophet seems to be quoting some of the peoples' objections to prophets' preaching.

Verse 7's challenging Hebrew sentence apparently says, "Is it asked, O house of Jacob, 'Has the Lord become impatient?' If these are his doings [that is, the things spoken of in the first five verses] will not my words do good unto him who walketh uprightly?"

Apparently the prophet is saying that nothing goes well in Israel any more—there is no security, no consideration for women and children, no regard for prophets; people only want to hear about indulgence, wine, and strong drink. Disrespect and maltreatment of women and children, especially, will "destroy you, even with a sore destruction" (v. 10).

It is difficult to tell whether verses 12–13 contain a prophetic promise that the Lord will lead them back out of captivity some day, or whether it is a bitter warning that because of the foregoing conditions the Lord will lead them and their king *into* captivity.

Micah 3

Since Israel's leaders or princes were not literally butchers and cannibals, we might conclude that they were "feeding" themselves by taking advantage of the poor. Because of their callous injustice in taking advantage of people, in their own time of need the Lord would "hide his face from them" and not listen to their pleas. As their "night" approached, they would not get any enlightenment from God.

On the other hand, as the true prophet prophesied, Zion would be plowed and the Temple Mount would look like a wilderness. Though spared for over a century more, Zion (Jerusalem) was eventually desolated (v. 12) by the armies of Babylon, and centuries later, the Temple Mount was literally plowed by the Roman soldiers of Titus. You will see in Jeremiah 26:18–19 testimony that the people listened and responded to Micah's prophecy, thus postponing the promised punishment.

Micah 4:1–5

According to the prophetic pattern (see commentary at Amos 9:11–15), Micah now shifts from doom and devastation to a message of hope. Though Zion (Jerusalem) would certainly become a heap of ruins, just beyond that dark cloud a ray of hope would shine. Zion (inhabitants of Jerusalem) would "go even to Babylon [but] there shalt thou be delivered; there the Lord shall redeem thee from the hand of thine enemies" (4:10). Zion had to return from Babylon; she could not remain in the strange land. Before other great prophecies could be fulfilled, she had to be reestablished in her own land.

Micah projected his vision into the latter-day future when the mountain of the house of the Lord (the Temple) would be established in the top of the mountains. Many people and nations would flow to the Temple to be taught the ways of the God of Jacob, when the law would go forth from Zion and the word of the Lord from Jerusalem. Micah went on to preview the millennial era, when instruments of war will be turned into implements of agriculture and nations will not "learn war any more," when "they shall sit every man under his vine and under his fig tree" (v. 4)—a figurative, formulaic expression of living comfortably, safely, and securely.

Isaiah voiced almost identical predictions of an era of peace and prosperity (Isaiah 2:1–3). As contemporaries, Micah and Isaiah likely knew each other's writings, but it is not known whether one of these prophets originally gave utterance to this millennial scenario and the other prophet borrowed it. As is often the case, the Lord may have inspired both prophets to utter the same glorious principles and promises.

Micah 4:6–10

In that day the Lord shall be King, reigning from Jerusalem. The essential meaning of "redeem" is to rescue, to save. Just as in our latter day, the suffering peoples of Israel in the days of their travail would find some comfort in knowing of an imminent time of peace with their Prince of Peace coming to rule and reign as King on this glorified sphere.

Micah 4:11–13; 5:7–15

This is another picture of the contrast between the days of Israel's degradation and their future days. It is used also as a comfort for Israel on another continent, in 3 Nephi 20:15–21. Two passages from the Old Testament prophet Micah were referred to by the Savior when he appeared to his people in the land Bountiful. The first is from Micah 4:12–13 (cited in 3 Nephi 20:18–19), where the Lord, after bringing the exiles back from Babylon, and finding other nations gathering against Jerusalem and eyeing her as prey, assures his people of ancient Israel that his purposes will be fulfilled. They will return from exile; they will be planted again in their land; they will exert their strength (as iron, brass, "beating in pieces," etc.) with the protection of the Lord, because his people Israel must continue in the land in order to realize the promises to the fathers—for instance, that the Messiah would be born in Bethlehem (Micah 5:2) and would minister to his people in their land.

The other passage from Micah is 5:7–15 (cited in 3 Nephi 20:16–17; 21:12–21), and it is similar in tone to the previous one. But contrary to the threatening, forceful imagery of some of the verses, one verse in Micah states that "the remnant of Jacob shall be in the midst of many people as a dew from the Lord, as the showers upon the grass" (Micah 5:7). In biblical imagery, dew and showers always suggest nourishment, peace, relief, and blessing. Apparently the remnant of Jacob in the latter days will also be a blessing to the Gentiles and promote the righteous life.

In ancient America, however, the Savior focused on the might and terror which he, through a remnant of Jacob, would strike into the hearts of their adversaries among the Gentiles (3 Nephi 20:16–19; 21:12–21).

Many of the predictions of the ancient prophets of Israel like Micah, Isaiah, and others, have multiple fulfillments or multiple adaptations. Prophetic utterances are sometimes used in different contexts in different dispensations. We have already seen how Hosea's words, "When Israel was a child, then I loved him, and called my son out of Egypt" (Hosea 11:1), applied to both the Israelite exodus from Egypt and the young life of Jesus (Matthew 2:14–15). Micah's words about the remnant of Israel could very well apply both to antiquity and futurity, but the Lord has not chosen to make the intent of these verses any clearer to us at the present time.

Micah 5:1–6

Micah again turned his prophetic eye to the future, this time somewhat closer to his own day. The Messiah would come to earth, and Micah specified the location of his birth. All of the prophets wrote and prophesied of the Messiah (see Jacob 7:11 and Mosiah 13:33), but no one except Micah in the biblical writings that have come to us preserved the specific prediction of the Savior's birthplace. There can be no mistake: there is only one Bethlehem in Judah, and there is only one ruler in Israel whose origins are from eternity. Even the chief priests and scribes of Jesus' day understood the prophecy clearly; they quoted it when

Herod inquired where the Messiah should be born. Herod was obviously convinced of the possibility since he proceeded to issue his infamous order to exterminate the children around Bethlehem: "And they said unto him, In Bethlehem of Judaea: for thus it is written by the prophet, And thou Bethlehem, in the land of Juda, art not the least among the princes of Juda: for out of thee shall come a Governor, that shall rule [Greek, meaning 'shepherd, tend, nurture'] my people Israel" (Matthew 2:5–6).

Consider "Assyria" (Micah 5:5–6) in the latter days to be representative of future opponents of God's work, whose evil ways will be vanquished, totally overcome by the forces of good.

Micah 6:1–8

Possibly the most sublime counsel the prophet Micah penned for the benefit of all generations was his rhetorical question of the Lord's expectation for his children, and the prophet's answer: "Will the Lord be pleased with thousands of rams, or with ten thousands of rivers of oil [as sacrificial offerings]? . . . He hath shewed thee, O man, what is good; and what doth the Lord require of thee, but to do justly, and to love mercy, and to walk humbly with thy God?" This language is reminiscent of Moses' charge to the house of Israel in one of his last sermons (Deuteronomy 10:12–13).

The importance of Micah's counsel in Judaism is demonstrated by the following excerpt from the Talmud (the codification of Jewish oral law and lore): "Rabbi Simlai lectured: 613 commandments were handed down to Moses; 365 of them are prohibitions, corresponding to the days of the year; 248 of them are laws of action, corresponding to the bones and limbs of man. Rabbi Hamnuna said: When David came, he reduced the commandments to eleven, for we read in Scripture [he then quoted Psalm 15]. . . . When Isaiah came, he reduced the commandments to six; for it is said:

"He that walketh righteously and speaketh uprightly,
"he that despiseth the gain of oppression,
"that *shaketh* his *hand from* holding of *bribes*,
"that stoppeth his ears from hearing of blood,
"and *shutteth* his *eye from* looking upon *evil*,

"he shall dwell on high (Isa. 33:15–16).

"When Micah came, he reduced the commandments to three; as it is said: It hath been told thee, o man what is good and what the Lord doth require of thee:

"Only to *do justly,*

"And to love mercy,

"And to *walk humbly with* thy *God* (Micah 6:8)" [Talmud Makkot 23–24] (quoted in Trepp, *History of the Jewish Experience,* 94–95).

Here Micah does not denigrate the importance of sacrifice but raises Israel's sights to a higher plane. The prophet Samuel said it a little differently: exact obedience is better than a myriad of sacrifices (1 Samuel 15:22).

Micah 6:9–16

This is another summary of sin and its results—a listing of the people's crimes and consequent punishments. The "statutes of Omri" and the "works of the house of Ahab" were apostate laws and practices. Therefore, says the Lord, he would make Israel a desolation.

Micah 7

Micah lamented the evil conditions that permeated Israel in his day. He used an analogy: looking for good and upright people at this juncture in Israel's history was like looking for summer fruit after the harvest had already ended. Yet, though the chapter begins on a note of gloom, the prophet ends with prayer, praise, and promises. Notwithstanding the crime and punishment, God would show his people how to be just and also how to be merciful. Perhaps it is at this point where Micah's name figures in his message: "Who is like Jehovah" for greatness and mercy and compassion? (v. 18). In the end Jehovah will fulfill all his covenants; he will bestow all the promised blessings upon Abraham, Isaac, and Israel, and their righteous posterity. There is no power like Jehovah's power, and there is no king like this King.

ISAIAH

Isaiah is one of the greatest prophets ever to have lived. He is usually, and justifiably, regarded as the greatest of the prophets of the Old Testament whose writings have been transmitted to us. Isaiah was brilliant as well as an inspired servant of God. Besides being a prophet, he was a scholar, poet, and historian. He used at least twenty-five Hebrew words that none of the other writing prophets used. And he used a total Hebrew vocabulary of almost 2,200 words—more than any other Old Testament writer.

Isaiah was the son of Amoz, not to be confused with the prophet Amos, of whom Isaiah was a contemporary, as well as of Hosea and Micah. The beginning of Isaiah's ministry is dated to 740 B.C., and its forty-year span (740–700 B.C.) paralleled the reigns of at least four kings (see commentary on Isaiah 6:1). We have no scriptural information about Isaiah's birth, childhood, maturation, his personal appearance, or his death (though Jewish rabbinical writings do record traditions of his death in the reign of Manasseh—Yebamoth 49b and Sanhedrin 103b and the pseudepigraphical book called the Martyrdom of Isaiah (see *Apocrypha and Pseudepigrapha of the Old Testament*, 2:162); and Martyrdom 5:1 records Manasseh's killing the prophet by "sawing him asunder").

We know that Isaiah was married and the father of at least two sons, to whom he gave highly symbolic names: *Shear-jashub,* literally, "a remnant shall return" (7:3), and *Maher-shalal-hash-baz,* literally "quick to the plunder, swift to the spoil" (8:3). Isaiah spent most of his life in Jerusalem and had tremendous influence on the southern kingdom of Judah during the reign of King Hezekiah. He was a court counselor, advisor, and source of godly wisdom.

Isaiah's book focuses on four major themes: the first and

second comings of Jesus Christ to the earth, the last days, and the Millennium. Isaiah was the great prophet of the Messiah's advent, the coming of God to this earth. To denote God, Isaiah consistently used the name-title "the Holy One of Israel" some twenty-five times in his writings (there are only thirty-one attestations of this name-title in the whole Old Testament). It is a phrase that influenced the prophets and peoples of the Book of Mormon (thirty-eight times). This name-title signifies that Jesus Christ is both the embodiment of holiness (an important concept for Isaiah) and the very God of Israel.

As a writer, Isaiah was fond of using the technique of personification throughout his work—ascribing human thoughts and actions to inanimate objects. For example, "the faithful city [is] become an harlot" (Isaiah 1:21), or "the moon shall be confounded, and the sun ashamed" (24:23), or "the mountains and the hills shall break forth before you into singing, and all the trees of the field shall clap their hands" (55:12).

Isaiah is magnificent. We will be blessed by paying the price to study his writings. Elder Bruce R. McConkie inquired in a landmark article: "If our eternal salvation depends upon our ability to understand the writings of Isaiah as fully and truly as Nephi understood them—and who shall say such is not the case!—how shall we fare in that great day when with Nephi we shall stand before the pleasing bar of Him who said: 'Great are the words of Isaiah'? (3 Ne. 23:1)" (*Ensign*, Oct. 1973, 78).

WHY SHOULD WE STUDY ISAIAH?

Better than any other source we possess, the Book of Mormon helps us to understand why we should study Isaiah. The following scriptural passages attest to this truth.

3 Nephi 23:1–3

The first and best reason to study Isaiah is that we have been commanded to search his writings, and the commandment has been repeated several times (see also 3 Nephi 20:11 and Mormon 8:23). A commandment, of course, is something for which we will all be held accountable; for our good he demands that we make special study of the words he gave to this particular prophet.

Isaiah gave revelations concerning all things and all stages of the great plan of salvation. His prophecies have been and will be fulfilled; they have dual, and in some cases, multiple fulfillments (in modern parlance, they are reusable or recyclable prophecies). Things which have been and will be are often called types. Isaiah's teachings may have one particular true *interpretation* but multiple *applications*. Every reader should watch for personal application in his or her own life.

Time, rather than being linear, is circular: "one eternal round" (see Ecclesiastes 1:9; 1 Nephi 10:19). The creation and population of worlds are cyclical, that which has been done over and over again. The work of dispensations is also cyclical, each having a beginning, an apostasy, a warning period, and "latter days."

Apocalyptic revelation (as in Lehi and Nephi's dream, and some writings of Isaiah, Ezekiel, Daniel, Zechariah, and John) can often be seen in terms of timelessness; for a brief moment all things are before the prophet—past, present, and future.

Typical actors, in all ages, are a dragon, a beast, a serpent, a great and abominable church, a spiritual Babylon, a mother of harlots, a pit, darkness, angels, stars, servants, saints, sheep, water, light, individuals arrayed in white, and so forth.

Zion and Babylon, the righteous and the wicked, are foils, or contrasts; Assyria and Egypt represent superpowers at the end of time.

The use of symbols is important. They can *conceal* meaning, but understanding the symbols can *reveal* meaning.

1 Nephi 19:23

Jesus Christ is the central message of Isaiah (recall that the prophet's name means "Jehovah saves"). Isaiah provides a greater testimony of the Redeemer, and the study of Him is certainly for our profit and learning (see also 2 Nephi 25:23, 26).

2 Nephi 6:4–5

By searching the writings of Isaiah we learn about God and glorify him. Isaiah's teachings apply to us. They are not just history lessons but lessons from history. It has been said, history is what happened; literature is what happens. And the book of Isaiah is great literature. Isaiah gives us views of what lies ahead. We are quite accustomed these days to pushing a button and getting an "instant replay." Some day we will understand how we can push a button and get an "instant preplay."

2 Nephi 11

We can learn much from eyewitnesses of the Redeemer. Joseph Smith wrote, "Could you gaze into heaven five minutes, you would know more than you would by reading all that ever was written on the subject" (*Joseph Smith* [manual], 419). Isaiah is one of the great prophets who gazed into heaven, and he can teach us much. We can come to believe more fully in the God of heaven and delight in his coming; we can learn the typologies and attributes of him—all of which will enable us to lift up our hearts and rejoice for all men.

HOW CAN WE UNDERSTAND ISAIAH?

1 Nephi 19:23

Isaiah is a spiritual workout. Proper study of his writings can sharpen us mentally and spiritually. We are encouraged to liken his writings to our own personal situations, for our profit and learning.

2 Nephi 25:1, 5

We can become acquainted with the manner of writing among the Jews, coming to understand their literary mechanisms for better comprehension. Isaiah in particular wrote with sophisticated artistry; more than 90 percent of his writings is in poetic form (poetry is saying one thing and also meaning another). Types, figures, and symbols usually have a surface meaning but also a deeper, underlying meaning. Coming to understand the form is important—for example, the similes, metaphors, personification, and parallelisms (learning to read in couplets).

Knowing King James English helps us to understand Isaiah, so we are grateful for the language notes in the LDS edition of the King James Version of the Bible. The more we read and study it, the more familiar it becomes. Knowing Hebrew also helps us to understand Isaiah better, so we are likewise grateful for the Hebrew language notes in the LDS edition of the King James Bible.

2 Nephi 25:4

Understanding Isaiah requires us to be filled with the spirit of prophecy, which, according to John, is "the testimony of Jesus" (Revelation 19:10). There is an obligation of personal worthiness for every student of Isaiah. Only by sincerely inquiring of the Lord, in faith, and keeping his commandments, will the comprehension of his writings be opened to us. Each one must pay the price (see 1 Nephi 10:19; Alma 26:22; 12:9–10).

2 Nephi 25:6

Learn something of the history and geography of the Holy Land. Goethe wrote in *Faust*: "*Wer den Dichter will verstehen, muss in Dichters Lande gehen*" ("whoever wants to understand a poet must go to the poet's homeland"). If you want to understand Wordsworth, go to his homeland, and you will understand his writings better. If you want to understand Isaiah, a poet par excellence, go to his homeland, and you will relate better than ever to his imagery. Nephi lived in the same land and city as Isaiah, so he understood Isaiah's figurative language. The land is a natural commentary on the writings that come from it. Just as Jesus did in his mortal ministry, Isaiah constantly drew examples and illustrations from the objects of daily living and from the "regions round about."

Since not everyone can afford the time and money to travel to the other side of the world to visit the physical settings of biblical scripture, we are greatly blessed in modern times to have books, documentary films, and an inexhaustible supply of Internet sites that can help visually acquaint us with Old Testament lands and sites.

2 Nephi 25:7–8

We can benefit from Nephi's plainness, in which "no man can err." Nephi intentionally avoided the manner of prophesying among the Jews; the Book of Mormon prophets do not follow all the Hebraic literary styles. Isaiah is difficult only because the Jews desired it (Jacob 4:14–18). Knowing the prophecies in our day, we can see them fulfilled. For example, Isaiah 29 // 2 Nephi 27 includes a conversation between two men in New York City that was foreseen and recorded twenty-five hundred years before it happened! (see commentary at Isaiah 29:11–12). Isaiah's prophecies are of great worth, particularly to us in the last days. The phrase "in that day" appears forty-three times in Isaiah. His teachings are recorded for our good, to help us be prepared and involved in bringing about the great purposes of God.

In "Ten Keys to Understanding Isaiah," Elder Bruce R. McConkie gave us valuable learning tools to help us study Isaiah (*Ensign*, Oct. 1973, 80–83):

1. Gain an overall knowledge of the plan of salvation and of God's dealings with his earthly children.
2. Learn the position and destiny of the house of Israel in the Lord's eternal scheme of things.
3. Know the chief doctrines about which Isaiah chose to write.
4. Use the Book of Mormon.
5. Use latter-day revelation.
6. Learn how the New Testament interprets Isaiah.
7. Study Isaiah in its Old Testament context.
8. Learn the manner of prophesying used among the Jews in Isaiah's day.
9. Have the spirit of prophecy.
10. Devote yourself to hard, conscientious study.

Isaiah 6:1 (2 Nephi 16:1)

We begin with chapter 6 because Isaiah's call in a vision from the Lord is contained in it. We do not know why the compiler put it there instead of at the very beginning. Isaiah's early prophecies were mostly pertinent to his lifetime and home country. He then frequently took a seeric or prophetic flight into the past, or to future times like the meridian of time and the last days to tell of ultimate things. This is part of "the manner of prophesying among the Jews"—to relate things of their times to things past and future. To aid in understanding these prophetic words, we often refer to the Book of Mormon, the world's greatest commentary on Isaiah. Likewise, the notes at the foot of each page of Isaiah increase our understanding; more such notes have been included with this book of scripture than any other—for our profit and learning.

Tomb plaque of King Uzziah. "Now the rest of the acts of Uzziah, first and last, did Isaiah the prophet, the son of Amoz, write. So Uzziah slept with his fathers, and they buried him with his fathers" (2 Chronicles 26:22–23)

The year that King Uzziah died was sometime between 750 and 740 B.C. He is known by two names in the Old Testament: *Uzziah*, which in Hebrew means "strength of the Lord," and *Azariah*, which means "help of the Lord." More on this king of Judah is found in 2 Chronicles 26:16–21. His leprosy was the result of unauthorized assumption of priesthood functions (compare Nadab and Abihu, Uzzah, and King Saul). Interestingly, a tomb plaque of Uzziah dating from the Second Temple period was found in the ancient cemetery on the Mount of Olives. The plaque bears an inscription explaining that the bones of King Uzziah had been transferred from their original burying place to a new plot on the Mount of Olives (see 2 Chronicles 26:23), thus providing tangible corroboration of the fact that this ancient king mentioned during the ministry of Isaiah really lived, died, and was buried in old Jerusalem.

"The vision was a divine revelation. It was a revelation given to the prophet in time and space upon this earth, and not in a vacuum. It is to be expected, therefore, that in a formal sense it would have a point of contact with the religious paraphernalia which the prophet would understand. In a formal sense there are relations between the contents of this vision and practices and customs to be found in other religions of antiquity. What was essentially new was the fact that this vision was a revelation from God. It must also be remembered that the pagan religions of antiquity were degenerations from the true, and indeed were imitative of it. . . . The idea of the Temple is derived from the well-known earthly Temple, and merely serves as a background for the vision" (Young, *Book of Isaiah*, 1:239, 250).

Isaiah saw the Lord (probably the experience Nephi referred to in 2 Nephi 11:2). Isaiah was an eyewitness. His vision dispels the sectarian notion of a God without body, parts, and passions; the Lord was sitting on a throne and his train (the skirts of his robe)—or his glory—filled the Temple. He was "high" and "lifted up," the latter concept being especially rich in symbolism; the Savior was lifted up on the cross and then lifted up to exalted position to rule and reign forever.

Isaiah saw an actual Being. Scriptures do teach anthropomorphism—not "God in the image of man" but "man in the image of God," just as Genesis 1:27 says: man was created in the image of God. We have bodies; he has a Body. The Bible itself notes that God has various body parts: He has a face (Exodus 33:20, 23; Deuteronomy 5:4); he has eyes (Deuteronomy 11:12); ears (Ezekiel 8:18); a mouth (Numbers 12:8; Deuteronomy 8:3); arms (Exodus 15:16; Isaiah 52:10); hands (Job 10:8; 12:9; Isaiah 11:11); fingers (Exodus 8:19; 31:18); a heart (Genesis 6:6; 8:21); and feet (Isaiah 60:13; 66:1). Paul constantly wrote about the resurrection of Jesus Christ, emphasizing that He has a glorified body (Romans 8:17; 1 Corinthians 15:12–29; Philippians 3:21). Luke recorded his witness of the risen Lord: "handle me, and see; for a spirit hath not flesh and bones, as ye see me have" (Luke 24:39). The Prophet Joseph Smith testified: "That which is without body, parts and passions is nothing. There is no other God in heaven but that God who has flesh and bones" (McConkie and Ostler, *Revelations of the Restoration*, 1086).

Isaiah 6:2–3 (2 Nephi 16:2–3)

The Book of Mormon properly uses the term *seraphim* (there should be no final "s" as in the King James Version's *seraphims;* it is already plural in Hebrew). The cross-reference is to the Topical Guide "Cherubim," meaning angelic beings in God's presence. Wings symbolize power and motion (D&C 77:4; 109:79; see also Bible Dictionary, "Seraphim"). The covering of the face and feet signifies reverence and obeisance toward God. Hebrew *saraph* means "fiery one" or "burning one." Those who dwell in the presence of the Lord dwell in "everlasting burnings" or, in other words, in the radiance, brilliance, or glory of that kingdom (*Joseph Smith* [manual], 53, 221).

Isaiah 6:4 (2 Nephi 16:4)

"Smoke" in Hebrew can mean smoke or cloud (see Exodus 19:18, where Mount Sinai was "on a smoke"; 1 Kings 8:10–11). The glory of the Lord filled his House, just as his glory fills the earth. The Lord has said that his work and glory is seeing his creations become immortal and eternal (Moses 1:39), so the earth and at least some of the Father's children will bring him additional glory.

Isaiah 6:5 (2 Nephi 16:5)

Those who see God sometimes fear and feel unworthy. Isaiah's lips may have been unclean, but his heart was not, for he had a willing heart. The Lord has worked out in a wonderful way this problem of feeling fear and unworthiness. He teaches us according to our ability to receive his teachings, and we learn as we are ready, willing, and worthy. Peter felt unworthy when the Lord cleansed his feet; to a degree we all feel unworthy of the Lord's cleansing and atoning blood, but we must accept it and apply it anyway.

Isaiah 6:6–7 (2 Nephi 16:6–7)

A seraph (singular of *seraphim*) took a burning coal or glowing stone and touched Isaiah's mouth, symbolic of cleansing, a "baptism by fire"—the "refiner's fire." From ancient times metals have been cleansed from impurities by submitting them to extreme heat.

In this case, the cleansing was literal, but the process was symbolic or figurative. When God commissioned Jeremiah, He touched his lips (Jeremiah 1:9), symbolic of cleansing the inner man. The lips are an apt metaphor. The Savior later said that it was that which came out of the mouth, uttered by the lips, which defiled a person (Matthew 15:11). The heart and the lips are linked: "for of the abundance of the heart his mouth speaketh" (Luke 6:45).

Repentance does involve pain. If we have not suffered, we have not really repented. Isaiah's sin was "purged"; the Hebrew term *t'khuppar* means "atoned for." As he was purged, he was qualified and strengthened for the work.

Isaiah 6:8 (2 Nephi 16:8)

Isaiah's call to serve is recorded, along with further instructions he received. Note the question, "Who will go for *us?*" It is the work of the Father and the Son (recall Genesis 1:26). Isaiah responded to the call for missionary service, echoing Jehovah's response to the Father in the Grand Council in Heaven. Young men, women, and couples by the tens of thousands these days repeat the same sentiment when accepting mission calls: "Here am I; send me."

Isaiah 6:9 (2 Nephi 16:9)

This verse reads quite differently in the Book of Mormon: "Hear ye indeed, but *they understood not;* and see ye indeed, but *they perceived not*" (emphasis added). This is a prophesied reaction of the people to Isaiah's preachment. It is not what the Lord desires, of course, but he knew beforehand how the people would generally respond to Isaiah's call to repentance. Isaiah's ministry would have the ironic effect of causing rebellious Israel to harden their hearts. This was later true also of the Messiah's time.

Isaiah 6:10 (2 Nephi 16:10)

The message is presented in the form of an inverted parallelism, or chiasm:

a Make the *heart* of this people fat,

   b and make their *ears* heavy,

      c and shut their *eyes*—

    c lest they see with their *eyes,*
    b and hear with their *ears,*
    a and understand with their *heart*

For more light on the rejection of the prophetic call to repent, compare Zechariah 7:11–12; Matthew 13:10–17; Jacob 4:14; Alma 12:9–11; and 3 Nephi 18:32. Isaiah was instructed to make the true doctrine so plain that his people would have to accept it or harden their hearts against it and reject it. The same would happen in these last days.

Question: Why would the Lord send a prophet to a people he knew would reject the message? *Answer:* (1) As a warning to them *and* to us in the latter days, (2) as a testimony or witness against them, (3) so people could prove themselves *to themselves,* and (4) some would believe, and they would be grateful to Isaiah.

Isaiah 6:11–13 (2 Nephi 16:11–13)

The message of hope pertains both to ancient Israelite days and to the latter days. The scattering and gathering were prophesied. The tree (Israel) still has potential to grow even when its leaves have fallen and are scattered. A tenth (a remnant) will return (see footnote *b* to Isaiah 6:13).

Isaiah 1:1

The book of Isaiah is not a sequential narrative; it is more like sections in the Doctrine and Covenants. Chapter 1 may be called the "Preface," an introductory statement to the entire book. It is like a court scene, a great arraignment, where the Lord accuses his people of various crimes. Amulek taught that everyone will be "arraigned before the bar of Christ . . . to be judged according to their works" (Alma 11:44).

Verse 1 is a headnote, or introduction, to the entire book of Isaiah. Other verses that apply to whole books, such as Amos 1:1, Hosea 1:1, Micah 1:1, and Zephaniah 1:1, are similar in form to Isaiah 1:1.

Isaiah 1:2–6

These verses begin the accusation, featuring Israel's list of sins. "Hear, O heavens, and give ear, O earth" (compare Deuteronomy 32:1 and D&C 76:1). The Lord laments that he has raised children who have not just fallen away but actually rebelled against him.

If ox and ass are more loyal and obedient to their provident master, then Israel is brutish and rebellious indeed. Israel doesn't even recognize their own God.

"They are gone away backward" (v. 4)—the phrase at first sounds awkward, but the image is appropriate and poignant. Israel had not just turned their backs on the Lord and pursued evil, but they were backing away from him, keeping their eyes on him, and doing evil while looking at him.

The consequences of sin without repentance are inevitable. Every time we sin there is a loss of power. The Lord's castigation or chastisement was supposed to bring humility, submission, and penitence—but Israel only sinned more aggressively.

"The whole head is sick, and the whole heart faint"—their thoughts and feelings were perverted and infecting society. Festering sores were repulsive to the Lord, as they are to us. On-going sin, like festering wounds, results in guilt that can eat away at the soul of a person, causing much pain and endless torment if left untreated. Today, an abscess of the physical body may be treated by first lancing it so the infection can drain out. It is then rinsed several times with antibacterial solution, and antibiotics are administered to help keep the infection from returning. Comparing this process to that of repentance, we can see that we must undergo a procedure that fully rids us of the impurities of sin as well as guarding us against its recurrence. The Lord gave a prescription to cure these sins: "Wash you, make you clean" (v. 16). The gospel of repentance is the antidote for the diseases described in verses 5 and 6. If "used as directed," it is a proven cure for all ills.

The "ointment" in verse 6 refers to olive oil, which was well-known anciently for its curative and antiseptic properties (compare Luke 10:34).

Isaiah 1:7–9

Verses 7–15 constitute a "wake-up call" to the children of Israel; they speak of immediate judgments against the sinful nation. They had apostatized; that is, willfully revolted from and mocked the Holy One of Israel.

Verse 8 contains similes of destruction. Jerusalem, the great Temple City, is left as a mere booth (Hebrew, *sukka*), or hut, in a cucumber patch.

With no promise of a remnant, they would be annihilated as were Sodom and Gomorrah. But God is merciful; by his grace, his loving kindness, he would spare and preserve a remnant of his people.

Isaiah 1:10–15

There were problems in the religious establishment. Isaiah called the leaders "rulers of Sodom" and the people, "people of Gomorrah." On the Lord's view of these Israelites' sacrifices, see 1 Samuel 15:22 and Jeremiah 6:20. There was a semblance of religiosity, but it was hypocritical; they had a form of godliness, but their hearts were far from him. They were merely "going through the motions." Ritual or ceremony is not the end but a means to an end (see also 1 Corinthians 13:1–3). Isaiah clearly taught the futility of mindless and spiritless religious activity. We must bring not only our physical bodies to Church but our spirit bodies too. Empty worship is hypocrisy.

Verse 12 begins literally, "When ye come to see *my face*"—that is, when you go up to the Temple and "tread my courts," it is not just to multiply statistics. We could say that Temple-treading is Hebrew for Church-going.

President John Taylor said: "We are told that 'Many will say to me in that day, Lord, Lord, have we not prophesied in Thy name and in Thy name have cast out devils, and in Thy name done many wonderful works?' Yet to all such he will say; 'Depart from me, ye that work iniquity.' You say that means the outsiders? No, it does not. Do they do many wonderful works in the name of Jesus? No; if they do anything it is done in the name of themselves or of the devil. Sometimes they will do things in the name of God; but it is simply an act of blasphemy. This means you, Latter-day Saints, who heal the sick, cast out devils and do many wonderful things in the name of Jesus. And yet how many we see among this people of this class, that become careless, and treat lightly the ordinances of God's house and the Priesthood of the Son of God; yet they think they are going by and by, to slide into the kingdom of God; but I tell you unless they are righteous and keep their covenants they will never go there. Hear it, ye Latter-day Saints!" (Salt Lake Stake Conference, Jan. 6, 1879, in Smith and Sjodahl, *Doctrine and Covenants Commentary,* 462–63).

Our scripture study, fasting, praying, partaking of the sacrament, home and visiting teaching, and tithe-paying need to be done with full purpose of heart and not as "vain oblations"—the *heart* is what God wants. Inner motives are more important than outer motions.

Not only the ritual sacrifices but also the *prayers* of Israel were rejected. Multiplication of prayers is no substitute for obedience. "Your hands are full of blood"—that is, of murders and blood-guiltiness. Their hands were symbolically full of blood because of their sins; they were also full of blood because of their spiritless sacrifices—an interesting double-edged image.

Isaiah 1:16–20

These verses contain the promise of pardon, on the condition of repentance and obedience. Indeed, repentance was the remedy for all their social and religious ills. Such cleansing is still available to us (D&C 19:15–20; 58:42–43).

In verse 18, like a concerned parent, the Lord says "let us reason together." The similes of cleansing and sanctification are superb. Scarlet comes from insects' eggs in the oak tree—in Arabic *kirmiz,* which is translated in English as "crimson." Why the use of scarlet? Black, not scarlet, is the opposite of white. Rich symbolism is involved here: blood is a dark, red color like scarlet and crimson. Throughout scripture we see the cycle of staining and purifying. Israel was continually staining her beautiful garments with sin. Even the smallest scarlet stain on white is very noticeable, and such a stain is almost impossible to remove. Yet the Lord promises that our sin-stained souls, like the whole house of Israel, may be made completely white through his atoning blood. But we must be willing to give up the scarlet and accept the white. "For because of their faith in the Lamb of God their garments are *made white in his blood*" (1 Nephi 12:10; emphasis added).

Did ancient Jerusalemites experience *snow?* Did they understand the prophet's use of such an image of whiteness while living on the edge of the great Judean Desert? Indeed, Jerusalem, which sits at the top of the hills, averages two occurrences of snowfall each winter. One storm in January of 1992 brought eighteen inches of snow over the Holy City. Fresh-fallen snow is a beautiful image. It covers the dirt and paths of men.

We can eat or be eaten up (vv. 19–20). The key words are "willing" and "obedient" (v. 19)—not just obedient; they were being obedient, as they thought, but they must be *willing*, putting some heart into their obedience.

Isaiah 1:21–31

Here is the Judge's final sentencing, with problems in society enumerated and condemned. Righteousness formerly lodged in Jerusalem—at least during the era of Melchizedek, King of Righteousness, did righteous people reside in the city.

But now the harlot sells that which is priceless for meager quantities of money. The people were giving up million-dollar blessings for ten-cent pleasures. The Lord's people, to whom he was married, were prostituting their sacred relationship. Good things were being diluted and adulterated, as "wine mixed with water" (v. 22).

Now the leaders of Jerusalem were rebellious and dishonest; they accepted bribes and refused to help orphans and widows (recall verse 17). Treatment of orphans and widows is always a clear reflection of a society's conscience.

Verses 25–27 offer prophetic preview of a time, after the discipline of exile, that the covenant people will be restored—in a future messianic era of justice and righteousness.

Verses 28–31: While the righteous will be redeemed, the transgressors will be destroyed by burning, the sinners serving as tow (kindling) and spark, destroyed in their own perfidy.

Read Doctrine and Covenants 121:43 and reflect on the Lord's celestial method of bringing souls back to him—as illustrated here, in these writings of Isaiah.

Isaiah 2 (2 Nephi 12)

The Book of Mormon corrects and changes many verses of Isaiah in this chapter. The joys, blessings, and peace of the righteous in the Temples of the Lord are contrasted to the sorrows, woes, and inquietude of the wicked in the day of the Lord's coming.

Isaiah 2:1–2 (2 Nephi 12:1–2)

Isaiah's prophecies are given in order to lift the spirits of his people. The "word" (Hebrew, *davar*) may also be translated "thing" or "message." "Saw" (Hebrew, *khazah*) means "envisioned." Again, Isaiah's father, whose name is anglicized in the King James Version as Amoz, is not the same person as the prophet Amos, Isaiah's contemporary.

Isaiah received the word concerning Judah and Jerusalem, though there is actually very little about the rest of Judah in Isaiah; his focus is Jerusalem. So the word was for Judah and Jerusalem in his day, "*and* it shall come to pass *in the last days* . . ."—then and now indicates dual fulfillment.

In verse 2 the italicized "that" in the King James Version is rendered "when" in the Book of Mormon, which more properly fits the context of the previous phrase. The word "mountain" is both a literal and figurative reference to the Temple of God. The mountain-temple connection in ancient Israel is well established. A common name for the Jerusalem Temple was *har ha-bayit,* "mountain of the house." Regarding the mountain abode of God and its relationship to the Temple, see Psalm 68:16; Isaiah 8:18; Doctrine and Covenants 84:2–4; 133:12–13. Mountains were among God's first Temples. Through the ages prophets have had glorious, revelatory experiences on top of mountains, for example, Enoch (Moses 7:2–4), the brother of Jared (Ether 3:1; 4:1), Moses (Moses 1:1, 27–28), Nephi (1 Nephi 18:3), and Peter, James, and John (Matthew 17:1, 9; D&C 63:21).

Isaiah's prophecies often focus on the place where God chose to put his name: the Temple (1 Kings 8:29; 9:3; 2 Kings 21:4; compare D&C 97:15; 109:26). The prophet saw the latter-day Temple (see chapter headnote), the "mountain of the Lord's house."

The Prophet Joseph Smith asked: "What was the object of gathering the Jews, or the people of God in any age of the world? . . . The main object was to build unto the Lord a house whereby He could reveal unto His people the ordinances of His house and the glories of His kingdom, and teach the people the way of salvation; for there are certain ordinances and principles that, when they are taught and practiced, must be done in a place or house built for that purpose" (*History of the Church*, 5:423).

This passage of Isaiah can have multiple meanings:

1. The Salt Lake Temple in the Rocky Mountains. President Wilford Woodruff mentioned this Isaiah passage in the Salt Lake Temple dedicatory prayer (*Discourses of Wilford Woodruff*, 337)
2. The New Jerusalem Temple in Independence, Missouri (D&C 57:1–3 and headnote)
3. The Old Jerusalem Temple (D&C 133:12–13)

Elder Bruce R. McConkie wrote: "Thus Israel gathers for the purpose of building temples in which the ordinances of salvation and exaltation are performed for the living and the dead. And thus it comes as no surprise to find the ancient prophets speaking of the temples of the Most High and doing it in the setting of the gathering of Israel. 'And it shall come to pass in the last days,' saith Isaiah, 'that the mountain of the Lord's house shall be established in the top of the mountains, and shall be exalted above the hills; and all nations shall flow unto it.' This has specific reference to the Salt Lake Temple and to the other temples built in the top of the Rocky Mountains, and it has a general reference to the temple yet to be built in the New Jerusalem in Jackson County, Missouri. Those in all nations, be it noted, shall flow to the houses of the Lord in the tops of the mountains, there to make the covenants out of which eternal life comes" (*New Witness*, 539).

Mountain may also mean meeting place as well as holy place. Compare Nephi's experience in the mountain, where the Lord showed him "great things" (1 Nephi 18:3). In a metaphorical sense, *mountain* may also mean nation or people (see commentary at Isaiah 2:12–18). An alternate translation of verse 2, then, may be "when the nation of the Lord's house shall be established as the head of the nations."

"All nations" shall flow unto it, that is, many people from all nations. The Lord's House will be a means of unifying the peoples of the earth. In his House "all nations" may learn the mysteries of his kingdom.

Isaiah 2:3 (2 Nephi 12:3)

"Let us go up to the mountain of the Lord"—in sacred high places God teaches us of his ways, how to walk in the path to godhood.

Two Jerusalems—two headquarters—are clearly indicated (compare 3 Nephi 20) using what biblical literary scholars call synthetic or complimentary parallelism, suggesting two places. Modern prophets have explained that there are multiple fulfillments of this passage; see also, later in Isaiah, "thy holy cities . . . Zion [and] . . . Jerusalem" (64:10).

Several definitions of Zion have been suggested by modern prophets and apostles. Some indicate that "out of Zion shall go forth the law [teaching, doctrine]" through general conferences from the current headquarters.

President Harold B. Lee wrote: "I have often wondered what that expression meant, that out of Zion should go forth the law. Years ago I went with the brethren to the Idaho Falls Temple, and I heard in that inspired prayer of the First Presidency a definition of the meaning of that term 'out of Zion shall go forth the law.' Note what they said: 'We thank thee that thou hast revealed to us that those who gave us our constitutional form of government were men wise in thy sight and that thou didst raise them up for the very purpose of putting forth that sacred document [the Constitution of the United States; see D&C 101:80]. . . .

"'We pray that kings and rulers and the peoples of all nations under heaven may be persuaded of the blessings enjoyed by the people of this land by reason of their freedom and under thy guidance and be constrained to adopt similar governmental systems, thus to fulfill the ancient prophecy of Isaiah [and Micah] that " . . . out of Zion shall go forth the law and the word of the Lord from Jerusalem"'" (*Teachings of Harold B. Lee*, 377).

The Prophet Joseph Smith explained: "You know there has been great discussion in relation to Zion—where it is, and where the gathering of the dispensation is, and which I am now going to tell you. The prophets have spoken and written upon it; but I will make a proclamation that will cover a broader ground. The whole of America is Zion itself from north to south, and is described by the Prophets, who declare that it is the Zion where the mountain of the Lord should be, and that it should be in the center of the land. When Elders shall take up and examine the old prophecies in the Bible, they will see it" (*History of the Church,* 6:318–19).

Zion is also defined as the city of the living God, the New Jerusalem (D&C 76:66; 84:2; 133:12–13; see also Ogden and Skinner, *Book of Mormon,* 1:144–45.).

In summary, the law of the Lord may go forth out of Zion through worldwide broadcasts of the Church's general conferences, through passage of constitutional laws out of the United States of America, and through preaching God's word to all the world from all of the Americas, and specifically from Zion, the New Jerusalem (on Zion, the New Jerusalem, see further commentary at Isaiah 52:8–10; 54:11–12; Malachi 3:1–4).

Isaiah 2:4–5 (2 Nephi 12:4–5)

Swords, spears, plowshares, and pruning hooks represent instruments of war and peace. There will be an abrupt change from present political machinations: no more war! In preparing for that great day, we as individual members of the kingdom should also beat our swords of personal revenge into the plowshares of peaceful reconciliation. The work of the Prince of Peace is to bring peace to nations and to individuals.

The word "come" in verse 5 is a gentle invitation to walk in the Light, to walk with him.

Isaiah 2:6–22 (2 Nephi 12:6–22)

These verses summarize the basic spiritual problems that troubled ancient Israel and that will prevail again before the Second Coming. Isaiah knew what would plague people in the last days because he knew what was afflicting Judah in his day. He knew basic human nature, or the nature of fallen man, and he knew the consistent strategies, themes, and tools that Satan uses to carry out his aims. For example, some seek after the philosophies of men and set God at naught. Setting God *at naught* means ignoring, disregarding, avoiding, rejecting, disobeying, and reviling against him, deeming him worthless—not important to us (see 1 Nephi 19:7, 9; 2 Nephi 28:16; 33:2; Helaman 4:21; 12:6; D&C 3:4).

Isaiah 2:7–8 (2 Nephi 12:7–8)

Some seek after material things. Materialism runs rampant. When people are full of the world, it is difficult to find place for God. There is no end of our "chariots" on the freeways. Could the prophet have envisioned a modern shopping mall with its myriads of stores and "treasures," the "work of their own hands"?

Isaiah 2:9–11 (2 Nephi 12:9–11)

The Book of Mormon changes the text: "The mean man boweth *not* down, and the great man humbleth himself *not*, therefore, forgive *him* not." Pride is always an obstacle to spiritual progress. As Malachi would later prophesy, at the Lord's second coming the proud and all that do wickedly shall be consumed as stubble (Malachi 4:1), and then the meek will inherit the earth—none of the proud will be around to contest the inheritance.

The Book of Mormon adds "O ye wicked ones" to begin verse 10.

The Lord alone will be exalted in that day (vv. 11, 17); verse 18 tells that idols are utterly abolished—the antithesis of the Lord being exalted. How the idols are disposed of is described in verse 20.

Isaiah 2:12–18 (2 Nephi 12:12–18)

The proud and lofty will be cut down in that day, the day of the Second Coming; cedars and oaks are symbolic of the proud and lofty. Mountains and towers are also symbols of the high and lofty. Second Nephi 12:14 adds: "and upon all the nations which are lifted up, and upon every people"—nations and people being parallel with mountains and hills.

The Greek Septuagint has one phrase from verse 16, and the traditional (Masoretic) Hebrew text the other phrase; but the Book of Mormon has both (see footnote 16*a*).

Isaiah 2:19–22 (2 Nephi 12:19–22)

The wicked flee from the God of righteousness. They separate themselves; they feel like hiding because of sins and the resultant guilt. Verse 22 counsels humans against trusting in the arm of flesh.

Isaiah 3 (2 Nephi 13)

In this chapter, historically speaking, Isaiah moved from prophesying about Ephraim's problems at the hands of the Assyrians to prophesying of Judah's and Jerusalem's demise at the hands of their oppressors, the Babylonians, beginning around 600 B.C. Verses 1–3 describe the deportation of Jerusalem's upper classes during the Babylonian siege under Jehoiachin (2 Kings 24:14–15). The second half of chapter 3 moves to a discussion of circumstances of the last days, with verse 11 perhaps being the transition. However, all of chapter 3 applies to our day as well.

Isaiah 3:1–4 (2 Nephi 13:1–4)

Economic prosperity is gone. Bread and water are both literal and symbolic, as Amos explained: "Not a famine of bread, nor a thirst for water, but of hearing the words of the Lord" (Amos 8:11). True leadership is also gone, with only incompetent leaders left.

Isaiah 3:5–7 (2 Nephi 13:5–7)

General collapse of social order ensues; lawlessness and insolence against elders, gangs of youth walking the busy streets with rebellion and violence, and families torn apart. The desperate condition of society is illustrated by the demand of one who has a simple article of clothing to rule over his peers.

Isaiah 3:8–11 (2 Nephi 13:8–11)

Note the use of future perfect tense verbs, as if future events and conditions are accomplished realities. The grammatical and prophetic use of the past tense in place of the future occurs when an action is "not yet completed but so viewed by the speaker. Hence he speaks as though it were already completed. A perfect of certainty even though not yet done in time" (Young, *Grammar of the Hebrew Language*, 184). This is frequent in the poetic discourse of prophets: compare Numbers 24:17; Isaiah 5:13; especially 9:1–6; also Genesis 15:15 and Judges 15:3.

"This is put when the speaker views the action as being as

good as done. This is very common in the Divine prophetic utterances: where, though the sense is literally future, it is regarded and spoken of as though it were already accomplished" (Bullinger, *Figures of Speech Used in the Bible*, 518).

Such use of the prophetic tense shows the absolute certainty of things spoken. "The great Jehovah contemplated the whole of the events connected with the earth, pertaining to the plan of salvation, before it rolled into existence . . . ; the past, the present, and the future were and are, with Him, one eternal 'now'" (*Joseph Smith* [manual], 406). The implications of this fact are staggering and must cause some of us to readjust our thinking. If God the Father knew of the certainty of the Savior's atoning act millennia before it physically occurred—and he did—it means that one aspect of the concept of predestination is true. All those who will be saved can be saved only through the Atonement of Jesus Christ (Ephesians 1:5). There is no other way.

Our ultimate objective, of course, is to have God's image engraven in our countenance (Alma 5:14, 19). Our outward appearance reflects our inner character. People are openly and willfully sinning, not even trying to hide it, as at Sodom; sin is visible in their faces. Immorality is blatantly promoted in society—then and now. Some actively endeavor to change laws to legalize, in order to facilitate, their sins and perversions.

The righteous and the wicked will always get what they deserve (D&C 29:27–28).

Isaiah 3:12 (2 Nephi 13:12)

President Ezra Taft Benson saw the fulfillment of this verse in our day: "Today the undermining of the home and family is on the increase, with the devil anxiously working to displace the father as the head of the home and create rebellion among the children. The Book of Mormon describes this condition when it states, 'As for my people, children are their oppressors, and women rule over them.' And then these words follow—and consider these words seriously when you think of those political leaders who are promoting birth control and abortion: 'O my people, they which lead thee cause thee to err, and destroy the way of thy paths' (Isaiah 3:12; 2 Nephi 13:12)" (*Teachings of Ezra Taft Benson*, 541).

Isaiah 3:13–15 (2 Nephi 13:13–15)

The Lord will take the stand to accuse and prosecute the case against his people. Perhaps verse 15 refers to greedy and unconscionable institutions in the world today.

Isaiah 3:16–24 (2 Nephi 13:16–24)

After condemning the male leaders (Isaiah 3:1–15), the Lord turned to rebuke the "daughters of Zion." It is clear that he expected more of the women. The pride and haughtiness that goad men in their vain ambitions may be manifested in women through their outward adornment and apparel. If women are corrupt, society is inevitably suffering its death throes. Here are described the "flirtatious fashion slaves"—those who parade the "who's wearing what?" and "who's showing off what?" mentality, with their eyes painted and their bodies bedecked with ornaments (see Ezekiel 23:40). Name-brand clothes, earrings, nose rings, tongue rings, and other body piercings, expensive haircuts, tanning salons, and plastic surgery seem to be an obsession, greater than the lasting virtues of genuine womanhood. (However, an increasing number of males in modern culture are also obsessed with manipulating the human body. Such behavior is surely not expressive of the highest ideals of manhood either.) The Lord's first epithet is "haughty"; he goes on to explain in detail their offensive behavior.

Archaeologist Gabriel Barkay's 1986 report of his excavations along the west side of Jerusalem's Hinnom Valley describes findings from the richest sepulchre opened:

"The abundant jewelry found in the tomb provides the first material evidence to support the frequent allusion in the Bible to the wealth of Jerusalem during the First Temple period. Isaiah had mocked the ostentation of Jerusalem's society ladies when he wrote: 'On that day the Lord will take away the finery of their anklets, the head bands and their crescents; the pendants, the bracelets and the scarfs; the headdresses, the armlets, the sashes, the perfume boxes and the amulets; the rings and the nose jewels.' The tomb produced six gold items and 95 silver items as well as jewelry made of rare stones, glass and faience—many of them of great beauty including earrings, rings, beads and pendants. This is the first time that a representative selection of jewelry worn by the women of Jerusalem at the end of the First Temple period forms part of an archaeological assemblage" (*Jerusalem Post Magazine*, July 18, 1986, 11).

The women are concerned about their physical appearance, and they are devoted to drawing attention to it. The word "wanton" in verse 16 means excessive, unrestrained, licentious. These "daughters of Zion" were also types of the future, as indicated by "in that day" in verse 18, meaning the last days. Their immodesty will result in total indecent and inhumane exposure.

In the vanity and merriment of debauchery, health is destroyed, and social diseases result.

Isaiah 3:25–4:1 (2 Nephi 13:25–14:1)

Note that in the Hebrew text and in the Joseph Smith Translation, Isaiah 4:1 is the last verse in chapter 3, where it properly fits.

War reduces the male population; women want to remove the reproach of barrenness and childlessness. Lacking seed (offspring) is deemed a curse.

President Wilford Woodruff recorded the following vision: "I had been reading the revelations . . . [when] a strange stupor came over me. . . . I arose to speak and said . . . I will answer you right here what is coming to pass shortly. . . . I then looked in all directions . . . and I found the same mourning in every place throughout the Land. It seemed as though I was above the earth, looking down to it as I passed along on my way east and I saw the roads full of people principally women with just what they could carry in bundles on their backs . . . It was remarkable to me that there were so few men among them. . . . Wherever I went I saw . . . scenes of horror and desolation rapine and death . . . death and destruction everywhere. I cannot paint in words the horror that seemed to encompass me around. It was beyond description or thought of man to conceive. I supposed that this was the End but I was here given to understand, that the same horrors were being enacted all over the country . . . Then a voice said 'Now shall come to pass that which was spoken by Isaiah the Prophet 'That seven women shall take hold of one man saying [. . . and so forth]'" (Journal of Wilford Woodruff, June 15, 1878; in Ludlow, *Isaiah*, 109).

Elder Bruce R. McConkie wrote: "'And in that day'—the millennial day—'seven women shall take hold of one man, saying, We will eat our own bread, and wear our own apparel: only let us be called by thy name, to take away our reproach,' the reproach of being without a husband, without children, without a family of their own. This shall come to pass after the destruction of the wicked, and it is one of many scriptural intimations that the generality of women are more spiritual than are most men. The inference is that far more women will abide the day of his coming than will be the case with men. And they, being clean and upright, and desiring family units and children and the exaltation that grows out of all these things, will turn to the marriage discipline of Abraham their father so they may be blessed like Sarah of old" (*Millennial Messiah*, 655).

Isaiah 4 (2 Nephi 14)

At the end of time come the promised reinstatement, restoration, and redemption.

Isaiah 4:1–3 (2 Nephi 14:1–3)

The branch of the Lord and the fruit of the earth symbolize the Messiah himself and people who live under his rule during the millennial era. His people, the remnant of Israel, are a holy people living in a holy city in a holy land—all of which means, in the Hebrew expression, that they will be a people of holiness living in a city of holiness in a land of holiness, with the Holy One of Israel reigning among them. Those who remain to live into this glorious era are the elect, those whose names are written in the Lamb's book of life (see Topical Guide and Bible Dictionary, "Book of Life").

Isaiah 4:4 (2 Nephi 14:4)

Note the strong wording: the Lord has to cleanse the *filth* of the daughters of Zion and purge the blood on the hands of his people (Isaiah 1:15). The people are "washed" as with the fuller's "soap" and purged by "burning" as with the refiner's "fire." Purification comes by the spirit of burning, or as we sing, "The Spirit of God like a Fire Is Burning" (*Hymns*, 2); the Spirit, the Holy Ghost, cleanses and burns away evil waste.

A watchtower in Samaria. "My wellbeloved hath a vineyard in a very fruitful hill: And he fenced it, and gathered out the stones thereof, and planted it with the choicest vine, and built a tower in the midst of it" (Isaiah 5:1–2)

Isaiah 4:5–6 (2 Nephi 14:5–6)

On the "cloud [of] smoke" and "flaming fire," compare the cloud of smoke and fire that guided and protected the Israelites in Sinai (Exodus 13:21–22). The second image signaling protection for the righteous is a tabernacle (the Hebrew word means "booth") in the vineyard, providing shade from the harsh summer sun and cover from the pounding winter rains. The two figures depict the total safety and comfort—in all seasons, under all conditions—for those deserving of God's watchful care.

Isaiah 5 (2 Nephi 15)

Isaiah wrote this song (vv. 1–7), which is an allegory of the Lord's vineyard—the land of Israel. (Whereas a parable is an expanded simile, an allegory is an expanded metaphor, a series of implied comparisons.) Compare 2 Samuel 12:1–8 and Matthew 21:33–45; the meaning is hidden until the end, which is more effective than direct accusation.

192

Isaiah 5:1–4 (2 Nephi 15:1–4)

The Lord protected his vineyard by fencing it, and he gathered out the stones, or evicted the wicked previous tenants. He planted it with the finest, choicest plants (his covenant people of Israel; see also Jeremiah 2:21). The Lord does all he can, but moral agency is guaranteed; some choose to be wild.

What more could have been done? (The same question is asked in Jacob 5:41.) We have a courtroom scene again; this is a pleading question.

Isaiah 5:5–6 (2 Nephi 15:5–6)

Resultant curses are listed: the protective hedges and walls around his vineyard are broken down and removed, and thorns and thistles replace them. The clouds will release no rain upon the land. The ancients knew that rain came not from the sky but from heaven; spiritual rain was revelation, necessary to keep them spiritually alive (compare Deuteronomy 11:8–17).

Isaiah 5:7 (2 Nephi 15:7)

The interpretation of the allegory includes the use of paronomasia (a play on words). In Hebrew: "he looked for *mishpat*, but behold *mishpakh*; for *tsdakah*, but behold *ts'akah*." In English: "he looked for *equity*, but behold *iniquity*; for a *righteous nation*, but behold *lamentation*" (Bullinger, *Figures of Speech Used in the Bible*, 313).

Isaiah 5:8–12 (2 Nephi 15:8–12)

These verses describe the ills in society. The religious establishment must have considered Isaiah's prophecy as rank heresy, and the political establishment, as treason. But Isaiah spoke the truth, and the truth was painful—to him as well as to the people.

Verse 8: greed in acquisition of real estate, especially the wealthy taking from the poor

Verse 9: desolated lands and properties

Verse 10: unproductive lands and properties

Verse 11: drunkenness, riotous living

Verse 12: musical revelry (compare Amos 6:5–6 and Isaiah 24:8–9)

Isaiah 5:13 (2 Nephi 15:13)

The nation is taken captive and destroyed because of lack of knowledge (compare Hosea 4:6). The people were famished and thirsty because they had not turned to the Bread of Life and the Living Water (compare again Amos's famine and thirst for hearing the word of the Lord in Amos 8:11). The Lord's people, of their own will and choice, were suffering from spiritual malnutrition. In our present world, which is virtually overflowing with knowledge—with the Internet and all the universal, sophisticated information and communication systems and devices—we are, ironically, dying from a widespread famine of spiritual knowledge.

Isaiah 5:14–19 (2 Nephi 15:14–19)

Doom is proclaimed through a host of woes and judgments.

Verse 14: A gaping hell (Hebrew, *sheol*, "death and spirit prison") awaits the rebels to swallow them up.

Verses 15–16: This is the same message as Isaiah 2:11, 17; 2 Nephi 12:11, 17.

Verse 17: The once-flourishing vineyard has become mere grazing land.

Verse 18: When we willingly tie ourselves to our sins (like beasts tied to their burdens), it is difficult to later free or disentangle ourselves from those sins. "Whosoever committeth sin is the servant of sin" (John 8:34). Sin is a slave driver, and it is oppressive; 2 Peter 3:3–4 calls such people "scoffers."

Verse 19: Hypocrisy and sarcasm are offered by individuals who seem to say, "Fine. Let this 'Holy One of Israel' bring on his work—so we can see and know for sure."

Isaiah 5:20 (2 Nephi 15:20)

A critical purpose of this earth life is to learn to distinguish between good and evil. Some people in the world are working hard at blurring our view of what is right and what is wrong. There *are* moral absolutes. Woe to those who call evil good, and good evil (see 2 Nephi 28:20). Examples are plentiful. Some claim that marriage is unnecessary; that homosexual relations are normal; premarital and extramarital sex are expected; movies and magazines glamorize and celebrate infidelity; pornography destroys sacred marital and family relationships with grossly cheap substitutes;

and abortion is justified and even encouraged ("pro-choice" advocates presume to do a noble service in protecting and preserving women's rights). So much of what we call enlightenment is really the opposite—darkness. Much of our sophistication is really degradation.

On a very personal level, this verse is a stark warning. God knows what we know. He knows what is in our hearts, our intentions. Baptized members of the Church cannot rationalize wrong behavior on the grounds of ignorance or political correctness. President Spencer W. Kimball said, "I challenge any normal baptized person who says he did not know he was doing wrong" (*Love versus Lust*, 7).

Isaiah 5:21–25 (2 Nephi 15:21–25)

Compare verse 21 to 2 Nephi 9:28–29.

Verse 22: It is ironic that Judah's men of valor were mighty not in the battle but in the bottle.

Verse 23: They acquit the wicked for a bribe, and deny justice to the innocent.

Verse 24: Isaiah eloquently illustrates from nature the dire consequences of Israel's rejection of the law and the word of their God. Just as the weed or waste part of the grain is consumed by fire, so Israel's root—from which all the rest of the tree is supposed to receive nourishment—is full of rotten decay, and therefore its blossoms (its potential for fruit) are blown away by the winds of corruption. A later prophet similarly described the tragedy: "For behold, the day cometh, that shall burn as an oven; and all the proud, yea, and all that do wickedly, shall be stubble . . . that it shall leave them neither root nor branch" (Malachi 4:1).

Verse 25: The Lord was angry with them and had smitten them with drought, famine, plague, pestilence, earthquake, and war (Amos 4:6–11). "For all this his anger is not turned away, but his hand is stretched out still" (see commentary at Isaiah 9:8–14).

Isaiah 5:26–30 (2 Nephi 15:26–30)

Hope is proclaimed ("in that day," the last days).

Ensign means "standard" or "banner," something to rally around. The gospel and the Book of Mormon are to hiss forth (2 Nephi 29:2; Moroni 10:28). In the scriptures the word "hiss" is sometimes used to express ideas or feelings in a negative, condemnatory way, but in this case it signifies the dissemination of God's truth as a blessing—to serve and save the souls of men. For hissing forth through missionary work, see Doctrine and Covenants 115:5–6. Zion will be a refuge from the storm (compare Isaiah 4:5–6).

"They [the missionaries] shall come with speed swiftly." Does a swift journey suggest travel by jet aircraft?

Elder LeGrand Richards, a great apostle-missionary ministering twenty-seven centuries after Isaiah, gave these verses a prophetic application in modern days: "Since there were no such things as trains and airplanes in that day, Isaiah could hardly have mentioned them by name, but he seems to have described them in unmistakable words. How better could 'their horses' hoofs be counted like flint, and their wheel like a 'whirlwind' than in the modern train? How better could 'Their roaring . . . be like a lion' than in the roar of the airplane? Trains and airplanes do not stop for night. Therefore, was not Isaiah justified in saying 'none shall slumber nor sleep; neither shall the girdle of their loins be loosed, nor the latchet of their shoes be broken'? With this manner of transportation the Lord can really 'hiss unto them from the end of the earth,' that 'they shall come with speed swiftly'" (*Marvelous Work and a Wonder*, 230).

Isaiah 5:28–30 (2 Nephi 15:28–30)

"Whose arrows are sharp, and all their bows bent." Could this be an airplane from top or bottom view? Arrows, bows, horses, and prey depict war imagery. We often sing about a battle that is raging in this world: "Behold! A Royal Army," "Hope of Israel, Zion's Army," "Onward, Christian Soldiers," "We Are All Enlisted," and "We Are Marching On to Glory" (*Hymns*, nos. 251, 259, 246, 250, 225).

"Prey" may mean converts. Note that the missionary lions are out to rescue the prey from their enemy, to carry them away to safety.

Darkness reigns because the children of light depart, and the Lord withholds his light because of wickedness.

Isaiah 7 (2 Nephi 17)

To understand this chapter of Isaiah, it is essential to read or review 2 Kings 15:27–17:24. Those verses contain important background material to the historical and political events recounted here.

Isaiah 7:1–7 (2 Nephi 17:1–7)

"In the days of Ahaz" means about 735 B.C. onward. The nations, capitals, and rulers involved are as follows:

Nation (alternate name)	Capital	Ruler
Judah	Jerusalem	Ahaz
Israel (Ephraim)	Samaria	Pekah, son of Remaliah
Syria (Aram)	Damascus	Rezin

See these place-names on Bible Maps 9 and 10.

Syria and Israel had formed a coalition to block the armies of the Assyrian Tiglath-pileser III as they advanced westward. They wanted Judah to join also, but Ahaz refused. Syria and Israel then decided to march on Jerusalem and replace Ahaz with a man of their own persuasion. Verse 2 says King Ahaz's "heart was moved" or shaken.

Isaiah 7:3 (2 Nephi 17:3)

Shear-jashub means "the remnant shall return," which was a prophecy at the time of Isaiah's call (see Isaiah 6:13). This is a familiar motif throughout Isaiah: despite the forthcoming exile, a remnant would return to the promised land to accomplish the Lord's purposes (see for example, Isaiah 10:20–22 // 2 Nephi 20:20–22).

"The end of the conduit of the upper pool in the highway of the fuller's field" meant either at the Gihon Spring or to the south near the one-time spring called En-rogel (now a well; see Bible Map 12). The fuller needed water for his work of cleaning and whitening cloth.

Isaiah 7:4–7 (2 Nephi 17:4–7)

The bold prophet commanded the king not to worry about the two kingdoms to the north, the "smoking firebrands." If they are smoking, then their fire is out. The political ploy of Israel and Syria against Judah would not be accomplished; it would fail.

Isaiah 7:8 (2 Nephi 17:8)

Prophecy: Within sixty-five years, the northern tribes of Israel would be scattered.

Fulfillment: By 733–32 B.C. northeast Israel and trans-jordanian Israel were exiled; by 722–21 B.C. the rest of the kingdom of Israel was exiled to Assyria, and even scattered beyond there (what we often call the "lost ten tribes"). This twelve-year period was the time when the Galilee region of the Holy Land was cleaned out by the Assyrians. Most of Israel was taken away, and foreign populations imported. This is significant because of the messianic prophecy in Isaiah 9 (2 Nephi 19):1–3, which describes the religious "darkness" that engulfed the region of Galilee for a long time.

Isaiah 7:9 (2 Nephi 17:9)

Again, paronomasia is used—a prophetic play on words: "If ye will not believe [*im lo taaminu*], surely ye shall not be established [*lo teamenu*]." In English the play on words could be: "If ye will not understand, ye shall not . . . stand" or, "If ye have no belief, . . . ye shall have no relief" or, "No confiding, no abiding" (Bullinger, *Figures of Speech Used in the Bible*, 313).

Isaiah 7:10–13 (2 Nephi 17:10–13)

Ahaz was told, as a command, to ask for a sign (meaning an evidence or spiritual confirmation). He rejected the prophecy, and would not trust the Lord. Why wouldn't he? He either didn't care, as "Esau [who] despised his birthright" (Genesis 25:34), or else he didn't want the Lord interfering with his political plans to ally with Assyria. Ahaz intentionally set himself up as wiser and more politically astute than God.

"And he [Isaiah] said . . . Is it a small thing for you to weary men [meaning himself, Isaiah], but will ye weary my God also?" A more colloquial translation would be, "O house of David! is it not enough to try the patience of men, but will you try the patience of God also?"

Old Testament scholar Franz Delitzsch wrote: "He [King Ahaz] studiously brought down upon himself the fate denounced in [Isaiah 6 // 2 Nephi 16], and indeed not upon himself only, but upon all Judah as well. For after a few years the forces of [Assyria] would stand upon the same fuller's field . . . and demand the surrender of Jerusalem. In that very hour, in which Isaiah was standing before Ahaz, the fate of Jerusalem was decided for more than two thousand years" (*Prophecies of Isaiah*, 1:215).

Biblical scholar Edward Young wrote: "Ahaz' wickedness is seen in the fact that by his stubbornness he was in fact rejecting the very foundation of the covenant. God had promised to be a God and a Deliverer to His people. Syria and Israel, therefore, will not overthrow the Davidic dynasty, for if they could succeed in so doing, the promises of God would be rendered void and salvation would not ultimately be accomplished through the Messiah. In effect, Ahaz, by his refusal, is asserting that God is not faithful to His promise" (*Book of Isaiah*, 1:283–84).

Isaiah 7:14–15 (2 Nephi 17:14–15)

Messianic prophecy: The apostle Matthew understood these verses to be a foreshadowing of Jesus. Historically it may have been talking about Isaiah's wife (Isaiah 8:3) who bore him a second son, but Matthew was inspired to see its eternal import. The phrase "a virgin" is Hebrew *ha-alma*, or, in English, "the [note the definite article] young woman," though *ha-alma* appears to be the only Hebrew noun that definitely applies to an *unmarried woman*. The Septuagint, the Old Testament in Greek, renders the word "virgin," and the New Testament and the Book of Mormon both refer to her as a virgin. She shall conceive, and bear a son. If the birth is not a miraculous virgin birth, given as a sign, then what is so unusual about a young woman having a son? The prophecy clearly suggests miraculous and divine intervention to ensure its accomplishment (see Ogden and Skinner, *Book of Mormon*, 1:51–53).

Fulfillment: There are at least two possibilities for interpreting this messianic prophecy. First, in the spirit of 2 Nephi 11:4—all things are the typifying of Jesus Christ—a young woman in

Isaiah's day (possibly his wife, the "prophetess"), bears a son, who is given a symbolic name, Immanuel, meaning "God [is] with us," thus prophesying that God himself would come down, or condescend, to dwell among mortals (Isaiah 8:8, 10). The young woman in Isaiah's day becomes a type of the young virgin in Nazareth (compare Hosea and his wife being a type, or similitude, of the Lord and his people; also compare the language of verses 14 and 16 to 8:3–4).

Or, second, this is a direct prophecy of the virgin Mary and God the Father having a Son, Jesus (Matthew 1:23; Luke 1:27; 1 Nephi 11:13–20; Alma 7:10).

Butter (curds, yogurt) and honey are symbolic of a humble diet.

Isaiah 7:16–25 (2 Nephi 17:16–25)

These final verses of the chapter contain the word of the Lord concerning contemporary events.

Isaiah 7:16 (2 Nephi 17:16)

Prophecy: "Before the child [or *a* child] shall know to refuse the evil, and choose the good [possibly an idiomatic reference to the age of accountability, that is, within eight years], the land that thou abhorrest shall be forsaken of both her kings."

Fulfillment: Syria and Israel were plundered, and both Pekah and Rezin were killed within three years.

Isaiah 7:17 (2 Nephi 17:17)

The nation of Judah would eventually have a Redeemer, but the king of Judah will imminently have a destroyer—the king of Assyria. What Ahaz wanted is what he got.

"The day that Ephraim departed from Judah" was in the mid-tenth century before Christ, at the division of Solomon's kingdom into north and south.

Prophecy: "The Lord shall bring upon thee . . . the king of Assyria."

Fulfillment: Sennacherib laid siege to Judah and Jerusalem in 701 B.C.

Isaiah 7:18–19 (2 Nephi 17:18–19)

Judah was a bone of contention between Egypt (the fly, *zebub*) and Assyria (the bee, *dvorah*); they would swarm all over Israel. An attacking bee can sting, and a fly can carry plague.

Isaiah 7:20 (2 Nephi 17:20)

Isaiah used a metaphor to indicate that the Lord would use Assyria as an instrument of his chastisement against his chosen but wayward people. By making an alliance and paying tribute to Assyria, Ahaz hired the razor called Assyria to cut off Syria and Israel. The Lord then used the same razor to cut off part of the people of Judah. Shaving captives is symbolic of humiliation, but it is also literal: cutting off the beard was a sign of degradation to Israelites (compare 2 Samuel 10:4–5); "the hair of the *feet*" in the Hebrew text is hair of the *legs*, a euphemism for the genital area.

Isaiah 7:21–25 (2 Nephi 17:21–25)

The once prosperous agricultural land will be overrun by briers and thorns and serve only as grazing land.

Isaiah had prophesied that if the people ("ye"; plural, vv. 9, 13) did not believe and hearken, they would not be established permanently in the land, though he made it clear that Judah would not be totally destroyed. A remnant would return to the land and to their God, for the Messiah would come through Judah, which was comforting assurance of their destiny despite the temporary setbacks.

Isaiah 8 (2 Nephi 18)

Isaiah gave more messianic prophecies and prophecies for his own day.

Isaiah 8:1–3 (2 Nephi 18:1–3)

The name of Isaiah's child (the longest proper name in the Old Testament) means "quick to the plunder, swift to the spoil," referring to the speed of the Assyrian destruction of Syria and Israel. The imminent future of Jerusalem was parallel to the city's future in the meridian of time, which Isaiah foreshadowed in the previous chapter.

The two "witnesses" were two apparently well-known,

Isaiah's vision of Jesus' birth. "Moreover the Lord said unto me, Take thee a great roll, and write in it with a man's pen . . . And I took unto me faithful witnesses to record, Uriah the priest, and Zechariah the son of Jeberechiah" (Isaiah 8:1–2)

prominent citizens, Uriah and Zechariah. The names in Hebrew mean "my light is Jehovah" and "remember Jehovah," respectively. "The prophetess," in this case at least, was the prophet's wife and not necessarily a prophetic office.

Isaiah 8:4 (2 Nephi 18:4)

"As in [Isaiah] 7:15, 16 the infancy of the Messiah was made the measure of the time that Judah would suffer from her two adversaries, so here the infancy of Maher-shalal-hash-baz is made the measure of the time that would elapse before the king of Assyria would devastate Damascus and Syria. . . .

"There is thus a formal relationship between the two prophecies. There is, however, an even deeper relationship. Men could verify the prophecy concerning Isaiah's son; they could witness its fulfillment. It would thus become as it were a pledge or earnest of the prophecy of the virgin's Son. Seeing that Maher-shalal-hash-baz had been born in accordance with the prophecy, they could be sure that in His own good time God would fulfill the promise concerning the virgin, and that she would bear a son" (Young, *Book of Isaiah*, 1:303, 304).

Prophecy: "Behold, the child shall not have knowledge to cry, My father [*Abi,* 'Daddy'], and my mother [*Imi,* 'Mommy'], [an idiom meaning two or three years, or a short time], before the riches of Damascus and the spoil of Samaria shall be taken away before the king of Assyria" (JST Isaiah 8:4).

Fulfillment: Damascus was conquered in 732 B.C. Samaria was besieged in 733 and then destroyed in 721 B.C. The prophecy was literally fulfilled (2 Kings 16:9; 15:29–30).

Isaiah 8:5–8 (2 Nephi 18:5–8)

After the fall of the northern kingdom of Israel, the prophet turned to the fate of Judah. Water is life in the land of Shiloah (or Shiloh, the Messiah), and the people of Judah rejected their source of life. Jerusalem's water supply was the Gihon Spring, and the waters "that go softly" may refer to the channel that flows from that spring and waters the Kidron Valley. Instead of rejoicing in the Lord, Judah rejoiced only in the defeat of her two enemies to the north.

Contrast the "waters of Shiloah that go softly" (the blessings of the Lord) with the "strong and many" waters (the flooding Euphrates, which symbolizes the destructions of the Assyrian army).

After the flooding waters reach to the neck, the image abruptly changes to the outspread wings of a bird of prey.

Calling the land by the name of Immanuel amounts to calling it the land of Jehovah, or the land of the Lord, who is Jesus. Again, Immanuel means "God with us."

Isaiah 8:9–10 (2 Nephi 18:9–10)

Just as destruction was assured by the symbolic name of Isaiah's child, deliverance was assured by the symbolic name of the virgin's Child. Salvation from all enemies, mortal and spiritual, is available only when God is with us, "*Immanuel.*"

Isaiah 8:11–18 (2 Nephi 18:11–18)

Instructions are given to Isaiah and to Judah.

Verses 12–13: Judah must not rely on alliances with foreign powers for safety but rely on the Lord and reverence him.

Verses 14–15: The Lord can be a sanctuary, but he can also be a stone of stumbling, a rock of offence, for both houses of Israel (Israel and Judah). For similar descriptions in the writings of Peter, Paul, and Jacob, see 1 Peter 2:8; Romans 9:33; 1 Corinthians 1:23; and Jacob 4:15.

Verse 16: The testimony is the book of the Prophets, and the law is the Torah, or five books of Moses. Together the testimony and the law constitute the scriptures (see also v. 20). Isaiah was to write down and seal up his own witness account.

Verses 17–18: Isaiah trusted in the Lord. He and his family were "for signs and for wonders" to the house of Israel; they constituted a message from God in the form of a similitude or a type—just as Abraham and Isaac were types of the Father and Son, and Hosea and his unfaithful wife were types of the Lord and his unfaithful people. The prophet's name, *Isaiah,* signified that salvation was in Jehovah, *Shear-jashub* meant that a remnant of Judah would return following the chastisement of exile, and *Maher-shalal-hash-baz* foreshadowed the imminent and speedy destruction of a large part of Israel.

"The Lord of hosts . . . dwelleth in mount Zion"—the House of the Lord was on Mount Zion, or the Temple Mount.

Isaiah 8:19 (2 Nephi 18:19)

Seeking God was commendable, of course, but not through diabolical mediums. In times of crisis certain men of Judah were advocating turning to soothsayers and diviners for answers and help, rather than to the Lord's prophets. There are "witches of Endor" in all ages—those who suppose they can approach God through spiritualism instead of spirituality.

"For the living to hear from the dead?" may also be rendered, "Why consult the dead on behalf of the living?" Should we not turn to the Lord's living prophets?

Isaiah 8:20 (2 Nephi 18:20)

Recall verse 16: The scriptures are the canon or standard by which we should measure the worth of all things. If our sources of information and influence do not measure up to what is written in the scriptures, it must be "because there is no light in them." Thus, verse 20 outlines the first test of any revelation: Does it speak the word of the Lord; is it filled with light? A second test: Is it in harmony with the teachings of the only man on earth called and authorized to speak for the Lord in everything—the president of the Church? (D&C 43:1–7; 132:7). A third test: Does it come by the Holy Ghost, and can it be felt in the heart? (2 Nephi 33:1; D&C 50:17, 23; 100:5–8).

Isaiah 8:21–22 (2 Nephi 18:21–22)

Members of the house of Israel would be taken captive, be hard-pressed and hungry, and in their distress, as they looked upward, they would blame and curse their king and their God. And as they looked downward, they would find no consolation on the earth—only trouble, darkness, and anguish; only gloom and depression.

Isaiah 9:1 (2 Nephi 19:1)

This verse belongs with chapter 8; it corresponds to 8:23 in the Hebrew Bible. During the period of trouble, darkness, and anguish, the tribal regions of Zebulun (the region around Nazareth) and Naphtali (the region of the Sea of Galilee) were afflicted by attacks from the Assyrian monarchs Tiglath-pileser III, Shalmaneser V, and Sargon II.

The "way of the sea" is called in Hebrew *Derekh HaYam* and in Latin *Via Maris,* the great international highway that passes along the Sea of Galilee and the Mediterranean. Why the Book of Mormon has "Red Sea" in this verse is not known.

"Beyond Jordan" in Hebrew is *Ever HaYarden,* or in Greek, *Perea.* "Galilee of the nations" is Hebrew *Galil HaGoyim,* or Galilee of the Gentiles, because it was formerly inhabited by non-covenant peoples.

Isaiah 9 (2 Nephi 19)

Some see fulfillment of this prophecy in Hezekiah, and others see it in some great Davidic figure before the Millennium, but consider the chapter headnote and footnotes, especially for verses 6–7. Isaiah is speaking of the coming Messiah.

Though the northern tribes of Zebulun, Naphtali, and others

would experience the dark affliction of captivity, being vexed by Assyrian kings, the prophet proclaimed that the people who walked in darkness would see a great light. After the severe, dark blow of foreign foes, a Light would come, a Child would be born, a Son would be given. Though the tribes of Israel were carried off and lost to Israelite history, the tribe of Judah would not be totally destroyed. A remnant must return to their homeland, for the Messiah was to come through Judah and be born in Bethlehem of Judah.

Isaiah 9:1–2 (2 Nephi 19:1–2)

Again, the land of Zebulun is Nazareth and vicinity. The land of Naphtali is the Sea of Galilee region. As a result of Assyria's invasion of northern Israel in 733 B.C., and again in 722 B.C., the Israelite peoples of these regions were deported and the areas repopulated with Gentiles who did not know the God of Israel or anything about the true Messiah. Hence, they walked in darkness. In the second or first centuries before Christ, Jews of a Davidic clan began resettling the region. Among this new Jewish population were the ancestors of Joseph and Mary. Mary's infant Son, Jesus, who was the Light of the world, the great light prophesied by Isaiah, thus was brought to the land of these Israelite tribes.

Messianic prophecy (using prophetic tense verbs as if already accomplished): The people who walked in the darkness of apostasy, those who lived in the land of the shadow of death (where the ancient armies of the Near East marched)—they are the people who will see the great Light, the Messiah.

Fulfillment: Jesus is the "great light" (Matthew 4:16).

Isaiah's description of "people that walked in darkness" and "dwell in the land of the shadow of death" refers not only to their living in the darkness of sin and apostasy but also to a very physical image. The Galilee is covered with dark volcanic basalt, spewed all over the region by several now-extinct volcanoes on the Golan, east of the lake, and the black stone casts a dark shadow across the land.

The people who dwell in the shadow of death are also all people who experience mortality, who live with the shadow of death hanging over them; it is a dark thing to us, able to be dispelled only by the Light of life.

Isaiah 9:3–5 (2 Nephi 19:3–5)

Second Nephi 19:3 and the Revised Standard Version of the Bible (following many ancient manuscripts) delete "not" in the second line of Isaiah 9:3. The Light brings an increase of joy to the people of Israel.

Reasons are given in verses 4–5 for the increase of joy spoken of. The yoke and staff and rod have been broken; the oppressors—enemy armies and sin—have been taken away.

The Book of Mormon deletes "as in the day of Midian" at the end of Isaiah 9:4. Perhaps Nephi saw little relevance in that phrase for his own people or for us in the future.

The battles that the hosts of Israel, God's people, are fighting, especially in these last days, certainly are "with confused noise."

Isaiah 9:6–7 (2 Nephi 19:6–7)

Isaiah exults in the coming of a royal son (or descendant) of David. The oppressors of Israel, the mortal antagonists and especially the dark foes of sin and death and hell, are ultimately taken away because a Child is born, a Son is given. Verses 4, 5, and 6 all begin with "For . . ."—these are all reasons for the rejoicing among God's people noted in verse 3. Verse 6 introduces the greatest cause for rejoicing ever given and is gloriously rendered in Handel's famous oratorio, *Messiah*.

The first line of verse 6 refers to the first coming of Jesus, but all the rest of verses 6 and 7 refer to the Second Coming. The full messianic mission of Jesus was known and prophesied long before his mortal birth; it has always been important to see that mission in its complete context, what the Messiah would accomplish in his first coming *and* in his second coming.

Messianic prophecy: A Child is born, a Son is given.

Fulfillment: Only Jesus, the Messiah, fulfills this prophecy. See footnotes and Topical Guide references for Isaiah 9:6–7: "Jesus Christ, Prophecies about"; "God, Manifestations of"; "Jesus Christ, Birth of"; "Jesus Christ, Divine Sonship"; "Jesus Christ, Authority of"; "Jesus Christ, Millennial Reign"; "Jesus Christ, Mission of"; "Jesus Christ, Power of"; and "Jesus Christ, Davidic Descent of."

Yet many in the scholarly world, having no belief in the possibility of prophetic preview and disavowing any divine design, regard Hezekiah as the fulfillment of this prophecy. But was Hezekiah a great light? the mighty God? the everlasting Father? the Prince of Peace? Was there *no end* to his government and peace? Was he on the throne of David with judgment and justice *forever*?

Hezekiah might in some other ways have been a *type* of the Messiah, but Hezekiah does not stand up to the description, nor could any mortal. This Son who was given to the people is unique. Take away the divine Sonship, and Christianity has no foundation.

On the title *Counsellor:* If people will turn to the Lord, *the* Counselor, or to his agent counselor, the ward bishop or branch president, they will be blessed. The Lord's celestial self-reparation package, called repentance, is better than all the earthly self-help and self-esteem-building seminars, recordings, and texts. In some situations, including pornography and other addictions, professional counselors are absolute necessities, along with full use of the gospel of Jesus Christ and his representatives. Jesus is also our counselor in a legal sense. He is our advocate with the Father. He will plead our case before him (1 John 2:1; D&C 29:5; 45:3; 110:4).

The name-title *the mighty God,* apart from all others, unquestionably defines the Subject of the whole prophecy. Despite the attempts of scholars to adjust the words to mean something like "one Mighty in Valor," possibly to accommodate some private interpretation of this great prophecy, there is no allowable digression from the meaning of *El gibbor*—it means "the mighty *God.*" God himself would one day come into the world as a Child.

On the title *everlasting Father:* Jesus Christ is both the Son *and* the Father—the Son because he was begotten by the Father and submitted to the will of the Father, but also the Father because he is the Creator or Father of the earth; he is the Father of our flesh because our flesh is made from the dust or elements of the earth, which he created; he is the God or Father of the Old Testament, the great Jehovah, and the Father or Author of our salvation; he has all the attributes of the Father; and by divine investiture he serves the role of the Father in all things relative to our salvation. By his sacrifice he became even more than our Savior, he became our covenant Father, and as we are spiritually reborn we become the children of Christ (Mosiah 5:7; 27:25; Ether 3:14; D&C 25:1; 34:3; 39:4).

On the title *Prince of Peace:* The Lord Jesus Christ is the personification of real peace; he leaves his kind of peace with us, not the world's kind of "peace" that is won at the negotiating table or on the battlefield (John 14:27). Jesus fulfilled the typology established thousands of years before his mortal life: the city to which he would eventually come was a place originally called Peace (*Shalem* or *Salem*), and the man who reigned and ministered there was Melchizedek ("King of Righteousness"), who was a type of the future Messiah and the first mortal referred to as "Prince of peace" (JST Genesis 14:33). For the present time, Melchizedek's name-title is substituted when we refer to the Savior's power—the priesthood—out of reverence for the name of the Son of God. The Melchizedek Priesthood is the power by which all peace is established. The Prince of Peace came in the meridian of time to the City of Peace (*Uru Shalem,* or Jerusalem) but was rejected. Since then, there has been no lasting peace in that place. He will come again, and he will establish enduring peace for all lovers of peace to enjoy.

Some years ago on a BBC television program, renowned Christian theologians were interviewed, followed by Elie Wiesel, the Nobel Prize–winning Jewish author. Asked about Christianity, Wiesel quipped, "One thing we know. When Messiah comes there will be peace; Jesus came, and there is no peace" (in Harvey, Seminar on Christ). From that perspective, the Author of true Christianity is relegated to dismal failure due to lack of peace in this world. But Christ himself remonstrated, "Think not that I am come to send peace on earth: I came not to send peace, but a sword" (Matthew 10:34). Inherent in the great plan of happiness is a period of testing, when the war between good and evil—begun in the premortal world—continues, and the absence of total peace persists until the adversary is confined eternally to outer darkness and all flesh is brought under the Savior's dominion. The title "Prince of Peace" is, therefore, a prophecy of that millennial era, which assuredly will come.

On the expression "the throne of David," see Luke 1:32–33. Jesus, a direct descendant of David, was entitled to the throne of David, and his kingdom will last forever (see also Daniel 2:44*a*).

Isaiah 9:8–10:4 (2 Nephi 19:8–20:4)

Four evils among the people are denounced and four warnings pronounced.

Isaiah 9:8–14 (2 Nephi 19:8–14)

"The Lord sent *his* word" (2 Nephi 19:8) to Jacob, or Israel.

Evil number one: *pride.* Israelites felt confident that they could handle any losses and that they could rebuild. They had high regard for their own abilities and little regard for God. Enemies would gather against them.

Read verse 12 as if standing in the middle of the country, looking eastward: Syrians are "before," on the east, and Philistines are "behind," on the west.

Four times (in verses 12, 17, 21, and 20:4) Isaiah uses the following formulaic parallelism, almost as a chorus to his poetic pronouncement of condemnation:

> *For all this his anger is not turned away,*
> *but his hand is stretched out still.*

Is this synonymous parallelism (saying the same thing twice) or is it antithetic parallelism (saying the opposite), or could it be both kinds of parallelism? Footnote *d* to Isaiah 9:12 says: "In spite of all, the Lord is available if they will turn to him." However, the context of this parallel thought is that since the Lord's people are still unrepentant, his anger is still directed against them (see the previous occurrence also, in Isaiah 5:25). Bullinger indicates that the *hand stretched out* is an idiom, meaning "to send judgments upon," "to inflict punishment" (*Figures of Speech Used in the Bible,* 879). And verses 13–14 say: "the people turneth not unto him. . . . Therefore will the Lord cut off from Israel head and tail, branch and rush"—that is, great and small.

Perhaps this critical couplet is either synonymous or antithetic parallelism, with the two opposite meanings, *depending on the response of the people.* The Lord's hand, like his word, can be a sharp two-edged sword providing either protection and salvation or destruction and damnation. His hand is like a stone, which can be used to build or to crush. The Lord's hand may sometimes be construed as a hand offering relief, though here Isaiah seems to be describing the back of the Lord's hand slapping wrath against those who have rejected his open palm.

For the hand of justice, see Isaiah 5:25; 9:12, 17, 21; 10:4; 14:26–27. For the hand of mercy, see Isaiah 59:1–2; 65:1–2.

Isaiah 9:15–17 (2 Nephi 19:15–17)

Evil number two: *errant leaders.* Isaiah specified some who will be cut off. The words "and honourable" in Isaiah 9:15 are deleted in 2 Nephi 19:15 because there is nothing honorable about a devious leader.

Isaiah 9:18–21 (2 Nephi 19:18–21)

Evil number three: *wickedness* (spreading as a forest fire). Ugly scenes of civil and family strife are envisioned.

Isaiah 10 (2 Nephi 20)

The first part of this chapter identifies the fourth evil. Then Isaiah identifies the instruments the Lord will employ to inflict punishment for evil behavior in ancient days and in the last days.

Isaiah 10:1–4 (2 Nephi 20:1–4)

Evil number four: *neglecting the poor and the needy.* Verse 3 asks, "What will ye do in the day of visitation, and in the desolation which shall come from far?" The Hebrew word rendered "desolation" is *shoah,* meaning holocaust.

Isaiah 10:5–19 (2 Nephi 20:5–19)

Doom is pronounced. Note the irony that Israel's mortal enemy, Assyria, is being used to punish her. Just as the Lord used Lamanites as a scourge against the Nephites, to humble them and get them to repent and keep them in remembrance of him, so he would use the Egyptians, then the Assyrians, then the Babylonians (the Lord even called Nebuchadnezzar "my servant"; Jeremiah 27:6), and later the Romans and others to scourge his people for the same reasons in the Old World. Assyria would punish unfaithful Israel, but Assyria would also be punished (see commentary at Nahum 2–3). "Behold, the judgments of God will overtake the wicked; and it is by the wicked that the wicked are punished" (Mormon 4:5).

Isaiah 10:5–8 (2 Nephi 20:5–8)

The footnote of Isaiah 10:5 renders this verse in parallel form:

Assyria is the rod of my anger,
and my wrath is a staff in their hand.

The description in Isaiah 1:2–3 portrays Judah as a disobedient child; here the parent (the Lord) punishes the child with a whipping, and Assyria is the stick he uses (see Hayes and Irvine, *Isaiah, the Eighth-Century Prophet,* 196).

"To take the spoil, and to take the prey" is related to the symbolic name Isaiah and his wife gave their son, Maher-shalal-hash-baz (Isaiah 8:1–3). Assyrians did conquer and plunder Israel, but Assyria did not see itself as an instrument in God's hands; it boasted in its own power to overthrow many nations.

Isaiah 10:9–11 (2 Nephi 20:9–11)

The Lord was watching those who deserved punishment, the cities of Israel and Judah as well as other cities the Assyrians had conquered. Compare Amos 9:8: "Behold, the eyes of the Lord God are upon the sinful kingdom." Note also Assyria's arrogant attitude expressed in 2 Kings 18:33–35. Calno and Carchemish, Hamath and Arpad, Samaria and Damascus were all neighboring kingdoms destroyed by the Assyrians between 740 and 720 B.C.

Isaiah 10:12–14 (2 Nephi 20:12–14)

After Israel's exile, there was a scare also for Judah with the Assyrians' intent to humble the southern kingdom (Sennacherib's invasion in 701 B.C.). Finally, after administering justice to Jerusalem, insolent Assyria would also be punished. The Assyrian Empire, who had plucked unprotected eggs out of the nest of nations, had altered the borders of the nations more than any previous empire. And Judah could hardly make a peep or do anything about it.

Isaiah 10:15–16 (2 Nephi 20:15–16)

The ax, saw, rod, and staff are metaphors referring to the Lord's cutting Israel down, with Assyria serving as the tool he used. Regarding proud boasting, the Lord has said: "In nothing doth man offend God, or against none is his wrath kindled, save those who confess not his hand in all things, and obey not his commandments" (D&C 59:21).

"His fat ones" refers to the soldiers of the Assyrian king. "Under his glory" refers to the "glory" of the Assyrian. Kindling a "burning like the burning of a fire" could refer to, at least in part, the feverish plague in the Assyrian camp in the fateful year 701 B.C., when the Lord began to cut down the mighty empire.

Isaiah 10:17–19 (2 Nephi 20:17–19)

The Holy One of Israel, the "Light" and the "Fire" of Israel, can raise up a nation in a day, and he can destroy a nation in a day. The entire nation was not destroyed just yet, but the surviving members of the Assyrian army would be so few that a child could count them.

Isaiah 10:20–34 (2 Nephi 20:20–34)

Hope is proclaimed "in that day."

Verse 20: There will come a day when the remnant of Israel will cease relying on the arm of flesh and turn to the merciful arm of God. The remnant shall return, in truth. The Hebrew verb *lashuv* means both to return and to repent. The meaning of the Hebrew concept of repentance is to come back (to God).

Verse 21: "The remnant shall return" is in Hebrew *Shear-jashub*, the prophetic name of Isaiah's son. There are two remnants: the historic remnant of the past and the prophetic remnant of the future. The eschatological message (the message for the last days) is embodied in the remnant's return to "the mighty God," which is a messianic prophecy already laid down in Isaiah 9:6. Hosea also voiced this prophetic truth: "Afterward shall the children of Israel return, and seek the Lord their God . . . and shall fear the Lord and his goodness *in the latter days*" (Hosea 3:5; emphasis added).

Verses 22–23: The hand of God is in the "consumption decreed" upon all nations in the last days (see also D&C 87:6), and though the people of Israel become numerous, yet only a remnant will truly repent and return to their God.

Verses 24–26: Consoling words from a loving God—yes, there is a consumption decreed and an overflowing scourge will be felt by all nations, but fear not. "Assyria," the figurative title for a superpower in the latter days, will again strike as an instrument in the hands of the Lord of hosts, but the smiting is measured and will, in the Lord's due time, cease. The people that dwell in the future Zion will be rescued, and "Assyria" will be scourged just as Gideon punished the Midianites (Judges 7).

Verse 27: "The yoke shall be destroyed because of the anointing" clearly has messianic connotation. It is the Anointed One who makes all burdens or yokes light and eventually takes them away (Matthew 11:28–30).

Verses 28–32: Isaiah described, as if standing on the wall of Jerusalem, the progress of the Assyrian army toward Jerusalem, featuring in Hebrew a superb example of alliteration. "Another Assyrian unit apparently marched against Jerusalem via the province of Samaria, conquering a series of towns as it passed through the district of Benjamin" (Aharoni, *Land of the Bible*, 339). This idealized sequential conquest narrative apparently symbolizes also the future siege called Armageddon (see commentary at Isaiah 40:1–2; 51:19–20; Ezekiel 38–39).

Verses 33–34: Historically this was fulfilled as leaders of Assyria were lopped off and hewn down, but the figure is also future (see Zechariah 14:2; Revelation 11). The Lord of hosts will do the cutting down in both eras.

Isaiah 11 (2 Nephi 21)

Isaiah was the prophet foretelling the Restoration. Joseph Smith was the prophet fulfilling the prophecies of the Restoration. It should not surprise us, therefore, that Isaiah foresaw and wrote about the latter-day prophet who would be the Lord's instrument in fulfilling his prophecies. In fact, Isaiah may have appeared to Joseph Smith (see Woodruff, *Journal of Discourses*, 16:266–67). The Prophet Joseph Smith, the gathering of Israel, the restoration of the gospel, and the great Millennium would, of necessity, be significant themes in Isaiah's writings.

On September 21, 1823, Moroni quoted Isaiah 11 to Joseph Smith (Joseph Smith–History 1:40) and told him that this prophecy was "about to be fulfilled." Doctrine and Covenants 113 is important for interpretation.

Isaiah 11:1, 10 (2 Nephi 21:1, 10)

The perpetuity of the house of Jesse is illustrated with a dramatic metaphor from the fields of Israel: "There shall come forth a rod out of the stem of Jesse, and a Branch shall grow out of his roots"; or, as the parallelism translates directly from the Hebrew, "There shall come forth a branch [*khoter*] out of the trunk of Jesse: indeed, a shoot [*netzer*] from his roots shall bear fruit." The terms *khoter* and *netzer* can be used interchangeably, though in this case *khoter* is a branch or shoot from the trunk of the tree, whereas *netzer* is a shoot from the root system, and only a shoot or branch from the root can start new life.

Matthew may have referred to this prophecy when he saw in Jesus the fulfillment of what was spoken by the prophets: "He shall be called a Nazarene" (Matthew 2:23). *Nazarene* in Hebrew is *notzri*, the same root word used by Isaiah and variously translated "branch" or "shoot." The olive tree is one of the few trees that can have apparently dead branches and even a dead trunk and still produce, sometime later, new life from the root. Characteristics of the olive tree are called to bear witness that the Messiah, a descendant of David, son of Jesse, would grow from the original root of the family tree of the royal house of David.

The "stem of Jesse" (Hebrew, *geza Yishai*) is Jesus Christ (D&C 113:1–2). The "rod" (Hebrew, *khoter*) is Joseph Smith, a descendant of Jesse and Ephraim (D&C 113:4; see Topical Guide, "Joseph Smith").

The "branch" (Hebrew, *netzer*, in Matthew 2:23) is Jesus Christ. As with footnotes to other scriptures in which this word appears—for example, Jeremiah 23:5 and Zechariah 3:8—the Topical Guide references indicate that this word refers to the Savior.

Matthew sees fulfillment of a messianic prophecy in Jesus' connection with Nazareth. There is no specific reference in biblical literature to prophets declaring that the Messiah would be a Nazarene, unless Matthew is telling us he sees one in Isaiah 11:1 or he had access to writings now lost. Isaiah foreshadowed that a "branch" (Hebrew, *netzer*) would grow out of the root of Jesse—that is, from the Davidic line—and thus Jesus would be a Nazarene (Hebrew, *notzri*). Both Hebrew words come from the same root word.

Elder James E. Talmage taught, "As made known to the prophet [Isaiah] and by him proclaimed, the coming Lord was the living Branch that should spring from the undying root typified in the family of Jesse" (*Jesus the Christ*, 44). Likewise, Elder Bruce R. McConkie taught that the Branch and the King are the Lord Jesus Christ when he returns to earth to reign as King of kings and Lord of lords (see *Promised Messiah*, 192–95).

The "root of Jesse" (Hebrew, *shoresh Yishai*, v. 10) is Joseph Smith. Doctrine and Covenants 113:6 explains the fulfillment as follows:

1. A descendant of Jesse and Joseph on whom was laid much power. President Brigham Young taught that "the Book of Mormon came to Ephraim, for Joseph Smith was a pure Ephraimite, and the Book of Mormon was revealed to him, and while he lived he made it his business to search for those who believed the Gospel" (*Journal of Discourses*, 2:269; see also Smith, *Doctrines of Salvation*, 3:253).

2. A rightful heir to the priesthood.

3. A holder of the keys of the kingdom.

4. His work would be an ensign to the nations.

5. His work would help gather Israel in the last days.

Thus Isaiah 11:1–5 and 10 refer to Jesus Christ and to Joseph Smith.

The stem and the branch of Jesse are Jesus; the description in Isaiah 11:2–5 could only be of Jesus, the same Being described in Isaiah 9:6. He is the personification of wisdom, understanding, counsel, might, knowledge, reverence, judgment, righteousness, equity, and faithfulness.

The rod and the root of Jesse are Joseph Smith; the description in Doctrine and Covenants 113:6 could only be of Joseph Smith.

The "root of Jesse" may also have additional meanings. For example, note *b* to Romans 15:12 cross-references the "root of Jesse" to Topical Guide, "Jesus Christ, Davidic Descent of," and Revelation 5:5 and 22:16 refer to Jesus as the "Root of David."

Isaiah 11:6–9 (2 Nephi 21:6–9)

These verses provide a refreshing description of the peacefulness of the millennial reign of Christ (compare D&C 101:24–32). The Messiah's kingdom will far exceed the peace of any and all mortal kingdoms. All enmity and hostility will cease. As in the beginning, animals and humans will be helpful to each other. "A little child shall lead them" reminds us of the Savior's injunction to become as little children.

During Zion's Camp, while journeying from Kirtland to Missouri, the Prophet Joseph Smith wrote: "In pitching my tent we found three . . . prairie rattlesnakes, which the brethren were about to kill, but I said, 'Let them alone—don't hurt them! How will the serpent ever lose his venom, while the servants of God possess the same disposition, and continue to make war upon it? Men must become harmless, before the brute creation; and when men lose their vicious dispositions and cease to destroy the animal race, the lion and the lamb can dwell together, and the sucking child can play with the serpent in safety'" (*History of the Church*, 2:71).

Isaiah 11:8 (2 Nephi 21:8)

An asp is a viper, one of the deadly snakes in the Holy Land. The cockatrice is another venomous serpent. To appreciate the peaceful period when a little child may, without worry, play on the hole of a viper, consider the following episode.

One of our students, a thirty-eight-year-old male, large and sturdy, was working in the banana fields of a kibbutz, a collective farming settlement, near the Sea of Galilee. One day he tried to save a snake from the hands of other students who uncovered it and intended to kill it. When he picked it up with his fingers to remove it from danger, the viper somehow elongated itself, swung around, and sank its fangs into his forefinger.

Kibbutz personnel immediately rushed him to a nearby hospital, where he remained for three days of observation. They released him, and after he spent a few hours at the BYU Jerusalem Center, the pain in his finger was still so intense that he was rushed in the middle of the night to the emergency room of the Hadassah Hospital in Jerusalem. The student remained in the hospital for twelve more days. Doctors tried every kind of painkiller to ease his periodic agony. Now and then his whole body writhed with pain from his finger. The finger increased to double its normal size, and the tissues inside turned a black color. We feared that they might have to amputate his finger and maybe even his hand.

The student was released from the Jerusalem hospital to fly back to the United States with his group, and there he was admitted to another medical center. Several months passed before he recovered completely from those venomous fangs that had sunk just a fraction of an inch into his finger. The poison might have killed a smaller, more fragile individual.

That experience with a viper highlights the extraordinary changes that will prevail in the millennial era when formerly dangerous creatures will be pacific and playful.

Isaiah 11:9 (2 Nephi 21:9)

The reason for all the remarkable changes in the new world of peace is the overflowing knowledge of the Lord, meaning that he will be seen and known and that the knowledge that he has, his wisdom, understanding, counsel, judgment, righteousness, equity, and faithfulness will be available to all his creations. They will not only know *about* him but will know him.

Elder Orson Pratt taught that "the earth will be made new, and great knowledge will be imparted to the inhabitants thereof, as predicted in the 11th chapter of the prophecy of Isaiah. The knowledge of God will then cover the earth as the waters cover the mighty deep. There will be no place of ignorance, no place of darkness, no place for those that will not serve God. Why? Because Jesus, the Great Creator, and also the Great Redeemer, will be himself on the earth, and his holy angels will be on the earth, and all the resurrected Saints that have died in former dispensations will all come forth, and they will be on the earth. What a happy earth this creation will be, when this purifying process shall come, and the earth be filled with the knowledge of God as the waters cover the great deep!" (*Journal of Discourses*, 21:324–25).

Isaiah 11:10 (2 Nephi 21:10)

In the latter days the root of Jesse, who is Joseph Smith, will stand as an ensign to the people (see commentary at Isaiah 11:1, 10), and to him (not "it," as in the King James Version) will the

Gentiles seek. When his work is complete, his rest will be glorious, as was confirmed by Lucy Mack Smith, the Prophet's mother. She described what happened when she saw her martyred sons: "I sank back, crying to the Lord in the agony of my soul, 'My God, my God, why hast thou forsaken this family!' A voice replied, 'I have taken them to myself, that they might have rest.' . . . I seemed almost to hear them say, 'Mother, weep not for us, we have overcome the world by love; . . . ours is an eternal triumph'" (*History of Joseph Smith by His Mother*, 324–25).

Isaiah 11:11–12 (2 Nephi 21:11–12)

Joseph Smith taught, "The time has at last arrived when the God of Abraham, of Isaac, and of Jacob, has set His hand again the second time to recover the remnants of his people, which have been left from Assyria, and from Egypt, and from Pathros, and from Cush, and from Elam, and from Shinar, and from Hamath, and from the islands of the sea, and with them to bring in the fulness of the Gentiles, and establish that covenant with them, which was promised when their sins should be taken away" (*History of the Church*, 1:313).

The Lord set his hand the first time to reprove his people; this second time he will recover his people and gather a remnant of them. Though in Isaiah's day there had not yet been any wide dispersion of his people, the prophet used the language of prophetic preview. Nations from antiquity were used as symbols for the future. The gathering will be from all directions, from the four corners of the earth.

Isaiah 11:12–13 (2 Nephi 21:12–13)

The ensign may be the Book of Mormon (2 Nephi 29:2), or the gospel, or the Church. President Joseph Fielding Smith wrote: "In the little town of Fayette, Seneca County, New York, the Lord set up an ensign to the nations. It was in fulfillment of the prediction made by the Prophet Isaiah. . . . That ensign was the Church of Jesus Christ of Latter-day Saints, which was established for the last time, never again to be destroyed or given to other people. It was the greatest event the world has seen since the day that the Redeemer was lifted upon the cross and worked out the infinite and eternal atonement. It meant more to mankind than anything else that has occurred since that day" (*Doctrines of Salvation*, 3:254).

"Ephraim shall not envy Judah, and Judah shall not vex Ephraim" is a daring prophecy of healing, reconciliation, and cooperation, considering the bitter enmity between the two peoples in Isaiah's day. The historic rivalry between blood relatives within Israel will yet be resolved by the Messiah and his ensign. Only the eternal truths of the gospel of Jesus Christ can overcome conflict and establish peace.

A pleasant illustration of verse 13 occurred at the dedication of the Orson Hyde Garden on the Mount of Olives in 1979. Jewish and Latter-day Saint leaders not only shook hands but at one point were linked arm in arm as they walked down the mount. One Church leader said at that moment he could not help but think of Isaiah 11:13: "Ephraim shall not envy Judah, and Judah shall not vex Ephraim."

Isaiah 11:14–16 (2 Nephi 21:14–16)

Unity among the people of Israel, the covenant people of the Lord, helps to spiritually subdue surrounding peoples in the world. Again, representative nations during Isaiah's time were used as symbols for the future. The enemies of God, in the western world and in the eastern world, will be spiritually overrun by united Israel, the covenant people.

The people cannot accomplish the work of God by themselves. The Lord intervenes in miraculous ways to gather his people.

"Assyria" represents all nations from which the remnant of Israel will be gathered. The Lord will provide a way (a "highway") to deliver his people, as in the day of the great Exodus, and he will provide a way for them to come back to him. Doctrine and Covenants 133:25–33 gives details of this remarkable scenario.

Isaiah 12 (2 Nephi 22)

Just as Moses wrote a song of praise for deliverance (Exodus 15), so Isaiah presents two psalms of praise (vv. 1–3 and 4–6) for salvation in the millennial day. In fact, one could call all of Isaiah 12 a millennial hymn. After writing about Jesus Christ and Joseph Smith, there was reason to sing praises! How true for our day as well. Read this short chapter aloud and with feeling.

Isaiah 12:2 (2 Nephi 22:2)

This verse may be translated literally as follows:

Behold El is my salvation,
I shall trust and not be afraid;
For my strength and my song is Yah, Yahweh,
And he has become my salvation.

As Jesus himself would later testify, he *was* the great Jehovah, the Law and the Light, who came to earth to provide eternal life (3 Nephi 15:5–9). He literally became salvation, as Isaiah prophesied.

El is the singular of *Elohim,* but the word seldom occurs in the Bible in singular form. In the King James Version of the Bible both singular and plural are rendered by the word *God. Yah* is a contracted form of *Yahweh,* or Jehovah, which in the Bible is usually rendered in English as LORD. Here, to avoid LORD LORD, the translators rendered it LORD *Jehovah.* This is one of only four times the name is written out fully as Jehovah in the King James Version. We are not exactly sure why the King James Bible translators chose to do this. The short form *Yah* also occurs in Hebrew in Exodus 15:2 and Psalm 118:14, which passages reflect a similar tone of praise.

Moses, a type of the Messiah, was a great lawgiver and a great deliverer; the Messiah himself was *the* great Lawgiver and *the* great Deliverer. The Messiah is Jehovah, and Jehovah is our strength and our song; he is our salvation. It was Jesus Christ who gave his life for our salvation. Jehovah, therefore, could be none other than Jesus Christ, our Lord.

Isaiah 12:3 (2 Nephi 22:3)

In the desert world of the Israelite prophets, water was life. In Sinai, Moses smote the rock and water gushed forth to save a thirsty people. In the millennial earth the Messiah will provide the water of life; his people will symbolically draw water from the wells of salvation, water that springs up unto eternal life. Compare the language of John 4:13–14; 7:38; 1 Corinthians 10:4; and Revelation 21:6; also Isaiah 41:17–18.

Isaiah 12:4–6 (2 Nephi 22:4–6)

Hebrew *Hallelujah,* or *Hallelu Yah,* means literally "praise ye the Lord." Every tongue will praise his excellent works and cry out and shout everlasting thanksgiving, especially for the greatness of his atoning sacrifice. Read Doctrine and Covenants 84:98–102 for more exulting praise and thanksgiving.

Isaiah 13 (2 Nephi 23)

Isaiah 13–23 contains "burdens" on ten different nations— the Lord's warning voice to other peoples (see Amos 3:7) and his judgments upon them. "Burden" is used to translate the Hebrew word *massa,* which means something lifted up, an "oracle" or "message." These oracles against the nations demonstrate that the sovereignty of the Lord God is universal, and that he is involved in the history of all his people. Heavenly Father is mindful of all his children, and he is concerned about wickedness everywhere. Compare Amos 1–2; Jeremiah 46–51; and Ezekiel 25–32.

Isaiah 13–14 // 2 Nephi 23–24 are about *Babylon.* Although Assyria was the superpower in Isaiah's time, through the spirit of prophecy he foresaw that mighty, wicked Babylon would threaten his homeland. These two are the only chapters of Isaiah 13–23 quoted in the Book of Mormon, which says something about their relative value.

Isaiah 13:1 (2 Nephi 23:1)

"Babylon" is a type, a symbol of the whole wicked world (Revelation 14:8; D&C 133:14; see also Revelation 16:19; 17:5; 18:2–4, 10, 21; D&C 1:16; 35:11; 64:24; 86:3; 133:5, 7).

Brigham Young University professor of ancient scripture Richard D. Draper wrote: "Babylon incarnates arrogance, pride, and insatiable corruption in opposition to God and his kingdom. It stands in contrast to the heavenly city, the New Jerusalem, where the law of God thrives. . . .

" . . . Babylon represents a real historical organization. . . . it is composed of more than one entity. . . . Seeing spiritual Babylon as only one association, either at its inception or today, would therefore be wrong. It symbolizes all leagues that may be properly called Antichrist, that pervert the right way of the Lord or promote antichristian principles and lifestyles.

"The arrogant Babylonians combined purely sensual and material principles with the lofty striving within the soul of man. Out of this grew the principle of spiritual fornication. Men mistook lust for joy, sought happiness through passion, and pursued security through materialism. The bit of graffiti, 'He who dies with the most toys wins,' could have been written as easily in Babylon as in New York, or Las Vegas. Today many still seek to find heaven through drugs, lust, money, success, or power. People continue to try to escape the deadly round of daily life through material and immoral means. . . .

"God has provided a solution: flee Babylon. The command demands a complete severing of relations. God allows no association whatsoever. There is good reason. Babylon is not to be converted but destroyed: 'We would have healed Babylon, but she is not healed: forsake her' (Jer. 51:9, KJV). Any that linger in Babylon will be taken with her plagues, 'For after today cometh the burning . . . and I will not spare any that remain in Babylon' (D&C 64:24)" (*Opening the Seven Seals,* 189–90, 204–5).

Isaiah 13:2 (2 Nephi 23:2)

The Hebrew word *nes* is variously translated as "banner," "ensign," and "standard." This ensign or standard is a rallying point for God's "warriors" in a day to come.

Isaiah 13:3–5 (2 Nephi 23:3–5)

"Sanctified ones," "holy ones," and "saints" translate two Hebrew words: *kadosh,* or plural, *k'doshim,* used ten times in the Old Testament, and *hassid,* or plural, *hassidim,* used nineteen times in the Old Testament.

Second Nephi 23:3 corrects the statement as it appears in the King James Version: "I have also called my mighty ones, for mine anger *is not upon* them that rejoice in my highness."

Can we identify the "sanctified ones," the "mighty ones" who are called and set apart (mustered) for the battle, as the missionary force of the latter-day kingdom? Anyone who has been in the middle of the royal army assembled at the Missionary Training Center in Provo, Utah, has possibly felt power unequalled in any other single place in the world. These warriors of God do come from distant places ("from a far country, from the end of heaven"), and they are certainly going forth to conquer on life's great battlefield, to overthrow the whole wicked world, to destroy evil by establishing righteousness.

That "mighty army of the Lord," however, is only part of what he calls the "sanctified ones"; all the Saints, the citizens of his kingdom, are involved in the battle, including help from the other side of the veil.

Isaiah 13:6–18 (2 Nephi 23:6–18)

Judgments come upon the earth's inhabitants at the Second Coming, "the day of the Lord."

Verses 6–8: The destructions sent forth from the Almighty (Hebrew, *Shaddai*) will cause faint-heartedness in the wicked; fear, pain, and faces enflamed with embarrassment and anxiety will characterize the disobedient. Paul later envisioned the same scene: "For when they shall say, Peace and safety; then sudden destruction cometh upon them, as travail upon a woman with child; and they shall not escape" (1 Thessalonians 5:3).

Verse 9: "The day of the Lord cometh . . . and he shall destroy the sinners thereof out of it"—all telestial people and things will be removed from this earth at the beginning of His millennial reign.

Verse 10: The sun will be darkened, the moon and stars will give no light. Could this happen as the earth moves back into its previous orbit and becomes terrestrial? Notice what Doctrine and Covenants 29:14 and 133:49 tell us about the sun, moon, and stars. Those heavenly spheres seem to act strangely—being darkened, refusing to give light—because of their relative impotence next to the Source of all light. The Lord God of heaven and earth is described as "above the brightness of the sun," whose "brightness and glory defy all description" (Joseph Smith–History 1:16–17). When he comes, those other luminaries will appear totally insignificant, just as the moon is hardly visible when the sun is shining.

Verse 11: Two sets of parallel statements detail how God's judgments will be executed. He will punish the world (meaning the wicked; compare Joseph Smith–Matthew 1:4), and he specifically identifies one type of wicked person—the proud—as the primary object of his wrath (Malachi 4:1).

Verse 12: The parallelism teaches that relatively few men will survive the promised judgments. Ophir, probably in the southern Arabian peninsula, was a land famous for its gold (see Bible Dictionary, "Ophir").

Verse 13: Two more sets of parallel statements foreshadow God's use of earthquakes; the Hebrew phrase "remove out of her place" may be translated into English as *quake*. See also Joseph Smith–Matthew 1:29; Revelation 6:12; 16:18.

Verse 14: Like the hunted roe and the shepherdless sheep, so those who have lived without God in the world will be helpless in the day of the Lord's visitation.

Verse 15: "Every one that is *proud* shall be thrust through; and every one that is joined *to the wicked* shall fall by the sword" (italics indicate changes in 2 Nephi).

Verses 16–18: These verses, in addition to depicting horrible vengeance to be meted out at the Second Coming, take us back also to the original type, less than two centuries after Isaiah's time, when the Medes would overrun the Babylonians with viciousness and cruelty. In 539 B.C. the Lord did indeed stir up the Medes (and Persians), who, uninterested in monetary gain, wreaked merciless vengeance upon those who opposed them.

Isaiah 13:19–22 (2 Nephi 23:19–22)

"Babylon the great is falling; / God shall all her towers o'erthrow" (*Hymns,* no. 7). Babylon truly was "the glory of kingdoms." The Hanging Gardens of Babylon were one of the seven wonders of the ancient world. Yet, Babylon fell without a struggle before the armies of Cyrus of Persia. He and his men dug a canal into which they diverted the waters of the Euphrates, which normally flowed into Babylon, so they could penetrate into the heart of the city via the dry river bed. By this means vegetation ceased growing in the city, and the city began deteriorating, leading to the fulfillment of Isaiah's prediction that it would be uninhabited; there wouldn't even be an Arab to pitch a tent or a shepherd to make a sheepfold there. Total desolation was predicted, and it was an accurate prophecy. Isaiah's prophecy was gradually but literally fulfilled within a few centuries, by the Roman period.

The vivid description of Babylon's destruction fits both

the terrain at the southern end of the Dead Sea, where Sodom and Gomorrah once flourished in wickedness, and the land of Babylon. Both places foreshadow the eschatological (latter-day) devastation of spiritual Babylon.

Isaiah poetically employs two fictional beasts usually associated with superstitious traditions in this description of desolation. "Satyrs" are in Hebrew *seirim*, meaning "hairy" or "rough" ones. In mythology a satyr is half man and half goat. "Dragons" are jackals or wild dogs.

Isaiah 14 (2 Nephi 24)

Isaiah spent a lot of time describing the scattering of Israel. He discussed the gathering in this chapter. In one of the great overriding themes of the writings of Isaiah, the prophet proclaims his main message: Babylon, historical and symbolic, must be destroyed (chapter 13) and Israel must be gathered and saved (chapter 14). Jehovah will be just, but he will also be merciful.

Could "strangers" (v. 1) mean converts or proselytes? Gentiles certainly are accepting the gospel and joining spiritual Israel, being grafted or adopted into the covenant people. Note the topics associated with this verse in footnote *e* to Isaiah 14:1: "Conversion" and "Israel, Mission of." "And I will bless them through thy name; for as many as receive this Gospel shall be called after thy name, and shall be accounted thy seed" (Abraham 2:10).

In another sense, with reference to the physical gathering to the land of Israel in the last days, could Arab Palestinians also be among the inhabitants of the Holy Land? See Genesis 16:12 (descendants of Ishmael) and Ezekiel 47:22.

Isaiah 14:2 (2 Nephi 24:2)

This prophecy finds fulfillment in 538 B.C. and in the latter days. Other people or nations will take Israel and "bring them to their place [Joseph Smith Translation addition: *and they shall return to their lands* (plural) *of promise*]: and the house of Israel shall possess them [that is, *the strangers*] in the land of the Lord for servants and handmaids: and they shall take them captives, whose captives they were; and they shall rule over their oppressors."

Isaiah 14:3 (2 Nephi 24:3)

Second Nephi has "It shall come to pass in *that* day," which is a change from Isaiah in the King James Version, which reads "*the* day.*" "Hard bondage" may be literal, meaning the servitude of the Babylonian captivity (586–538 B.C.), but may also refer to the captivity and the chains with which we shackle ourselves when we serve sin. This kind of salvation, deliverance from sin, far exceeds the deliverance from captivity in ancient Egypt or Babylon.

Isaiah 14:4–23 (2 Nephi 24:4–23)

These verses contain a satirical or taunting song against the king of Babylon, which title symbolizes Satan.

Verses 5–8: The whole earth, humankind and even the trees, rejoice when the longest-reigning, cruelest subjugator of all, the devil himself, is bound and put away (see also Revelation 20:1–3; 1 Nephi 22:15, 26; D&C 101:28).

Verses 9–11: The inhabitants of hell react as Satan is consigned there. Even the bygone, wicked rulers of nations who once were appareled in luxurious robes, note that the king of Babylon, their evil sponsor, the devil himself, is now symbolically covered only by worms.

Verses 12–15: These verses apply to the king of Babylon and also to Lucifer, the prototype of Babylon's king. In other words, ancient Babylon's fall is symbolic of Lucifer's fall. Undoubtedly, that is why Isaiah thought of Lucifer after describing Babylon's fall. Lucifer is the king of Babylon, meaning the whole wicked world. *Lucifer* is Latin, and the Hebrew is *hellel;* both mean "shining one." "Son of the morning" is *ben shakhar,* "son of dawn." Lucifer's fall in the premortal life is recorded also in Revelation 12:7–9 and Moses 4:1–4. He sought to take away our agency—a warning to all of us not to get overanxious or overzealous in coercing or compelling others (see also Jacob 4:18; D&C 76:25–28).

The history of this world began with a war. We engaged in that war and we won, but the war continues in this world. Lucifer imported it to planet Earth. It is the longest war ever on Earth, lasting six thousand years now. We are fighting in this war with evil, and we will win again. The final battle is still ahead, and we are assured that good will always prevail. A number of our hymns teach us about the war: "Onward, Christian Soldiers" (no. 246), "Behold! A Royal Army" (no. 251), "We Are All Enlisted" (no. 250), and "Hope of Israel" (no. 259), and others (see Ogden and Skinner, *Book of Mormon*, 2:60–63). We sing about war, battles, conflicts, soldiers, armies, the foe, the battlefield, banners, swords, helmets, bucklers, shields, signals, war cries, and victory—all in an eternal context. Ours is a battle not to save physical bodies, for all physical bodies will eventually be resurrected to an immortal condition, but to save the souls of humankind. In wartime we cannot sit back complacently while the enemy surrounds us with his formidable weaponry. Entering any day of our lives without prayer and scripture study is like a warrior charging into battle without his armor.

Verse 14: "I will be like the most High." Ambition is pride's first cousin. Lucifer aspired to ascend to heaven, to have a throne higher than the stars of God, to be like God—all of which was ambitious indeed. It appears that he felt he could displace God. His selfish ambition ruined his eternal existence. Jesus said, "whosoever shall exalt himself shall be abased" (Matthew 23:12) and "that which is now exalted of itself shall be laid low of power" (D&C 49:10). The higher up we are, the farther we can fall; Lucifer apparently fell from a very high position. He is described as "an angel of God who was in authority in the presence of God" (D&C 76:25).

Verses 15–17: When all the children of God see Lucifer as he is consigned to his ultimate fate, they will squint at him with disgust and amazement and wonder aloud: Is this the person who caused such incredible physical and spiritual devastation in the world? this spiteful, pathetic figure of misery and degradation?

Verses 18–22: We are promised that if our eye is single to the glory of God, we can be filled with light (D&C 88:67). Lucifer wants the glory for himself and, therefore, has no light in him, only darkness. Even mortal wicked people have something to glory in, their physical bodies, but Satan has *none;* there is no grave for Satan—he has no body. The great irony is that he sought superior power and glory and in the end will have *none,* all of which is another warning to us.

Verse 23: Babylon (representing worldly wealth, power, and glory) will become a "possession for the bittern" (a heron) and stagnant marshes, and it will be swept with the broom of destruction; that is, the world will be cleansed and renewed.

Isaiah 14:24–27 (2 Nephi 24:24–27)

The previous verses applied also to the evil empire Babylon. Now the scene changes back to her infamous predecessor. In the year 701 B.C., Assyria attacked Judah and succumbed to catastrophe at the hand of the Lord himself (Isaiah 36–37). Isaiah's vision of historical events is like the panoramic vision of John the Revelator in that both move back and forth through periods without too much concern for strict chronology.

The alternate parallelisms of verses 26–27 attest that God's punishing hand will inevitably fall on Assyria and on all other rebellious nations.

Isaiah 14:28–32 (2 Nephi 24:28–32)

In the year that king Ahaz died, ca. 715 B.C., the prophet received an oracle (a revelation) against Philistia.

Verse 29: The King James Version's "Palestina" is Latin for Philistia, later called Palestine.

Some think that historically the "serpent's root" may have been Shalmaneser V, and the "cockatrice" that followed was Sennacherib.

Verse 31: The gate, and the city which it represents, will howl and cry and ultimately be dissolved by a power coming down from the north, Assyria and then Babylon.

Verse 32: The whole prophecy against Philistia revolves around the final thought, the central message: there is no future in any temporal state, for the Lord has founded Zion; the poor in spirit (meaning the humble) and the meek will always turn to the Lord, and Zion will be established. That foundation is sure.

Isaiah 15–17

A most important lesson comes from these chapters of Isaiah: those who exalt themselves will be humbled, and those who humble themselves will be exalted—whether nations or individuals. There is no room for God in a person full of himself. Pride brings nations and individuals down.

With remarkable insight C. S. Lewis wrote:

"There is one vice of which no man in the world is free; which every one in the world loathes when he sees it in someone else; and of which hardly any people . . . ever imagine that they are guilty themselves. I have heard people admit that they are bad-tempered, or that they cannot keep their heads about girls or drink, or even that they are cowards. I do not think I have ever heard anyone . . . accuse himself of this vice. And at the same time I have very seldom met anyone . . . who showed the slightest mercy to it in others. There is no fault which makes a man more unpopular, and no fault which we are more unconscious of in ourselves. And the more we have it ourselves, the more we dislike it in others.

"The vice I am talking of is Pride or Self-Conceit: and the virtue opposite to it . . . is called Humility. You may remember, when I was talking about sexual morality, I warned you that the centre of Christian morals did not lie there. Well, now, we have come to the centre. According to Christian teachers, the essential vice, the utmost evil, is Pride. Unchastity, anger, greed, drunkenness, and all that, are mere fleabites in comparison: it was through Pride that the devil became the devil: *Pride leads to every other vice: it is the complete anti-God state of mind.*

"Does this seem to you exaggerated? If so, think it over. I pointed out a moment ago that the more pride one had, the more one disliked pride in others. In fact, if you want to find out how proud you are the easiest way is to ask yourself, 'How much do I dislike it when other people snub me, or refuse to take any notice of me . . . or patronise me, or show off?' The point is that each person's pride is in competition with every one else's pride. It is because I wanted to be the big noise at the party that I am so annoyed at someone else being the big noise. Two of a trade never agree. Now what you want to get clear is that Pride is *essentially* competitive—is competitive by its very nature—while the other vices are competitive only, so to speak, by accident. Pride gets no pleasure out of having something, only out of having more of it than the next man. We say that people are proud of being rich, or clever, or good-looking but they are not. They are proud of being richer, or cleverer, or better-looking than others. If everyone else became equally rich, or clever, or good-looking there would be nothing to be proud about. It is *the comparison* that makes you proud: the pleasure of being above the rest. Once the element of competition has gone, pride has gone. . . . *Nearly all those evils in the world which people put down to greed or selfishness are really far more the result of Pride* (*Mere Christianity*, 121–23; emphasis added).

"There are few passages in the O.T. which convey so little meaning to the modern reader as do [Isaiah 15–16]" (*Interpreter's Bible*, 5:267). They speak of the destruction of Moab in the historic past and the prophetic future (compare Jeremiah 48). Isaiah paints a woeful scene of devastation throughout Israel's neighbor to the east. At least twenty places are mentioned along with pertinent circumstances in and around the land of Moab, suggesting that Isaiah was well versed in geography, history, and current events. Chapter 16 verse 5 contains a prophecy of the Messiah sitting upon the throne of David.

Isaiah 17

Verses 1–3 describe the destruction of Damascus, the capital of Syria, in the historic past and the prophetic future. Are we nearing the fulfillment of that prophetic future?

Verses 4–5: The prophetic eye turns to the northern kingdom of Israel; although there was a time of richness and fatness, now Israel is lean and impoverished—through her disobedience and rejection of God.

Verse 6: Few will be left after God's punishments upon Israel; compare Amos's image of two legs and piece of an ear (Amos 3:12).

Verse 7: After the chastening hand of God has shaken his people, some will be humbled and return to him.

Verse 8: Those who turn to God with full purpose of heart will utterly abandon the accoutrements of idolatry—the altars, the images, and the "groves," which were *asheroth*, or fertility goddesses.

Verses 9–11: Isaiah continues with imagery from planting. The basic message is, as always: we reap what we sow.

Verses 12–14: The phrase "rolling thing" (v. 13) is translated from the Hebrew *galgal*. The galgal plant begins its rapid growth in March when its first leaves have sprouted and young flower buds appear. Within a few short weeks this innocent-looking galgal turns into a thorny monster, its leaves and buds covered with wickedly sharp thorns. As summer progresses, it begins to dry up but continues to look so firmly entrenched and menacing it seems there is no way to get rid of it. When the galgal seems to be at its peak, a curious thing happens below ground between its stalk and roots: the plant cells between the two detach, so that with one puff a summer wind blows away the whole galgal plant. This was Isaiah's message: just as the galgal looks threatening but is easily blown away by the wind, so it will be with Israel's enemies. They look very threatening, but they have no real roots in the land, and so they shall be swept away "like the galgal before the wind." And it will happen quickly: "At eveningtide trouble; and before the morning [it] is not." Compare also the play on words in Joshua 5:9, and see also Mosiah 12:12 (for a drawing of the galgal plant, see Ogden and Chadwick, *Holy Land*, 51–52).

Isaiah 18:1–7

According to most interpreters of the Bible, this chapter is enigmatic and obscure, an anomaly because it is a prophecy of hope in the midst of prophecies of destruction.

We have a possible resolution of the enigma: modern prophetic interpretation suggests reference to *missionaries going forth from America* to gather the remnants of Israel to Zion. Because of America's important role in the last days, it should not surprise us to find Isaiah commenting on it. Nephi also saw key events concerning America.

Verse 1: "The land shadowing with wings" may be a poetic description of the continental outline of the Americas. Hyrum Smith said in general conference, April 1844: "North and South America, are the symbols of the wings" (*History of the Church*, 6:322).

"Beyond the rivers of Ethiopia": In biblical Hebrew there is no word for ocean; ancient Israelites used words meaning "river," "sea," "many waters," etc.

Verses 2, 7: The ambassadors or messengers are part of the "coming forth of my church out of the wilderness—clear as the moon, and fair as the sun, and terrible as an army with banners" (D&C 5:14; 105:31).

Verse 3: The ensign has been lifted up; the trump is sounding throughout the earth (Isaiah 5:26 // 2 Nephi 15:26; Isaiah 11:12 // 2 Nephi 21:12). Zion shall be "an ensign unto the people, and there shall come unto her out of every nation under heaven" (D&C 64:42).

Verses 4–5: Another example of metaphorical language; late winter pruning produces more fruitful branches (see John 15:2).

"In verse 5, Isaiah describes a special vine-pruning. A vineyard must be pruned twice each year. The more severe pruning comes late in winter, just before the dormant limbs develop their spring growth. The non-producing branches from the previous season and most of the vines are then cut off. The second and less severe pruning occurs after the grapes have formed, when the vine dresser cuts off the nonbearing branches and those with small, green, bitter fruit. The result is a vine whose remaining branches are stronger, are in full sunlight, and are able to produce more ripe fruit (see Buttrick, *Interpreter's Dictionary of the Bible*, 3:941; 4:785).

"In a similar fashion, just before the harvest of the Millennium, the Lord of the vineyard will prune out the non-productive, bitter limbs of the house of Israel so that the strong branches can produce a full, sweet fruit. (See Matt. 13:24–43; Jacob 5.)" (Ludlow, *Isaiah*, 209).

Verse 6: Birds and beasts feed year round on the refuse of the vineyard; see Doctrine and Covenants 29:20 for literal application of the same idea.

Verse 7: The Prophet Joseph Smith taught that the Saints "have labored without pay, to instruct the United States [and now the world] that the gathering had commenced in the western boundaries of Missouri, to build a holy city [Zion], where, as may be seen in the eighteenth chapter of Isaiah, the present should 'be brought unto the Lord of Hosts'" (*History of the Church*, 2:132).

Summarizing Isaiah 18, President Joseph Fielding Smith wrote: "This chapter is clearly a reference to the sending forth of the missionaries to the nations of the earth to gather again this people who are scattered and peeled [v. 7]. The ensign has been lifted upon the mountains, and the work of gathering has been going on for over one hundred years. No one understands this chapter, but the Latter-day Saints, and we can see how it is being fulfilled" (*Signs of the Times,* 54–55).

Isaiah 19:1–25

Here we have the most important prophecies about Egypt in the Old Testament. Verses 1–18 forebode doom and destruction, but verses 19–25 foretell hope and redemption.

Verse 1: The Lord's judgment is pronounced on Egypt. The idols there will *shake* at his coming, presaging destruction.

Verses 2–3: Civil war ensues among the people of Egypt, and, as a result of abandonment of God, they turn to spiritualistic mediums (compare King Saul, when bereft of the Spirit, turning to a sorceress: 1 Samuel 28).

Verse 4: We wonder if this is "a cruel lord, a fierce king" of the past, or yet future.

Verses 5–10: Could these problems with the Nile River waters result from the modern Aswan Dam? (see Ludlow, *Isaiah,* 214–16).

Verses 11–17: Chaos and degradation are rampant in governmental circles. Zoan or Tanis was a prominent city in the Delta; Noph or Memphis, about ten miles south of modern Cairo-Giza, was once the greatest city of the ancient world. Jeremiah also foresaw its desolation (Jeremiah 46:19). Even the mention of Judah in that day will strike fear and dread into the hearts of the Egyptians.

Verses 16, 18, 19, 23: Note the use of the eschatological signal "in that day," meaning in the last days.

Verse 18: In that day "five cities" of Egypt will be speaking the language of the residents of Canaan; that is, they will be converted to the worship of the true God, and swear allegiance to him.

Verses 19–22: An altar representing and suggesting a Temple of the Lord will be erected in the land of Egypt. Just as the numerous dynasties of Egyptian kings will one day give way to the King of kings, so also the prodigious temple complexes all along the Nile will give way to the true Temple or House of the Lord. The people of Egypt will then have opportunity to come to know their true Savior, and worship him. The smiting hand of the Lord will have its proper effect on them (see Helaman 12:3), and they will be healed as they repent and return to the Lord.

Verse 23–25: These verses present an incredible possibility: Assyria, Egypt, and Israel allied. Isaiah could have written political textbooks that would guide the nations of the world in their foreign policy decisions. Here, however, Isaiah is not talking politics. In the day of the Lord, long-standing animosities will be dissolved as the latter-day descendants of these former inveterate enemies come to a knowledge of their true God and recognize each other as brothers and sisters. The three nations will become as one, and will bless each other. "My people," "the work of my hands," and "mine inheritance" now apply not only to Israel but to those strangers and foreigners adopted into covenant Israel.

Isaiah 20–23

Chapter 20 seems to be purely historical. In 712 B.C. Tartan (the name of a position, as a chief captain or general under the king) crushed a revolt that the coastal city of Ashdod had led against Assyria. Isaiah's three-year mission to preach to Judah half-naked and barefoot symbolized the fall of Egypt. Judah saw Egypt succumb to the might of Assyria and understandably wondered how she herself could survive (v. 6). Fortunately, ten years later Judah's King Hezekiah wisely chose to follow Isaiah's counsel and trusted in Jehovah for deliverance (see Isaiah 36–37).

Chapters 21–23 are quite obscure. Five burdens are presented, and two personal condemnations. Miscellaneous judgments are decreed for wickedness, greed, and selfishness.

Isaiah 22:1–14

The "valley of vision" evidently here means Jerusalem. Reference is made in verse 10 to King Hezekiah breaking down houses to build or fortify a great wall. To prepare Jerusalem for an Assyrian retaliatory invasion, Hezekiah began refortifying the main city wall. A two hundred foot section of Hezekiah's wall has been uncovered in recent years in today's Jewish Quarter of the Old City of Jerusalem. The "Broad Wall," as it is called later in Nehemiah 3:8 and 12:38, is twenty-two feet wide, testimony of the serious fortification-works of Judah's king (see photo in commentary at 2 Kings 18:1–8). As archaeologists cleared away the debris of centuries, they exposed to view houses which were destroyed along the course Hezekiah laid out for the protective wall,

Royal steward's inscription. "Shebna . . . thou hast hewed thee out
a sepulchre here, as he that heweth him out a sepulchre on high, and that
graveth an habitation for himself in a rock" (Isaiah 22:15–16)

just as Isaiah noted. On the water conduit alluded to in verse 11, see 2 Kings 20:20 and 2 Chronicles 32:2–4. Verses 12–14 explain the reasons the city will have to weep and lament.

Isaiah 22:15–19

Shebna was a kind of secretary of state. In the twentieth century, archaeologists found the Royal Steward's Inscription, dating to about 700 B.C., in the necropolis (the cemetery) of the City of David, and it appears to be an inscription referring to this very man—the only contemporary individual condemned specifically in the book of Isaiah, again providing corroboration of a biblical text (see Shanks, "Nahman Avigad," 48–49). Though Shebna had carved out a sepulchre in Jerusalem (v. 16), he would be buried elsewhere (v. 18).

Isaiah 22:20–22

"Eliakim" in some ways appears to be a type of the Messiah. The name means "God shall cause to arise," foreshadowing the Resurrection. On verse 22, see also Genesis 49:10 and Revelation 3:7. The "key of David" represents the absolute power of the Messiah.

Isaiah 22:21–25

Besides alluding to the Resurrection, there seems also to be some sacred Temple imagery in these verses: "clothe him," "robe," "girdle" (v. 21); "the key of the house of David" (priesthood involved in the resurrection?; v. 22); "a nail in a sure place"

236

(prophecy of the Crucifixion; v. 23; Ezra 9:8 says nail in the *holy* place); "the sure [or holy] place be removed, and be cut down, and fall" (perhaps the Savior and his Temple; v. 25).

In one way or another, these images center on Jesus Christ and his power and authority to remove the burden of physical and spiritual death through his crucifixion, resurrection, and atonement. These aspects of the Savior's ministry are at the heart of Latter-day Saint worship in holy places (see Skinner, "Two Crucified Men," 384–86).

Isaiah 23:1–18

This chapter of Isaiah "foretells the destruction of the Phoenician port city of Tyre. Tyre, the marketplace of the nations [v. 3], was one of the most important and prosperous cities of the world, because it controlled much of the trade in the eastern Mediterranean. Its wealth had led to pride, which is abhorrent to the Lord. In Isaiah's day, Tyre was an island off the Phoenician coast [see Bible Map 9]. Although the city was forced to pay tribute several times during the Assyrian and Babylonian periods, it was not captured or destroyed until almost four centuries after Isaiah, when in 332 B.C. it fell to Alexander the Great. The oracle concludes with the prophecy that Tyre will one day be dedicated to the work of the Lord: 'Her merchandise and her hire shall be holiness to the Lord' [v. 18]" (Seely, "Lord Is Our Judge," 117–18).

Isaiah 24–27

After the burdens, hope is again held out to Israel. In these chapters we find some apocalyptic or eschatological writings similar to the later writings of Daniel, Zechariah, and John, events at the time of the Second Coming, Zion being established, the Resurrection, and the Millennium.

"The word *apocalypse* literally means 'from hiding' and refers to prophetic discourse or revelation in general. The common definition of this word, however, is derived from the New Testament, in Revelation 1:1, in which it refers to the vision given to John the Beloved on the Island of Patmos concerning the events surrounding the latter days, the Second Coming, and the end of the world. Today *apocalyptic* is used as a virtual synonym of *eschatology* (Greek, 'teachings about last things') and also denotes visions and revelations about events of cosmic destruction and the end of the world. The absolute nature and the finality of the language in Isaiah 24 through 27 is clearly eschatological, and the fulfill- ment of these prophecies is best looked for in the last days" (Seely, "Lord Is Our Judge," 118).

In chapter 24 we have several clues showing that these proph- ecies are for the latter days. Cataclysmic punishments will come.

Isaiah 24:1–18

Judgments are pronounced on the whole wicked world; they include earthquakes (vv. 1, 18–20), drought (4), a curse that de- vours the earth with burning (6), desolation and destruction (12), and flood (18).

Isaiah 24:2

All of the inhabitants will suffer: people and priests, servant and master, maid and mistress, buyer and seller, lender and bor- rower, and taker and giver of usury. Each of these expressions is a merism, a rhetorical device in which two members of a set (often opposites, as in "buyer and seller," "lender and borrower") are juxtaposed to mean a whole. In other words, *everyone* will suffer.

Isaiah 24:5–6

"Thus after this chosen family [Israel] had rejected Christ and His proposals, the heralds of salvation said to them, 'Lo, we turn unto the Gentiles;' and the Gentiles received the covenant, and were grafted in from whence the chosen family were broken off: but the Gentiles have not continued in the goodness of God, but have departed from the faith that was once delivered to the Saints, and have broken the covenant in which their fathers were established (see Isaiah xxiv:5); and have become high-minded, and have not feared; therefore, but few of them will be gathered with the chosen family. Have not the pride, high-mindedness, and unbelief of the Gentiles, provoked the Holy One of Israel to with- draw His Holy Spirit from them, and send forth His judgments to scourge them for their wickedness? This is certainly the case" (Smith, *History of the Church*, 1:313–14).

Who *can* break the "everlasting covenant"? For the Latter- day Saint concept of this everlasting covenant see Doctrine and Covenants 1:11–17 and 133:57. Note the dire warning to those who profess to have it but do nothing to fulfill it (D&C 112:24–26).

Unfaithful inhabitants of the earth will be burned; telestial people and things will be burned at the Second Coming.

Isaiah 24:16–17

In English, the Hebrew paronomasia (play on words) could be rendered: "skinny me, skinny me—pity me!" And "plunderers plunder . . . even with plunder do plunderers plunder" (Young, *Book of Isaiah,* 2:174). Notice in verse 17 another play on words in Hebrew: fear (*pakhad*), pit (*pakhat*), and snare (*pakh*). Isaiah uses many masterful literary devices to teach.

Isaiah 24:19–20

Catastrophic changes at the Second Coming portend cleansing and renewal. "Earth shall reel to and fro like a drunkard" (see D&C 49:23; 88:87); the Hebrew means "sway like a hut."

Isaiah 24:21–23

The "high ones that are on high" are the followers of Satan, who will be gathered into a pit—shut up in prison—and after many days be visited (D&C 138; Smith, *Doctrines of Salvation,* 2:155). The kingdoms of the earth—Egypt, Assyria, Babylon, Persia, Macedonia, Rome, and others—"are become the kingdoms of our Lord . . . ; and he shall reign for ever and ever" (Revelation 11:15).

There will be no need of moon or sun; God and the Lamb, the Father and the Messiah, will be there. Their glory will overshadow all other lights, as the sun in the daytime sky obscures all stars. God's light is superior; all others seem dark in comparison (see Revelation 21:23; D&C 133:49). The Lord of hosts will reign from two Jerusalems—one old and one new—each having a throne and a Temple.

Isaiah 25:1–5

Chapter 25 is a psalm of praise and thanksgiving for deliverance. These verses refer to those who are made strong through their trust in the Lord. We wonder if verses 4–5 give a hint of atomic warfare (blast, heat, noise, and shadow of cloud). In a general conference address in April 1979, Elder Bruce R. McConkie stated: "It may be . . . that nothing except the power of faith and the authority of the priesthood can save individuals and congregations from the atomic holocausts that surely shall be" (*Ensign*, May 1979, 93).

Isaiah 25:6–10

The "feast of fat things" is the gospel feast, when the righteous will partake of more of the mysteries of godliness. This is the great supper of the Lord in Mount Zion, the New Jerusalem (compare D&C 58:8–12). All are invited, but only those who are clean and properly dressed will be allowed to stay and sup (JST Matthew 22:14).

"'Sacral, communal meals are carried out in connection with temple ritual, often at the conclusion of or during a covenant ceremony.' The evidence for such practices in ancient temple ritual is very widespread.

"The presence of a communal meal at the conclusion of a covenant ceremony, all within a temple context, is expressed very clearly in the Old Testament. The parade example of this point is the meal which 'Moses, and Aaron, Nadab, and Abihu, and seventy of the elders of Israel' partook of with the Lord following the covenant ceremony that was sealed with the blood of the sacrificial animal (see Exodus 24:7–11). We find the same principle in the dedicatory prayer offered by Solomon at the completion of the building of the temple in Jerusalem. This prayer and the building of the temple, both of which clearly serve as symbols of the renewal of the covenant between the Lord and the Israelites which had existed for many centuries, were concluded with an enormous feast to which the entire congregation of Israel was invited. . . . (See 1 Kings 8:62–66.)

"The ultimate sacramental meal was the one celebrated in honor of the Savior, who 'by his own blood . . . entered in once into the holy place, having obtained eternal redemption for us' (Hebrews 9:12). In this setting the temple imagery is very clear. Indeed, there is to be yet another messianic sacramental meal, and this too is spoken of in the scriptures within the context of the temple. We read in Revelation 19:9, 'Blessed are they which are called unto the marriage supper of the Lamb.' And earlier in the same book: 'Therefore are they before the throne of God, and serve him day and night *in his temple:* and he that sitteth on the throne shall dwell among them. . . . For the Lamb which is in the midst of the throne *shall feed them,* and shall lead them unto living fountains of waters: and God shall wipe away all tears from their eyes.' (Revelation 7:15, 17; emphasis added.) This same conjunction of concepts is found in the Doctrine and Covenants, where we read of '*a supper of the house of the Lord,* well prepared, unto which all nations shall be invited. . . . And after that cometh the day of my power; then shall the poor, the lame, and the blind, and the deaf, come in unto the *marriage of the Lamb, and partake of the supper of the Lord,* prepared for the great day to come' (D&C 58:9, 11; emphasis added). It is within this context of a millennial supper, to be enjoyed in the temple ('on this mountain') by all those who have entered into holy temple covenants with the Lord, that I believe the passage in Isaiah is to be understood" (Lundquist, "Temple Symbolism in Isaiah," 41–43).

"Lees" are sediment, or dregs.

Verses 8–9: There is sublime emotion in these images: "God will wipe away tears from off all faces" (compare Revelation 7:17; 21:4), and "This is our God; we have waited for him." "The rebuke of his people" in verse 8, which God will take away, may be the Fall—overcome by God himself in the Atonement (also Alma 7:12). "Glad" in verse 9 is Hebrew *nagila,* as in the Israeli song "*Hava Nagila,*" "Let's Be Glad."

Verse 10: "This mountain" connotes Jerusalem, where the Temple and government headquarters are. "Moab" connotes the enemies, the adversaries.

Isaiah 26:1–2

Isaiah 26 is a song of praise and thanksgiving that will be sung "in that day"—in these last days. "Open ye the gates" and let the righteous in.

Isaiah 26:3–4

The righteous will trust and find strength in the Lord; they will be in "perfect peace" (Hebrew, *shalom shalom*). President Joseph F. Smith testified: "We are in perilous times, but I do not feel the pangs of that terror. It is not upon me. . . . I propose to live so that I shall be immune from the perils of the world, if it be possible for me to so live, by obedience to the commandments of God and to his laws revealed for my guidance. No matter what may come to me, if I am only in the line of my duty, if I am in fellowship with God, if . . . I can stand spotless before the world, without blemish, without transgression of the laws of God, what does it matter to me what may happen to me? I am always ready, if I am in this frame of understanding, mind, and conduct. It does not matter at all. Therefore, I borrow no trouble nor feel the pangs of fear" (*Improvement Era*, July 1917, 827).

Isaiah 26:9, 16

"When thy judgments are in the earth, the inhabitants of the world will learn righteousness" and "they poured out a prayer when thy chastening was upon them. Parallel teachings are found in Helaman 12:3 and Doctrine and Covenants 101:8.

Isaiah 26:18

Israel brought forth no fruit, just gas. They failed in their holy mission; they didn't help others to be born again, and they haven't borne fruit for two thousand years. But they will yet bear fruit, as Isaiah 27:6 boldly exclaims.

Isaiah 26:19

The doctrine of resurrection was definitely taught in the Old Testament, though Sadducees later, believing only what was written in their Hebrew scriptures, verbatim, managed to find little in the Hebrew Bible on resurrection, so they didn't believe in it (Acts 23:8). Reflect also on Isaiah 25:8 as clear evidence of the resurrection. Not only will the dead arise and live again but they will awake and sing!

Isaiah 26:20–21

Stand in holy places until the indignation has passed over (as at the original Passover time). Selective punishment will allow the righteous to be spared.

Isaiah 27:1–13

This chapter preserves another of Isaiah's songs of deliverance, this one a song of the vineyard. Throughout the scriptures, covenant Israel is often depicted in agricultural, horticultural, and viticultural terms (agriculture is cultivating crops in *fields;* horticulture is cultivating plants in *gardens;* viticulture is cultivating grapes on *vines;* see Psalms 80:8–13; Jeremiah 2:21; Ezekiel 15; Hosea 10:1; Matthew 21:33–43; Mark 12:1–11; Luke 20:9–17; Jacob 5; and many more).

"Leviathan" (see footnote 27:1*c*), the "serpent" and the "dragon" are all symbols of forces opposing God, especially Satan (see also Revelation 12:9; 20:2).

Verses 2–4: Just as the destruction of the people had been couched in the images of harvesting, so restoration and gathering is expressed as planting a vineyard, watering it, weeding it, and rejoicing in its fruitfulness. By "watering" our testimonies, they grow.

Verse 11: Dried up, unproductive branches will be broken off and gathered to be burned; see the parallel image in John 15:6.

Verses 12–13: This refers to the gathering of Israel in the latter days, and their worship of the Lord in the "holy mount at Jerusalem" and in many other holy mounts (Temples) worldwide.

Isaiah 28:1–13

Isaiah prophesies against the northern kingdom of Israel (and future Israel)—the wealth, glory, and carnal security of political and religious leaders. The veritable irony is that the powerful would lose their crowns, and the meek would wear them. They will go from pleasure to poverty, hilarity to humiliation, ecstasy to exile.

"A mighty and strong one" the Lord used back in those days was Assyria. That empire came "as a flood of mighty waters overflowing" (compare Isaiah 8:7).

Verses 5–6 contain an interlude foreshadowing a glorious future for a righteous remnant.

In verses 7–8 Isaiah turned on the religious leaders. If he envisioned a party where all participants were drunk, he gave us here an appropriate description. Drinking impairs judgment and it blurs vision (both physically and spiritually); in some cases it also causes physical illness accompanied by vomiting. Isaiah may not have had access to modern medical studies on the effects of alcohol, but he had seen enough abuse of it in his own day to understand its damaging influence on bodies and spirits.

Isaiah 28:10, 13

"Precept upon precept; line upon line" suggests that perfection is a process, not an event. The principle involved is *patience.* We are not expected to run faster than we have strength. These veiled minds of ours need time to ingest and eventually understand the mysteries of godliness. If we were to receive all knowledge in one giant spoonful, we could certainly choke on it.

Line upon line is the way that Satan, the great imitator and great distorter, also works: little by little, until there's no turning back. See more details about the scriptural definition of perfection and what we mortals are expected to attain in this life, in "The Concept of Perfection in the Scriptures" in the commentary at Genesis 17:1–8.

Isaiah 28:14–15

Isaiah turns to warn Jerusalem and all Judah. Verse 15 describes the inevitable result of their behavior: making a covenant with death and hell brings eternal anguish; as Paul later wrote, "the wages of sin is death" (Romans 6:23). An "overflowing scourge" is further identified in Doctrine and Covenants 5:19 and 45:31. "Lies" and "falsehood" refer to idols—anything that distracts people from their true God.

Because of the overflowing scourge, the Messiah is sent (see v. 16). Compare Doctrine and Covenants 1:17, which tells us that because of calamity, Joseph Smith is sent.

Isaiah 28:16–29

Read the messianic prophecy in verse 16 in connection with Isaiah 8:14–15. On the stone of Israel, see also 1 Peter 2:6 and Jacob 4:15–18. In the final line, "shall not make haste" is rendered in 1 Peter 2:6 "shall not be confounded" and in Romans 9:33 "shall not be ashamed."

Building imagery is used in verses 16–17. The line and

plummet, or plumb line, measures uprightness or straightness (in this case, of the people).

Verse 21: The mention of Mount Perazim may refer to either the episode in 2 Samuel 5:19–20, or possibly to Exodus 19:16–24. Regarding the valley of Gibeon, see Joshua 10:8–14. His "strange act" is the Lord's restoring his gospel, pouring out his Spirit, and bringing forth the Book of Mormon, as prophesied in Isaiah 29 (see also D&C 95:4; 101:95).

Verse 22: For the "consumption, even determined upon the whole earth," see Doctrine and Covenants 87:6.

Verses 23–29: A man in the field is a type of the Master Husbandman (see footnote 29a). Does he plow all day? (v. 24). No, just enough to prepare the soil. Fitches (v. 25) are spices, either black cummin or dill.

Verses 24–29: The lesson presented here in allegorical form is that our own "threshing" or testing is done appropriate to each individual—only what each person can handle.

Isaiah 29 (2 Nephi 26:15–27:35)

Isaiah 29 has been quoted more often by General Authorities of the Church than any other chapter in Isaiah. In the Bible, Isaiah 29 has 24 verses. Nephi's version has 54 verses. Either Nephi's record of Isaiah's writings was longer or else Nephi added commentary. This is one of the great prophetic visions of Isaiah that would be understood only when it finally occurred: "in the days that the prophecies of Isaiah shall be fulfilled men shall know of a surety, at the times when they shall come to pass" (2 Nephi 25:7). Note the chapter heading for Isaiah 29 in the Bible.

Isaiah 29:1–10

Verses 1–2: Usually Ariel is translated "Lion of God," but more correct is "Hearth of God." Ezekiel 43:15 has Harel, meaning "Mountain of God," and Ariel, meaning "Altar of God." Ariel represents Zion (specifically, Jerusalem).

Regarding the "woe" pronounced on Ariel, Elder Orson Pratt taught: "After the Messiah came and was sacrificed for the sins of the world, the Jews continued to 'kill sacrifices,' when they should have been done away; they added 'year to year' to the law of Moses, until they brought down 'heaviness and sorrow,' and great 'distress' upon their beloved city. The Roman army encompassed the city—cast a trench about it, and, finally, brought it down 'even with the ground.' The principal part of the Jews perished, and a remnant was scattered among the nations, where they have wandered in darkness unto this day" (*Orson Pratt's Works*, 270).

Verse 4: Voices from the dead are heard by Saints in the latter days (as detailed in 2 Nephi 26:15–17). The original meaning of Hebrew *'ov,* "a familiar spirit," is obscure (see commentary at 1 Samuel 28:3–25).

Elder Orson Pratt testified: "One of the most marvelous things connected with this prediction is, that after the nation should be brought down, they should 'speak out of the ground.' . . . Never was a prophecy more truly fulfilled than this, in the coming forth of the Book of Mormon. Joseph Smith took that sacred history 'out of the ground.' It is the voice of the ancient prophets of America speaking 'out of the ground'; their speech is 'low out of the dust'; it speaks in a most familiar manner of the doings of bygone ages; it is the voice of those who slumber in the dust. It is the voice of prophets speaking from the dead, crying repentance in the ears of the living. In what manner could a nation, after they were brought down and destroyed, 'speak out of the ground'? Could their dead bodies or their dust, or their ashes speak? Verily, no: they can only speak by their writings or their books that they wrote while living. Their voice, speech or words, can only 'speak out of the ground,' or 'whisper out of the dust' by their books or writings being discovered" (*Orson Pratt's Works*, 271).

In verses 5–10 judgments are pronounced on the wicked. Verse 8 attests that those who fight against Zion will suffer spiritual famine. Verse 10 is rendered differently in 2 Nephi 27:5: "For behold, the Lord hath poured out upon you the spirit of deep sleep. For behold, ye have closed your eyes, and ye have rejected the prophets; and your rulers, and the seers hath he covered because of your iniquity." Between verses 10 and 11, the Book of Mormon (2 Nephi 27:6–14) adds nine additional verses.

Isaiah 29:11–12 (2 Nephi 27:15–20)

These verses contain a specific prophecy of the Book of Mormon, the "book that is sealed." The 1828 meeting of

Martin Harris with Charles Anthon in New York City is reported in Joseph Smith–History 1:63–65. This episode in latter-day Church history was, at least in part, seen, heard, and recorded by the prophet Isaiah twenty-five hundred years before it happened. The "learned" was the renowned professor of classical languages, Charles Anthon, from Columbia College, now Columbia University. The one "not learned" was Joseph Smith, who had received only about three years of formal education and who, during the translation of the Book of Mormon record, enlisted others to serve as scribes for him (see Joseph Smith–History 1:61–65).

Isaiah 29:13–14 (2 Nephi 27:25–26)

As recorded in verse 13, Isaiah prophesied of the Apostasy. "With their lips do honour me": Lip service, without the heart, is hypocritical and insulting to the Lord (see again Isaiah 1:11–13).

As recorded in verse 14, Isaiah prophesied of the Restoration—"a marvellous work and a wonder." "I will proceed"— interestingly, the word "proceed" in Hebrew is *Yosef* (English, Joseph). *A Marvelous Work and a Wonder* is the title of Elder LeGrand Richards's highly popular twentieth-century book about the restored gospel.

"The wisdom of their wise men shall perish, and the understanding of their prudent men shall be hid"—to many biblical scholars, Isaiah 29 is still sealed.

Isaiah 29:15–17 (2 Nephi 27:27–28)

These verses describe the proud, the skeptics, the modern antagonists of the work of God, who, like pottery vessels boasting themselves against the potter, are the created boasting themselves against their Creator. Just so, the proud and worldly "forest of Lebanon" (1 Kings 10:17, 21; 2 Chronicles 9:16, 20) will, in the final day, be replaced by the more humble and spiritually-minded "fruitful field."

Isaiah 29:18–19 (2 Nephi 27:29–30)

The spiritually deaf and blind will hear and see the Book of Mormon, and the meek and poor will rejoice in the Lord. This prophecy may be interpreted both symbolically and literally (for example, sophisticated hearing aids, audio recordings, scriptures in Braille, etc.).

Isaiah 29:20–24 (2 Nephi 27:31–35)

The Lord's promise is that Satan and his minions will be cut off. They who offend with their words, or who try to entrap those who carry out proper business transactions and legal matters (where such matters were conducted anciently, at the city gate), or who pervert justice for trivial kickbacks will all be cut off.

The descendants of Abraham and Jacob, God's covenant people, will not be embarrassed or ashamed but will sanctify the name of the Holy One of Israel and fear (revere) the God of Israel.

All who have erred and have harbored critical feelings may finally come to understanding and learn true doctrine through the Book of Mormon. "The book" is the marvelous instrument to bring people to Christ.

Isaiah 30–31

These chapters contain Isaiah's contemporary warning against trusting in Egypt. The prophet had warned Ahaz about allying with Assyria; now he warns Hezekiah about ties with Egypt. His message was trust in the Lord! Today the same applies; real peace and security are available only through the Lord.

Isaiah 30

Verse 7: "Egyptians shall help in vain, and to no purpose"; their boast is idle.

Verses 8–17: People were rebelling against seers and prophets. As in ancient times we are interested in receiving new revelations without really living the present ones. We don't want to hear what's wrong with us. We prefer "smooth things," the "feel-good" philosophy.

Verses 18–33: Blessings are foreshadowed for Israel at Restoration time, when they are living in Zion.

Verses 19–20: After the discipline of adversity they will walk with God. Regarding "bread of adversity" and "water of affliction," President Spencer W. Kimball wrote: "Being human, we would expel from our lives physical pain and mental anguish and assure ourselves of continual ease and comfort, but if we were to close the doors upon sorrow and distress, we might be excluding our greatest friends and benefactors. Suffering can make saints of people as they learn patience, long-suffering, and self-mastery" (*Faith Precedes the Miracle*, 98).

The word "teachers" in verse 20 should be singular, and with a capital: *Teacher.* It is a messianic prophecy.

Isaiah 31:1

"Woe to them that go down to Egypt for help . . . they look not unto the Holy One of Israel, neither seek the Lord!" Do we "go down to Egypt for help" today? On what do we rely for security? President Spencer W. Kimball assured us that "if we are righteous the Lord will either not suffer our enemies to come upon us . . . or he will fight our battles for us" (*Ensign*, June 1976, 6; see also our commentary at Deuteronomy 1:19–46).

Isaiah 31:4–5

The Lord had promised Israel that he would serve as a protective shield for them; he would fight their battles for them. This is a powerful simile. There are some species of birds that will fight to the death and give up their own lives before they will let a predator kill their young. The Savior is the ultimate example of someone who would die for his children.

Compare the image of birds hovering over their nests to Jesus' lament over Jerusalem (Matthew 23:37); the word "hen" in the New Testament is Greek *ornis*, meaning a *bird* or fowl (not necessarily a hen). The image of God hovering over his offspring certainly found at least partial fulfillment in 701 B.C., when he protected Jerusalem from the predator, Assyria (see Isaiah 38).

Isaiah 32

Verses 1–2: The millennial government will be a kingdom. King Messiah (the Lord Jesus Christ) will rule and reign with princes (ecclesiastical governors) sharing the rule under his direction. "A man" in verse 2 is the King, and a series of pleasant similes depicts the security and prosperity of the glorious millennial kingdom.

Verses 13–15: The Holy Land will remain desolate until the Spirit returns to it.

"Fruitful field" (v. 15) is Hebrew *carmel* (also in Isaiah 29:17), literally "vineyard of God."

Verse 18: "Sure [Hebrew, *b'tuakh*, "secure"] dwellings . . . quiet [Hebrew, *sha'anan*, "secure"] resting places." Compare this safe and serene portrayal of future Zion with Isaiah 33:20.

Isaiah 33

Verse 6: "Add to your faith knowledge, etc. The principle of knowledge is the principle of salvation. This principle can be comprehended by the faithful and diligent; and every one that does not obtain knowledge sufficient to be saved will be condemned. The principle of salvation is given us through the knowledge of Jesus Christ" (Smith, *History of the Church*, 5:387).

Verses 14–15: Those who will dwell in "devouring fire" and "everlasting burnings" or, in other words, those who will dwell with God, are those who keep the commandments, speak no evil of others (avoiding faultfinding), who refuse to profit from extortion or bribes, who refuse to tolerate violence or evil of any kind (compare Psalm 24:3–4); "that stoppeth his ears from hearing of blood"—for example, refraining from watching violent video games (see D&C 130:6–8; on the "fire" or "burning" of the Lord, see Ogden and Skinner, *Book of Mormon*, 2:88; 215–16).

Verses 20–22: Zion, the city of God, is compared to a tabernacle or tent, an immovable tent, with its stabilizing stakes (see also Isaiah 54:2–3; compare D&C 94:1; 96:1). In verse 22 the Lord is characterized as Judge, Lawgiver, King, and Savior—the judicial, legislative, and executive branches in a theocratic kingdom. Joseph Smith said verse 22 should be the political motto of Israel (*History of the Church*, 5:64). Indeed, one motto of the United States of America is "In God We Trust"; how blessed we would be if we, as a nation, really believed that.

Isaiah 34

Verses 1–10: These verses possibly foreshadow nuclear warfare in a battle we often call Armageddon (see commentary at Isaiah 25:1–5). When the Lord returns to earth at the Second Coming, he may find the wicked destroying themselves, and he will rescue the righteous. Isaiah describes the polluted rivers, the burning pitch and smoke—all of which sounds like modern warfare. The prophet could hardly have predicted these events in such detail had he not seen them.

Verse 4: At the Second Coming the heavens will be rolled together as a scroll.

As part of the physical changes occurring at the Second Coming, several scriptures symbolically note that the heavens and/or the earth will be changed or transfigured (D&C 63:21); they will be wrapped or "rolled together as a scroll" (Mormon 5:23); see other examples in Revelation 6:14; 3 Nephi 26:3; Mormon 9:2; and Doctrine and Covenants 88:95.

Brigham Young elaborated: "If anybody wants to know what the Priesthood of the Son of God is, it is the law by which the worlds are, were, and will continue for ever and ever. It is that system which brings worlds into existence and peoples them, gives them their revolutions—their days, weeks, months, years, their seasons and times and by which they are rolled up as a scroll, as it were, and go into a higher state of existence" (*Discourses of Brigham Young*, 130).

Commenting on Isaiah 34:4, Professor Daniel H. Ludlow wrote: "At least three possible interpretations might explain the phrase 'the heavens shall be rolled together as a scroll': 1. The weather phenomena of the last days (D&C 43:25; 133:69) or the manifestations in the skies. (Rev. 6:14; D&C 29:14.) 2. The sealing of the heavens after the completion of one phase or glory of the earth; or the opening of the veil of heaven, indicating a new age. (D&C 77:8; 133:69.) 3. The completion of the work of the telestial world in anticipation of the Millennium and the Second Coming. (D&C 88:95; 101:23.)" (*Companion*, 298).

Verses 5–8: The Lord's sword will fall in judgment; his sword will be bathed in heaven (see also D&C 1:13); that is, prepared to destroy the wicked. *Idumea* is the English version of the Latin rendering of *Edom*, meaning "the whole wicked world" (D&C 1:36). This connotation doubtless arose out of the historical fact that Edom was an inveterate enemy of ancient Israel.

Verse 7: Interestingly, while Joseph Smith prepared his inspired revision of the biblical text, he came to the fictitious beasts referred to in our King James Bible as "unicorns," and the

Prophet simply inserted the Hebrew word into the text: *re'em* (which is Hebrew for wild ox or bull).

Verses 11–15: Definitions of these birds and animals are still tentative. A world with birds of prey, wild beasts, noxious weeds, and thistles: this is not a vacation adventure spot.

Verse 14: A satyr is a fictitious literary creation combining goat and man. The Hebrew term is *seir* (which is also another name for Esau), meaning hairy; that is, a "he-goat" or ram.

Verse 16: The Joseph Smith Translation of this verse reads "Seek ye out of the book of the Lord, and read *the names written therein;* no one of these shall fail, none shall want *their* mate; for my mouth it hath commanded, and *my Spirit* it hath gathered them." On the book of the Lord, see Revelation 20:12–15; Doctrine and Covenants 1:37; 85:9; 128:6–7. "Their mate" suggests exaltation in a celestial kingdom *with companions.*

Isaiah 35:1–10

These events happen after the restoration of the Church, in preparation for a millennial earth, a paradisiacal world.

Verses 1–2: Blessings are poured out on the land, with deserts blossoming as a rose. Although our Utah pioneers in America and Israel's pioneers in Israel have reclaimed the lands, we have probably seen only the beginning of what is anticipated in verse 1. And those who will yet prepare the New Jerusalem will establish it with verdure, richness, and prosperity—symbolized by the best examples from Isaiah's world: the Lebanon and Carmel mountains and the plains of Sharon.

Verses 3–10: Blessings are also poured out on the people. Verses 3–4 contain beautiful counsel for home teachers and visiting teachers—for any real Latter-day Saints—desiring to lift and strengthen others.

Verse 8: The "highway . . . The way of holiness" is provided for those who follow God's anointed servants; they will be guided onto such a highway that leads to Zion and God. The popular Primary song entitled "Follow the Prophet" reminds us that if we listen to the prophets, we will not stray from the path of righteousness (*Children's Songbook,* 110). Read more about the highway in Doctrine and Covenants 133:26–34. Is the highway literal, or figurative, or possibly both?

Verse 10: In the glorious day of restoration of all things, the ransomed or redeemed will be secure in two Zions, or two Jerusalems—both of which will be under the Redeemer's control:

"Our western tribes of Indians [Native Americans] are descendants from that Joseph which was sold into Egypt, and . . . the land of America is a promised land unto them, and unto it all the tribes of Israel will come, with as many of the Gentiles as shall comply with the requisitions of the new covenant. But the tribe of Judah will return to old Jerusalem. The city of Zion spoken of by David, in the one hundred and second Psalm, will be built upon the land of America, 'And the ransomed of the Lord shall return, and come to Zion with songs and everlasting joy upon their heads' [Isaiah 35:10]; and then they will be delivered from the overflowing scourge that shall pass through the land. But Judah shall obtain deliverance at Jerusalem" (Smith, *History of the Church*, 1:315).

Isaiah 36–39

This historical interlude reminds us that God intervenes in national life (chapters 36–37 describe the Lord's rescue of his people under King Hezekiah) and that God also intervenes in personal life (chapters 38–39 describe Hezekiah's sickness and subsequent promise of recovery and fifteen more years of life). See commentary at 2 Kings 18–20 for virtually the same material.

Isaiah 40–66

A great theme of chapters 40–49 is the redemption of Israel and the world through the Lord. Chapters 50–59 focus on the wickedness and fall of Israel, followed by the suffering of the Redeemer for the wickedness of man and the way to awaken and be redeemed. Chapters 60–66 depict the future glory of Zion and the new heaven and earth.

THE AUTHORSHIP OF ISAIAH

Isaiah 40–66 is considered by many scholars to be the work of another prophet writing much later than Isaiah (or even several later authors). The reason for that view is that these later chapters deal with the exiled Jews in Babylon and their return to rebuild Jerusalem, which is a period of history two hundred years after the ministry of Isaiah in Jerusalem. The Persian king, Cyrus, who would set in motion this return of the exiles is even mentioned by name (44:28; 45:1). The modern trend in the scholarly world is to discount prophetic preview of events and simply assign such chapters to a later time when those events were happening. Latter-day Saints, on the other hand, believe that prophets all through the ages (for example, Adam, Enoch, the brother of Jared, Abraham, Moses, Nephi, John the Revelator, and others) have seen and foreseen events in all periods of the world's existence. The Church also stands by New Testament writers who quote from all parts of Isaiah (including 40–66) and attribute them to Isaiah. Of approximately thirteen quotations in the New Testament that are ascribed to Isaiah, six originate in what we call chapters 1–39 and seven originate in chapters 40–66.

The Book of Mormon provides clear evidence that Isaiah, living in Jerusalem in the eighth century before Christ, is responsible for the entire sixty-six chapters because whole chapters from all parts of Isaiah are quoted from the brass plates, which Lehi took from Jerusalem about 600 B.C., thus showing that the whole book of prophecy was compiled and recorded before the prophecies were fulfilled and before Cyrus was even born.

If no one can see into the future, as some claim, we would have to discard all references to the First Coming, the Second Coming, the last days, the Millennium, and so forth, even by a "Second Isaiah."

The book of Isaiah has admittedly not come down to us uncorrupted; it is clear that there are flaws in the text, but that does not argue against Isaiah's authorship of all of the book. Differences in writing style are also evident. Isaiah 1–35, the prophet's earlier prophecies, are more factual, more *specific* in focus and orientation. However, Isaiah 40–66, his later prophecies, are more *devotional* in nature and would understandably feature a different descriptive style and vocabulary (compare our own personal journals featuring changes of style, diction, and syntax, over the years). For differences in style, compare the Gospel of John and the book of Revelation, which were both written by the same person!

Isaiah 40:1–2

This announcement anticipates the end of Jerusalem's warfare and her restoration. The messages of Isaiah 40 accomplish the Lord's directive, "Comfort ye, comfort ye my people." After all the woe pronounced in previous chapters, the whole idea of *comfort* sounds particularly inviting.

"Her warfare is accomplished" clearly refers to the very last days and the beginning of a new era of peace.

Question: Why would Jerusalem receive double for all her sins?

Answer: She is more accountable and responsible because she had a greater witness. Was there not a double scattering?

"In the days ahead some of the faithful will gather again within her walls and shall build the promised temple, a temple whose functions and uses will be patterned after the house of the Lord in Salt Lake City. Thereafter two prophets—valiant, mighty witnesses of the Lord Jesus Christ—will teach and testify and prophesy in her streets for three and a half years, at which time they will be slain, resurrected, and caught up to heaven. In the midst of the great war of Armageddon then in progress, Jerusalem will fall, the Lord will come, and the remnant of Judah that remains will accept the Nazarene as their King. . . .

"Jerusalem has been and yet again will be destroyed for her iniquities. When Nebuchadnezzar pillaged and burned and slew and carried the Jews into Babylon, it was because they had rejected Jeremiah and Lehi and the prophets. It was because they walked in an evil course. When Titus tore her asunder, slew most of her citizens, and made slaves of the rest, it was a just retribution because she had crucified her King. And when she falls again, amid the horror and brimstone and blood and fire of Armageddon, it will be because she has again slain the prophets . . .

"Once again the cup of her iniquity will be full, and she shall fall as she fell before. Then, having been cleansed by blood, she shall rise to become the millennial capital from which the word of the Lord shall go forth to all the earth" (McConkie, *Millennial Messiah*, 462–64).

Isaiah 40:3

The Hebrew parallelism reads literally: "A voice is crying, In the wilderness prepare ye the way of the Lord; make straight in the desert a highway for our God."

John the Baptist's ministry in New Testament times is one application of the prophecy (Matthew 3:3; John 1:23; 1 Nephi 10:8–9), but it has dual application (see Topical Guide, "Jesus Christ, Prophecies about" and "Jesus Christ, Second Coming of"). One who would cry that Jerusalem's warfare is finished would certainly be crying before and at his Second Coming. John the Baptist came at the Savior's first coming, and he has come before His second coming (see JST Luke 3:4–11; Joseph Smith–History 1:68–74).

Isaiah 40:4–5

These cataclysmic changes heralded by the voice in the wilderness should prepare the world for renewal, and for the Messiah's second coming.

Isaiah 40:6–8

This metaphor on the transitoriness of man is also found as a simile in Psalm 103:15–16 and 1 Peter 1:24, and is the same image perpetuated in modern scripture (D&C 124:2–3, 7; see commentary at Isaiah 51:12). We humans really are as the grass of the field: once having started to sprout, our growth is cut off permanently if we fail to receive nourishment from deepening our roots and accepting the promised rain or dew from heaven.

Isaiah 40:9–11

"O Zion, that bringest good tidings": The phrase in Hebrew is *Mevasseret Zion* (the name of one of modern Jerusalem's suburbs). *Besora*, translated "good tidings," means the gospel.

Elder Orson Pratt declared: "Something about Zion now, before the Lord comes—'O Zion, that bringest good tidings, get thee up into the high mountains.' Did you come up into these high mountains, you people of the latter-day Zion? What did you come here for? Because Isaiah predicted that this was the place you should come to, you should get up into the high mountain. He foretold it, and you have fulfilled it. 'O Zion, that bringest good tidings.' What good tidings? What tidings have you been declaring

. . . to the nations and kingdoms of the earth? What have you testified to, you missionaries? Your missionaries have gone from nation to nation and from kingdom to kingdom, proclaiming to the people that God has sent his angel from heaven with the everlasting Gospel to be preached unto all people upon the face of the whole earth. This is what you have been proclaiming. Is not the everlasting Gospel glad tidings to the children of men? I think it is, and especially when it is brought by an angel to prepare the way for the great and glorious day of the coming of the King of kings and Lord of lords. It is good tidings that people who receive this everlasting Gospel, are commanded to get up into the high mountain. You have fulfilled it . . . coming up from the eastern slope, from the great Atlantic seaboard, and gradually rising and ascending until you have located yourselves in a place upwards of four thousand feet above the level of the sea" (*Journal of Discourses,* 18:150).

George Frideric Handel drew from these verses some of the text for his masterpiece, *Messiah.* Verse 11 features a beautifully tender image, "He shall feed his flock like a shepherd"; compare the equally beautiful and tender images in Psalm 23 and John 10.

Isaiah 40:12–17

The greatness of God is contrasted with the nothingness of man. Consider this alternate translation from the authors: "Who has measured the waters in the palm of his hand, or marked off the heavens with a span [the width of the extended hand], or enclosed the soil of the earth in a small container, or weighed the mountains in scales, the hills in a balance?"

Verses 13–14: Is there *anything* any man can teach God? (Compare Romans 11:33–35.)

Verses 15–17: If you stand next to the tallest buildings in New York City or Chicago, and look up, the view is imposing and impressive. On the other hand, if you fly over the same buildings, from high in the air they look fairly insignificant, like legos. So is the Lord's point of view regarding the nations. Even the dust of the earth obeys the Lord but nations do not. On the concept of *nothingness,* see Moses 1:10; Mosiah 4:11; Helaman 12:7; on the other hand, consider the teachings "I am a child of God" (*Children's Songbook,* 2) and "the worth of souls is great" (D&C

18:10). Notice that Isaiah says the *nations* are less than nothing; he does not say an individual soul is nothing in the sight of God.

Isaiah 40:18–31

God is incomparably great, especially compared to idols made by human hands. It seems that, over the ages, those who refused to trust in God Almighty tried to insure some sense of permanence or immortality for themselves by creating stone and metal images that live on after them. Do we try to amass wealth or any kind of earthly possessions or "accomplishments" that may live on after us? These may be our idols, and they do for us what gold and silver idols did for the ancients—nothing. Reflect on the profound lesson expressed by the great English poet, Percy Bysshe Shelley, as he described the extraordinary attainments of Ramses II (in Egyptian, his name is Ozymandias), the great pharaoh who was responsible for perhaps half of all the colossal statues, monuments, and temples spread along Egypt's Nile river valley:

Ozymandias

I met a traveller from an antique land
Who said: Two vast and trunkless legs of stone
Stand in the desert. Near them, on the sand,
Half sunk, a shattered visage lies. . . .
And on the pedestal these words appear:
"My name is Ozymandias, king of kings:
Look on my works, ye mighty, and despair!"
Nothing beside remains. Round the decay
Of that colossal wreck, boundless and bare,
The lone and level sands stretch far away.
(Hutchinson, Complete Poetical Works of Percy Bysshe
Shelley, *550)*

Just as there is no tree good enough to make a righteous idol, there are no earthly materials beautiful enough, expensive enough, or praiseworthy enough to take the place of God.

Verse 31: On eagles' wings, see also Doctrine and Covenants 124:18, 99. Elder Orson Pratt elaborated: those who would "mount up with wings as eagles" would be renewed with the light of truth, and be enabled to move from place to place at accelerated velocity, even with the speed of light (see *Journal of Discourses*, 3:104).

Isaiah 41–44

For these chapters there is no particular historical setting; they are timeless, and their message is universal.

The Servant(s) of the Lord, often referred to in the scholarly literature as *Ebed-Yahweh* ("servant of the Lord"), may be defined as (1) a collective figure: Israel, or the prophets of Israel; (2) an individual figure: the Messiah; and/or (3) the Latter-day Saints: "servants of the Lord, even the children of Ephraim" (D&C 133:32).

There are sometimes questions about the *identity* of the Servant or servants, but more important is the *characterization*, what we can learn from all those who serve the Lord. This is similar to another dilemma: we always want to know when the Second Coming will occur instead of learning the signs of the Second Coming.

Isaiah 41:1

"Islands" (Hebrew, *iyyim*), are land areas bordered by water, or continents. "Renew their strength" is related to the previous verse (40:31). Here again we have a courtroom scene, a divine cosmic court headed by the Judge of all (as in Isaiah 1:18): "Come now, and let us reason together."

Isaiah 41:2

The righteous one from the east (Hebrew, *mizrakh;* Latin, *oriente)* could be adapted and understood in several different contexts: *Abraham* as a type of the Messiah (a ruler; see Abraham 3:22–23); *Cyrus* as a type of the Messiah; notes 2*a* and 2*b* both suggest Cyrus (see also Isaiah 46:11; 45:1); or the *Messiah* himself, coming from the east in his triumphal entry, and at his second coming (see Isaiah 63).

Isaiah 41:10–29

Verse 10 was inspiration for a verse of the Latter-day Saint hymn "How Firm a Foundation" (*Hymns*, no. 85). The rest of the chapter identifies some characteristics of the servant of the Lord:

Verse 10: fearless, trusting

Verse 14: humble (admission of "nothingness")

Verses 15–16: courageous, valiant in battle ("mountains" represent nations or enemies)

Verses 17–20: able to control the elements (by use of priesthood)

Isaiah 42

Verses 1–4: Servant Song 1 (the other Servant Songs are found at 49:1–6; 50:4–9; and 52:13–53:12). "My servant" is Jesus, the Redeemer of Israel (Matthew 12:14–21).

Following is another curious interpretation of these verses of Isaiah. Near the end of his seafaring career Christopher Columbus studied holy scripture and other literature to find evidence of divine guidance in his discoveries. He cited more than twenty passages from Isaiah in connection with his life's work. In his introductory letter to the monarchs of Spain, Columbus indicated that the enterprise to the Indies "all turned out just as our redeemer Jesus Christ had said, and as he had spoken earlier by the mouth of his holy prophets." Later in the same letter, he pointed out that "for the execution of the journey to the Indies I was not aided by intelligence, by mathematics or by maps. It was simply the fulfillment of what Isaiah had prophesied." Columbus didn't specify exactly which prophecy he had in mind, but 42:1–4 was among those cited: "Behold my servant: I will uphold him. My elect: my soul lighteth in him. I have given my spirit upon him . . . and the islands shall wait for his law" (West and Kling, *Libro de las profecias of Christopher Columbus,* 107, 111, 171).

CHARACTERISTICS OF THE SERVANT

Verse 1: Spiritual, fair in judgment

Verse 2: Humble

Verse 3: Tender, full of integrity; "bruised reed" is in Hebrew *kane* (English, *cane*). "Early Christians saw in Jesus the fulfillment of Isaiah's visions of the Suffering Servant. Isaiah 42 begins with the prophet speaking messianically, describing him as the epitome of gentle tenderness, unwilling to harm even the weakest plant. . . . The Greek word for flax was *linen,* which is one of the products prepared from the fibrous plant. Flax was grown in various parts of the Near

East anciently, especially in Egypt. . . . The 'smoking flax' is a reference to the wick of an oil lamp. The gentleness of the Messiah would figuratively disallow his even putting out the smoking linen wick used in a lamp" (Ogden, *Where Jesus Walked,* 89).

Verse 4: Persevering, positive, just

Verse 6: Caring, trusting

Verses 6–7: These verses describe the mission of Israel (the Latter-day Saints are the covenant people of Israel in our day). After quoting Isaiah 42:7, the Prophet Joseph Smith explained: "It is very evident from this that He not only went to preach to them, but to deliver, or bring them out of the prison house" (*Joseph Smith* [manual], 406; see also 1 Peter 3:18–19; D&C 138:30).

The Lord, as a loving father, said to the people of Israel, in effect, I will "hold thine hand" when you take your first faltering steps toward obedience. Through another prophet he indicated that he had taught Ephraim how to walk, "taking them by their arms." He lovingly and kindly guided their first steps along the path of righteousness (see Hosea 11:3).

Verse 12: Praiseworthy

Verse 13: Zealous

Verse 16: Faithful, loyal

Verses 19–23: The Joseph Smith Translation says the servant is not blind but the people are. Read Joseph Smith's translation of Isaiah 42:19–23 in the Bible Appendix (v. 20 especially fits the topic "Man, Potential to Become like Heavenly Father" in the Topical Guide).

Isaiah 43

This chapter is in first person; the Lord is speaking. It is addressed to covenant Israel—in the modern day, the Latter-day Saints.

The "Jacob-Israel" combination appears seventeen times in Isaiah 40–49. Just as Jacob becomes Israel, so sinful Israel becomes glorified Israel.

Verses 1–21 describe the glorious destiny of redeemed Israel.

Verses 22–28 describe the present pathetic condition of sinful Israel.

Isaiah specifies a series of *name-titles* of his God, and the sum total of all these name-titles teaches us clearly who he is.

Verse 1: Creator, Redeemer (Hebrew, *go'el*).

Verse 3: Lord, God, Holy One, Savior (*Mashiakh;* this is the word's first occurrence in Isaiah).

Verse 7: Creator.

Verse 11: Savior.

Verse 14: Redeemer, Holy One.

Verse 15: Creator, King.

In addition, these chapters refer to Him as a Servant. Compare the lesson Jesus taught in the Upper Room (John 13:12–16). Though he is our Master, he came to show us how to be a Servant. As the Savior was a Servant, so Israel should be a servant—that is the mission of God's covenant people: to serve others.

Verses 1 and 7 use the Hebrew terms *baurau* and *yatzar,* two verbs of creation in Genesis that are used again here. "I have redeemed thee"—once again the future perfect tense is used (see commentary at Isaiah 3:8–11).

Verse 2: Compare Doctrine and Covenants 122. Our loving, personal God reassures each of us: "When thou passest through the waters [of affliction], I will be with thee . . . when thou walkest through the [refiner's] fire, thou shalt not be burned."

Verse 3: Jehovah promises to come as Savior.

Verse 4: Again, the loving nature of the Servant is identified.

Verses 5–6: A worldwide gathering is foreseen (through missionary work).

Verse 8: Again, the court scene.

Verse 10: "Ye are my *witnesses*" (in court); we are Jehovah's or Jesus' witnesses; compare Acts 1:8, "Ye shall be *witnesses* unto me"; and in the sacrament ordinance we promise to *witness.* Why does such a congregation of witnesses exist? To be "a light of the Gentiles" (42:6) and to "shew forth my praise" (43:21).

Because of Isaiah's remark that "before me there was no God formed, neither shall there be after me" some have asked how the Latter-day Saints can believe in multiple Gods, and even our own potential to become Gods, as President Lorenzo Snow taught. The answer is actually quite simple. Looking closely at the whole chapter 43, it is obvious that the Lord is explaining, in some detail, who he is—that all those idols of stone, wood, and metal that the people had made to worship were sheer nonsense. The Egyptians, Mesopotamians, Canaanites, and at times, even the Israelites, had a serious problem with idolatry. The Lord is arguing his case as their only true God: the Creator and Redeemer (v. 1), the Lord, God, the Holy One of Israel, the Savior (v. 3), the Lord, Redeemer, the Holy One of Israel (v. 14), the Lord, the Holy One, the Creator of Israel, their King (v. 15). His point is that he is the only Being in the universe—always has been and always will be—the only Person who can save them . . . because he paid the price for their sins! This chapter is simply a great discourse defending his position as their only, true God, in the face of all that ridiculous idolatry. He argues: "I, even I, am the Lord; and beside me there is no saviour" (v. 11; compare D&C 76:1). From the premortal council in heaven to the eternities yet ahead, we will always hold him dear as our only Savior, the only God with whom we have to deal for the salvation of our souls. All this, of course, under the direction of the Father and as guided by the Holy Ghost. Those Three are the only Gods who are involved in our eternal exaltation.

Verse 12: "The power of God unto salvation is found here in the tops of these everlasting hills; and this glorious truth is spreading out to all the nations of the earth as rapidly as people in them accept the testimony and witness that is borne and believe the truths that our fellow representatives proclaim. This is a day of which God has said that all of gathered Israel shall be witnesses of his name. ' . . . ye are my witnesses, saith the Lord, that I am God'" (McConkie, *Ensign*, July 1972, 110).

Verse 21: Again, the mission of Israel is noted.

Verse 25: The Savior blotted out or atoned for our transgressions. In one sense, he forgives us for *his* sake. Anyone who is unforgiving is the one who really suffers injury and hurt, so by refusing to remember our sins, the Savior rids himself of the heavier burden of holding a grudge, thereby freeing himself for love and faith in our potential. We can know this same freedom by following his example in forgiving.

Verse 26: Again, we see the loving parent: "let us plead together."

Verse 28: Some of the curses and reproaches over the centuries have been called Assyrians, Babylonians, Greeks, Romans, and Nazis.

Isaiah 44

Verse 2: God does form us from the womb; his hand is involved in the miracle of human creation from conception. *Jesurun* means "upright, righteous" from Hebrew *yashar* (see Deuteronomy 33:26).

Verse 6: Isaiah gives us additional descriptive titles for God: *Lord, King, Redeemer, Lord of hosts (Lord of Sabaoth), the First and the Last (Alpha and Omega).* "I am the first, and I am the last"— The phrase "I am" is an eternal statement of being. It implies no beginning, for to have a beginning means there was a time when he was not. There never was such a time, for, he says, *I AM,* and always have been.

Verse 8: Could we have here a taste of divine humor? "Is there a God beside me? yea, there is no God; I know not any."

Verses 9–20: Idols are ridiculed.

Verses 22: Sins have been covered, from Hebrew *kappar* (as in Yom Kippur, Day of Atonement). Isaiah scholar Edward J. Young wrote: "A command to repent is given, because God Himself has paid a price to purchase His people. It is that concept that lies at the heart of the matter. . . . The reference is not to the return from exile, for that act could not really be designated a redemption paid by God; the reference is to a ransom paid for deliverance from sin and guilt, and the price God paid for that deliverance was His own Son, in whom we have redemption through His blood, the forgiveness of sins" (*Book of Isaiah,* 3:184).

Verses 26–28: Here Cyrus (Hebrew, *Koresh*) is mentioned by name, which mention forms the basis for the "deutero-Isaiah" hypothesis (see also 45:1). That his name was known two hundred years before his birth is no problem for Latter-day Saints; there are other examples of those whose names were known before they were born: Joseph Smith Jr. and Sr. (2 Nephi 3:15); John (1 Nephi 14:27); Moses (2 Nephi 3:9–10, 17); and Mary (Mosiah 3:8; Alma 7:10). Denial of predictive prophecy is the ideology espoused by Sherem (Jacob 7:7) and Korihor (Alma 30:13).

The Lord foreordained his servant Cyrus to instigate the rebuilding of Jerusalem and the Temple.

Isaiah 45

Verse 1: Deliverance through Cyrus typifies the Lord's universal salvation. Cyrus was "anointed." *Where* was he anointed? He was foreordained in the premortal world of spirits. Compare Jeremiah 25:9 and 27:6, where Nebuchadnezzar is called "my servant."

Joseph Smith wrote: "That we may learn still further that God calls or elects particular men to perform particular works, or on whom to confer special blessings, we read, [Isaiah 45:4], 'For Jacob my servant's sake, and Israel mine elect, I have even called thee [Cyrus] by thy name,' to be a deliverer to my people Israel, and help to plant them on my holy mountain" (*History of the Church*, 4:257).

Cyrus was a type of the Messiah, the Anointed One, the Deliverer:

"Cyrus is the only Gentile king who is called God's 'anointed.' Since this is the translation of the Hebrew word which we spell in English as *Messiah*, Cyrus is in a sense a type of the Anointed One, the Lord Jesus Christ. Typology is often misunderstood and abused. A type is a divinely appointed prophetic symbol, usually of Christ. When a person or a thing is called a type, that does not alter its literal meaning or deny its historical reality. Cyrus was a Persian king, and we have no evidence that he ever really knew the true God, although the Persian religion was relatively free from the gross idolatries of the Babylonians. Consequently when it is asserted that Cyrus is a type of Christ, it is not said that he was like the Lord Jesus Christ in every respect. The only intended resemblance is in the fact that Cyrus was the anointed one who delivered the people of Israel from their captivity. As such he points us to the greater Anointed One who saves His people from their sins" (Alfred Martin, *Isaiah, the Salvation of Jehovah*, 77–78, as cited in *Old Testament* [student manual], 2:186).

The Jewish historian Josephus wrote:

"In the first year of the reign of Cyrus, which was the seventieth [year] from the day that our people were removed out of their own land into Babylon, God commiserated the captivity and calamity of these poor people, according as he had foretold to them by Jeremiah the prophet, before the destruction of the city, that after they had served Nebuchadnezzar and his posterity, and after they had undergone that servitude seventy years, he would restore them again to the land of their fathers, and they should build their temple, and enjoy their ancient prosperity; and these things God did afford them; for he stirred up the mind of Cyrus, and made him write this throughout all Asia:—'Thus saith Cyrus the King:— Since God Almighty hath appointed me to be king of the habitable earth, I believe that he is that God which the nation of the Israelites worship; for indeed he foretold my name by the prophets, and that I should build him a house at Jerusalem, in the country of Judea.'

"This was known to Cyrus by his reading the book which Isaiah left behind him of his prophecies; for this prophet said that God had spoken thus to him in a secret vision:—'My will is, that Cyrus, whom I have appointed to be king over many and great nations, send back my people to their own land, and build my temple.' This was foretold by Isaiah one hundred and forty years before the temple was demolished. Accordingly, when Cyrus read this, and admired the divine power, an earnest desire and ambition seized upon him to fulfil what was so written; so he called for the most eminent Jews that were in Babylon, and said to them, that he gave them leave to go back to their own country, and to rebuild their city Jerusalem, and the temple of God, for that he would be their assistant, and that he would write to the rulers and governors that were in the neighbourhood of their country of Judea, that they should contribute to them gold and silver for the building of the temple, and, besides that, beasts for their sacrifices" (*Antiquities of the Jews*, bk. 11, chap. 1, paras. 1–2).

Although Cyrus is thought to have been a Zoroastrian, a follower of Zarathustra—which would require allegiance to the monotheistic worship of the Lord of Wisdom, Ahura Mazda— he may have been a religious eclectic, something of a polytheist, wishing to do the will of any and all gods of the lands he conquered; he built temples to other gods also. There are significant resemblances between Ahura Mazda and Jehovah and their respective religions, which would have impressed King Cyrus and motivated him to do the bidding of Israel's God (see Rasmussen, *Ensign*, Nov. 1971, 32–38).

Verse 7: "I make peace, and create *evil*"—God, of course, does not literally create evil. Other definitions of the Hebrew word are woe or calamity, which are the antithesis of peace. Note the parallelism: light// darkness, peace// evil. Darkness is absence of light; calamity is absence of peace.

Verse 8: "Truth shall spring out of the earth [the Book of Mormon]; and righteousness shall look down from heaven" (Psalm 85:11).

The Prophet Joseph Smith declared: "And now, I ask, how righteousness and truth are going to sweep the earth as with a flood? [and how will the heavens pour down righteousness?] I will answer. Men and angels are to be co-workers in bringing to pass this great work, and Zion is to be prepared, even a new Jerusalem, for the elect that are to be gathered from the four quarters of the earth, and to be established an holy city, for the tabernacle of the Lord shall be with them" (*Joseph Smith* [manual], 188–89).

Salvation—Isaiah uses the Hebrew root word thirty-eight times in his writings (in addition to the fifteen times used as part of his own name). The word is *Yeshua*, and it was the name by which the Savior was known in mortality (English, Jesus). Isaiah undoubtedly knew what his name would be, just as Adam and Enoch (Moses 6:52, 57; 7:50), Nephi (2 Nephi 25:19; 31:10), and others knew.

Verse 9: Compare Isaiah 29:16 and Romans 9:20.

Verse 12: The Old Testament student manual for institute classes makes interesting comments on this verse: "Men and organizations often deal with the things of the earth in terms of ownership. 'I own a large home,' one might say, or 'I built this business up through my own labors; therefore it is mine.' If these statements were really true, then one could understand their reluctance to share it with others or to pay the Lord his required tenth. But men cannot speak of ownership. Through Isaiah, the Lord reminded Israel that he is the creator of the earth and therefore only he can properly refer to it in terms of ownership. In language similar to Isaiah's, the Lord reminded the Latter-day Saints that he created the earth and that men are only stewards over his property (see D&C 104:13–14, 54–57). Then he gave this reminder: 'And let not any among you say that it is his own; for it shall not be called his, nor any part of it' (D&C 104:70).

"Elder Spencer W. Kimball asked some pointed questions concerning this subject: 'Do you feel generous when you pay your tithes? Boastful when the amount is large? Has the child been generous to his parents when he washes the car, makes his bed? Are you liberal when you pay your rent, or pay off notes at banks? You are not generous, liberal, but merely honest when you pay your tithes.' [Isaiah 45:12.]

"'Perhaps your attitudes are the product of your misconceptions.

"'Would you steal a dollar from your friend? a tire from your neighbor's car? Would you borrow a widow's insurance money with no intent to pay? Do you rob banks? You are shocked at such suggestions. Then, would you rob your God, your Lord, who has made such generous arrangements with you?

"'Do you have a right to appropriate the funds of your employer with which to pay your debts, to buy a car, to clothe your family, to feed your children, to build your home?

"'Would you take from your neighbor's funds to send your children to college, or on a mission? Would you help relatives or friends with funds not your own? Some people get their standards mixed, their ideals out of line. . . . Would you supply gifts to the poor with someone else's money? The Lord's money?' (In Conference Report, Apr. 1968, p. 77.)

"Honestly answering these questions may reveal to the modern Saint how dangerously close he is to walking the same foolish path chosen by ancient Israel" (*Old Testament* [student manual], 2:186–87).

Verses 15–25: Isaiah bears his testimony of the Lord Jehovah, or Jesus.

Verse 17: "World without end" (compare D&C 76:112) means "everlasting salvation" (same verse) or "throughout all ages" (Ephesians 3:21).

Verse 19: Compare Acts 26:26, "this thing was not done in a corner." The Lord does not speak in secret or in dark places, nor do prophets. They let their light shine, and those who find themselves in the darkness of sin but are willing to listen will enter into the light and rejoice in it.

Verse 21–23: Compare Philippians 2:9–10. Jehovah and Jesus are clearly one and the same.

Verse 23: Every knee shall bow, and every tongue confess to God (Romans 14:11; Philippians 2:10–11; D&C 88:104).

Isaiah 46

Idols are ancient and modern. Place no trust in earthly objects or powers.

Isaiah's message is similar to Elijah's on Mt. Carmel (1 Kings 18:17–39). What are the idols we encounter in our modern, sophisticated world?

President Spencer W. Kimball wrote:

"Idolatry is among the most serious of sins. There are unfortunately millions today who prostrate themselves before images of gold and silver and wood and stone and clay. But the idolatry we are most concerned with here is the conscious worshiping of still other gods. Some are of metal and plush and chrome, of wood and stone and fabrics. They are not in the image of God or of man, but are developed to give man comfort and enjoyment, to satisfy his wants, ambitions, passions and desires. Some are in no physical form at all, but are intangible. . . .

"Modern idols or false gods can take such forms as clothes, homes, businesses, machines, automobiles, pleasure boats, and numerous other material deflectors from the path to godhood. What difference does it make that the item concerned is not shaped like an idol? Brigham Young said: 'I would as soon see a man worshiping a little god made of brass or of wood as to see him worshiping his property.'

"Intangible things make just as ready gods. Degrees and letters and titles can become idols. Many young men decide to attend college when they should be on missions first. The degree, and the wealth and the security which come through it, appear so desirable that the mission takes second place. Some neglect Church service through their college years, feeling to give preference to the secular training and ignoring the spiritual covenants they have made.

"Many people build and furnish a home and buy the

automobile first—and then find they 'cannot afford' to pay tithing. Whom do they worship? Certainly not the Lord of heaven and earth, for we serve whom we love and give first consideration to the object of our affection and desires. Young married couples who postpone parenthood until their degrees are attained might be shocked if their expressed preference were labeled idolatry" (*Miracle of Forgiveness*, 40–41).

Verse 1: Bel and Nebo were Babylonian idol-gods. Bel was the chief of their pantheon (compare Canaanite Baal). Nebo was a god of wisdom and divine guidance; note Babylonian names using Nebo or Nabu: Nebuchadnezzar, Nabopolassar. Bel and Nebo were apostate versions of Jehovah and the Holy Ghost.

Verses 3–4: Compare Matthew 20:27–28.

Verse 8: "Shew yourselves men"; compare 2 Nephi 1:21: "arise from the dust, my sons, and be men."

Verse 11: "A ravenous bird from the east" is figurative for Cyrus and his rapid conquest. On the "east," recall 41:2; and again compare the Messiah in Isaiah 63:1.

Verse 12: "Stouthearted" means stubborn of heart.

Isaiah 47

Read the footnotes. This is a song of taunting, a prophecy of Babylon's destruction, and a type of what will happen to spiritual Babylon (see D&C 133:14). In a symbolic way, Zion is the spiritual offspring of Jehovah; Babylon is the evil offspring of Lucifer.

Verse 1: The prophecy was fulfilled in 539 B.C. when Cyrus conquered Babylon; compare Jeremiah 50:9–10.

Verse 2: Those who are taken into captivity by sin will experience exposure, humiliation, and shame. Those who refuse to succumb to sin, or hastily retreat from sin when they have tasted its bitter fruit, will wear the garment of the holy priesthood and remain physically and spiritually covered and clothed.

Verse 7–9: Compare Revelation 18:7–8.

Verse 10: An "open mind" may be like a fertile garden that is capable of nourishing not only the fruitful vine but also all sorts of weeds, which can flourish and choke the vine. Read the vital warning in 2 Nephi 9:27. We must be careful to cultivate wholesome knowledge and, at the same time, leave room in our minds for the Lord to plant new seeds.

Verse 13: Many programs of pop psychology, motivational seminars, psychic and astrological hot lines will eventually weary those sincerely seeking truth—they are telestial and terrestrial approaches at best. The gospel of Jesus Christ protects against the confused noises of the world and provides celestial comfort, security, and stability.

Verse 15: Compare Revelation 18:3.

Isaiah 48 (1 Nephi 20)

The first two chapters of Isaiah quoted in the Book of Mormon (1 Nephi 20 and 21), describe Nephi's reading of Isaiah 48 and 49 to his brothers. Isaiah 48 is largely a discussion of ancient Israel's waywardness and their disloyalty to the Redeemer of Israel. Isaiah 49 is the prophet's announcement of a special servant to come forth, who would possess several significant and special characteristics, and fulfill unique roles. Three things become obvious: first, Isaiah possessed a panoramic perspective on Israel's history and destiny; second, Nephi knew well and appreciated this section of Isaiah because of the parallel it presented between Israel and his own brothers, Laman and Lemuel; third, only two beings fit Isaiah's very specific and unusual qualities: the Lord Jesus Christ and the Prophet Joseph Smith.

Notice that after hearing these two chapters Nephi's brothers came to him and asked, "What meaneth these things?" (1 Nephi 22:1). Fortunately, Nephi gave further explanation.

Isaiah scholar Claus Westermann claimed that Isaiah 48 has serious textual difficulties, "and so far editors have not succeeded in finding any convincing solution" (*Isaiah 40–66,* 195). Now we have a solution: the Book of Mormon.

Isaiah 48:1 (1 Nephi 20:1)

Notice that the very first word in this first chapter of Isaiah that Nephi quotes is not *hear* but *hearken*—supplementing the passive hearing with active obeying.

In the 1840 printing of the Book of Mormon, the Prophet Joseph Smith added after "the waters of Judah": "or out of the waters of baptism." This refers to those who have taken on themselves the covenant of baptism, thus indicating that baptism was an essential ordinance performed in Old Testament times (though known more by the term *immersion* than by the later Greek term *baptism*).

Isaiah 48:2 (1 Nephi 20:2)

"They call themselves of the holy city." As hypocrites said in Jesus' day: "we have Abraham [for] our father" (Luke 3:8); "we be Abraham's seed" (John 8:33). They thought themselves worthy of some preferential status, but they did not stay themselves on [that is, depend on, rely on, trust in] the God of Israel. Brigham Young University professors Joseph McConkie and Robert Millet wrote of this verse: "Salvation is not obtained by living in a particular place, but rather by living in a particular way. There are no holy cities without a holy people" (*Doctrinal Commentary*, 1:152).

Isaiah 48:3–9 (1 Nephi 20:3–9)

The Lord revealed future things before his wayward people could claim that idols did them.

Verse 7 addition in the Book of Mormon: "even before the day when thou heardest them not *they were declared unto thee.*"

Verse 9 addition: "for my praise will I refrain *from* thee."

Isaiah 48:10 (1 Nephi 20:10)

The phrase "but not with silver" in Isaiah disrupts the meaning of the verse, and the Book of Mormon omits it.

This is great doctrine, this idea of being refined and chosen in the furnace of affliction. Just as gold is smelted in the fire to remove impurities, so God has tried his people with fire to remove impurities. The Lord is working hard to draw impurities out of us. Just as a diamond is carefully faceted and polished to reveal its inner beauty, so has Israel been shaped and polished. Trials are not punishment inflicted by a vengeful God but tests by a loving Father who wants us to be refined and polished. Our impurities (weaknesses, faults) are burned away *if* we can withstand the heat and pressure of our trials. Refineries heat up the metal to its melting point, at which time the impurities separate. In a similar way God "turns up the heat" until we reach the point where we become refined so we can be of use to him. The temperature necessary to refine each of us is different. Refinement is customized for each of us by a perfect and omniscient Father. And it helps to know that our troubles and trials are purposeful; we endure them for good reasons.

We are here on earth to be refined, and this earth is one big furnace! All of these metaphorical expressions about the refiner's fire give new meaning to the statement of the prophet Brigham Young: "Learn everything that the children of men know, and be prepared for the most *refined* society upon the face of the earth" (*Journal of Discourses*, 16:77; emphasis added).

Isaiah 48:11 (1 Nephi 20:11)

Note the Book of Mormon change from the King James Version: "for *I will not suffer my name to be polluted.*"

Isaiah 48:13 (1 Nephi 20:13)

Right hand: "Showing favor to the right hand or side is not something invented by man but was revealed from the heavens in the beginning. . . . There are numerous passages in the scriptures referring to the right hand, indicating that it is a symbol of righteousness and was used in the making of covenants" (Smith, *Answers to Gospel Questions*, 1:156–57).

Isaiah 48:14–15 (1 Nephi 20:14–15)

The pronouns *he* and *him* are somewhat confusing; it seems to be Jehovah speaking but talking about himself. He is delivering the message of the Father about himself, so the prophecy is about Jesus, who is using the third-person form. He is speaking as the Father—either as God the Father or in his role as Jehovah, it is the same.

Isaiah 48:20 (1 Nephi 20:20)

"Go ye forth of Babylon." In one of our hymns we sing about the importance of bidding Babylon farewell (see *Hymns*, no. 319). On the eve of Babylon's destruction we have a new exodus, a type of the old. Doctrine and Covenants 133:14 certainly refers to a spiritual exodus, but could it also be referring to a physical exodus? Unlikely. Our God wants us to flee from the spiritual wickedness around us but not isolate ourselves physically from the rest of humankind. We have to stay among them to show them the way, to be a light to all people. Ralph Waldo Emerson made an interesting observation: "It is easy in the world to live after the world's opinion; it is easy in solitude to live after our own; but the great man is he who in the midst of the crowd keeps with perfect sweetness the independence of solitude" (*Essays*, 31).

Isaiah 48:22 (1 Nephi 20:22)

Book of Mormon addition: "And notwithstanding he hath done all this, and greater also."

There is no peace for the wicked. The Holy Ghost does not comfort the wicked. No one comforts the wicked. See also Alma 41:10: "wickedness never was happiness."

Isaiah 49 (1 Nephi 21)

The best way to study this chapter is alongside the inspired commentary and interpretations of Nephi (in 1 Nephi 22:1–12) and Jacob (in 2 Nephi 6:4–18 and 2 Nephi 10:1–22).

This chapter is directed to the modern covenant people of Israel: "The revelations that are in the Bible, the predictions of the patriarchs and prophets who saw by vision and revelation the last dispensation and fulness of times plainly tell us what is to come to pass. The 49th chapter of Isaiah is having its fulfillment" (Wilford Woodruff, as cited in Smith, *Signs of the Times*, 112).

Isaiah 49:1–6 (1 Nephi 21:1–6)

This is one of the great Servant Songs of Isaiah, speaking of an individual or a group who will make salvation accessible for those who diligently seek it. Possibilities for the servant are Isaiah himself; Jehovah (Jesus Christ); Israel, particularly Ephraim; and Joseph Smith. Maybe all of the above are applicable, but especially Jesus Christ and Joseph Smith.

Isaiah 49:1 (1 Nephi 21:1)

The first half of the verse is missing in the King James Version; Nephi adds, "And again: Hearken, O ye house of Israel, all ye that are broken off and are driven out because of the wickedness of the pastors of my people; yea, all ye that are broken off, that are scattered abroad, who are of my people, O house of Israel."

Isles means habitable ground or dry land as opposed to water, or in other words, islands and continents.

America is referred to (see 1 Nephi 22:7–8).

"Called me from the womb"—that is, the servant was fore-ordained. All servants of the Lord are foreordained (compare Jeremiah 1:5).

Isaiah 49:2 (1 Nephi 21:2)

"Mouth like a sharp sword": To the wicked, the servant's words are cutting like a sword (1 Nephi 16:2; D&C 6:1–2).

Elaborating on the concept of a polished shaft, the Prophet Joseph Smith exclaimed: "I am like a huge, rough stone rolling down from a high mountain; and the only polishing I get is when some corner gets rubbed off by coming in contact with something else, striking with accelerated force against religious bigotry, priestcraft, lawyer-craft, doctor-craft, lying editors, sub-orned judges and jurors, and the authority of perjured executives, backed by mobs, blasphemers, licentious and corrupt men and women—all hell knocking off a corner here and a corner there. Thus I will become a smooth and polished shaft in the quiver of the Almighty, who will give me dominion over all and every one of them, when their refuge of lies shall fail, and their hiding place shall be destroyed, while these smooth-polished stones with which I come in contact become marred" (*History of the Church,* 5:401).

"In his quiver hath he hid me": The servant is hidden or pro-tected until the appropriate time for the Lord to pull him out to fight in the cause of righteousness. The arrow of truth will be shot out into the world and will pierce the hearts of the wicked.

Isaiah 49:5 (1 Nephi 21:5)

Of Joseph Smith the Lord said: "Fools shall have thee in deri-sion, and hell shall rage against thee; while the pure in heart, and the wise, and the noble, and the virtuous, shall seek counsel, and authority, and blessings constantly from under thy hand" (D&C 122:1–2). And "God shall exalt thee on high" (D&C 121:8).

Isaiah 49:6 (1 Nephi 21:6)

The mission statement of the covenant people of Israel is identified: to be a light to the Gentiles, to bring them to salvation. "Salvation" in Hebrew is *Yeshua* (Jesus). The Savior, the prophet, and every true servant of the Lord are lights to the Gentiles.

Isaiah 49:7 (1 Nephi 21:7)

The world despised the Lord Jesus Christ and the Prophet Joseph Smith, but kings and princes will indeed bow and honor these noble and great ones.

Isaiah 49:8 (1 Nephi 21:8)

"Have I heard thee, *O isles of the sea*"—isles are the far islands or continents beyond Asia.

"And give thee *my servant* for a covenant of the people"—that is, Joseph Smith.

A SPECIAL SERVANT

Isaiah announced a special servant of God who would come forward in the future, possessing several significant and unusual characteristics. In 1 Nephi 21, Nephi once again described this prophetic figure. He would be someone—

- whom "the Lord hath called . . . from the womb" (1 Nephi 21:1).
- who would say that the Lord "formed me from the womb" to do a special work, or in other words, someone who *knew* he had been foreordained (21:5).
- whose "mouth [was] like a sharp sword," or in other words, someone who spoke with authority (21:2).
- who was hidden "in the shadow of [the Lord's] hand" (21:2).
- who was "made . . . a polished shaft; in his quiver hath he [the Lord] hid [him]" (21:2).
- who would say, "I have labored in vain" (21:4).
- who would authoritatively say, "And now, saith the Lord" (21:5).
- whose life's work would be "to bring Jacob again to [the Lord]—though Israel be not gathered" (21:5).
- who would be the Lord's "servant to raise up the tribes of Jacob, and to restore the preserved of Israel" (21:6).
- whom the Lord would "give . . . for a light to the Gentiles" (21:6).
- "whom man despiseth," but at the same time, someone whom "kings shall see and arise, princes also . . . worship" (21:7).
- who will be given to Israel "for a covenant of the people, to establish the earth, to cause to inherit the desolate heritages,"

who will free the prisoners and enlighten those who sit in darkness, and who will shepherd the chosen people (21:8–9).

Though various specific aspects of this list could probably fit a number of individuals, taken together they apply to only two beings. One is obviously Jesus, but the other is Joseph Smith. Consider the following:

- Joseph Smith was indeed called "from the womb," or foreordained.
- He knew through revelation, now recorded as Doctrine and Covenants 127:2, that he had been chosen to be the prophet of the Restoration. On another occasion he also said: "Every man who has a calling to minister to the inhabitants of the world was ordained to that very purpose in the Grand Council of heaven before this world was. I suppose that I was ordained to this very office in that Grand Council. It is the testimony that I want that I am God's servant, and this people His people" (*Joseph Smith* [manual], 511).
- Joseph Smith spoke as a "sharp sword" because he spoke the words of the Lord (D&C 18:35–36; 21:5), which are described as "quick and powerful, sharper than a two-edged sword, to the dividing asunder of both joints and marrow" (D&C 6:2).
- Joseph Smith was "hid" by the Lord (D&C 86:9).
- Joseph Smith became a "polished shaft" in the quiver of the Almighty, as his own characterization of himself testifies.
- Joseph Smith at times became discouraged and felt that he labored in vain (D&C 121:2).
- Not only did Joseph Smith have the authority to speak for God but on numerous occasions he validated those messages by uttering the very words Isaiah predicted he would say: "Thus saith the Lord" (for example, D&C 52:1; 54:1; 60:1; 87:1).
- Joseph Smith's life work was to bring the house of Israel again to the Lord (Mormon 8:16; D&C 5:9–10; 6:6; 109:67).
- Joseph Smith was also commissioned to "raise up the tribes of Jacob" and "restore" them by overseeing the latter-day gathering of Israel (D&C 110:11).
- Joseph Smith is spoken of in the scriptures as "a light unto the

Gentiles" (D&C 86:11). Only one other person can claim that distinction: the Lord himself (Isaiah 42:6).

- Joseph Smith was both despised and revered, just as the Lord had predicted (Joseph Smith–History 1:33). Joseph was also promised that the gospel he restored would be preached before "kings and rulers" (D&C 1:23).

- Joseph Smith was the servant through whom the eternal gospel covenant was reestablished (D&C 1:17–22). Surely it is not just coincidence that Doctrine and Covenants 1, the revelation by which the Lord introduces Joseph Smith to the world, begins with the same language as Isaiah 49:1. Just as Isaiah had foretold, the Prophet Joseph was also commanded to "proclaim the acceptable year of the Lord, and the gospel of salvation" (D&C 93:51).

Isaiah 49:9 (1 Nephi 21:9)

Salvation for the dead is taught in the Old Testament. How do we know that Isaiah understood this vital doctrine? "And Isaiah, who declared by prophecy that the Redeemer was anointed to bind up the broken-hearted, to proclaim liberty to the captives, and the opening of the prison to them that were bound, [was] also there [in the spirit world when the Savior visited between his death and resurrection]" (D&C 138:42).

Isaiah 49:14, 21, 24 (1 Nephi 21:14, 21, 24)

Israel remonstrates with a series of complaints:

Verse 14—complaint 1: The Lord forsook and forgot Israel. Some in Israel felt wronged by the Lord. They felt severely punished through their sufferings due to political oppression, exile, famine, plague, and more.

Verses 14–16—from the Book of Mormon comes this answer from Nephi: "*but he will show that he hath not.*" A powerful attachment is expressed: graven on the palms of his hands are the nail wounds in the Savior's hands. Far from forsaking them, he gave his all for them. "Greater love hath no man than this, that a man lay down his life for his friends" (John 15:13). Christ paid the ultimate price for our sins. He cannot forget us because he has the evidence of that price in his hands and feet (see D&C 6:36–37).

Verse 18—the covenant people of Israel will eventually be clothed and ornamented (that is, prepared) as a bride for the Bridegroom, as reflected in various scriptures; see, for example, Matthew 25:1–10; D&C 33:17; 133:10, 19.

Verse 21—complaint 2: Israel has lost all her children.

Verses 22–23—answer: The Lord will raise a standard or ensign (for example, the Church, the Book of Mormon, and the everlasting covenant) and bring the children of Israel back to their promised inheritance.

Is the Lord talking about Jews in the Holy Land or the Israelites broken off inhabiting the Americas? (see 1 Nephi 22:6). Isaiah speaks to *all* Israel, which assures multilevel fulfillment.

Kings and queens, and other political leaders, will be nursing fathers and mothers in helping restore the remnants of Israel to their covenant lands. Note one fulfillment of this prophecy in the following excerpt from Elder Orson Hyde's dedicatory prayer given October 24, 1841, on the Mount of Olives in Jerusalem:

"Let the land become abundantly fruitful when possessed by its rightful heirs; let it again flow with plenty to feed the returning prodigals who come home with a spirit of grace and supplication . . . Incline them to gather in upon this land according to Thy word. Let them come like clouds and like doves to their windows. Let the large ships of the nations bring them from the distant isles; and let kings become their nursing fathers, and queens with motherly fondness wipe the tear of sorrow from their eye.

"Thou, O Lord, did once move upon the heart of Cyrus to show favor unto Jerusalem and her children. Do Thou now also be pleased to inspire the hearts of kings and the powers of the earth to look with a friendly eye towards this place, and with a desire to see Thy righteous purposes executed in relation thereto. Let them know that it is Thy good pleasure to restore the kingdom unto Israel—raise up Jerusalem as its capital, and constitute her people a distinct nation and government" (Smith, *History of the Church*, 4:457).

Verse 24—complaint 3: Israel is prey; she is held captive.

Verses 25–26—answer: Read 2 Nephi 6:16–18. The Mighty God shall deliver his covenant people.

Isaiah 50 (2 Nephi 7)

Jacob, Nephi's brother, explained why he quoted these Isaiah chapters in the Nephite record: "I speak unto you these things that ye may rejoice, and lift up your heads forever, because of the blessings which the Lord God shall bestow upon your children" (2 Nephi 9:3).

Isaiah 50:1 (2 Nephi 7:1)

Jacob quotes Isaiah 50, where Isaiah is speaking messianically. Notice the questions the Lord raises right up front. The first question is found only in the Book of Mormon; it is not in the King James Bible. If a man found uncleanness (infidelity) in his wife, he could put her away with a bill of divorcement (see the Mosaic law in Deuteronomy 24:1–4).

Here again we have marriage imagery: God is married to his people, but they had estranged themselves because of their wickedness. Recall the complaint (Isaiah 49:14) that the Lord had forsaken and forgotten them, but he would show that he had not. They were separated but not divorced.

The Lord does not forsake us when we sin. We forsake him. He does not "sell" us. We sell ourselves when we decide to give up our eternal souls for the pleasures of the moment (compare Moses 8:15).

It is easy to see why Isaiah used the symbolism of divorce and slavery to describe the relationship between Christ and Israel. When the people of Israel (ancient or modern) commit sin, they are slaves in the "bondage of sin" (D&C 84:49–51). In ancient Israel, idolatry was regarded as spiritual adultery, and Jesus Christ, the Bridegroom, deserves unadulterated fidelity.

Isaiah 50:2–3 (2 Nephi 7:2–3)

The text of 2 Nephi makes some of Isaiah's questions declarative sentences; consult also Doctrine and Covenants 133:64–73. Christ's first coming was to his own, and he was rejected; at his Second Coming he will call again, offering another opportunity for deliverance and redemption.

Isaiah 50:4–10 (2 Nephi 7:4–10)

Here is another Servant Song (see the previous one in Isaiah 49:1–6). The servant is likely not ancient Israel as a people, because the suffering is undeserved; this could only be the Savior.

Incidents in Jesus' life are prophesied, as also in Isaiah 53:4–9 (Mosiah 14:4–9). See also Matthew 5:39; 26:67; 27:26.

To set one's face "like a flint" (a very hard stone) means to be firm, steadfast, and determined.

The "fear" mentioned in verse 10 means reverence or honor.

Isaiah 50:11 (2 Nephi 7:11)

"Walk in the light of your fire." Compare Doctrine and Covenants 1:16: "Every man walketh in his own way, and after the image of his own god."

Isaiah 51 (2 Nephi 8)

Verses 1–2: Abraham is the rock, and Sarah is the quarry. We must live up to the covenant called after Abraham. Ultimately, the covenant is centered on the Rock of our Salvation, which is Jesus Christ. Just as a rock will have the same physical properties and composition as the mountain from which it is taken, so we have the potential to become like our Father and his Son, our only sure foundation.

One student of Isaiah wrote: "The image is of a quarry; we are just smaller pieces of the parental rock. We are made of the same stuff as Abraham, and we are also made of the same stuff as Christ and God since we are children of God. There is a reason why the Lord wants us to do our genealogy and know 'from whence we are digged.' We know several reasons, such as baptism and eternal marriage for the dead. But are there other reasons? In France, a woman told me that her daughter had been counseled by a psychiatrist to do her genealogy as therapy: it would help her know who she is and to feel more self-worth and a sense of belonging in this world. Through modern genetics it is known that we physically inherit traits from our parents and that all of us contain a large number of identical genes, indicating a common ancestor. We should not forget those who went before us, because that is what links us all together as a world family. That is what makes it possible to love those around us and to love ourselves without being prideful. Therefore, 'from whence we have been digged' affects us physically, mentally, and spiritually."

Isaiah 51:3–5 (2 Nephi 8:3–5)

Both Isaiah and Jacob knew the future. Earth will return to paradisiacal glory, as stated in Article of Faith 10. The Book of Mormon is certainly part of the law that will proceed from the Lord in the last days, a portion of the restoration of all things that will enlighten all who look for light.

Law, Light, Righteousness, Salvation, and Judge are all name-titles for the Savior of the world, the one Person in whom we can implicitly trust.

Isaiah 51:6 (2 Nephi 8:6)

Peter also saw the day when the heavens and the earth would pass away with great noise, fire, fervent heat, and melting elements (2 Peter 3:10–13). President Joseph Fielding Smith wrote, "The earth, as a living body, will have to die and be resurrected, for it, too, has been redeemed by the blood of Jesus Christ" (*Doctrines of Salvation*, 1:74). The Lord provides life for eternity.

Isaiah 51:7–8 (2 Nephi 8:7–8)

The Lord extends assurance and confidence to his faithful followers (compare D&C 6:33–37), whereas reviling men will be consumed.

Isaiah 51:9–10 (2 Nephi 8:9–10)

"Rahab" and "the dragon" also appear in the creation story of Ugarit, one of Israel's neighbors to the north in Old Testament times. In that story they represent the forces of chaos that God subdued through the order of his creations. God has power over all elements and all enemies.

"Put on strength": "What is meant by the command in Isaiah, 52d chapter, 1st verse, which saith: Put on thy strength, O Zion—and what people had Isaiah reference to? He had reference to those whom God should call in the last days, who should hold the power of priesthood to bring again Zion, and the redemption of Israel; and to put on her strength is to put on the authority of the priesthood, which she, Zion, has a right to by lineage; also to return to that power which she had lost" (D&C 113:7–8).

Isaiah 51:11 (2 Nephi 8:11)

"The redeemed of the Lord" are the true Latter-day Saints (D&C 45:71; 101:18–19), and the era of restoration and redemption and the establishment of Zion will be a joyful time for them.

Isaiah 51:12 (2 Nephi 8:12)

Do not be afraid of man. Man is compared to grass, suggesting the transitory nature of life. From a psalmist and from the prophet Isaiah, we learn the symbolism of grass, which persists through both the Old and New Testaments.

"As for man, his days are as grass: as a flower of the field, so he flourisheth. For the wind passeth over it, and it is gone; and the place thereof shall know it no more" (Psalms 103:15–16).

"All flesh is grass, and all the goodliness thereof is as the flower of the field: The grass withereth, the flower fadeth: because the spirit of the Lord bloweth upon it: surely the people is grass. The grass withereth, the flower fadeth: but the word of our God shall stand for ever" (Isaiah 40:6–8).

Grass was a physical similitude of the transitoriness of man. With the heavy rains of wintertime, grass flourishes and even spreads its velvety green carpet over the barren desert; but with the coming of the hot, dry winds off that desert, it is gone. The blades are thriving and vigorous one day and vanished the next. So is the life of man.

But some things, like the word of God, are more timeless and permanent, as the chief apostle declared: "All flesh is as grass, and all the glory of man as the flower of grass. The grass withereth, and the flower thereof falleth away: But the word of the Lord endureth for ever. And this is the word which by the gospel is preached unto you" (1 Peter 1:24–25).

The same image appears also in the Doctrine and Covenants: "Make a solemn proclamation of my gospel . . . This proclamation shall be made to all the kings of the world, . . . to the honorable president-elect, and the high-minded governors of the nation in which you live, and to all the nations of the earth. . . . Call ye, therefore, upon them with loud proclamation, and with your testimony, fearing them not, for they are as grass, and all their glory as the flower thereof which soon falleth" (D&C 124:2–3, 7).

Isaiah 51:13–16 (2 Nephi 8:13–16)

There is no need to forget the Lord and fear the oppressor and the destroyer. Righteous captives are released from exile and protected and covered, as he says, "in the shadow of mine hand," and allowed to participate in establishing Zion.

Isaiah 51:17–18 (2 Nephi 8:17–18)

Jerusalem had indeed "drunk at the hand of the Lord the cup of his fury" and been "wrung out" to the very last drop. As Isaiah exclaimed, "she hath received of the Lord's hand double for all her sins" (Isaiah 40:2).

But why so much suffering, and why for so long? The Lord declared, "As one generation hath been destroyed among the Jews because of iniquity, even so have they been destroyed from generation to generation according to their iniquities" (2 Nephi 25:9). If they continue to reject their God, they continue to suffer for it.

Verse 18 explains that there would be no priesthood leadership in Judah; there would be no prophets.

Isaiah 51:19–20 (2 Nephi 8:19–20)

Isaiah 51:19 has "these two things"; the Hebrew simply says "these two." On the other hand, 2 Nephi 8:19 has "these two sons," who have the priesthood. These are the two witnesses, the two prophets in Jerusalem at the end of days, the time of Armageddon. John the Revelator also saw these two prophets.

JOHN THE REVELATOR'S VISION
OF THE TWO PROPHETS

Revelation 11:3. "And I will give power unto my two witnesses, and they shall prophesy a thousand two hundred and threescore days, clothed in sackcloth."

The ministry of the two witnesses or prophets in Jerusalem will last for a period of 1,260 days (three and a half years). The number may be literal or symbolic. Three and a half is half of seven, the number of perfection or completion. Thus we understand that their mission will be cut short.

Elder Bruce R. McConkie described their ministry in greater detail: "Who are these witnesses, and when will they prophesy? 'They are two prophets that are to be raised up to the Jewish nation in the last days, at the time of the restoration, and to prophesy to the Jews after they are gathered and have built the city of Jerusalem in the land of their fathers.' (D&C 77:15.) Their ministry will take place after the latter-day temple has been built in Old Jerusalem, after some of the Jews who dwell there have been converted, and just before Armageddon and the return of the Lord Jesus. How long will they minister in Jerusalem and in the Holy Land? For three and a half years . . . The Jews, as an assembled people, will hear again the testimony of legal administrators bearing record that salvation is in Christ and in his gospel. Who will these witnesses be? We do not know, except that they will be followers of Joseph Smith; they will hold the holy Melchizedek Priesthood; they will be members of The Church of Jesus Christ of Latter-day Saints. It is reasonable to suppose, knowing how the Lord has always dealt with his people in all ages, that they will be two members of the Council of the Twelve or of the First Presidency of the Church" (*Millennial Messiah,* 390).

Revelation 11:4–5. "These are the two olive trees, and the two candlesticks standing before the God of the earth. And if any man will hurt them, fire proceedeth out of their mouth, and devoureth their enemies: and if any man will hurt them, he must in this manner be killed."

The prophet Zechariah also saw these two witnesses. He referred to them symbolically as two olive trees or two candlesticks (Zechariah 4:3, 11–14). Olive oil helps to heal, and candlesticks give light. The glory ("fire") of these two prophets will be miraculously displayed in protecting them and destroying their enemies.

Revelation 11:6. "These have power to shut heaven, that it rain not in the days of their prophecy: and have power over waters to turn them to blood, and to smite the earth with all plagues, as often as they will."

The two witnesses will have powers similar to two of the great ancient Hebrew prophets: shutting the heavens so that it does not rain, as Elijah did (1 Kings 17:1), and sending plagues on the earth, as Moses did (Exodus 7–11).

Revelation 11:7–13. "And when they shall have finished their testimony, the beast that ascendeth out of the bottomless pit shall make war against them, and shall overcome them, and kill them. And their dead bodies shall lie in the street of the great city, which spiritually is called Sodom and Egypt, where also our Lord was crucified. And they of the people and kindreds and tongues and nations shall see their dead bodies three days and an half, and shall not suffer their dead bodies to be put in graves. And they that dwell upon the earth shall rejoice over them, and make merry, and shall send gifts one to another; because these two prophets tormented them that dwelt on the earth. And after three days and an half the Spirit of life from God entered into them, and they stood upon their feet; and great fear fell upon them which saw them. And they heard a great voice from heaven saying unto them, Come up hither. And they ascended up to heaven in a cloud; and their enemies beheld them. And the same hour was there a great earthquake, and the tenth part of the city fell."

The two witnesses will be killed, and their bodies will lie in the streets for three and a half days, with nations viewing their bodies. Then they will be resurrected and ascend into heaven while a great earthquake strikes the city.

Isaiah 51:21–23 (2 Nephi 8:21–23)

The cup of trembling and fury passes to those who afflict God's covenant people.

Isaiah 52:1–3 (3 Nephi 20:36–38)

This passage is quoted three different times in the Book of Mormon, and explanation is given in Doctrine and Covenants 113:7–10. Zion, the New Jerusalem, is to "put on thy strength" and "put on thy beautiful garments," which represent the authority of the priesthood. Doctrine and Covenants 113:10 indicates that the remnants are exhorted to return to the Lord. Recall that Isaiah's son was named *Shear-jashub*, meaning "the remnant shall return"—return not only to the land but to the Lord. Hebrew *lashuv* means both "to return" and "to repent," the idea being that backsliding Israel will come back to her God. The bride, the Lord's wife, will return from playing the harlot and repent and adorn herself with beautiful, clean wedding garments as she prepares for the coming of the bridegroom, her husband, the Savior (Jeremiah 3:14; Matthew 22:1–14; 25:1–13; D&C 133:10, 19).

Israel is to rise up from her dejected position and sit down in a more glorious and honored place, the New Jerusalem, the redeemed Zion.

To loose herself from the bands of her neck means to repent and remove herself from "the curses of God upon her . . . [in her] scattered condition among the Gentiles" (D&C 113:10); in other words, to flee Babylon, the wicked world, and free herself from the captivity of the devil.

Israel had sold herself, as a harlot, having prostituted her sacred relationship with her Husband, "for nought"; that is, she had betrayed her God, searching for the worthless lusts of the flesh and pleasures of worldliness. Nevertheless, she can be "redeemed without money" through the Atonement of her Savior, whose loving invitation comes "without money and without price" (2 Nephi 9:50).

Isaiah 52:4–5

These two verses are omitted in the Book of Mormon and the Doctrine and Covenants, probably because they deal with local historical events about Egyptian and Assyrian oppression.

Isaiah 52:6 (3 Nephi 20:39)

Some seem to think that God's existence depends on people's belief in him. This means that if someone believes in him, then he is real for that person. If another person does not believe in God, however, he is as unreal to that person as he is real to the first. In this verse, however, the Lord teaches us that whether or not we choose to believe in him and follow him, the time will come when we will have to acknowledge him as our Lord.

Isaiah 52:7 (Mosiah 12:21; 3 Nephi 20:40)

Isaiah's words "how beautiful upon the mountains" appear seven times in the Book of Mormon: four times in Mosiah

287

15:14–18, and also in 1 Nephi 13:37; Mosiah 12:21; and 3 Nephi 20:40.

Those who bring good tidings, who publish peace and salvation, who testify "Thy God reigneth!" or "God lives!" are, particularly, the missionaries of The Church of Jesus Christ of Latter-day Saints (see also Ogden and Skinner, *Book of Mormon*, 1:356–57).

Medical doctors assisting missionaries conclude that of all the parts of the body that they treat for ailments, the feet are among the most frequent victims. Over the ages, and again in this last dispensation, many tired, blistered, and swollen feet have carried the glad tidings of great joy. It is significant that the two most dramatic ordinances of the gospel involve the feet and are polar opposites of each other: the washing of the feet (the ultimate ordinance of *commendation* in mortality), and the dusting of the feet (the ultimate ordinance of *condemnation* in mortality). The feet are so important because they take the mind and heart to the places they have contemplated.

"How beautiful" in Hebrew is *mah nauvoo*. This is the source of the name *Nauvoo*, the city the Saints built on the banks of the Mississippi River. The name was probably first seen by the Prophet Joseph Smith in his study of Professor Joshua Seixas's grammar *A Manual Hebrew Grammar for the Use of Beginners*, from which he studied in the School of the Prophets in Kirtland, January to March 1836 (50, no. 53 [2]).

"Him that bringeth good tidings" is one word in Hebrew (*m'vaser*), containing the same root word as *besora*, which is "gospel."

Once again, "salvation" is in Hebrew *Yeshua*—in English, "Jesus." Declaring salvation, then, is declaring Jesus.

Isaiah 52:8–10 (Mosiah 12:22–24; 15:29–31; 3 Nephi 16:18–20; 20:32–35)

These verses from the writings of Isaiah are quoted four times in the Book of Mormon. Watchmen are those who publish the good tidings—the gospel of Jesus Christ. They are the prophets and all servants of the Lord who are called to teach, testify, and bring people to Christ.

Two Jerusalems are spoken of: the first is the famous Old Jerusalem in the Holy Land and the second is the New Jerusalem, also called Zion. New Jerusalem, or Zion, will be built in Independence, Jackson County, Missouri. Joseph Smith wrote:

"I received, by a heavenly vision, a commandment in June [1831], to take my journey to the western boundaries of the State of Missouri, and there designate the very spot which was to be the central place for the commencement of the gathering together of those who embrace the fullness of the everlasting Gospel. Accordingly I undertook the journey, with certain ones of my brethren, and after a long and tedious journey, suffering many privations and hardships, arrived in Jackson County, Missouri, and after viewing the country, seeking diligently at the hand of God, He manifested Himself unto us, and designated, to me and others, the very spot upon which he designed to commence the work of the gathering, and the upbuilding of an 'holy city,' which should be called Zion—Zion, because it is a place of righteousness, and all who build thereon are to worship the true and living God, and all believe in one doctrine, even the doctrine of our Lord and Savior Jesus Christ. 'Thy watchmen shall lift up the voice; with the voice together shall they sing: for they shall see eye to eye, when the Lord shall bring again Zion' [Isaiah 52:8]" (*Joseph Smith* [manual], 185).

The lyrics of the song that will be sung have been revealed (see D&C 84:99–102). On the Lord's coming to the New Jerusalem and all the earth seeing his salvation, see Doctrine and Covenants 133:2–5.

Isaiah 52:11 (3 Nephi 20:41)

The command here is to flee from the wicked world. Live in the world but do not be of the world. Avoid the world's contaminating influences (for example, many of Hollywood's movies, and books, magazines, and many Internet sites that specialize in pornographic materials that degrade and destroy moral and spiritual character)—"touch not that which is unclean," the Lord teaches in 3 Nephi. "Go ye out of the midst of her; be ye clean that bear the vessels of the Lord."

Handling any of the instruments in a hospital, a nurse must

first wash and sterilize her hands. The tools she handles are for the vital operations of healing. If a nurse gets washed just to "bear the vessels" or instruments of a doctor, how much more sterilizing does one need for handling the things of the Lord? Our society expects certain standards of physical cleanliness and spends great sums of energy and money to achieve them, but the expectation of moral cleanliness and insistence on it seem to be lacking. Those who bear the vessels of the Lord can and must be a light to the world. That is the whole point of being a covenant people, chosen to show others how to be clean in a filthy world.

Isaiah 52:12 (3 Nephi 20:42)

The Lord of Hosts will go before his people and will also protect them from behind (be their "rearward"), but he expects us to do our part in moving the work forward. Presiding elders of the Church in Missouri issued the following counsel in July of 1833: "For the disciples to suppose that they can come to this land without ought to eat, or to drink, or to wear, or anything to purchase these necessaries with, is a vain thought. For them to suppose that the Lord will open the windows of heaven, and rain down angel's food for them by the way, when their whole journey lies through a fertile country, stored with the blessings of life from His own hand for them to subsist upon, is also vain. For them to suppose that their clothes and shoes will not wear out upon the journey, when the whole of it lies through a country where there are thousands of sheep from which wool in abundance can be procured to make them garments, and cattle upon a thousand hills, to afford leather for shoes, is just as vain. . . . Do not conclude from these remarks, brethren, that we doubt in the least, that the Lord will provide for His Saints in these last days. . . . We know that the Saints have the unchangeable word of God that they shall be provided for; yet we know, if any are imprudent, or lavish, or negligent, or indolent, in taking that proper care, and making that proper use of what the Lord has made them stewards over, they are not counted wise; for a strict account of every one's stewardship is required, not only in time, but will be in eternity. . . . 'Let not your flight be in haste, but let all things be prepared before you' [D&C 133:15]" (*History of the Church*, 1:382–83).

Isaiah 52:13–15 (3 Nephi 20:43–45)

Here is another prophecy with dual fulfillment: Jesus Christ and Joseph Smith were both marred at the hands of wicked men (3 Nephi 21:8–11; D&C 135:1–3).

The word *sprinkle* in 3 Nephi 20:45 was changed to *gather* by the Prophet Joseph Smith in his inspired revision of the biblical text (footnote *a;* see JST Isaiah 52:15). The high-minded leaders of men will be astonished, and speechless, when they finally recognize and acknowledge the glorious work of the Savior of the World and the Prophet of the Restoration (see also 3 Nephi 21:8).

Isaiah 53 (Mosiah 14)

Isaiah 53 is a prophecy of the Atonement of Jesus Christ. It is one of the plain and precious things *not* taken out of the Bible, though many have tried to distort its meaning and weaken its powerful witness through humanistic and academic devices.

This chapter of Isaiah shows that the Old Testament does indeed testify of Jesus the Messiah, and it does teach the basic principles of the Atonement. Almost all of Isaiah 53 is reproduced in the New Testament, applying to Jesus. It also forms the foundation of the prophet Abinadi's teachings in the New World (see Mosiah 14–15).

Philip, an early Christian Church leader and missionary, encountered on one occasion an officer of the Ethiopian court, returning to his homeland from Jerusalem. The officer was reading Isaiah 53 when Philip met him on the road, and Philip asked him if he understood what he was reading. After looking at several verses, the officer asked Philip, "I pray thee, of whom speaketh the prophet this? of himself, or of some other man?" (Acts 8:34). It was not immediately apparent to the Ethiopian who the subject of Isaiah's prophecy was. "Then Philip opened his mouth, and began at the same scripture, and preached unto him Jesus" (Acts 8:35).

Elder Bruce R. McConkie wrote: "As our New Testament now stands, we find Matthew (Matt. 8:17), [John (John 12:37–41)], Philip (Acts 8:27–35), Paul (Rom. 4:25), and Peter (1 Pet. 2:24–25) all quoting, paraphrasing, enlarging upon, and applying to the Lord Jesus various of the verses in this great 53rd chapter of Isaiah. How many sermons have been preached, how many lessons have been taught, how many testimonies have been borne—both in ancient Israel and in the meridian of time—using the utterances of this chapter as the text, we can scarcely imagine" (*Promised Messiah*, 235).

Isaiah 53:1 (Mosiah 14:1)

The question "who hath believed our report?" suggests that few have believed or understood the prophecies that the Messiah would come in the form of a meek mortal. This belief and understanding comes only to those to whom the "arm of the Lord," or the power of God, is revealed, for the things of God can only be understood by the Spirit of God (1 Corinthians 2:11).

Many do not respond to the Spirit because of hard-heartedness (John 12:39–41); that is, unwillingness to listen to the prophets. Thus, the apostle John reported, "But though he had done so many miracles before them, yet they believed not on him: That the saying of Esaias [Isaiah] the prophet might be fulfilled, which he spake, Lord, who hath believed our report? and to whom hath the arm of the Lord been revealed?" (John 12:37–38).

In the case of Abinadi and the priests of Noah, Abinadi testified that God would come in the "form of a man, and go forth in mighty power upon the face of the earth" (Mosiah 13:34). The priests of Noah did not believe his report.

Isaiah 53:2 (Mosiah 14:2)

Jesus was the "root," as he himself testified in the last chapter of the last book in the Bible: "I Jesus . . . am the root and offspring of David" (Revelation 22:16).

In the first volume of *The Mortal Messiah* in a chapter entitled "The Soil in Which the Root Was Planted," Elder Bruce R. McConkie wrote that our Savior "was to be planted in arid soil; to grow up as a tender plant, as a root out of dry ground. Babylonia, Persia, Egypt, Syria, Greece, and Rome—each in turn—had ploughed in the fields of [Canaan, or Israel]. Each had reaped harvests without dunging the land. The early rains of revelation and the latter rains of prophetic guidance had not watered the soil for centuries. The thistles and weeds and briers of sin encumbered the vineyards. There was a famine of hearing the word of the Lord" (*Mortal Messiah*, 1:295).

One characteristic of dry ground that once was wet is that it becomes very hard. This is especially true of certain soils that become sunbaked; they become hardened and impenetrable. The Lord, as the fountain of living waters (Jeremiah 2:13), would come to irrigate the arid soil so that "the desert [could] rejoice, and blossom as the rose" (Isaiah 35:1). To those whose souls become hard, like the baked earth, the Living Water runs off without penetrating.

Just as the rock was smitten to bring forth water for thirsting Israelites (Numbers 20:11), so the Lord himself was smitten to provide the living water of eternal life for all who would come and drink.

"No form . . . no beauty"—Jews expected supernatural glory in their Messiah. Some imagined that their King would be fabulously wealthy, handsome, and in every way attractive, and that he would come with great fanfare and applause. Almost all came to expect a powerful, military ruler, in the mold of King David, who would subdue all of Israel's physical enemies—all attackers and oppressors. His purposes would be well-known and publicized, and there would be no question about who he was. Everyone would recognize him at a glance. President Joseph Fielding Smith wrote: "It is expressed here by the prophet that he had no form or comeliness, that is, he was not so distinctive, so different from others that people would recognize him as the Son of God. He appeared as a mortal man" (*Doctrines of Salvation*, 1:23).

Isaiah 53:3 (Mosiah 14:3)

Isaiah clearly foretold the attitude of many in Israel regarding their Savior. Ironically, in rejecting these very words as a prophecy of the Messiah, his people were fulfilling them by despising and rejecting him.

Some of his own family members failed to accept him as Messiah at first (John 7:5); people in his hometown tried to kill him (Luke 4:16–30); his own countrymen rejected him (John 1:11); one of his best friends betrayed him (Luke 22:48). In the end "all the disciples forsook him, and fled" (Matthew 26:56), and his enemies demanded his execution (Matthew 27:22–23). The people of Israel would hide their eyes from their God and not esteem his salvation (compare 1 Nephi 19:7–9).

PROPHECIES OF THE MESSIAH

Why would Jews generally reject Jesus as their long-awaited Messiah? Glance through the following sample of prophecies to understand what concept of Messiah should have prevailed among his own people (emphasis added):

Genesis 49:10. "The *sceptre* shall not depart from Judah . . . until Shiloh come."

Numbers 24:17. "There shall come a Star out of Jacob, and a *Sceptre* shall rise out of Israel."

Psalm 22:1. "My God, my God, why hast thou forsaken me?"

Psalm 22:16. "They pierced my hands and my feet."

Psalm 34:20. "He keepeth all his bones: not one of them is broken."

Psalm 69:21. "In my thirst they gave me vinegar to drink."

Psalm 118:22. "The stone which the builders refused is become the head."

Isaiah 7:14. "A virgin shall conceive, and bear a son . . . Immanuel."

Isaiah 9:6. "Unto us a child is born, . . . the *government* shall be upon his shoulder."

Isaiah 9:7. "Of his government . . . there shall be no end."

Isaiah 50:6. "I gave my back to the smiters."

Isaiah 53:5. "He was wounded for our transgressions."

Isaiah 61:1. "Anointed me to preach good tidings."

Jeremiah 23:5. "A *King* shall reign and . . . execute judgment and justice."

Daniel 9:26. "Shall Messiah be cut off."

Micah 5:2. "Beth-lehem . . . , out of thee shall he come forth . . . to be *ruler* in Israel."

Zechariah 9:9. "Thy *King* cometh unto thee . . . riding upon an ass."

Zechariah 11:13. "I was prised at . . . thirty pieces of silver."

Zechariah 13:6. "I was wounded in the house of my friends."

All the prophetic suggestions of royalty, rulership, and kingship would eventually be fulfilled at the Lord's *second* coming;

meanwhile, look again at the other passages for what kind of a Messiah he would be at his *first* coming.

Elder Bruce R. McConkie reminds us of the belief prevalent at the time of Jesus' birth: "No single concept was more firmly lodged in the minds of the Jews in Jesus' day than the universal belief that their Messiah would be the Son of David. . . . They looked for a temporal deliverer who would throw off the yoke of Roman bondage and make Israel free again. They sought a ruler who would restore that glory and worldwide influence and prestige which was enjoyed when the Son of Jesse sat on Israel's throne. The true concepts of deliverance from spiritual darkness, of being freed from the bondage of sin, of a kingdom which is not of this world—all made possible through an infinite and eternal atonement—all this was lost and unknown doctrine to them" (*Promised Messiah*, 188).

Isaiah 53:4 (Mosiah 14:4)

This may be the single greatest verse of scripture in the Old Covenant (the Old Testament) on the essential principle of the Atonement: substitution, or proxy. In his vicarious sacrifice the Savior took upon himself not only all of our sins but also our pains and sorrows—in this way he knows how to succor his followers in their hour of emotional and spiritual need (compare Alma 7:11–12; 2 Corinthians 5:21; Hebrews 2:18).

Some would think that the Savior was "stricken, smitten of God" because of his personal sins, but Isaiah taught otherwise: "he was wounded for *our* transgressions, he was bruised for *our* iniquities" (v. 5; emphasis added).

Isaiah 53:5 (Mosiah 14:5)

Christ's sufferings at Gethsemane and Golgotha are described. He took upon himself the pains and sins of the world to heal and redeem the Father's children.

Referring to Jesus' suffering for "*our* transgressions" and "*our* iniquities," Isaiah makes us aware of our personal involvement and responsibility for the oppression and affliction of the Savior. Jacobus Revius, a Dutch poet and theologian (1586–1658), powerfully teaches the same poignant lesson that Isaiah teaches:

He Bore Our Anguish

It was not the Jews, Lord Jesus, who crucified you,
Nor the traitors who dragged you to the law,
Nor the contemptuous who spit in your face
Nor those who bound you, and hit you full of wounds,
And it was not the soldiers who with evil hands
Lifted up the reed or the hammer,
Or set that cursed wood on Golgotha,
Or cast lots and gambled for your robe;
It is I, O Lord, it is I who have done it,
I am the heavy tree that overburdened you,
I am the rough hands that bound you,
The nail, the spear, and the cords that whipped you,
The bloodied crown that tore your head:
All this happened, alas! for my sins.
(In BYU Studies *15, no. 1 [Autumn 1974]: 103)*

"The chastisement of our peace was upon him"—the English word "peace" is used here to translate the Hebrew *shalom,* which carries the connotation of wholeness and reconciliation. This is not the common greeting of "shalom" that the world extends but the deeper doctrine of justification to dwell in God's presence. The Savior suffered the chastisement so that we could be reconciled to the Father and become whole.

"With his stripes we are healed"—his "stripes" refer to his scourging, both the physical flogging and also the spiritual flagellation caused by the sins of the world. Until we accept his stripes, we are spiritually sick; we need to follow the prescription of the Master Physician to be healed. It is ironic that we are healed through his stripes; our peace comes through his pain. Peter testified of this doctrine: "Who his own self bare our sins in his own body on the tree, that we, being dead to sins, should live unto righteousness: by whose stripes ye were healed" (1 Peter 2:24).

Isaiah 53:6 (Mosiah 14:6)

The verse "All we, like sheep, have gone astray; we have turned every one to his own way" symbolizes the need for all to be saved by the Atonement of Christ (compare Matthew 9:36; Alma 5:37; D&C 1:16).

Isaiah 53:7 (Mosiah 14:7)

These images prophetically foreshadow events during the hearings or "trials" of Jesus before Jewish and Roman leaders. While being accused and interrogated by the chief priests, Jesus gave no answer (Mark 15:3; John 19:9), and while standing before Herod Antipas, Jesus answered him nothing (Luke 23:9). When the time came to be brought as a lamb to the slaughter, "the Lamb slain from the foundation of the world" (Revelation 13:8) opened not his mouth—just as a sheep is dumb, or mute, in the hands of the shearers.

Isaiah 53:8 (Mosiah 14:8)

The Hebrew text implies that he was taken *by arrest* and *by judgment*. Think about the combined meaning of all the adjectives Isaiah used to describe the Messiah: stricken, smitten, afflicted, wounded, bruised, and oppressed. Now the prophet even declares that he would be "cut off out of the land of the living," which was certainly not the way Jews centuries later viewed the purpose and mission of their Messiah.

In the Old Testament the value of a person's life was often measured by his posterity, who would perpetuate his name, works, and merits. Inasmuch as Christ would be "cut off" or killed, who would "declare his generation"? Who would be his posterity to carry on his work and glory? Who would declare the life and atoning mission of Jesus the Messiah? Abinadi testified "that when [Christ's] soul has been made an offering for sin he shall see his seed" or posterity (Mosiah 15:10). Abinadi then taught that Christ's seed are those who believe in him and are redeemed through him: the prophets and those who believe on their words (Mosiah 15:10–12). They become his children, his sons and daughters, who will perpetuate his words and works in the earth.

Isaiah 53:9 (Mosiah 14:9)

Transpose the two nouns, to read that his *death* was with the wicked (he was crucified between two thieves; see Matthew 27:38), and he was with the rich in his *grave* (he was buried in the borrowed grave of wealthy Joseph of Arimathea; see Matthew 27:57–60).

This verse may give us insight into why the leaders of the Jews wanted to kill Jesus. Isaiah wrote, "because he had done no violence [Abinadi: "no evil"—Mosiah 14:9], neither was any deceit in his mouth." Few things can stir up anger in the unrighteous as much as a good example. Recall Laman and Lemuel. Why didn't Laman and Lemuel just get up one morning and make the hike back to Jerusalem? Why was their incessant effort to kill Lehi and Nephi and *then* go back to Jerusalem? They knew that their father and brother were telling the truth, and they were angry because of it. They were jealous and envious and proud. Some of the Jewish leaders had the same problem with Jesus. No one welcomed them into the city by throwing down palm fronds in their path. Nobody was being healed by them. There were no great crowds flocking around them to hang on their every word. Something had to be done about this righteous person who always spoke the truth. They had him crucified.

Isaiah 53:10 (Mosiah 14:10)

"Yet it pleased [satisfied, gratified] the Lord to bruise him"— this phrase has at least two possible interpretations. First, "Lord" may be a reference to Elohim, the Father, thus teaching that this was a willing offering by the Father and the Son (John 3:16).

Elder Melvin J. Ballard wrote: "In that hour I think I can see our dear Father behind the veil looking upon these dying struggles until even he could not endure it any longer; and, like the mother who bids farewell to her dying child, has to be taken out of the room, so as not to look upon the last struggles, so he bowed his head, and hid in some part of his universe, his great heart almost breaking for the love that he had for his Son. Oh, in that moment when he might have saved his Son, I thank him and praise him that he did not fail us, for he had not only the love of his Son in mind, but he also had love for us. I rejoice that he did not interfere, and that his love for us made it possible for him to endure to look upon the sufferings of his Son and give him finally to us, our Savior and our Redeemer. Without him, without his sacrifice, we would have remained, and we would never have come glorified into his presence. And so this is what it cost, in part, for our Father in Heaven to give the gift of his Son unto men" (*New Era*, Jan. 1976, 11).

Another interpretation of verse 10 is that Isaiah may be differentiating between the two roles of the Savior: it pleased Jehovah, the God of the Old Testament, to bruise Jesus, pointing to the fact that the great Jehovah would come in the person of Jesus, and that they are, indeed, one God (compare Mosiah 15:2–4).

"When thou shalt make his soul an offering for sin, he shall see his seed"—"his" and "he" in this verse are usually taken to mean Christ, while the pronoun "thou" is thought to refer to either God the Father or to those receiving the prophecy. In either case the message is the same for all: when one is forgiven of sins through the Atonement, one is spiritually begotten of Christ and becomes "his seed," or child (compare Mosiah 15:10–12; D&C 84:36–38).

"He shall prolong his days"—Christ will be resurrected and become immortal.

Isaiah 53:11 (Mosiah 14:11)

Luke asked, "Ought not Christ to have suffered these things, and to enter into his glory?" (Luke 24:26). Jesus' crown of thorns came before his crown of glory. Having shown the way, he later taught that "after much tribulation come the blessings" (D&C 58:4; see also Alma 26:27; 7:5; 17:11; 28:8).

The Savior will "justify many," meaning that he will make righteous and reconcile many. The use of *many* rather than *all* suggests that some, the unrepentant, will not be justified, that is, put back into a right relationship with God the Father (compare D&C 19:16–19).

Isaiah 53:12 (Mosiah 14:12)

"He shall divide the spoil with the strong"—the strong and faithful will become joint-heirs with the Savior, possessing with him the fulness of the Father; that is, all that the Father has (Romans 8:17; D&C 50:26–28; 76:50–60; 88:107; 93:15–30; 132:20).

Christ's atonement was active rather than passive suffering. "By saying that *he poured out his soul* unto death, Isaiah may be suggesting why it was important for him to die on the cross—for this manner of death allowed him time to do the pouring out.

If he had been beheaded, hanged, run through with a sword, or stoned, he would have died instantaneously without having had any time to use his volition in giving up his life. When they put him on the cross to see that he died, all they needed to satisfy their desires was time. Given time, he would die. But by giving him time, they gave him control over the giving. He could decide at what point to lay down his life. Thus, as a priest sacrificing a lamb, he performed the sacrifice. And as a Lamb, he became his own victim. (Heb. 8:1–2; 9:11–16, esp. v. 14.) This crucial detail was known to Isaiah when he said that the righteous servant would pour out his own soul unto death" (Meservy, "Isaiah 53," 171).

The grand purpose of Jesus' suffering is for us to become his seed and declare his generation. Jesus came to earth to be a suffering Servant, and his was a unique service to all humankind. Isaiah's description of Jesus' service is also unique; no one else could possibly fulfill such an appointed service except the Son of God himself.

Isaiah 54 (3 Nephi 22)

Isaiah 54 was quoted by the Savior to his righteous disciples in the western hemisphere during his postresurrection appearance to them (see 3 Nephi 22).

In many cultures, when a woman marries a man, she takes his name and is then legally his heir and represents his name as long as she is married to him. So it is in the relationship between God and his bride, his people. Israel, the wayward and estranged wife, is invited to return and resume her proper relationship with the Lord.

"In Isaiah 54:1–3 the Lord addresses his barren bride Israel: 'Sing, O barren, thou that didst not bear.' Marriage as a metaphor for the covenant—the Lord being the groom and Israel the bride—occurs frequently in the Old Testament (e.g., Hosea 1–3; Jer. 2–3; Ezek. 23). Israel, as the unfaithful spouse, is guilty of adultery and is a harlot. Certainly these are grounds for divorce, and the penalty for adultery is death. The Lord punished Israel with death, destruction, and scattering by the Assyrians in 721 B.C., by the Babylonians in 587 B.C., and by the Romans in A.D. 70. Many suffered the penalty of death, but the Lord in his mercy spared Israel's posterity and scattered them throughout the earth. In Isaiah's metaphor, there was no divorce ('where is the bill of your mother's divorcement'; Isaiah 50:1) but a separation. The Lord explained, 'For thy Maker is thine husband . . . for a small moment have I forsaken thee . . . in a little wrath I hid my face from thee for a moment; but with everlasting kindness will I have mercy on thee' (Isa. 54:5–8). The Lord in his love and mercy, as dramatized by Hosea when he forgave his unfaithful wife (Hosea 1–3), will take back his bride, and her barrenness will be replaced with productivity as the Lord begins to gather their posterity (Isa. 54:7)" (Seely, "Lord Will Bring Salvation," 155).

"Children of the desolate"—a prophecy about scattered Israel and Gentiles in the last days: those who had been desolate or apostate are now gathered and blessed.

The scattering and gathering of Israel is not merely a process of moving people about (or moving "trees"; Jacob 5) but of bringing people to Christ, of establishing Zion. There is such a thing as divine positioning. The Lord puts people where he needs them, to help facilitate the "at-*one*-ment," the gathering in and becoming one with him.

Isaiah 54:2 (3 Nephi 22:2)

The gathering of Israel's posterity will necessitate enlarging the family tent, lengthening the cords, and strengthening the stakes. The tent signifies refuge from storms. Stakes (this is the origin of the name of our Church unit), must be strong to stabilize the whole tent, which is the Church and kingdom of God on earth, made up of families. Compare Isaiah 33:20 and Doctrine and Covenants 82:14. In some of the Semitic languages the words for "tent" and "family" come from the same root. "Tent dwellers" means "families" (Holladay, *Lexicon of the Old Testament*, 6).

Isaiah 54:2–3 (3 Nephi 22:2–3)

Zion expands worldwide; see also Doctrine and Covenants 133:7–13; Moroni 10:31. "Break forth on the right hand and on the left" suggests expansion. To "inherit the Gentiles" suggests Latter-day Saints in all the world.

Isaiah 54:4 (3 Nephi 22:4)

In the early years of the nation, Israel departed from her God and slew her Husband, causing the "reproach of thy widowhood"; all of that will be forgotten when she is mercifully gathered into his arms once again.

It is we mortals, in all ages, who have deserted our God and find it incumbent on ourselves to repent and return to him, yet it is he who first makes the conciliatory effort to gather us. He is tireless in his efforts to bring us back into his arms.

"Thou shalt forget the shame of thy youth" is an injunction for ancient Israel but also for us individually. There were two great Josephs whose lives teach us a valuable principle: the foolish, shameful, or simply immature mistakes we make in our youth can be forgiven and forgotten; we can rise above and beyond our past. Joseph, son of Jacob, who was later sold into Egypt, was, while a teenager, rather unwise in broadcasting the dreams of his future greatness to his family members who would someday bow down to him (Genesis 37). And a Joseph in our day said of himself: "I frequently fell into many foolish errors, and displayed the weakness of youth, and the foibles of human nature; which, I am sorry to say, led me into divers temptations, offensive in the sight of God. In making this confession, no one need suppose me guilty of any great or malignant sins. A disposition to commit such was never in my nature. But I was guilty of levity [light-mindedness], and sometimes associated with jovial company, etc., not consistent with that character which ought to be maintained by one who was called of God as I had been" (Joseph Smith–History 1:28). The Lord will help us "forget the shame of [our] youth" as we repent and show penitence through many good works during our mature years on earth.

Isaiah 54:5–6 (3 Nephi 22:5–6)

There is no mistaking who the Husband is. He is plainly identified as the Lord of Hosts, the Redeemer, the Holy One of Israel, the God of the whole earth. Zion, the New Jerusalem, is the bride (Isaiah 61:10; Revelation 21:2).

Isaiah 54:7 (3 Nephi 22:7)

The adversities and afflictions experienced during the time away, when the wayward wife was separated ("scattered") from her Husband, shall appear to be—in the eternal perspective—only "a small moment" (see also D&C 121:7). Actually, the Lord has never forsaken any of his people; it may just seem that way as he tries and tests us. We understandably feel God-forsaken when we abandon him and his Spirit.

Isaiah 54:8–10 (3 Nephi 22:8–10)

When Israel, the covenant people, forsook her Maker—her Husband—she suffered the consequences of her abandonment and incurred his "little wrath" for a moment, but his kindly, merciful promise to gather Israel is as sure as his promise to send no more flood. Verse 9 confirms the historicity of the flood at the time of Noah. Besides the biblical account, we have an additional three witnesses of the Flood in Alma 10:22; 3 Nephi 22:9; and Ether 6:7; 13:2.

Kindness is a good measure of the greatness of a person, and God is great.

Isaiah 54:11–12 (3 Nephi 22:11–12)

Compare this description of future Zion, the New Jerusalem, with the even more detailed description in Revelation 21:19–21; compare also the words of our hymn "Beautiful Zion, Built Above" (*Hymns*, no. 44).

Isaiah 54:13 (3 Nephi 22:13)

Elder M. Russell Ballard exclaimed: "Peace. What a marvelous, desirable blessing to bring to the souls of our children. If they are at peace within themselves and secure in their knowledge of Heavenly Father and His eternal plan for them, they will be able to cope better with the unrest in the world around them and be prepared better for reaching their divine potential" (*Ensign*, Apr. 1994, 60).

Isaiah 54:14–17 (3 Nephi 22:14–17)

These verses attest how the Saints of Zion will survive and prosper in the face of the high-tech weaponry of the world and how they will escape oppression and "terror . . . [that] shall not come near thee."

Referring to verse 16, Elder Gerald N. Lund wrote: "Joseph was surely the smith who forged the instrument by which the Lord's people continue to prepare individually and collectively for the Savior's return—and that instrument is The Church of Jesus Christ of Latter-day Saints" (*Ensign*, Jan. 1997, 54).

The assurances in verse 17 are repeated by the Lord in our day: "There is no weapon that is formed against you shall prosper; and if any man lift his voice against you he shall be confounded" (D&C 71:9–10). This greatest cause on earth will continue to roll forth until it fills the whole earth, as the Prophet Joseph Smith prophesied:

"The Standard of Truth has been erected; no unhallowed hand can stop the work from progressing; persecutions may rage, mobs may combine, armies may assemble, calumny may defame, but the truth of God will go forth boldly, nobly, and independent, till it has penetrated every continent, visited every clime, swept every country, and sounded in every ear, till the purposes of God shall be accomplished, and the Great Jehovah shall say the work is done" (*History of the Church*, 4:540).

Isaiah 55:1–3

Here is our invitation to eat and drink, and what is the food and drink? See Isaiah 55:10–11 and 2 Nephi 9:50–51. On "living bread" and "living water" see John 6:51 and 7:37–39. We are encouraged to feast upon the word, search and ponder the scriptures, and treasure them up. In fact, the Lord seldom encourages or commands us to merely read the scriptures. He and his prophets use such terms as "search" (John 5:39; 3 Nephi 23:1, 5; D&C 1:37); "meditate" (Joshua 1:8; 1 Timothy 4:15; D&C 76:19); "study" (D&C 11:22; 26:1; 88:118); "ponder" (2 Nephi 4:15; 3 Nephi 17:3; D&C 88:62, 71; 138:1, 11); "reflect upon" (D&C 138:2; Joseph Smith–History 1:12); "feast upon" (2 Nephi 31:20; 32:3; Alma 32:42); and "treasure up" (D&C 84:85; Joseph Smith–Matthew 1:37). The Lord will indeed show unto us great things, as we do our part: praying over and studying and reflecting upon the words of scripture, and taking the time to be "in the Spirit."

"There are a number of passages in the Old and New Testaments that speak of springs of water issuing from underneath the temple of the Lord. The passages are Joel 3:18; Ezekiel 47:1; Zechariah 14:8 ('living waters shall go out from Jerusalem'); and Revelation 22:1 ('a pure river of water of life, clear as crystal, proceeding out of the throne of God and of the Lamb'). All of these passages are millennial in time reference, with the exception of the passage in Revelation, which seems to be celestial in reference. The Prophet Joseph Smith spoke in a similar vein, stating that 'Jerusalem must be rebuilt.—& Judah return, must return & the temple water come out from under the temple—the waters of the dead sea be healed . . . & all this must be done before Son of Man will make his appearance [sic].' The theme of 'messianic water' is very strongly emphasized within the context of a covenantal meal in Isaiah 55:1–3" (Lundquist, "Temple Symbolism in Isaiah," 52).

Spiritual food is free; it is accessible to all of us, though in a sense, there is a price to pay. The price is faithfulness and valiance.

On "the sure mercies of David" mentioned in verse 3, see 2 Samuel 7:15–16.

Isaiah 55:4–5

The titles "witness," "leader," "commander," and "Holy One of Israel" all refer to the Lord of hosts, who is the Lord Jesus Christ (John 18:37).

Isaiah 55:6–7

In addition to searching, pondering, and treasuring up his words, we are encouraged to call upon him—pray to him (see also D&C 88:62–63). We must return unto the Lord. The Hebrew word for repent, *lashuv*, means "to return," to come back to God.

Isaiah 55:8–9

Isaiah puts us in our place. God's thoughts and ways are far above ours (see also Jacob 4:8). Compare man's nothingness (Isaiah 40:15, 17). The intent is that we remember that we are fallen man, and conceived in sin. It is absurd to feel proud.

Human understanding operates at frequencies, similar to the wavelengths of light. Visible light only covers a range of 4000 to 7000 Angstroms. Beyond that there is ultraviolet, infrared, radio, microwave, and other wave lengths of light that our eyes are not tuned to see. Man's thoughts and comprehension remain at the visible wavelengths, but God's thoughts and comprehension cover them all, including ours.

Isaiah 55:10–13

The constancy of God and his word is affirmed. His word waters fertile soil and produces in us fruit (compare Moses 4:30). Life can be abundant where water is plentiful; where there is little water, there is little life.

The word of God was given to long-ago Israel with the intent to bear fruit yet in the latter days. Seeds are placed in the ground long before they bear fruit. In fact, seeds appear to have no effect on the ground in which they are initially planted. The tiny, tender seed takes time to germinate and eventually gains strength enough to begin pushing its way through the crusty, trampled soil. When it has broken through it will need nourishment and light to continue growth. The Light of Life and the Water of Life bring rapid growth, and the plant becomes fruitful and fulfills the purpose of its creation.

Isaiah 56:1–2

Through the next chapters Isaiah continues to focus on key gospel doctrines. After teaching about scripture study and prayer, he emphasized keeping the Sabbath day holy and Temple worship. "Keep[ing] the sabbath" means honoring and properly observing all holy days (in the Jewish mind all the holy days were considered sabbath days, and there were also sabbath years). The Sabbath was a sign of God's covenant people (Exodus 31:12–17). How to properly observe the Sabbath is powerfully described in Isaiah 58:13–14.

Isaiah 56:3–4

Strangers (foreigners) and eunuchs (emasculated males) were considered ritually unfit for Temple worship, but Israelites were obligated to treat all strangers or foreigners with civility and kindness (Exodus 22:21; Leviticus 19:34). They, too, are children of our Heavenly Father and are invited to be faithful to him and merit eternal blessings.

Isaiah 56:5

"A place and a name" in Hebrew is *Yad Vashem,* which is the name of modern Israel's Holocaust Memorial in Jerusalem. Those outside the covenant are also invited to make themselves worthy and enter the holy place and receive a special name. "I will give them [or endow them with] an everlasting name" (compare Revelation 3:12). Compare also the Kirtland Temple Dedicatory prayer: "establish the people that shall worship, and honorably hold *a name and standing* in this thy house, to all generations and for eternity" (D&C 109:24; emphasis added). Those who obey the Lord will receive a new name that will be everlasting. This is a better name than that of sons and daughters, because everyone is a son or daughter of God, while not everyone will be honored to receive an everlasting name and inheritance with God.

Isaiah 56:6, 8

Sons of the stranger join themselves to the Lord and take hold of the covenant. See Abraham 2:10; Isaiah 60:3; and Ogden and Galbraith, "What are the reasons behind the long-standing conflicts in the Holy Land, and how should Latter-day Saints view such conflicts?" *Ensign,* Sept. 1993, 52–53.

Isaiah 56:7–8

"Even them will I bring to my holy mountain": Adopted Gentiles will participate fully in Temple ordinances and blessings (compare the parable in Luke 14:16–24).

Regarding the "house of prayer for all people," see Matthew 21:13. As Isaiah previously testified, the future Temples in the Old and New Jerusalems will fit this description of a holy mountain for all people (Isaiah 2:2–3).

Isaiah 56:9–57:12

We have here an abrupt change of subject: After expounding on righteous Temple worship, Isaiah contrasts perverted heathen temple practices. The prophet employs a brilliant juxtaposition of

Temple worship—what is proper worship of God—with idolatry, what is not proper worship of God.

Isaiah 56:10–12

Spiritually, what good is a *blind* and *dumb* watchman? He cannot see and cannot warn. Reference is metaphorically made to indolent, greedy, and gluttonous shepherds or leaders. Jesus later made a stark contrast between them and himself, when he referred to himself as "the *good* shepherd" (John 10:14; emphasis added).

Isaiah 57:1–12

These verses are a continuation of the previous chapter; idolatrous practices are described in vivid detail.

Verses 1–2: The righteous who die are taken from the calamity or evil milieu to a state of peace in the spirit world.

Verse 4: "Against whom do you make faces and stick out your tongue?"

Isaiah 57:5

"Enflaming yourselves" means arousing sexual passion (see also v. 8). Cultic prostitution and child sacrifice were perversions of a true principle: sacrifice of animals was approved but not sacrifice of humans, who are the offspring of God.

Which is worse—this ancient practice of child sacrifice or the modern practice of abortion? And could it be that there is an even more widespread and insidious form of child sacrifice today than abortion? Some children in our societies are physically alive but are spiritually sacrificed by their parents to the gods of materialism or fashion or religious skepticism. Many parents abandon their children to the care of others in order to pursue their own interests. Even some who spend time with their children fail to provide them with moral and spiritual nourishment.

Isaiah 57:9

The word "king" here should be rendered Melech or Molech, a Canaanite god associated with child sacrifices. Israel and Judah embraced idol-worship at times, much to their detriment.

Isaiah 57:13–21

Hope and *peace* are promised to the righteous.

Verse 20 features a superb simile. The wicked (the proud, the critical, the apostate) are like the troubled sea, always agitated, casting up mire and dirt.

Verse 21: Peace is not freedom from conflict but a calm assurance of our good standing before God. The wicked cannot feel such assurance.

Isaiah 58

Continuing his series of great gospel doctrine lessons, Isaiah gives us a wonderful sacrament meeting talk on fasting and sabbath keeping. Compare the latter-day treatment of the same topics in Doctrine and Covenants 59. This chapter's discourse is in the form of a conversation between the Lord and his people, Israel.

Verse 2: Hypocrisy is disdained; recall Isaiah 1:11–13.

Verse 3: "Haven't you even noticed all our fasting; haven't you paid attention to our humility?"

Verses 5–7: On the purposes of fasting, see also Matthew 6:16–18.

Why should we fast? (1) Tens of thousands of children in many parts of the world who are under four years of age are dying each day from malnutrition and related diseases. Fasting and giving offerings help such unfortunate people. (2) We learn to control our bodies, mastering physical appetites. (3) We learn to control our desire for money. (4) We learn to fast from food and from sin.

Verse 5: Afflict means torment. Sackcloth is Hebrew *sak* or English *sack*.

Verse 6: Fasting helps "undo the heavy burdens, and to let the oppressed go free." Fasting can help lift the heavy burdens of sin that too many of us carry around for too long. It can help all of us with spiritual problems (for example, Alma fasted and prayed for his son; Mosiah 27:13–24).

Verse 7: Compare Matthew 25:35–40. On May 17, 1845, Orson Pratt read these words of a general letter from the Council of the Twelve to the Church: "Let this be an ensample to all saints, and there will never be any lack for bread: When the poor are starving, let those who have, fast one day and give what they otherwise would have eaten to the bishops for the poor, and every one will abound for a long time; and this is one great and important principle of fasts approved of the Lord. And so long as the saints will all live to this principle with glad hearts and cheerful countenances they will always have an abundance" (Smith, *History of the Church*, 7:413).

President Joseph F. Smith declared: "It would be a simple matter for people to comply with this requirement to abstain from food and drink one day each month, and to dedicate what would be consumed during that day to the poor, and as much more as they pleased. The Lord has instituted this law; it is simple and perfect, based on reason and intelligence, and would not only prove a solution to the question of providing for the poor, but it would result in good to those who observe the law. It would call attention to the sin of over-eating, place the body in subjection to the spirit, and so promote communion with the Holy Ghost, and insure a spiritual strength and power which the people of the nation so greatly need. As fasting should always be accompanied by prayer, this law would bring the people nearer to God, and divert their minds once a month at least, from the mad rush of worldly affairs and cause them to be brought into immediate contact with practical, pure and undefiled religion—to visit the fatherless and the widow, and keep themselves unspotted from the sins of the world" (*Gospel Doctrine*, 237–38).

Verses 8–12: Promised rewards for fasting are described.

HOW TO HAVE A MEANINGFUL FAST

1. Plan and prepare your schedule.
2. Have a particular purpose.
3. Start the fast with a private, vocal prayer.
4. Keep the Spirit; use Saturday evening as part of your fast period.
5. Fast a full twenty-four hours, refraining from all food and drink, if possible.
6. Plan specific activities: study the scriptures, write in your journal and attend church meetings; participate in a *family* testimony meeting.
7. Pay a generous fast offering.

8. Before concluding your fast, set aside some time to ponder and meditate.
9. Read Moroni 7 or 10, or Mosiah 4, or Isaiah 53, or some other particularly powerful chapter of scripture.
10. End the fast with a private prayer.

Verses 13–14: Observance of the Sabbath is one of the signs of the covenant people. Is Sabbath observance one of the top distinguishing characteristics of "Mormonism"? If not, why isn't it?

"The mouth of the Lord hath spoken it" is similar to our "in the name of Jesus Christ, amen."

Isaiah 59

Verses 1–2: Israel has deprived herself of blessings because of unworthiness. The Lord (the Bridegroom) never initiates a divorce. He places culpability squarely on the shoulders of his errant people (the bride).

Verse 3: A splendid example of how the Lord uses parts of the body to show their sinfulness.

Verse 5: The Lord also uses examples from the world of fauna (such as snakes and spiders) to depict their iniquities.

Verse 6: The righteous are always clothed with good works, but imagine the embarrassment of the wicked, not having good works to cover their nakedness, as if going before the people wearing only a spider's web.

Verses 16–21: These verses refer to the Savior.

Verse 17: "He will return as the Divine Warrior dressed with a breastplate of righteousness, the helmet of salvation, the garments of vengeance, and a cloak of zeal (Isa. 59:17)—an image that applies to the Redeemer both as he conquered sin and death and also as he returns to judge the world at the end of time. Vengeance will come upon the wicked, and the Spirit of the Lord will rise up against the enemy" (Seely, "Lord Will Bring Salvation," 158).

Verses 20–21: Read an explanation of this prophecy in Romans 11:25–27.

"Who will be that Deliverer? Certainly Jesus, when he came

311

eighteen centuries ago, did not turn away ungodliness from Jacob, for they then were filling up their cup with iniquity. They have remained in unbelief from that day to this; hence, there did not come a Deliverer out of Zion eighteen centuries ago. But the Zion of the last days, that Zion that is so frequently and so fully spoken of by the ancient prophets, especially by Isaiah, is the Church and kingdom of God; and out of that Church or kingdom or Zion is to come a Deliverer, who will turn away ungodliness from Jacob after the times of the Gentiles are fulfilled" (Pratt, *Journal of Discourses,* 14:64).

Verse 21: "My covenant" is defined in Abraham 2:11.

Isaiah 60–66

The best commentary on these final chapters of the book of Isaiah is Doctrine and Covenants 133:8–52. Section 133 includes more passages from Isaiah than any other section of the latter-day scripture.

Again we see the prophetic pattern: after the doom, desolation, and destruction, come reinstatement, restoration, and redemption.

Isaiah 60

"Isaiah 60 through 62 describes the building of the glorified Jerusalem/Zion and the reign of the Lord. These prophecies were partially fulfilled by the return of Judah beginning in 539 B.C. and the rebuilding of Jerusalem and the temple and also in many ways spiritually with the coming of the Messiah in the meridian of time. But the prophecies will only be completely fulfilled in the latter days, with the restoration of the gospel, the events leading up to the Second Coming, and the Millennium, when Christ will reign on the earth. . . . (Isaiah 60–62 should be read with Isa. 2 and 11 as well as Ezek. 40–48, Zech. 14, and Rev. 21.)" (Seely, "Lord Will Bring Salvation," 159).

Verses 1–5, 10–12: Zion will arise and cause the light of Christ to shine on the nations; Gentile nations will join with and serve Zion.

Verses 1–2: Elder Orson Pratt taught: "The passage . . . from Isaiah has reference to the latter-day Zion. . . . [Zion] is called to 'arise and shine; for the glory of the Lord is risen upon thee.' There is no one thing more fully revealed in the Scriptures of eternal truth, than the rise of the Zion of our God in the latter days, clothed upon with the glory of God from the heavens—a Zion that will attract the attention of all the nations and kindreds of the whole earth. It will not be something that takes place in a corner on some distant island of the sea, or away among some obscure people; but it will be something that will call forth the attention of all people and nations upon the face of the whole earth" (*Journal of Discourses*, 16:78).

The Prophet Joseph Smith added: "Consider for a moment . . . the fulfillment of the words of the prophet; for we behold that darkness covers the earth, and gross darkness the minds of the inhabitants thereof, that crimes of every description are increasing among men; vices of great enormity are practiced; the rising generation growing up in the fullness of pride and arrogance . . . the day of the Lord [is] fast approaching when none except those who have on the wedding garment will be permitted to eat and drink in the presence of the Bridegroom, the Prince of Peace!" (*Joseph Smith* [manual], 151).

Elder Orson Pratt further explained that the darkness may be caused "because the salt of the earth is gathered out; the children of light are gathered together to Zion, and those who are left behind are in darkness" (*Journal of Discourses*, 14:355).

Verse 3: Compare Isaiah 56:6. "Inquires one—'Is Zion going to become popular, so that Gentiles and kings and great men will come to her light?' Yes, certainly; and not only Gentiles, kings and great men, but many of all the nations of the earth have got to come to Zion" (Orson Pratt, *Journal of Discourses*, 18:153).

Verses 5–10: People come by sea and by air, from all directions, to help build up Zion. Gentiles ("sons of strangers"; v. 10) contribute to building the walls of Zion; compare Isaiah 56:3–6; 61:5. Interestingly, Arabs have done almost all the masonry work in Israel for decades.

Verse 11: Gates of the New Jerusalem will remain open; there will be no war, and no need of defenses. John describes the same gloriously safe condition in Revelation 21:25. Open gates signify trust, integrity, and security. Zion will consist of people who are pure in heart; see Doctrine and Covenants 45:65–67.

Isaiah elaborates on Zion more than any other writer in the Old Testament.

Verse 12: President Spencer W. Kimball exclaimed, "We continue to warn the people and plead with them, for we are watchmen upon the towers, and in our hands we have a trumpet which we must blow loudly and sound the alarm" (*Ensign,* Nov. 1975, 7).

Verses 13–17: The City of Zion is established, with Gentile nations assisting; its beauty and glory are set forth (see also 49:22–23). "Exactors" in verse 17 are taskmasters.

Verses 18–21: The Millennium is further described. There will be no violence, no war, no sorrow (see also Isaiah 35:10). A light brighter than the sun will illuminate the city of God; John saw the same glorious vision of the future as Isaiah (compare Revelation 21:22–23; 22:5).

"Zion will not need the sun when the Lord is there, and all the city is lighted up by the glory of his presence. When the whole heavens above are illuminated by the presence of his glory we shall not need those bright luminaries of heaven to give light, so far as the city of Zion is concerned. But there will be a great people round about, dwelling in other cities that will still have need of the light of the sun and the moon; but the great capital city where the Lord will establish one of his thrones—for his throne is not to be in Jerusalem alone, it will also be in Zion. . . . When therefore, he shall establish his throne in Zion and shall light up the habitations thereof with the glory of his presence, they will not need this light which comes from the bright luminaries that shine forth in yonder heavens, but *they will be clothed upon with the glory of their God.* When the people meet together in assemblies like this, in their Tabernacles, the Lord will meet with them, his glory will be upon them; a cloud will overshadow them by day and if they happen to have an evening meeting they will not need . . . lights of an artificial nature, for the Lord will be there and his glory will be upon all their assemblies. So says Isaiah the Prophet, and I believe it" (Orson Pratt, *Journal of Discourses,* 14:355–56; emphasis added).

Verse 22: "A little one shall become a thousand, and a small one a strong nation." Compare Matthew 13:31 (Matthew 13 was interpreted by Joseph Smith as a series of parables relating to the Gathering, or the future of the kingdom of God; the kingdom likened to a grain of mustard seed depicts the growth of the Church in the last days; see *History of the Church,* 2:264–272). Read also Doctrine and Covenants 133:58. With a membership of fifteen million (2013) and growing, the Church and kingdom of God now has more citizens than many small nations. This may be seen as fulfillment of Isaiah's prophecy and a vital sign of the millennium preceding the coming of the Lord. God himself testifies: "I the Lord will hasten it in my time" (JST Isaiah 60:22).

Isaiah 61:1–2

Read the account of the fulfillment of these verses in Luke 4:16–30. This passage is attributed by Luke to Isaiah, which contradicts the hypothesis of a "Second Isaiah" or a "Third Isaiah"; see "The Authorship of Isaiah" just before commentary on Isaiah 40.

Verse 1 was a messianic prophecy and was fulfilled with the Messiah's mortal ministry. "Opening of the prison" refers to the Savior's work for the spirits in prison (see notes to 1*k*)—work for the dead was definitely spoken of in the Old Testament. During his ministry in Nazareth, Jesus quoted only the first phrase of verse 2, because the second phrase would not be fulfilled until his Second Coming (compare Isaiah 9:6). Such kaleidoscopic compression of events into one verse is typical of the prophets.

The words that Jesus had given to Isaiah over seven centuries earlier, and which now he cited, as recorded by Luke, contained prophecies with dramatic messianic implications:

"The Spirit of the Lord is upon me, because he hath anointed me [Hebrew, *Mashiah,* and Greek, *Christos,* both mean 'Anointed One']

"To preach the gospel to the poor [he preached to the poor in spirit; Matthew 5:3; 3 Nephi 12:3];

"He hath sent me to heal the brokenhearted [not only the physically sick and maimed but also the emotionally broken and wounded],

"To preach deliverance to the captives [spiritually captive souls in this world and in the spirit world; 1 Peter 3:19; D&C 138:8, 31],

"And recovering of sight to the blind [both the physically and spiritually blind],

315

"To set at liberty them that are bruised [he would offer to liberate those who were physically, spiritually, and emotionally bruised],
"To preach the acceptable year of the Lord [the acceptable year or the acceptable day of the Lord is the time salvation is offered to the souls of men; D&C 93:51; 138:31]" (Luke 4:18–19).

Isaiah 61:3–62:12

As already referred to in Isaiah 2:1–2, the Prophet Joseph Smith explained that the main object of gathering the people of God in any age of the world was "to build unto the Lord a house whereby He could reveal unto His people the ordinances of His house and the glories of His kingdom, and teach people the way of salvation; for there are certain ordinances and principles that, when they are taught and practiced, must be done in a place or house built for that purpose" (*Joseph Smith* [manual], 416).

With an understanding of the supreme importance of the Temple and its instructions, covenants, and ordinances, notice the Temple and marriage imagery in these chapters of Isaiah: anointing oil, garments, priesthood, covenants, robes, jewels, crowns, diadems, and new name.

Isaiah 62:4 describes that in the last days even "thy land shall be married." Compare Doctrine and Covenants 133:22–24: all the land will come together. Genesis 10:25 was literal—all the continents were separated, but at the Lord's Second Coming the continents will be joined together again. Just as the lands come together, so God and his people shall come together.

Compare also Ezekiel 37: Bones come together (resurrection); sticks come together (scriptural unity); and people come together (gathering of Israel). So Isaiah 62: Lands come together (return to a paradisiacal glory), and the Lord and his bride come together (marriage of the Lamb).

Isaiah 62:5 is in the form of a parallelism: "As a young man marrieth a virgin, so shall thy *God* [JST] marry thee: and as the bridegroom rejoiceth over the bride, so shall thy God rejoice over thee" (see also Revelation 19:7–9). This will be an eternal marriage.

"Both the New Jerusalem, which shall come down from God out of heaven, and The Church of Jesus Christ of Latter-day Saints are called the *Bride of the lamb* and the *Lamb's wife*. (Rev. 21:2, 9–10; 22:17; D&C 109:72–74.) The bride celebrates the marriage supper with the Bridegroom, her Husband, and is cherished and honored by him. To the millennial saints the Lord promises: 'As the bridegroom rejoiceth over the bride, so shall thy God rejoice over thee' (Isa. 62:5.)" (McConkie, *Mormon Doctrine*, 106).

Isaiah 62:5–7: The Lord's watchmen are proclaiming the gospel, giving out invitations to the marriage of the Lamb with his people (at the Second Coming).

Isaiah 62:11–12: The phrase "daughter of Zion" reflects the prophet's personification of Jerusalem. "Thy salvation cometh"— "salvation" in Hebrew is *Yeshua* or in English, *Jesus*. This language refers to the Second Coming but parallels the acclamations at the time of Jesus' Triumphal Entry (Matthew 21:5). Just as when Jesus came in the meridian of time, when he comes again to Jerusalem it will be a Triumphal Entry. He will come to his people, and they will be "Holiness to the Lord." Finally there will be a holy people in a Holy Temple in a Holy City in a Holy Land.

Isaiah 63:1–6

Read verses 1–4 with Doctrine and Covenants 133:46–51. The Lord comes from the *east*, which is the priority direction in that ancient land, both in his first and in his Second Coming. Isaiah uses a meaningful play on words here: Edom is a land to the east, but *edom* also means "red" (compare verse 2). We learn from Doctrine and Covenants 19:15–18 and from Luke 22:44 that the Lord's redness came from bleeding in Gethsemane. The images used here are poignant: the redness of his garments is due to the atoning blood pressed from his body as the juice of grapes in a wine vat (the Hebrew word for wine vat or winepress is *gath*, which is part of the name Gethsemane, or *Gath-shemen*); also, the blood of the wicked will be spilled in the day of vengeance (the Second Coming). John envisioned the same event: "He was clothed with a vesture dipped in blood" (Revelation 19:13).

In verse 3 the Messiah says, "I have trodden the winepress alone"; in Gethsemane he was awfully alone. "I will . . . trample them in my fury; and their blood shall be sprinkled upon my garments." That is the image behind Julia Ward Howe's "Battle Hymn of the Republic" (*Hymns,* no. 60).

"Mine eyes have seen the glory of the coming of the Lord,

"He is trampling out the vintage where the grapes of wrath are stored."

Verse 4 clearly identifies that day as a day of vengeance (compare Isaiah 61:2), though there is a brighter destiny which follows. Notice also the duration of vengeance and redemption:

"The day of vengeance is in mine heart." Justice (for a "day").

"And the year of my redeemed is come." Mercy (for a "year").

Isaiah 63:7–64:12

These verses constitute something of a psalm or prayer of praise by the prophet, praising the Lord for bringing about the redemption He had promised. It uses the future perfect or prophetic tense, as though that redemption had already happened (see commentary at Isaiah 3:8–11).

Isaiah 63:7–19

As the prophet recalls historic situations from as far back as the time of Moses when the Lord had been a Savior to Israel, note the evidence he sees that they had the guidance of the "Holy Spirit" in the days of the wilderness wandering. Though the term "Holy Ghost" as such does not appear in the Old Testament, it is apparent that similar gifts are connoted in the above usage.

"In all their affliction he was afflicted" (v. 9). Jesus suffered for our sins but also for our sorrows and griefs. So it is in our own relationships: when we really love someone, if they hurt we hurt. As Alma put it, we are "willing to mourn with those that mourn" and to "comfort those that stand in need of comfort" (Mosiah 18:9). Such a capacity for empathy is a sign of divinity and holiness.

Compare the teachings of Paul and Alma: "For we have not an high priest which cannot be touched with the feeling of our infirmities; but was in all points tempted like as we are, yet without sin. . . . For in that he himself hath suffered being tempted, he is able to succour them that are tempted" (Hebrews 4:15; 2:18). "That he may know according to the flesh how to succor his people according to their infirmities" (Alma 7:12).

The Lord actually condescended *below* all our afflictions, and he did it *alone*.

Verse 11: Remembering former times when the Lord seemed to be more directly involved with the people (the Exodus and the Red Sea crossing), now they are asking "where is he?" Compare Gideon's question: "If the Lord be with us . . . where be all his miracles which our fathers told us of . . . ?" (Judges 6:13). The unequivocal answer is in Isaiah 64:6–7 and 59:2.

Isaiah 64:1–12

Note: Isaiah 64:1 is 63:19 in the Hebrew text; English versions have properly corrected the Hebrew.

Read verses 1–5 with Doctrine and Covenants 133:37–45. Verse 1 speaks of the condescension of God. How far was he willing to come down? He was baptized at the lowest spot on earth, and descended in the water below that. He became the servant of all, washing his disciples' feet. He was willing to become mortal and suffer indignities and a cruel death. He condescended not only *to* our condition but *below* it. Doctrine and Covenants 122:8 teaches: "The Son of Man hath descended below them all." At his Second Coming, he will descend with vengeance.

"That the mountains might flow down"—compare Doctrine and Covenants 49:23; 133:22; one interpretation suggests catastrophism at his coming.

President Charles W. Penrose eloquently wrote: "He comes! The earth shakes, and the tall mountains tremble; the mighty deep rolls back to the north as in fear, and the rent skies glow like molten brass. He comes! The dead Saints burst forth from their tombs, and 'those who are alive and remain' are 'caught up' with them to meet him [1 Thessalonians 4:17]. The ungodly rush to hide themselves from his presence, and call upon the quivering rocks to cover them. He comes! with all the hosts of the righteous glorified. The breath of his lips strikes death to the wicked. His glory is a consuming fire. The proud and rebellious are as stubble; they are burned and 'left neither root nor branch' [Malachi 4:1]. He sweeps the earth 'as with the besom of destruction' [Isaiah 14:23]. He deluges the earth with the fiery floods of his wrath, and the filthiness and abominations of the world are consumed.

319

Satan and his dark hosts are taken and bound—the prince of the power of the air has lost his dominion, for He whose right it is to reign [Hebrew, *Shiloh*] has come, and 'the kingdoms of this world have become the kingdoms of our Lord and of his Christ' [Revelation 11:15]" ("Second Advent," 583).

Another interpretation of mountains flowing down at his presence derives from the parallelism; verse 2 has the *nations* trembling or bowing down at his presence.

The "melting fire [that] burneth" (v. 2) is the glory, aura, radiance, or radiation of the Lord and the glorious ones who come with him: "for the presence of the Lord shall be as the melting fire that burneth, and as the fire which causeth the waters to boil" (D&C 133:41; see also 5:19; 101:25; Ogden and Skinner, *Acts through Revelation*, 383–86; *Book of Mormon*, 2:88, 215–16).

Verse 4: The glory of God is intelligence, or light and truth. In our present state we have a portion of that light to guide us, but our telestial environment and tendencies inhibit our extended learning. When the earth is renewed to a terrestrial state with the glorified presence of the Messiah to open our hearts and minds to the truth, we will grasp knowledge heretofore unimagined by mortals. For future knowledge available to those who are worthy, read Doctrine and Covenants 121:26–32. The tuition we pay for such knowledge is valiance, faithfulness (D&C 121:29; see also 101:32–34). See these fascinating treatises by Elder Orson Pratt: "The Increased Powers and Faculties of the Mind in a Future State," *Journal of Discourses*, 2:235–48, and "The Increased Powers and Capacities of Man in His Future State," *Journal of Discourses*, 16:353–68.

Verse 8: In this appealing prayer we have one of the rare occasions wherein Old Testament writers address the Lord as "our father." See also Isaiah 63:16 and 1 Chronicles 29:10. Book of Mormon writers also refer to Jehovah/Jesus as the Father: see Mosiah 5:7; 15:2; Alma 11:38–40.

Isaiah used a metaphor that his people understood well: "we are the clay" (Hebrew, *khomer*, "material") "and thou our potter" (Hebrew, from *yatzar*, "to create, to form"). The same metaphor is used in Jeremiah 18:1–6.

We, like the clay, must be malleable; in doctrinal terms, we must be willing, humble, yielding, and submissive (Mosiah 3:19). Clay, in itself, is nothing but clay. It cannot make anything else out of itself. It *needs* the potter. The Savior expressed the same principle using the metaphor of the vine: "I am the vine, ye are the branches: He that abideth in me, and I in him, the same bringeth forth much fruit: for without me ye can do nothing" (John 15:5).

Verse 10–11: Here the future perfect or prophetic tense is used again; Isaiah saw in advance the destruction of holy cities and the Temple. Note "holy cities" (*plural*) are mentioned: Zion and Jerusalem (compare Isaiah 2:3). "Our holy and our beautiful house" is the Temple, "where our fathers praised thee."

Isaiah 65–66

People of all ages have dreamed of and hoped for an ideal world where there is no war, no hatred, no death, not even sickness or disease. The Lord has promised that such dreams will become reality as Zion is established and his glorious return to earth ushers in the great millennial conditions.

Even now as knowledge of the Lord begins to cover the earth, medical science believes, for example, that the disease smallpox has been wiped off the face of the earth. There is a reward offered for information about any case.

The new, purified earth which the Lord is about to create will be an extraordinary place to live. After all the wicked are removed from this world, and after the tribulations which always precede the blessings (D&C 58:4), the Creator will establish a new order of things where peace, love, and harmony prevail. As far off as such a time would seem, it is near, even at the doors. With these final two chapters of Isaiah you may want to also read the following scriptures: 2 Peter 3:10–14; 2 Nephi 30:8–15; Doctrine and Covenants 29:1–29; and Revelation 20–21.

Isaiah 65

In this chapter Isaiah summarizes the matter: Israel had failed to stay close to the Lord, though they had sought him in superficial ways. But, Israel (true followers of the Lord) would yet rejoice—during the Millennium.

Verses 1–2: The Joseph Smith Translation has the following changes: "I am *found of them who seek after me, I give unto all them that ask of me;* I am *not* found of them that sought me not, *or that inquireth not after me.* I said *unto my servant,* Behold me, *look upon* me; *I will send you* unto a nation that *is* not called *after* my name, for I have spread out my hands all the day *to a* people *who* walketh *not* in my ways, and *their works are evil and* not good, *and they walk* after their own thoughts."

Verse 2: The Lord's hands have been spread out all the day—"the day" meaning a thousand years? (The patriarchal period to Isaiah was about a thousand years; Moses to Malachi was about a thousand years; Lehi to Moroni was about a thousand years.)

Verses 3–5: Ancient Israel's abomination and hypocrisy are detailed.

Verse 6: With this verse begins the announcement of God's retribution to requite the evil.

Verses 17–25: Isaiah describes the transformation of telestial earth into terrestrial earth, the renewal to paradisiacal glory, and the Millennium. Enoch, Isaiah, John, and Joseph Smith apparently had the same vision (Moses 7:62–65; Revelation 21:1–7; D&C 101:23–25).

Verse 17: The "new earth" may refer to the cleansed, glorified, terrestrial-level sphere that will be taken back into the orbit where it was first created, before the Fall. And the "new heavens" may refer to the view of solar systems and galaxies in Earth's new position near its original creative setting. "This earth will be rolled back into the presence of God and crowned with celestial glory" (*Joseph Smith* [manual], 258). Brigham Young taught that the earth will move through space to "return again unto the presence of the Father" (*Journal of Discourses,* 17:143).

Those growing up in the Millennium will not remember nor comprehend life in former centuries when pride, greed, selfishness, and hate prevailed.

WHAT WILL THE MILLENNIUM BE LIKE ACCORDING TO SCRIPTURE?

Isaiah 2:4. No more war.

Isaiah 11:6–9. No more enmity among animals; those which

now eat flesh will eat grasses and grains; knowledge of the Lord covers the earth.

Isaiah 65:17–25. New heavens and new earth; no more sorrow.

Daniel 7:27. Saints of the Most High will be given the kingdom.

Zephaniah 3:9. One universal language is spoken.

Revelation 20:1–4. Satan is bound; Christ reigns a thousand years.

Revelation 21:1–4. New heaven and new earth; God himself is on the earth; no more death, sorrow, or pain.

1 Nephi 22:26. Satan is powerless because of the righteousness of the Lord's people (besides the fact that the Lord *bound* him). The Millennium is ushered in by the Lord's power; it is also maintained by the righteousness of the people.

2 Nephi 30:18. All things are revealed; Satan is powerless.

Doctrine & Covenants 29:11. The Lord dwells with men on earth a thousand years; no wicked.

Doctrine & Covenants 29:22–23. After a thousand years some again deny their God; end of terrestrial earth, change to new heaven and new earth (celestial).

Doctrine & Covenants 29:26. All graves are opened and bodies come forth.

Doctrine & Covenants 43:29–33. Saints reign with Jesus during Millennium; Satan is bound (then released for a little season at the end; also 88:110–111); people changed in the twinkling of an eye (see also 63:51); earth passes away as by fire; wicked go away into unquenchable fire.

Doctrine & Covenants 84:100. Time is no longer (see also 88:110); all things are gathered together; New Jerusalem is established on earth and New Jerusalem (City of Enoch) comes down from heaven.

Doctrine & Covenants 88:100–101. The wicked live not again until the thousand years are ended.

Doctrine & Covenants 101:25–31. All things become new; the Lord's knowledge and glory abound on earth; enmity of man and beasts ends; Satan has no power to tempt; no sorrow, no death—change in the twinkling of an eye (immediate resurrection) to a glorious rest.

Doctrine & Covenants 101:32–34. All things are revealed,

hidden and precious things; for example, how the earth was made, matters of geology, life sciences, astronomy, etc.

Doctrine & Covenants 133:24–35. All the continents are joined together as before division; ten tribes returning from the north are blessed by Ephraim.

Moses 7:62–65. Zion, a New Jerusalem, and Enoch's city are united; earth rests a thousand years; the Son of Man dwells on earth.

Article of Faith 10. Christ reigns personally on a paradisiacal earth.

PROPHETS DESCRIBE THE GREAT MILLENNIUM

"We believe that we shall rear splendid edifices, magnificent temples and beautiful cities that shall become the pride, praise and glory of the whole earth. We believe that this people will excel in literature, in science and the arts and in manufactures. In fact, there will be a concentration of wisdom, not only of the combined wisdom of the world as it now exists, but men will be inspired in regard to all these matters in a manner and to an extent that they never have been before, and we shall have eventually, when the Lord's purposes are carried out, the most magnificent buildings, the most pleasant and beautiful gardens, the richest and most costly clothing, and be the most healthy and the most intellectual people that will reside upon the earth. This is part and parcel of our faith; in fact, Zion will become the praise of the whole earth . . . if there is anything great, noble, dignified, exalted, anything pure, or holy, or virtuous, or lovely, anything that is calculated to exalt or ennoble the human mind, to dignify and elevate the people, it will be found among the people of the Saints of the Most High God. . . . The people will be so perfected and purified, ennobled, exalted, and dignified in their feelings and so truly humble and most worthy, virtuous and intelligent that they will be fit, when caught up, to associate with that Zion that shall come down from God out of heaven" (Taylor, *Journal of Discourses*, 10:147).

"The world has had a fair trial for six thousand years; the Lord will try the seventh thousand Himself . . . Satan will be bound, and the works of darkness destroyed; righteousness will be put to the line, and judgment to the plummet, and 'he that fears the Lord will alone be exalted in that day'" (Smith, *History of the Church*, 5:64–65).

"It has been the design of Jehovah, from the commencement of the world, and is His purpose now, to regulate the affairs of the world in His own time, to stand as a head of the universe, and take the reins of government in His own hand. When that is done, judgment will be administered in righteousness; anarchy and confusion will be destroyed, and 'nations will learn war no more.' It is for want of this great governing principle, that all this confusion has existed; 'for it is not in man that walketh, to direct his steps;' this we have fully shown" (Smith, *History of the Church,* 5:63).

"Christ and the resurrected Saints will reign over the earth during the thousand years. They will not probably dwell upon the earth, but will visit it when they please, or when it is necessary to govern it. There will be wicked men on the earth during the thousand years. The heathen nations who will not come up to worship will be visited with the judgments of God, and must eventually be destroyed from the earth" (Smith, *History of the Church,* 5:212).

"Do you know what the Millennium is for, and what work will have to be done during that period? . . . To build temples. . . . What are we going to do in these temples? . . . In these temples we will officiate in the ordinances of the Gospel of Jesus Christ for our friends, for no man can enter the kingdom of God without being born of the water and of the Spirit.

"We will officiate for them who are in the spirit world, where Jesus went to preach to the spirits, as Peter has written in the third chapter, verses 18, 19, 20, of his first epistle. . . .

"We will also have hands laid on us for the reception of the Holy Ghost; and then we will receive the washings and anointings for and in their behalf, preparatory to their becoming heirs of God and joint-heirs with Christ" (Young, *Journal of Discourses,* 13:329–30).

"In the millennium, when the kingdom of God is established on the earth in power, glory and perfection, and the reign of wickedness that has so long prevailed is subdued, the Saints of God will have the privilege of building their temples, and of entering into them. . . . And we will have revelations to know our forefathers clear back to Father Adam and Mother Eve, and we will enter into the temples of God and officiate for them. Then man will be sealed to man until the chain is made perfect back to Adam, so that there will be a perfect chain of priesthood from Adam to the winding-up scene. This will be the work of the Latter-day Saints in the millennium" (Young, *Journal of Discourses,* 15:138–39).

Isaiah 65:20 reads in the Joseph Smith Translation: "*In those days* there shall be no more thence an infant of days, nor an old man that hath not filled his days: for the child shall *not* die, *but shall live to be* an hundred years old; but the sinner, *living to be* an hundred years old, shall be accursed." People will live to the age of one hundred then be changed in the "twinkling of an eye" (D&C 101:30–31; 63:50–51).

Will there be *sin* during the Millennium? Yes, verse 20 refers to "the sinner." There will still be agency and capacity to sin; note Doctrine and Covenants 76:71–79, which speaks of terrestrial beings who are honorable people but still resist living all celestial laws. Those who live an honorable life will be terrestrial, and those who live a valiant life will be celestial.

Verse 22: "As the days of a tree" is an idiom; see also Ether 2:17 for the use of trees as a standard of measurement. In both of these occurrences, the use of a "tree" is just as logical as our "mile" or "kilometer" or "bushel" or "quart" or other such arbitrary standard measures.

Verse 25 paints the same peaceful, millennial scene as Isaiah 11:6–9.

Isaiah 66

The Lord is talking about the hypocritical worshipers who were as obnoxious to him as were the more blatant sinners.

Verse 3 cites examples of proper worship but with accompanying perversions of the proper worship.

Verse 5: "Ye that tremble" is in Hebrew *haredim* (literally, "the shakers" or "tremblers"), signifying the righteous.

Verse 7: The millennial kingdom of God is born. See Joseph Smith's translation of Revelation 12:1–7 in the Bible Appendix.

Verse 8: Israel, as a covenant nation, will be "born in a day."

President Charles W. Penrose described this magnificent climactic event, the birth of a covenant nation "in a day":

"His next appearance will be among the distressed and nearly vanquished sons of Judah. At the crisis of their fate, when the hostile troops of several nations are ravaging the city and all the horrors of war are overwhelming the people of Jerusalem, he will set his feet upon the Mount of Olives, which will cleave and part asunder at his touch. Attended by a host from heaven, he will overthrow and destroy the combined armies of the Gentiles, and appear to the worshiping Jews as the mighty Deliverer and Conqueror so long expected by their race; and while love, gratitude, awe, and admiration swell their bosoms, the Deliverer will show them the tokens of his crucifixion and disclose himself as Jesus of Nazareth, whom they had reviled and whom their fathers put to death. Then will unbelief depart from their souls, and 'the blindness in part which has happened unto Israel' [Romans 11:25] be removed. 'A fountain for sin and uncleanness shall be opened to the house of David and the inhabitants of Jerusalem' [Zechariah 13:1], and 'a nation will be born' unto God 'in a day' [Isaiah 66:8]. They will be baptised for the remission of their sins, and will receive the gift of the Holy Ghost, and the government of God as established in Zion will be set up among them, no more to be thrown down for ever" ("Second Advent," 583).

Dr. David B. Galbraith, founding director of the Jerusalem Center for Near Eastern Studies (Brigham Young University–Jerusalem), describes the glorious winding-up scenes as follows: "Old Testament prophecies describe a 'mass conversion' of the Jews at a time in these last days when the Lord says he 'will gather all nations against Jerusalem to battle (Zechariah 14:2). At that moment when the Jews face utter annihilation at the hands of their enemies, their long-awaited Messiah will appear. This time, however, he will appear in glory, not as a carpenter's son, and he will 'go forth, and fight against those nations . . . and his feet shall stand in that day upon the Mount of Olives, which is before Jerusalem on the east' (Zechariah 14:3–4). The Jews of that day will, in the words of the Lord, "look upon me whom they have pierced' (Zechariah 12:10) and then shall they say, 'What are these wounds in thine hands and in thy feet?' (D&C 45:51; Zechariah 13:6); at that moment a great miracle, foreseen by so many of the great prophets of old, will take place.

327

"In that historic moment of moments, all the Jews who had gathered in unbelief and had survived the 'refiner's fire' (Zechariah 13:9) will 'know' (D&C 45:52) that their Messiah, the Savior of the world, stands before them. They will know, if not by the overwhelming majesty of his very being, then certainly by the piercing, penetrating power of his own testimony, for he will declare to all who will hear the heart-shattering news that 'those [are the wounds] with which I was wounded in the house of my friends' (Zechariah 13:6). That statement alone will suffice to convince the honest in heart, and for those who still doubt, he will be more specific: 'I am he who was lifted up' (D&C 45:52). The confusion that this statement will raise in all those blinded by the traditions of many centuries will prompt a further testimony but this time one that will bear no misunderstanding, for he will authoritatively assert: 'I am JESUS that was crucified.'

"The impact that this revelation will have on all who are privileged to be assembled there is almost impossible to comprehend. For most, it will be all too clear that the Messiah who has just saved them from a terrible destruction is none other than that same Jesus who was crucified. But there remains yet one last hurdle, one last testimony without which, all would be in vain.

"In one grand and magnificent announcement, the dark scales that had accumulated over centuries, blinding a whole people, will suddenly be swept away and a new era will be born. Those solemn words to be uttered from the top of Olivet will penetrate and purge the very soul of all who will believe. These words will be heard in every corner of the land and will reverberate across the waters and around the world among every kindred, tongue and people. But among the first to hear them will be his own people—the Jews. The words will be: 'I AM THE *SON OF GOD*' (D&C 45:52).

"With that soul-rending announcement, the remnant of the Jews, that had been especially preserved by the hand of the Almighty to witness the event, shall be reduced to an unfathomable grief for 'then shall they weep because of their iniquities; then shall they lament because they persecuted their King' (D&C 45:53). Zechariah, speaking of that event, writes: 'In that day there shall be a great mourning in Jerusalem' (Zechariah 12:11). But it does not stop there, for 'the Lord shall utter his voice, and all the ends of the earth shall hear it; and the nations of the earth shall mourn, and they that have laughed shall see their folly' (D&C 45:49).

"The belief in Jesus Christ as the Son of God, the long-awaited Messiah, the Savior of the world, in that instant becomes the *uniting* rather than the divisive force that it had hitherto been, welding back into the fold his chosen people, and 'they shall call on my name, and I will hear them: I will say, It is my people: and they shall say, The Lord is my God' (Zechariah 13:9). And a nation, as it were, shall be born in a day" (unpublished manuscript; used by permission).

Verse 12: "Be dandled upon her knees" means to play or enjoy—which portrays the tender love of God for his people.

Verses 15–16: "The Lord will come with fire, and with his chariots like a whirlwind"—just as Elijah left the earth (2 Kings 2:11; see also Abraham 2:7).

On his cleansing with fire, refer back to commentary at Isaiah 64:2; see also Zephaniah 3:8; 2 Thessalonians 1:7–8; Doctrine and Covenants 5:19; 63:34; 130:7; 133:41.

Verse 19: Again, the sign or ensign, the Book of Mormon and the gospel, would be taken to Tarshish (Spain?), to Lud (Lydia), to Tubal (Turkey), to Javan (Greece), and to the isles afar off (the Americas). In other words, the gospel and the Book of Mormon would be taken to the ends of the earth. The glory of the Lord is declared among the Gentiles through the Book of Mormon.

Verse 22: "The new heavens and the new earth" means the terrestrial earth and later, the celestialized earth (see D&C 29:22–23; see also Isaiah 65:17).

Verse 24: The ultimate fate of the wicked is described.

NAHUM

The book of Nahum presents a harsh description of the destruction of the Assyrian capital of Nineveh because of her wickedness, cruelty, and idolatry. Its tone is accusing and vengeful, seemingly bereft of ethical and theological empathy. Nahum's words almost burn with anxiety to see judgments poured out on the barbarous Assyrians. Yet, in the introductory section of the book, Nahum reminds us that for all his power to take vengeance on the wicked the Lord is still slow to anger (Nahum 1:3), cares for those who trust in him, and is a refuge to them in times of trouble (1:7). Therefore, we may rest assured that Assyria deserved what they got at the hands of another empire on the rise—Babylon.

Both Jonah and Nahum were called to pronounce a burden or message of doom upon Nineveh, to lift the warning voice to the children of Heavenly Father living there. For over two centuries the brutality and violence of the Assyrian warlords were widely known and widely despised, and they were famous for atrocities committed upon the people they conquered. Recall that Jonah at first wanted nothing to do with such an assignment. He was bitter toward Israel's enemy and was likely quite reluctant to give them opportunity to repent and be spared. We don't know about Nahum's personal attitude toward the Assyrians, but his prophecy does not fit the usual pattern of doom followed by hope. This may be intentional, because Nineveh would be destroyed forever. Unlike Israel, it would never enjoy a later restoration, so there was no hope to prophesy about in Nineveh's case. By this time Assyria was simply too far gone and so Nahum starkly foretells Nineveh's destruction, which was fulfilled in 612 B.C.

Nahum apparently lived during the last half of the seventh century before Christ (about 640–620 B.C.). As a way to help date the prophet's ministry, historians point to Nahum's mention of the fall of Thebes (called "No" or No-amon in the Bible), the great capital of Upper Egypt, which occurred around 663 B.C. (Nahum 3:8–10). *Nahum* means "full of comfort" and could relate to the comfort he brought to Judah in knowing that the threat of Assyria would forever end.

Nahum 1

After the Assyrians' cruelties perpetrated on Israelites during the decades prior to Nahum's ministry, the prophet was called to pronounce the Lord's condemnation on the Ninevites. Though the Israelite nation was militarily feeble and unthreatening, the God of Israel was still God of all the earth, and he was about to unleash his fury and vengeance on his adversaries (v. 2). The word of the Lord is always strong and harsh against wickedness. Verses 3–8 describe the great power of the Lord to do what he proposes.

As frequently happens in Hebrew poetry, antecedents to pronouns are only implied, but it is evident by the context which verses are addressed *to* the Assyrians of Nineveh and which statements are *about* them. Some items are also addressed to Israel or Judah.

The herald of "good news" in verse 15 should sound familiar (see Isaiah 52:7). Nahum also anticipated the ultimate peace that was foreseen by Isaiah. The visions of both prophets came, of course, from the same source. Assyria's demise resulted when the mother-city, Asshur (614 B.C.), and the capital city, Nineveh (in 612 B.C.) were conquered by Nabopolassar, father of Nebuchadnezzar of Babylon, and father of the Babylonian Empire.

Nahum 2

Since the Israelites had been "emptied out" and "marred" because of their evildoing before they were conquered (721 B.C.), the prophet suggested that Nineveh must anticipate the same consequences.

Nahum's high and polished poetry, fiery figures, and white-hot images graphically depict the deserved destruction Babylon inflicted in the streets of Nineveh. We can vividly conjure up the clashing chaos (in this chapter and in chapter 3): the chariots raging in the streets, jostling one against another and running like lightning, the noise of whips, of rattling wheels, of prancing horses and jumping chariots, horsemen with bright swords and glittering spears. Verses 3 and 4 describe the Babylonian attackers; verse 5 tells of feverish defensive efforts within the city; verse 6 describes the opening of the sluice gates of the city moats; verse 7 describes the capture and exile of the queen (perhaps also the city itself); verses 8–10 describe the plundering of the city. Finally, using metaphors of a lion pack, Nahum describes in verses 11–13 the end of the terrible king and the end of his dynasty.

Nahum 3

As chapter 1 decrees Nineveh's doom and chapter 2 tells how it was to be done, chapter 3 essentially tells why her destruction was *deserved*. The phrase "bloody city," literally "city of blood" in Hebrew (v. 1), aptly describes all the bloody terror inflicted by the Assyrians on her conquered neighbors. The endless number of corpses and carcasses spoken of (v. 3) is based in fact. Cruel Assyrian kings boasted of stacking piles of their dead resistors at the gates of their conquered cities. The Assyrian king Shalmaneser III boasted that he had created a pyramid of the severed heads of one group of people. Furthermore, the Assyrian empire was filled with whoredoms and witchcrafts. No wonder the Lord said he was against Assyria and would "cast abominable filth upon" it—just what Assyria had done to others (v. 6).

One of the foremost messages of Nahum is a warning to all nations against strident militarism, seeking to conquer and get gain. As we know from the earliest history of the human family, killing (murdering) to get gain is the foundation of Satan's kingdom, the great Mahanic principle (see Moses 5:31). Jesus later taught, "all they that take the sword shall perish with the sword" (Matthew 26:52).

Nahum's vision of the destruction of Nineveh is another illustration of the Book of Mormon teaching that "the words of truth are hard against all uncleanness" (2 Nephi 9:40) and the word of God "speaketh harshly against sin" (2 Nephi 33:5). Nahum's message, however, does not end there. It is clear from his writings that Nineveh is used as a type of things to come, just as Babylon was a type (see Isaiah 13; 1 Peter 5:13; Revelation 14:8; 17; 18; D&C 1:16; 133:5, 7, 14). The Lord declares several times in modern scripture, "What I say unto one I say unto all" (D&C 61:18, 36; 93:49). The hard message of Nahum to Nineveh is also hard to nations and peoples in all ages, particularly in these last days preceding the Second Coming (Nahum 1, headnote). As Rudyard Kipling poetically pleaded "Lo, all our pomp of yesterday is one with Nineveh and Tyre! / Judge of the nations, spare us yet, / Lest we forget, lest we forget" (*Hymns*, no. 80), Nahum's three chapters stand as a forceful warning to people everywhere to repent and walk in the path of the Lord or suffer the vengeance of a just God.

HABAKKUK

Just before Judah fell to the Babylonian Empire, many prophets appeared to sound one final warning to the people (1 Nephi 1:4). The prophets foretold the demise not only of Judah but also of the Assyrian and Babylonian empires. Habakkuk was one of these. Not much is known about Habakkuk. His ministry took place at the time that the reconstituted kingdom of Babylon was on the rise (1:6), about 609 B.C.

The book of Habakkuk begins very much as other prophetic books do: "the burden which . . . the prophet did *see*" (v. 1; emphasis added). However, it is different from many other prophetic records in that it is not a direct pronouncement of doom against Israel or Judah but a record of a discussion between the prophet and Jehovah.

The book of Habakkuk became especially popular during the intertestamental period, roughly 200 B.C. to A.D. 70. A commentary on the book of Habakkuk was among the first of the Dead Sea Scrolls to be discovered at Qumran in the middle of the twentieth century. The ancient inhabitants of Qumran believed that such biblical writers as Habakkuk were speaking about events of the last days and that the last days were upon them, as one authority notes:

"The Habakkuk Commentary (1QpHab) from Qumran explains [Habakkuk 2:1–2] this way: 'God told Habakkuk to write down that which would happen to the final generation, but He did not make known to him when time would come to an end. And as for that which He said, '*That he who reads may read it speedily*' . . . interpreted, this concerns the Teacher of Righteousness, to whom God made known all the mysteries of the words of His servants the Prophets' (Habakkuk Commentary, 7:1–5).

"Many New Testament passages evidence the same eschatological reading of biblical texts, interpreting them as if they foretold and applied directly to contemporary events. . . .

"Another instance of this is Habakkuk 2:4b: [KJV: 'the just shall live by his faith'], one of Paul's favorite proof texts. He uses it in Galatians 3:11 to support his argument that faith, not works, is the way to become right with God. . . .

"The Habakkuk Commentary from Qumran offers another angle on Habakkuk 2:4b: "Interpreted, this concerns those who observe the Law in the House of Judah, whom God will deliver from the House of Judgment because of their suffering and because of their faith in [or: fidelity to] the Teacher of Righteousness" (Habakkuk Commentary, 8:1–3). Interestingly, the same passage that for Paul dealt with a way of righteousness other than the path of the Law was at Qumran a verse that encouraged faithfulness to that Law and fidelity to the Teacher who expounded it correctly" (Shanks, ed. *Understanding the Dead Sea Scrolls*, 197–99).

Habakkuk 1:1–4

Here is an individual living about 600 B.C. with a "burden" he doesn't like. Several other prophets express concern about the same problem: Why do the righteous suffer, while the wicked seem to prosper? Other notable references to that dilemma are in Psalms 37:1, 7, 35–36; 73:3–7, 12; Job 21:7–15; Jeremiah 12:1.

Habakkuk presents a *theodicy*—a vindication or defense of God's goodness and omnipotence despite the existence of evil. Agency is an eternal principle carefully guarded by God himself. Minds operating freely are allowed to choose evil or good and promulgate what they have willed to become. Some choose to impose evils upon others, and that is allowed for a time.

In verse 2 Habakkuk wisely questions, as did Joseph Smith in our own day, not "why?" but "how long?" (see D&C 121:2).

Habakkuk 1:5–17

The Lord's indication that he would allow the Chaldeans (Babylonians) to destroy the wicked of Judah did not please Habakkuk.

Though the prophet could conceive that the Babylonians

might "punish" and "correct" some of Judah's ills, why could he not believe the Lord would permit Judah to be destroyed by such as they? See especially verse 13, which contains a classic statement on the problem of evil in the Judeo-Christian context: Why does a just and holy God allow evil to flourish?

Habakkuk 2

The prophet acknowledges that he is a watchman—as were others. He seems to employ a bit of courageous humor in verse 1 ("I'm curious to see what I will say about the Lord's purpose."). The Lord commanded his prophet to receive his vision and to record it plainly. The Hebrew word in verse 4 rendered "faith" meant not just "hope for things which are not yet seen" but more accurately "faithfulness, steadfastness, firmness" (see footnote, v. 4). Paul later taught this doctrine in Romans 1:17 and Galatians 3:11.

These verses seem to tell of the Lord's ultimate judgment that would come upon wicked Babylon—or perhaps upon all types of wicked people. Remember how the Dead Sea Scroll community interpreted this passage as noted above.

Verse 20 presents reassurance and admonition to true worship in words that were inscribed over an inner archway of the Idaho Falls Temple.

Habakkuk 3

This chapter is a hymn or psalm intended for singing. *Shigionoth* is a poetic or musical instruction meaning perhaps "free" or "diverse"; it might be parallel to an *ad lib* direction to the performer. *Selah* is thought to mark places where the chanting could make certain liturgical breaks. The subject and purpose of the song is to praise the Lord.

Because of the Lord's intention, the prophet feared the worst for his people, but still he trusted and rejoiced in the Lord. He had provided salvation for Moses and his people in Teman and Paran, and in the Sinai desert. In Joshua's day the sun and moon stood still (Joshua 10:12–13).

Thoroughly humbled but yet reassured by the Lord's answer, the prophet resolved to abide by the Lord's management of things and never doubt him again, no matter how bad things were and how hard the trials became.

Verses 17–19 reflect a particularly good attitude for troubled times ahead. Trust in the Lord, no matter what the circumstances. This is the great lesson of faith learned by the prophet Habakkuk. Compare Job (13:15–16; 19:25–27) and Joseph Smith (D&C 121).

OBADIAH

We know almost nothing about the prophet whose name is attached to this book. Obadiah (Hebrew, "servant of *iah* or *Yah* [Jehovah]") was a fairly common name in Old Testament times (see 1 Kings 18:3–16; 1 Chronicles 3:21; 7:3; 8:38; 9:16; 12:9; Ezra 8:9; Nehemiah 10:5). Evidence suggests he was a contemporary of Jeremiah, as Obadiah refers to the Babylonian Captivity (v. 11).

The vision of Obadiah concerns Edom. Compare these verses with Jeremiah 49:9–10a, 14–16. It is not known whether Obadiah quoted Jeremiah, Jeremiah quoted Obadiah, or both quoted a common source. To appreciate fully the conflict between Israel and Edom, remember the background of their forefathers, the twin brothers, Jacob (Israel) and Esau (Edom). It all began with events preserved in Genesis 25:21–23ff. Edom as a nation had often been an enemy of Israel and Judah, and as a result, the very name of Edom (or the later Greek form, *Idumea*) came to symbolize "the world" (D&C 1:36; compare Isaiah 34:5) and thus Babylon.

Obadiah 1:1–14

After sarcastically telling the Edomites they will suffer when the day of the Lord's vengeance comes upon them, the prophet lists the chief reasons for their deserving punishment. Obadiah's burden or message applied to the Babylonian empire of his day but also to later events in world history. Verses 11–14 specifically refer to Babylon's attacks on Jerusalem (605–586 B.C.). Edom stood by while his "brother," Judah, was carried away captive. Edom acted like a stranger without helping, and even rejoiced over Judah's destruction. In fact, Edom assisted the destroyers.

Obadiah 1:15–21

The prophet makes a sudden transition from immediate to ultimate things, to tell what will happen to the wicked (such as Edom had been) in "the day of the Lord." As Israel had "drunk of the wrath" earlier, the Edomites shall drink and be destroyed: "[Edom] shall be as though they had not been" (v. 16). In verses 18–19, Israelites will again possess the parts of the promised land which Edomites, Philistines, and others had once taken away.

In contrast to those who choose to remain outside the kingdom of God (the "heathen"), those within it will inherit the earth after it is cleansed by fire. Certain helpers, saviors, will "come up on mount Zion" in the day of the Lord. Some Jewish commentaries suggest these "saviors" will be the Messiah and his officers. "Saviors" is from Hebrew *moshi'im*, singular *moshia'*, from a verb that means "to help save, rescue." Members of The Church of Jesus Christ of Latter-day Saints have commonly adapted this unique expression of Obadiah's to refer to those who research family history records and perform Temple ordinances to help rescue their ancestors in spirit prison, providing for them the ordinances essential to exaltation, thus becoming "saviors on Mount Zion"—Mount Zion used here as a designation for the holy Temple of the Lord. In one sense, a "savior" is someone who does something for someone else that they cannot do for themselves. Therein we employ the sacred concept of substitution, or proxy. We follow the example of the Lord Jesus Christ in helping serve as a savior for others of Heavenly Father's children.

The Prophet Joseph Smith declared, "But how are they to become saviors on Mount Zion? By building their temples, erecting their baptismal fonts, and going forth and receiving all the ordinances, baptisms, confirmations, washings, anointings, ordinations and sealing powers upon their heads, in behalf of all their progenitors who are dead, and redeem them that they may come forth in the first resurrection and be exalted to thrones of glory with them; and herein is the chain that binds the hearts of the fathers to the children, and the children to the fathers, which fulfills the mission of Elijah" (*History of the Church,* 6:184).

President Howard W. Hunter likewise testified: "We who live

in this day are those whom God appointed before birth to be his representatives on earth in this dispensation. We are of the house of Israel. In our hands lie the sacred powers of being saviors on Mount Zion in the latter days" (*Teachings of Howard W. Hunter*, 233).

ZEPHANIAH

Zephaniah's book begins in a familiar way: "The word of the Lord . . . came unto Zephaniah." Zephaniah performed his ministry in the days of King Josiah (ca. 640–609 B.C.). Like other prophets ministering during the late 600s, he warned Judah of impending invasion and exile, but his prophecies extend also to the end of times and the Second Coming, the "day of the Lord." Zephaniah's predictions of doom upon Jerusalem and Judah, along with other contemporary nations, are expressed in terms relevant to the final destruction of the whole wicked world. His writings presage a time of restoration and herald the messianic era, when the Lord will be King.

Zephaniah 1

This prophet's great-great-grandfather was Hezekiah (the spelling here in King James Version is Hizkiah.) It is possible that this was Hezekiah the king (2 Kings 18:1), making Zephaniah of royal lineage.

As verses 4 through 11 indicate, though the people may have changed, come and gone, over the years, the same old problems remained: Baal worship; a corrupt priesthood (*Chemarims* in verse 4 means "idolatrous priests"); Milcom, "the abomination of the Ammonites" (1 Kings 11:5), who was also known as Molech, the fire god to whom children were sacrificed; wicked princes clothed in foreign, inappropriate dress; and merchants grown rich through corrupt practices.

Note in verses 12–13 that people who take a "God-is-dead" attitude, saying in their hearts, "The Lord will not do good, neither will he do evil," are threatened with punishment. Ordinarily in this temporal world wealth is power, but what will earthly riches avail anyone in "the day of the Lord"? Real power comes from God, as one LDS hymn teaches:

> . . . *pow'r by earthly standards*
> *Comes by rank or wealth or sword;*
> *But the pow'r above all others*
> *Is the priesthood of our Lord.*
> (*Hymns,* no. 320)

Zephaniah 2

There is only one way for nations (Hebrew, *goi'im*) and for individuals to find security when the Lord unleashes his vengeance and punishments. Only by seeking the Lord and his righteousness is it possible to "be hid [and be safe] in the day of the Lord's anger" (v. 3; compare Colossians 3:2–3). In other words, only true repentance and faithfulness to the Covenant bring security.

Zephaniah 2:4–15 records the Lord's pronouncements against specific foreign powers. Verses 4–7 are judgments against Philistia and four of her five capital cities. Verses 8–11 are judgments against Moab and Ammon. Verses 12–15 are against Cush and Assyria.

Zephaniah 3:1–13

Woe is pronounced on any city that is filthy, polluted, and oppressive, but especially, in this case, Jerusalem, the city of God, which was supposed to be holy.

At the end of time, after the preparatory cleansing of the earth by fire, a universal pure language will be established, helping bring peace and unity among all peoples, for as a modern-day slogan indicates, "one language means one heart."

The meek of the earth will finally enjoy peace and safety.

Zephaniah 3:14–20

During the Millennium, the Lord will reign from two world capitals, Zion and Jerusalem (the New Jerusalem in America and the Old Jerusalem in the Near East). Great privileges and blessings will be available to the covenant people of Israel, to those who trust in the Lord, whose faith causes them to be faithful, fully committed and valiant.

JEREMIAH

We know more about Jeremiah's personal life and challenges than about any of the other prophets in the Old Testament. Enduring hostile circumstances could well be proposed as the theme of his life. He was reviled, beaten, put in prison, and exiled in Egypt. Thus, he serves as a powerful type and shadow of Jesus Christ. His ministry began sometime around 626 B.C. and ended after the fall of the Judahite kingdom in 586 B.C. He was a contemporary of Lehi, Habakkuk, Obadiah, Daniel, and Ezekiel, whose own ministry began in Babylon after the early deportations of Judah's population. In terms of political rulers, his ministry spans half the reign of King Josiah (640–609 B.C.), and the complete reigns of Jehoahaz (609 B.C.), Jehoiakim (609–598 B.C.), Jehoiachin (598–597 B.C.), and Zedekiah (597–586 B.C.). For more on the history of this period, see commentary at 2 Kings 21:1–18; 22:1–20; 23:28–30; 24:1–7; and, especially, 2 Kings 24:17–20.

Jeremiah is regarded primarily as a prophet of doom (after all, Judah was doomed), which partly explains why he had few friends. His closest associate was Baruch, his scribe, who recorded the prophet's messages as he dictated them (see Jeremiah 36). The Lord commanded Jeremiah not to marry or raise children (because of the coming disasters of Jerusalem's destruction and Babylonian captivity). The absence of a wife and children would naturally have increased his feelings of aloneness.

Jeremiah spoke much about his personal struggles—his feeling of inadequacy, his anguish of spirit, and his frequent petitions to the Lord to redress wrongs and rebuke his personal enemies. In fact, the English word "jeremiad," referring to a prolonged lamentation, complaint, or denunciating tirade, finds its origins in the practices of the prophet Jeremiah.

We do not know with certainty how or when Jeremiah died. Jewish tradition ascribes his death to stoning while living in exile in Egypt after the Babylonian devastation of Judah.

Jeremiah 1:1–3

Jeremiah was a priest from Anathoth (Joshua 21:18), which was one of the Levitical cities. According to the span of the reigns of the kings mentioned here, Jeremiah's mission was about 626–586 B.C. (Jeremiah 25:3), a period of forty years, and the Book of Mormon mentions him. Laban, an elder of the Jews, must have been acquainted with him (1 Nephi 5:13; 7:14; Helaman 8:20). He is one of the "many prophets" in Jerusalem at the end of the seventh century before Christ (1 Nephi 1:4; see commentary at 2 Kings 24:17–20). All of Jeremiah's writings are, therefore, important background for early chapters of the Book of Mormon (see Bible Dictionary, "Jeremiah"; *Encyclopedia of Mormonism*, "Jeremiah, Prophecies of").

Jeremiah 1:4–5

Some Jewish and Christian commentators have understood these verses to imply that Jeremiah was foreordained, or destined, to be a prophet before he was born. Verse 5 reads as though it were a line from Jeremiah's patriarchal blessing. For other sources of the belief in foreordination, see Abraham 3:22–23; Topical Guide, "Foreordination."

One of our colleagues recalled a fictional scene described by another colleague in which Jeremiah and his contemporaries were called into the stake president's office. The stake president turned to Daniel and said, "I would like to call you to go into Babylon. You will live under the protection of the king, you will receive a fine education, and you will become a respected leader in Babylon for decades." Turning to Lehi, the stake president said, "I would like to call you to escape the destruction of Jerusalem. Along with your family you will be sustained and blessed in the wilderness, you will be led to a promised land, and you will help to fulfill the birthright promises given to Joseph." Turning to Jeremiah, the stake president said, "I would like to call you to stay in Judah during the Babylonian attacks. You will be beaten, put in prison, held up in front of the people in ridicule, and be expected to preach to a wicked and unresponsive people."

No prophetic call is easy, but Jeremiah must have been extraordinary to take on such a challenging assignment.

JEREMIAH AND JESUS CHRIST

Jeremiah's prophetic call was introduced by a marvelous and famous revelation in which the Lord described Jeremiah's premortal preparation (Jeremiah 1:5). Jeremiah was a type and similitude of Jesus Christ who, we are told, was also foreordained and prepared from the foundation of the world (1 Peter 1:20; Revelation 13:8; Ether 3:14).

As a similitude of Christ, Jeremiah faced the same kind of opposition, insults, and attempts on his life as Jesus did—all from members of the house of Israel. This fits the sobering warning found in the Book of Mormon. The greatest persecutors of the Lord and his special witnesses are, shockingly, members of the house of Israel: "And the multitude of the earth was gathered together; and I beheld that they were in a large and spacious building, like unto the building which my father saw. And the angel of the Lord spake unto me again, saying: Behold the world and the wisdom thereof; yea, behold the house of Israel hath gathered together to fight against the twelve apostles of the Lamb" (1 Nephi 11:35).

Jeremiah said that because the Lord revealed to him the evil intents and doings of the house of Israel and the house of Judah, he knew he would encounter trouble: "*But I was like a lamb . . . that is brought to the slaughter;* and I knew not that they had devised devices against me, saying, Let us destroy the tree with the fruit thereof, and let us cut him off from the land of the living, that his name may be no more remembered" (Jeremiah 11:19; emphasis added). In other words, because Jeremiah had no children (Jeremiah 16:2), by killing him, though he was as innocent as a lamb, persecutors thought his name would die with him.

One immediately recognizes that this circumstance articulated in Jeremiah 11:19 also applies to both Jesus Christ (Isaiah quotes it in Isaiah 53:7 when describing the Savior's suffering) and the Prophet

Joseph Smith. The latter lamented when he went to Carthage to surrender himself to the pretended requirements of the law that he was
"going like a lamb to the slaughter" (D&C 135:4). Jeremiah, Jesus,
and Joseph Smith all faced parallel circumstances in their deaths.

Both Jeremiah and Jesus tried to stem the tide of immorality, feelings of prideful superiority, and misplaced fanatical confidence in
God's favoritism. Their single-minded efforts earned them the wrath
of their countrymen.

One of the interesting and important parallels between Jeremiah
and Jesus that helps us to see Jeremiah more clearly as a similitude
of Jesus centers on the interaction between the two anointed leaders and the priests of the Temple. The following summary may be
helpful:

- Both Jeremiah and Jesus preached in the court of the Temple
  (compare Jeremiah 26:1–2 and Matthew 21:23–23:36).
- Both preached following a divine mandate but with no guarantee
  of success (compare Jeremiah 26:3–6 and Matthew 21:33–39).
- Both prophesied the destruction of the Temple (compare
  Jeremiah 26:4–7 and Matthew 24:1–2).
- Priests were involved in arresting both Jeremiah and Jesus and
  charging them with prophesying falsely (compare Jeremiah
  26:8–9 and Matthew 26:47, 59; Mark 14:43, 55–64).
- Both Jeremiah and Jesus received some kind of hearing or
  arraignment within the Temple precinct under priestly jurisdic-
  tion (compare Jeremiah 26:9 and Matthew 26:57; Mark 14:53).
- In the cases of both Jeremiah and Jesus, secular authority con-
  vened a court (compare Jeremiah 26:10 and Matthew 27:11;
  Mark 15:1–2).
- With both, the priests framed the case before secular authority
  (compare Jeremiah 26:11 and Matthew 27:12, Mark 15:3).
- Both Jeremiah and Jesus defended themselves by referring to
  divine mandate (compare Jeremiah 26:12 and Matthew 26:64).
- In both cases, the secular ruler declared his intention to exoner-
  ate the accused (compare Jeremiah 26:16 and Matthew 27:23;
  Luke 23:4, 13–14).
- In both cases, a comparison was made with another accused,
  whose fate was also hanging in the balance (compare Jeremiah

26:20–22 and Matthew 27:15–26; see Welch and Hall, *Charting the New Testament,* 10–16.)

It is significant that the foregoing parallels between Jeremiah and Jesus come from Jeremiah 26, which, though an account of Jeremiah's Temple sermon, is really a similitude of the Savior's arrest and arraignment. Of course, Jeremiah was not immediately executed as Jesus was. But in the end, Jeremiah was executed as well. And, thus, ultimately Jeremiah's life was a powerful similitude and fore-shadowing of the earthly life of the God that Jeremiah served with patience, fortitude, and steadiness.

Like Jesus, Jeremiah lived in turbulent times. Both witnessed a society spiraling downwards. Jeremiah, like Jesus, addressed a hard-hearted, stiff-necked people. Their messages fell on deaf ears, and destruction followed the unheeded warnings. The Jerusalem Temple was destroyed, and the Jews were scattered by a powerful empire. The events of 586 B.C. were replayed in A.D. 70 with even greater intensity and horror. Jeremiah's life was a pattern of Jesus' life; what happened in Jeremiah's day was repeated in the meridian of time.

Jeremiah 1:6–10

Jeremiah felt inadequate and unprepared for his calling (com-pare the responses of Enoch in Moses 6:31, and of Moses in Exodus 4:10). The Lord reassured, encouraged, and endowed him with authority and power to do His work and speak His words. In verses 7–8 the Lord is saying, essentially, "Whomever I call, I qualify," which we have heard modern prophets reiter-ate. Jeremiah didn't need to fear mortal, temporary leaders, for the prophet would be given power "over the nations and over the kingdoms." The Lord's act of touching Jeremiah's mouth to sanctify him for the ministry was paralleled by an angel in Isaiah's case (Isaiah 6:7). Verse 10 uses some key words which seem to be a major theme in Jeremiah's writings (see also 18:7–9; 24:6; 29:5; 31:4–5, 28; 42:10).

Jeremiah 1:11–16

Jeremiah used symbolic visions and symbolic acts to teach. For example, almonds and a boiling pot (chapter 1) and fig baskets (chapter 24), spoiling the linen cloth (chapter 13), spoiling the pottery vessel (chapter 18), smashing another pottery vessel (chapter 19), wearing the yoke (chapters 27–28), buying the field (chapter 32), burying the stones (chapter 43), and throwing the scroll into the river (chapter 51). All these things were seen and done to dramatize his message, to leave no room for doubt or misunderstanding. All teachers know the value of object lessons.

This symbol of a "seething" or boiling pot, literally "blown upon" or "fanned"—with reference to the fire under it (v. 13), is picturesque for us who have slang idioms about "what's cooking." Our expression, like this one, refers to something in preparation, something imminent.

Although Babylon was east of Israel, the Babylonian attack had to come down from the north, because the desert prevented direct east-to-west travel. Verse 15 may imply that many nations in the Babylonian empire would be involved in the siege upon Jerusalem.

Jeremiah 1:17–19

Jeremiah, with God's power, could be bold and direct. "Gird up thy loins" means to gather up the long robe usually worn by men, tuck it under the belt or sash they also wore, and get ready for action.

It would be a challenge to be *alone* against kings, princes, priests, and people! But the Lord protected Jeremiah and made him as safe as a "defenced" or fortified city for the time of his appointed ministry. Those who fought against Jeremiah would not prevail. The Lord's promises to Jeremiah remind us of the promises made to the Lord's servants in the latter days: "they shall go forth and none shall stay them . . . this is mine authority [power], and the authority of my servants" (D&C 1:5–6). (Here we hasten to reiterate that Jeremiah was not a lone prophet; there was a host of prophetic voices vigorously declaring the Lord's word and will to the people.) Later, we will see that Jeremiah actually wondered whether he was getting enough protection from the Lord to be able to endure it all.

Jeremiah 2:1–6:30

These chapters are undoubtedly Jeremiah's earliest discourses, delivered during the later reign of King Josiah. The theme is

Judah's backsliding and apostate ways (chapters 2–5), which became so bad that they led to God's chastisement through another invasion of a foreign military power—Babylon (chapter 6).

Jeremiah 2

This section of Jeremiah's opening speech gives a sample of Jeremiah's approach—very metaphorical. Israel was holy to the Lord, his first and special harvest. Those nations who would try to "devour" Israel would be held guilty in the Lord's eyes and disaster would overtake them (v. 3). This verse has specific reference to the Lord's guidance during the Exodus, Israel's wilderness sojourn, and conquest of the Holy Land, as verses 6–7 indicate. But Israel forsook the Lord and tried to change their God for "gods, which are yet no gods" (v. 11). Israel forsook the "living waters" (v. 13) and became bereft of spiritual wellsprings by using broken cisterns. How would a cistern—a broken cistern—compare with a fresh water spring? Idols are like the broken cistern because much is put in, and nothing is derived from them.

Cisterns and pools are artificially developed containers or reservoirs for storage of water from another source. They are subject to stagnation and pollution. Wells, springs, and rivers, on the other hand, may be "living," that is, *flowing*—a continual supply of refreshing and life-giving water.

Centuries before Jesus, Jeremiah saw the Lord lamenting the condition of people who had "forsaken me the fountain of living waters, and hewed them out cisterns, broken cisterns, that can hold no water" (v. 13). It appears that Israelites in the Assyrian and Babylonian periods had rejected their Source of ongoing revelation and guidance. The perpetual replenishment of their spiritual waters which God was willing to provide had been superseded by his peoples' desire to horde the waters of life which had already been given them and store them away in underground cisterns of tradition and ceremonialism. The waters stored away, though no longer a perennial supply, could still have sustained and satisfied them for a time had they been directed into undamaged cisterns, but alas, the cisterns themselves were marred and broken and could hold no water.

Jeremiah ridiculed the vanity of worshiping gods of stone and wood and abandoning the true God who had planted them in the land and protected them from aggressors. Their hope of support from Egypt or Assyria against Babylon was fruitless; the only hope of Israel was the Holy One of Israel.

Verse 16: Noph refers to Memphis, the ancient capital of Egypt. Tahpanhes is another Egyptian city in the Delta region, probably Tel Dafneh today.

Verse 19: Though the Lord continually led his people (v. 17) their "backslidings"—and their repeated wicked actions—led to the Lord's reproof or rebuke.

Verse 22: Nitre was one of the powerful cleansing agents in the ancient world, but even it could not remove the stain of iniquity.

Verse 27: A "stock" is an idol made of wood. This verse also contains a nice play on words denoting that the house of Israel turned *away* from God ("turned their back") and not *toward* God ("their face"). Indeed, the concept of repentance in Hebrew is represented by the word *lashuv*, to "turn," or "return."

Jeremiah 3

The covenant marriage relationship between the Lord and his bride had been adulterated (see vv. 14, 20, and 2:32; see also first paragraphs of commentary at Judges 2:11–23). Judah had gone off and played the harlot, with "many lovers." Because of the polluted nature of the land, the Lord had withheld the rains, one of the means he uses for humbling his people (see Deuteronomy 11:11–17 and Amos 4:7). Does drought sound familiar in the covenant land of America? Is there still a relationship between wickedness and the withholding of moisture?

Judah had been more blameworthy than Israel because she had Israel's example to warn her. Yet, she did not turn to the Lord. Jeremiah then pleaded for repentance and illustrated the Lord's merciful nature by describing what awaited both Judah and Israel in the future. Verses 11–14 indicate how and when northern Israel was to be gathered again. Verse 14 demonstrates how the Hebrew concept of repentance is embodied in the word "turn." The old "Ark of the Covenant"—representing the Mosaic Law, or the old covenant—will have no more function under the new covenant (v. 16).

In verses 17–19 Jeremiah continues his discussion of a future time of restoration just before the Millennium when Jerusalem would be the Lord's capital, when the lost Ten Tribes would return from the north, and be reunited with Judah in their land of inheritance. Jeremiah then returned to Judah's treacherous apostasy.

The weeping and supplications of the children of Israel were heard many times in ancient days and down through the centuries in many nations of the earth. They have been heard again in modern days, especially in Europe between 1939 and 1945, as the far-reaching effects of the Holocaust continue to cause weeping.

Jeremiah 4

Chapter 4 continues the prophet's call to repentance, and includes a lament over the consequences of Judah's wicked ways. Pain, alarm of war, destruction, and spoiling all came because "my people is foolish, they have not known me" (v. 22; compare Hosea 4:6 and JST Matthew 7:23). The earth will be made "empty and desolate" ("without form and void," as in the beginning, according to KJV Genesis 1:2) but yet not be brought to a "full end" (v. 27); this creation will actually have no end. It is destined to live on in higher glory forever and ever.

Jeremiah 5:1–29

Jerusalem in Jeremiah's time seems to have been worse than Sodom and Gomorrah in Abraham's time. A few were led away from those immoral cities of the plain, but the cities and inhabitants were destroyed. Now again, some were led away but then the wicked city must be destroyed. The Lord withheld the rains, causing famine conditions, and he brought on plagues and enemies to humble and correct his people, but they became "harder than a rock" and refused to "return" (Hebrew, *lashuv*) or repent. Punishment was inevitable, and Babylon would be the destroying agent, brought by the Lord himself "from far" (v. 15). Israel's sins had cancelled out not only the rains but many other good things, including an immediate future with happiness. Their evil deeds seemed to have no limits (read "surpass" in place of "overpass" in verse 28); did they really expect the Lord would ignore such wickedness?

Jeremiah 5:30–6:30

According to these verses and 6:14 and 8:8–11, a false sense of security was promoted by false priests and prophets, and "my people love to have it so." What would result? (see 8:20–22). The Lord warned, "behold, I will bring evil upon this people, even the fruit of their thoughts" (6:19)—that is, they will get their just desserts. In starkly intimidating language, the Lord also reiterated the nature of the "great nation" he was bringing upon Judah "from the north country" (v. 22). They were a vast war machine, possessing no restraint: "They shall lay hold on bow and spear; they are cruel, and have no mercy; their voice roareth like the sea; and they ride upon horses, set in array as men for war against thee, O daughter of Zion" (v. 23).

Though the prophets had been set as watchmen upon the watchtowers, to warn of impending doom, they had been rejected—so the Lord must reject the people who refused to heed the voice of warning.

Jeremiah 7:1–16

The book of Jeremiah constitutes a collection of his speeches given from time to time and place to place during the years of his ministry. The prophet repeatedly presented the people with opportunity to repent. Jeremiah advised the Temple-goers at the gate that their perfunctory offerings would not save them. Even the Temple workers must not think they can hide in the holy place, regarding it inviolate—unable to be destroyed. The holy Temple had become a virtual "den of robbers" (v. 11; compare Matthew 21:13). In verse 12, Jeremiah reminded his fellow citizens that Shiloh, the site of the Tabernacle during the period of the Judges, had been destroyed about 1050 B.C. by the Philistines, because of Israel's iniquities. They had been cast out, the same fate that was imminent for Judah. Amazingly, the Lord instructed Jeremiah not to pray for the people. They were beyond hope and the Lord would no longer listen to petitions for their spiritual welfare. We are reminded that normally, "the effectual fervent prayer of a righteous man availeth much" (James 5:16). But these people had crossed the same line we read about in Mormon's last epistle: "thou knowest the wickedness of this people . . . they are without principle, past feeling . . . I cannot recommend them unto God" (Moroni 9:20–21). Perhaps, Jeremiah felt the same way as Mormon. Indeed, as with the Nephites, so with Judah—"the day of grace was passed with them" (Mormon 2:15).

Jeremiah 7:17–34

In recent decades, archaeologists digging in ancient Jerusalem of this period have uncovered hundreds of cultic objects, figurines, and idols—the same that are condemned here. For the identity of the "queen of heaven" see footnote 18a. What the Lord is saying in verses 21–23 is that temple sacrifices are accepted of him only when offered in sincerity, repentance, and obedience. "Go ahead," he says, "put your burnt offerings with your other sacrifices and eat them yourselves because they are of no value to me." *Tophet* (v. 31) means places of burning. The people were carrying on repulsive rites of neighboring "religions," including child sacrifices in the Hinnom Valley just south and west of the city (see Bible Map 12). Could a parallel be made today regarding abortion and child abuse and neglect—some people sacrificing their unborn children and even the children that are born to them to the idols of worldliness, convenience, and pleasure-seeking?

Jeremiah 8:1–19

More dire pronouncements of ravages from the God-sent invaders; survivors will prefer death over life.

Verse 7 records an indictment against humankind: even the birds know their appointed times and places for migration back and forth using the great bird migration route between Eurasia and Africa over the land of Israel—but God's own children lack sense of direction; they seem unable to recognize direction from him. A similar indictment opens the book of Isaiah (Isaiah 1:3).

Jeremiah 8:20–9:26

"The harvest is past, the summer is ended, and we are not saved." At this point there was no soothing ointment like the balm of Gilead, nor was there any physician that could heal this rotting body of people. The people of Judah, were now—to borrow again some Book of Mormon language—"past feeling" (1 Nephi 17:45); they had deteriorated to a "fulness of iniquity"

(Ether 2:10); their "day of grace was passed" (Mormon 2:15). Finding themselves beyond the point of repenting and returning to God, it was indeed "everlastingly too late" (Helaman 13:38).

Jeremiah expressed deep grief for the wickedness and resulting desolation of his people. We will see more of his anguish in the book of Lamentations (plus, compare the agonizing feelings of Mormon and Moroni over their fallen people in Mormon 6:16–20). Since Jeremiah knows his countrymen and women will be killed in the Babylonian siege of the city, notice the war images he employs in describing their hypocrisy.

Jeremiah 10

This chapter contains the prophet's reflection on the greatness of God—akin to a psalm of praise to the Lord. Embedded therein is a plea to forsake the ways of heathen nations—brutish, ignorant, and idolatrous. Jacob, or Israel, was made for better things.

Cultic trees were common in ritual fertility worship of that day, and the heathen ways are here condemned. It is always shocking to the righteous that speechless and powerless idols can replace the living God in the hearts of some human beings. The prophet continues to hope and pray that the people will turn from their vanity and mockery.

Jeremiah 11

How quickly humans forget; how often we need reminders, and God's prophets are called to frequently and incessantly remind the children of God of their Father's ways—so that backsliding souls will repent and return to Him. Jeremiah decries the fact that idolatry had so thoroughly permeated Judah that the number of gods therein was equal to the number of Judahite cities, and the number of pagan altars equal to the number of streets in Jerusalem. The Lord's instruction not to pray for the people is repeated. Remember, these are Jeremiah's people, and the instruction must have pained him.

The Lord revealed to Jeremiah that the people of Anathoth, his own hometown, were plotting to kill him. He had been "like a lamb or an ox that is brought to the slaughter" (v. 19). Jesus later faced the same treatment in his own hometown (Matthew 13:54–58).

Jeremiah 12

Jeremiah asks the same weighty questions as did the psalmists (Psalms 35:17–28; 37:1, 7, 35–36; 73:3–7, 12), Job (21:7–17; 24) and Habakkuk (1:2–4, 13): Why do the wicked prosper? And why do those whose behavior is treacherous seem so happy? Answers may be temporarily uncomfortable in this world, but the Lord once again gives assurances of ultimate justice: the wicked will definitely be punished for their evil and the righteous will certainly be rewarded for their good.

In a section wherein God's answer to the prophet is recorded (vv. 5–13), the Lord told Jeremiah that even members of his own family wanted to kill him. And then he warned, "do not trust them even though they speak well of you."

Jeremiah 13

The prophet continued using object lessons and emotional pleadings with his fellow Judahites. In verses 22–23 the people cry out, in essence, "Why is all this happening to us?" And the answer is pathetically simple: "For the greatness of thine iniquity." Having forgotten their Lord, the children of Israel would be scattered.

Jeremiah 14

Jeremiah supplicated the Lord for relief from recurring drought, but heaven's response was no; the people were not worthy of help. One reason Jerusalemites were equivocating over their allegiance to Jehovah was the multitude of false prophets in the city. Verse 11 contains a third reiteration of the command that Jeremiah should not pray for the people. Verses 13–16 teach how the people can distinguish true prophets from false ones. In verse 22 the Lord again reminds the people that only the true, living, and righteous Creator of all things can control the elements. Jehovah can send rain because he created all the elements.

Jeremiah 15

The prophet and other faithful souls were pleading for the kingdom of Judah to be spared, but the Lord made it clear that even if Moses and Samuel supplicated for the people, he would not reverse the decreed punishment. Moses and Samuel had achieved temporary reprieve for their people because some of their people had repented (Exodus 32:30–35; 1 Samuel 7; compare also Ezekiel 14:14). However, few, if any, souls in Jeremiah's time were genuinely repentant. They would therefore be "removed into all kingdoms of the earth" (v. 4).

Jeremiah regretted that his mother ever brought him into a world of such wickedness (v. 10), and he was depressed and needed the Lord's comfort and strength to continue his discouraging work. He reminded the Lord that he "sat alone" because he would not join the assembly of mockers (not to mention the fact that he was about to be told not to marry). His emotional and mental anguish spilled over as he asked the Lord why his pain was "perpetual" and his "wound incurable" (vv. 17–18).

The Lord finally answered Jeremiah at his low point—much the same way He answered Joseph Smith at one of his low points in Liberty Jail (D&C 122–23).

Jeremiah 16

Because of vile societal conditions, the prophet Jeremiah was to carry on his work alone, without a wife for companionship or children for comfort in the future. He was not to attempt to raise up a righteous posterity in those despairing circumstances. Nevertheless, as is the pattern in the Lord's dealings with his people, after the doom comes hope. In the future the Lord promised to gather his scattered people from the north, and from all other directions. They will be gathered by the Lord's emissaries, one by one, by "fishers" and "hunters" searching the mountains, hills, and holes in the rocks (v. 16). That is likewise the method of missionaries in the latter-day restored Church, searching high and low for those interested in turning to the Lord their God.

Jeremiah 17

Jeremiah gave a brief talk on Sabbath keeping, as did Isaiah earlier (recall Isaiah 58). The essence of the commandment given originally, that individuals do no work on the Sabbath, was reiterated. The original recipients did not pay attention, just as the people in Jeremiah's day paid no attention. Some things never seem to change. Will modern-day Israel, God's covenant people, pay attention?

Jeremiah 18:1–6

Here is an impressive symbolic use of clay in this object lesson Jeremiah performed in the Hinnom Valley, just outside ancient Jerusalem. The Lord is the Master Potter, trying to mold his people Israel into their most beautiful and useful shape. The imagery fits every stage of pottery making. Some of our sins are "soft" and relatively easy to repent of. Other sins are comparable to dried but brittle greenware pottery. Still other sins have been placed in the furnace of habit and have been fired to such hardness that they withstand all but the most serious attempts at repentance. Read also Isaiah 64:8.

Jeremiah 18:7–23

"Repent of" in verse 8 is changed to "withhold" in the Joseph Smith Translation. Jonah (3:10) is an excellent example of how the Lord can turn the prophecy around. "I, the Lord, command and revoke, as it seemeth me good" (D&C 56:4).

The last six verses describe further dangers Jeremiah encountered and how he met them.

Jeremiah 19

The prophet performed another of his symbolic acts before the elders in the Hinnom Valley. Jeremiah recorded a catalog of crimes (some specifically against the Ten Commandments) and their consequent punishment.

Our fellow religious educator, Paul A. Hanks, pointed out the comparative crimes of our day: "The killing of unborn infants is no better than the killing of the 'innocents' (v. 4). We are witnessing today a strident and powerful lobby to worship sex, whether in the brothel, in the movies, or in the bedroom, where life is not valued and adultery and fornication are acceptable. The further perversion of this abominable activity is the sexual abuse of children. To one who has not experienced a miscarriage and seen the perfectly formed fetus that has been cast off by the body, [the practice of aborting babies] may not have much meaning. I have seen such a fetus that died at five months from strangulation by the umbilical cord. This tiny boy was perfectly formed, even to his little fingernails and toenails. There is no doubt that he was a living organism, and the tragedy of seeing him lifeless left an indelible impression on my mind. Abortion is taking innocent life, just as was sacrificing children to Molech or Baal. Public opinion and the press would rigorously condemn any nation that allowed child sacrifices, yet many condone abortion."

Jeremiah 20:1–6

The senior official in the Temple had Jeremiah arrested, beaten, and put in stocks near a northern gate to the Temple Mount. The prophet then had some sharp prophetic words against him (compare Amos's pronouncement against the chief priest at Bethel in Amos 7:17).

Jeremiah 20:7–18

Jeremiah poured out his anguished feelings about the treatment he was receiving in the city for doing what the Lord had instructed him to do. He wanted to quit.

Elder Richard L. Evans, then a member of the Quorum of the Twelve Apostles, taught that "he who speaks the mind and will of the Lord to the condemnation of the ungodly finds adversity multiplied. It is a task of terrifying proportions, which even men of strength and courage would avoid if they could, to stand out from the crowd and tell onrushing humanity toward what inevitable end it is headed. But this, under divine appointment, is what a prophet must do. . . . therefore, a prophet is seldom popular, and the cost of being a prophet is always great: for he may be called upon to say those things which are not pleasing, even unto himself; he may find himself fighting against a tide of mass misconception, and, as history records, he may be stoned, crucified, banished, ridiculed, or shunned—for the truth is not pleasing unto all men, and time has proved that majorities are not always right" (*Unto the Hills*, 134–35).

Verse 9 contains a powerful statement about why Jeremiah could not quit (compare Alma 26:27; Helaman 13:2–3; Acts 4:19–20). Brigham Young experienced something similar to Jeremiah. After receiving a copy of the Book of Mormon, he

studied it and investigated the Church for a year and a half. He
was not impressed with the physical appearance or the intellectual
ability of the missionaries of the Church, but he could not deny
the truths they taught and the Spirit that accompanied their testimonies. He said, "The brethren who came to preach the Gospel
to me, I could easily out-talk them, though I had never preached;
but *their testimony was like fire in my bones*" (*Journal of Discourses,*
9:141; emphasis added).

Jeremiah 21

Jeremiah proclaimed the Lord's starkly contrasting options to
the people: "I have set before you the way of life, and the way of
death"—just as Moses had presented to earlier Israelite people: "I
have set before thee this day life and good, and death and evil"
(Deuteronomy 30:15; see also 2 Nephi 10:23). The immediate
consequences of their choice were specific and terminal. Few individuals would make the right choice.

Jeremiah 22

The Lord told Jeremiah to leave the Temple, higher up on the
hill where the prophet was teaching, and go down to the king's
palace to command him to do what was just and right. The king
of Judah at this point was probably Zedekiah since his predecessors are mentioned, in proper sequence, later on in the chapter:
Josiah (vv. 10–11), Jehoahaz or Shallum (vv. 11–12), Jehoiakim
(vv. 13–19), and Jehoiachin or Coniah (vv. 24–30).

Verses 13–19 may refer to a palace of Jehoiakim at Ramat
Rahel at the southernmost point of modern Jerusalem. It is the
first palace of a Judahite king to be systematically unearthed, and
it is one of the most impressive royal citadels ever found in the
Holy Land.

The woes Jeremiah declared upon his people are the results of a long history of disobedience and defiance. "Ye have
been rebellious against the Lord from the day that I knew you"
(Deuteronomy 9:24; compare Jeremiah 22:21). What a tragic epitaph for a favored people who were supposed to be the covenant
people of the Lord, his prized possession, his special treasure!

The prophecy against King Jehoiachin was soon fulfilled, as
recorded in Jeremiah 24:1, just two chapters later.

Jeremiah 23

There are good shepherds (pastors) and there are bad shepherds. The people of Judah were the sheep. Following the woes pronounced on the bad shepherds, the Lord promised a future restoration with good shepherds and a righteous Branch of the royal line of Judah as King. In the day that the Branch and King, "THE LORD OUR RIGHTEOUSNESS," reigns and prospers, true covenant Israel will dwell safely in their eternal inheritance. So phenomenal will be the last gathering and restoration that the deliverance from Egypt under Moses will be eclipsed as the lost tribes gather from the north country and elsewhere.

The Lord does indeed fill the heaven and earth (v. 24) but not in the sense of the false notion that God himself is so big that he can fill the universe (see D&C 88:7–13). His Person resides in one place at a time, but his influence—like any source of light—can radiate far and wide.

Jeremiah 24

The time of this message was about 598 B.C., some two years after Lehi, Ishmael, and their colony escaped from Jerusalem, and within the decade after King Jehoahaz was killed and Daniel and his friends were hauled off to Babylon. (Jehoahaz's brother Jehoaiakim, father of Jehoiachin, had also been dethroned and killed and young Jehoiachin enthroned—but only to be taken away to Babylon within a year.)

Good figs were those exiled to Babylon "for their good" (v. 5); bad figs represented those who temporarily remained in the land but with the prospect of being removed into all the kingdoms of the earth "for their hurt" (v. 9).

Jeremiah 25

Jeremiah's prophecies have not been arranged chronologically in our Bible; this revelation was received prior to the previous four. The first year of Nebuchadnezzar was 605 B.C. (note that his name is sometimes also spelled Nebuchadrezzar, a variant transliteration of his Babylonian name). Jeremiah began his ministry about 628 B.C., and he continued prophesying right to the day Nebuchadnezzar entered Jerusalem in 586 B.C.—over forty years. Maybe some people were beginning to wonder about Jeremiah's prophecies when five whole years passed, then ten, then twenty. They could have become a little complacent, especially with false prophets uttering conflicting prophecies and predicting opposite, more comfortable results.

Compare "Nebuchadrezzar . . . my servant" (v. 9; 27:6) with Isaiah 44:28 and 45:1, where the Lord calls Cyrus his "anointed" and "my shepherd." Judahites were to be subjected to a seventy-year exile (v. 11 and 29:10), with Nebuchadnezzar serving as the Lord's exiling agent. Cyrus would be the Lord's restoring agent— seventy years later.

As is a familiar practice among the prophets, not just one wicked nation was condemned. All surrounding nations had judgments pronounced upon them (compare Amos 9:1–10). Jeremiah's vision was then extended to the last days, with its overflowing wickedness and accompanying universal upheavals and catastrophes, both natural and man-made.

Jeremiah 26

This is the first of twenty historical chapters recounting the prophet's experiences and persecutions during his ministry. Jeremiah taught in the Temple in the year 609 B.C. When he prophesied against the place, the people wanted to kill him (v. 9)— just as they later wanted to kill Jesus in the Temple (John 8).

Some wise counsel comes forth from certain princes and the people (vv. 16–19): be careful what you do with this man. Remember, they warned, that Micah prophesied over one hundred years earlier; the people listened and were saved. One Urijah (v. 20) is another example of the "many prophets" (1 Nephi 1:4) also prophesying against Jerusalem in the days of Lehi and Jeremiah.

The Joseph Smith Translation indicates that when the *people* repent, the Lord turns away the evil, or the calamity, pronounced against them.

For more on chapter 26, see "Jeremiah and Jesus Christ" at Jeremiah 1:4–5.

Jeremiah 27

Neighboring nations were advised that the Lord was going to permit Babylon as his "servant" to overrun them for a time, and false prophets were not to be trusted. The best course for Judah and all other peoples was to submit to Babylon, otherwise the Temple, with all its sacred vessels and treasures, would be hauled away.

Jeremiah 28

Another case of the prophetic condemnation of individuals is given: Amos condemned Amaziah (Amos 7); Jeremiah condemned Pashur (Jeremiah 20); and now he condemns Hananiah. The final verse is a tersely worded, matter-of-fact report of the fulfillment of Jeremiah's prophecy.

A modern example of the same kind of pointed prophecy Jeremiah pronounced against Hananiah is recorded in the *History of the Church*.

"On his return home from Ramus, on the 18th of May, 1843, the Prophet took dinner with Judge Stephen A. Douglas, at Carthage [Illinois], and gave him, at his request, a detailed account of the persecutions the Saints had suffered. He concluded his narrative with a prophecy which B. H. Roberts considers 'one of the most remarkable prophecies either in ancient or modern times' (*Hist. of the Church*, Vol. V., p. 395). The Prophet concluded as follows:

"'Judge, you will aspire to the presidency of the United States; and if ever you turn your hand against me or the Latter-day Saints, you will feel the weight of the hand of the Almighty upon you; and you will live to see and know that I have testified the truth to you; for the conversation of this day will stick to you through life.'

"Judge Douglas did aspire to the presidency so effectively that, on the 23rd of June, 1860, he was nominated by the Democratic party. Judging from appearances, his election was sure, for his party, in the preceding election, polled over half a million votes more than the opposing parties. But the Judge failed miserably. On the 12th of June, 1857, he turned his hand against the Latter-day Saints, in spite of the warning of the Prophet, when, in a speech delivered at Springfield, Ill., he accused the Latter-day Saints, then living in Utah, of all the crimes known to the penal code, well knowing that he did so falsely, to gain favor among the enemies of the Church. The result was as the Prophet had told him would be the case, he was defeated. Abraham Lincoln carried

18 States; Breckinridge, 11; Bell, 3; and Judge Douglas, only *one!* Less than a year after his nomination he died, disappointed, heartbroken, only 48 years of age (*Hist. of the Church*, Vol. V., pp. 293–8). The prophecy was fulfilled to the letter" (Smith and Sjodahl, *Doctrine and Covenants*, 819).

Jeremiah 29

Some common-sense advice that Jeremiah gave by letter to those already exiled in Babylon: Prepare to stay in Babylon for seventy years and make the most of life there. It is what some might call the politics of acquiescence; "pray for the peace of Babylon!" The Lord intended to preserve and prepare his people (the prophets Daniel and Ezekiel were there, and Jeremiah would continue to communicate with them in their exile), and then in seventy years the Lord would return them to their homeland. Just as Felix Mendelssohn wrote in his *Elijah* oratorio, Jeremiah promised his people that if with all their hearts they would truly seek the Lord, they would surely find him (v. 13). The great prophets Joseph and Moses had said centuries before, with Israel exiled in another neighboring land, "God meant it unto good, to bring to pass, as it is this day, to save much people alive" (Genesis 50:20), and "that he might humble thee, and that he might prove thee, to do thee good at thy latter end" (Deuteronomy 8:16).

Shemaiah, discussed in verses 24–32, was a false prophet who incurred the Lord's displeasure because he preached rebellion against Jehovah.

Jeremiah 30

Jeremiah 30:1–33:26 has been called Jeremiah's "book of consolation" because it describes the restoration of both Israel and Judah. It is the longest sustained passage in the prophet's writings that discuss the restoration of the Lord's chosen people and their future hope. The book of Jeremiah records frequent prophetic forecasts of the return of Israel to their land in the last days. "For I am with thee, saith the Lord, to save thee: though I make a full end of all nations whither I have scattered thee, yet will I not make a full end of thee: but I will correct thee" (v. 11; see also Hebrews 12:5–7, 9–11; D&C 95:1–3). "In the latter days" they would fully understand this (v. 24).

Jeremiah 31:1–32:44

Chapter 31 continues the theme of Israel's future restoration, both in the meridian of time and in the latter days. "Watchmen" in 31:6 is Hebrew *notzrim*, the same term later used for "Christians" (see further in Ezekiel 3 and 33). In 31:9 notice that the Lord refers to himself as Israel's father, and Ephraim as his "firstborn." This is an important verse because it refers to the ordering of spirits, and families of spirit children, in our premortal existence, with the tribe of Ephraim being given the obligation of leadership for the family of Israel. (It cannot refer to mortality since Ephraim was not the firstborn temporally just as Jesus Christ was not the firstborn in mortality.) That the tribe of Ephraim remains the tribe of leadership for the family of Israel, as well as the guardians of the covenants and ordinances for the whole world until the Second Coming, is a doctrine that was reemphasized to the Prophet Joseph Smith (see Doctrine and Covenants 133:18–34, especially verses 25–34).

In connection with Herod's extermination order to kill all babies two years of age and under, Matthew cites the prophecy of Jeremiah 31:15 that there would be great lamentation and mourning in Rama(h), "Rachel weeping for her children . . . because they are not" (Matthew 2:18). Matthew, who referred continually to former-day prophecies which he saw fulfilled in the life and labors of Jesus, used this poetic picture of the Babylonian exile and applied it to a more current circumstance. Finding multiple fulfillment in prophecy is a proper application of scripture (compare also Joel 2:28–32 and Hosea 11:1). Nephi taught us how to get the most out of the scriptures, and how to understand the prophets, when he wrote "I did liken all scriptures unto us, that it might be for our profit and learning" (1 Nephi 19:23). There are many cases where New Testament authors appropriately found fulfillment of Old Testament passages in the words and works of Jesus. Matthew alone makes reference to nearly ninety passages from ten Old Testament books. Many things in the Old Testament are regarded as *types* of things to come.

"And there is hope in thine end, saith the Lord, that thy children shall come again to their own border" (31:17). Though Judah would be given over to the Chaldeans (Babylonians), God would "bring again the captivity"—return the captives to their homeland.

Jeremiah 31:31–34 is often considered the high point of Jeremiah's prophecies from a Christian perspective. This text has reference to the new covenant and higher law reestablished by Jesus Christ during his mortal ministry—at least that is how the earliest Christians saw it. This passage constitutes the longest sequence of Old Testament verses quoted in the New Testament (see Hebrews 8:8–12 and 10:16–17), and verse 31 is the only Old Testament use of the phrase "new covenant" that is found in the New Testament.

In truth, many components of what Jeremiah calls the new covenant were in operation from the time of Adam up to Israel's wilderness sojourn after their Egyptian bondage, things like the Melchizedek Priesthood and Temple ordinances. The Lord through Moses sought to reestablish this covenant, with its grounding in the higher priesthood, the powers of godliness, and key of the knowledge of God, among the Israelites during the Exodus. "But they hardened their hearts and could not endure his presence; therefore, the Lord in his wrath, for his anger was kindled against them, swore that they should not enter into his rest while in the wilderness, which rest is the fulness of his glory. Therefore, he took Moses out of their midst, and the Holy Priesthood also; and the lesser priesthood continued, which priesthood holdeth the key of the ministering of angels and the preparatory gospel" (D&C 84:24–26). This lesser priesthood, the Aaronic Priesthood, was the priesthood in operation at the advent of our Lord, Jesus Christ. He then restored the Melchizedek Priesthood and higher law as part of his earthly ministry (see JST John 1:26–28).

Like Jesus Christ, Joseph Smith would also act as an Elias of the Restoration. As in the meridian dispensation, so too in the latter-days—a new covenant would be established, with conditions and promises. There will come a day when God's covenant people will truly be of "one heart" (32:39) and live the "one way"— God's way.

Jeremiah 32:1–44 describes Jeremiah's imprisonment at the hands of King Zedekiah. The prophet was told by the Lord to purchase a field from his cousin in his hometown of Anathoth to symbolize and foreshadow Israel's restoration and return to their lands of inheritance. Jeremiah did this, though apparently with some reluctance since Babylonian forces were beginning the siege of Jerusalem. This act remains a powerful reminder to us that the Lord will gather his people, even in the midst of turmoil, and fulfill all his promises. As he said: "Behold, I will gather them out of all countries, whither I have driven them in mine anger, and in my fury, and in great wrath; and I will bring them again unto this place, and I will cause them to dwell safely: And they shall be my people, and I will be their God" (32:37–38).

Jeremiah 33

More on the promises of restoration. Jeremiah, as other prophets (including Joseph Smith in our day), received revelation from the Lord while in prison. The Lord showed him "great and mighty things" (v. 3; compare 1 Nephi 18:3).

Joy, gladness, and praise are voiced for the Lord of hosts (v. 11). The Branch (the Savior) will bring justice and righteousness into the land, and "in those days shall Judah be saved, and Jerusalem shall dwell safely" (vv. 15–16)—clearly presupposing the peace of the millennial era.

Jeremiah 34

Prophetic words, political actions, and important historical records are preserved in this chapter. Recall striking archaeological evidences about the Babylonian siege of the fortified cities of Jerusalem, Lachish, and Azekah noted in verse 7 that have come to light in modern times, as explained in commentary at 2 Kings 25:1–7.

Belligerent disregard, disrespect, and disobedience of God's holy covenant assured the inhabitants of Judah that the words of the prophets would all be fulfilled: their land would be desolated and they and their posterity would "be removed into all the kingdoms of the earth" (v. 17).

Jeremiah 35

The descendants of Moses' brother-in-law (here called the Rechabites) were people of integrity and proved more faithful than the Israelites; they are used here as an example to Judah.

(If interested in these unusual people, follow the biblical cross-references back, or look up the following sampling of passages: Numbers 10:29–32; Judges 1:16, 4:11; 1 Samuel 15:6; 2 Kings 10:15; 1 Chronicles 2:55.) The Druze people of Lebanon, Syria, and Israel have traditions connecting them back to those ancient people, the family of Jethro.

Jeremiah 36

This is the one example in all the Old Testament showing how inspired writings were preserved, and how if lost, they could be restored. Compare it with modern accounts in Latter-day Saint history of the reception and recording of revelations.

Recall the stunning corroborative archaeological evidence that has come to light regarding names of actual persons spoken of in this chapter—especially Baruch, son of Neriah, and Gemariah, son of Shaphan—as explained in the commentary at 2 Kings 25:1–7. Verse 18 is the only mention of writing with "ink" in the Old Testament.

Jeremiah 37–38

Jeremiah continued to preach that the Lord would not save Jerusalem and Judah from the Babylonians and that anyone who wanted to be spared must surrender. He was accused of treason—siding with the enemy; the subsequent political and religious establishments wanted him put to death. Skim these chapters for Jeremiah's additional sufferings because of his stance: being cast into a dungeon and sinking in its mire, and a rescue by a courageous and kind man, an Ethiopian servant of the king. According to tradition, Jeremiah's dungeon was a cistern (Hebrew, *bor*), with a narrow opening at the top (37:16; 38:6).

The Babylonians had a stranglehold on the city at the time; there was "no more bread in the city" (38:9; also 2 Kings 25:3). A secret meeting was arranged between the king and the prophet, and unfortunately, the faithless king rejected the counsel of the Lord (although he did provide for the prophet a safe sanctuary until the city fell).

Jeremiah 39–40 (compare 2 Kings 25)

These chapters preserve the account of the fall of Jerusalem and the special treatment of Jeremiah accorded by Nebuchadnezzar. The Babylonian king viewed Jeremiah as a friend because Jeremiah had recommended that the king of Judah not try to save himself and his country by military resistance to Babylon's control. Actually Jeremiah had simply been trying to teach Judah's king and people that only through righteousness and trust in God could they be saved.

Jeremiah 39:6 records Zedekiah's sons being killed. One son, Mulek, escaped, and helped lead a colony of Jews to the other side of the world, as attested in the Book of Mormon (Helaman 8:21).

It seems that the Babylonian conquerors understood better than the Jewish conquered exactly why all this had happened: "the captain of the guard took Jeremiah, and said unto him, The Lord thy God hath pronounced this evil upon this place. . . . The Lord hath brought it, and done according as he hath said: because ye have sinned against the Lord, and have not obeyed his voice, therefore this thing is come upon you" (40:2–3).

The powerful king of Babylon made Gedaliah the governor over the remnant of the people left in Jerusalem and Judah, "the poor of the land" (40:7). Jerusalem and its environs were left to deteriorate.

Jeremiah 41–44

The new administrative center of the Babylonians in the land of Judah was about seven miles north of Jerusalem, at Mizpah. The Babylonian-appointed governor, Gedaliah, seems to have been a good man, according to Jeremiah's account (Jeremiah 40). However, one Ishmael, a descendant of the house of David, conspired against Gedaliah, and to the regret of most of the remnant of Judah left in the land, Ishmael slew Gedaliah and others. He himself was attacked and barely escaped to the Ammonites, but the remnants of the Judahites were so afraid of repercussions from Babylon that they fled to Egypt. Jeremiah advised against it but to no avail. The history of those who went to Egypt is particularly worth reading (Jeremiah 43–44). Some people believe that Jeremiah and the king's daughters (mentioned in Jeremiah 43:6) eventually fled Egypt and went to present-day Britain and that the royal daughters intermarried with the ancient peoples of that land. However, nothing of that is found in the Bible.

Jeremiah 46–51

In these chapters Jeremiah prophesies against foreign nations ("gentiles"). In Jeremiah 46:19, 25 even the great Egyptian cities of Memphis (Noph) and Thebes (No) would become desolate. Jeremiah then prophesied against Philistia. Chapter 48 is a detailed geography lesson in the land of Moab, which was also condemned. Ammon, Edom, Damascus, Kedar, Elam, and Babylon were all doomed.

Though their own wickedness was certainly not condoned, the Lord used Assyria as an instrument to punish northern Israelites who had abandoned their God. Then the Assyrians' evil empire was forever destroyed by the Babylonians. The Babylonians in turn were also used by the Lord to punish the remaining Israelites in the south who had also abandoned their God. The Babylonians' evil empire was subsequently destroyed by the Medes and Persians. Jeremiah's prophecy concerning the ultimate fate of Babylon (chapter 50) is written with a flair. In 50:2 Babylon's "idols" are referred to in the Hebrew text in very derogatory terms, literally, "her pieces of dung are terrorized." The Lord describes his own people as "lost sheep" (50:6), a passage that may have provided the language for Jesus' parable in Luke 15:3–7. Jeremiah 50:17–19 contains a marvelous prophecy of the ultimate destiny of God's covenant people, similar to the refrain that Latter-day Saints sing: "O Babylon, O Babylon, we bid thee farewell; we're going to the mountains of Ephraim to dwell" (*Hymns*, no. 319).

Jeremiah 52 (2 Kings 24:18–25:30)

Some details are found here beyond the description in 2 Kings 25 concerning the final fall of Jerusalem, and the valuable things taken from the Temple. What a horrible scene this must have been: famine set in, the city was broken up, most (though not all) of Zedekiah's sons were slain, and Zedekiah's eyes were put out.

LAMENTATIONS

The Lamentations of Jeremiah contain the prophet's eye-witness feelings over the destruction of Jerusalem. Compare Jesus' later lament over the same city, Jerusalem (Luke 13:34–35; 19:41–44) and Mormon's lament over his fallen people (Mormon 6:16–20).

The Hebrew title of the book is *Eikha,* meaning "How?" It is the first word found in chapters 1, 2, and 4. The title of the book in the Greek Septuagint is *Threnoi,* and the title in the Latin Vulgate is *Threni,* both meaning "tears." The Septuagint prefaces Lamentations with the following lines: "And it came to pass after Israel had been taken away into captivity and Jerusalem had been laid waste that Jeremiah sat weeping and lamented this lamentation over Jerusalem and said . . ."

The entire book of Lamentations is poetry, which employs an unusual literary technique called an acrostic. We find acrostics in English, too; for example, the word *radar* is an acrostic, or acronym, formed from the words *r*adio *d*etecting *a*nd *r*anging.

In the original Hebrew, the chapters of Lamentations form perfect acrostics. For example, chapter 1 has twenty-two verses, each succeeding verse beginning with the next of the twenty-two letters of the Hebrew alphabet. Chapters 2 and 4 also have perfect acrostics: twenty-two verses, each succeeding verse beginning with the next of the twenty-two letters of the alphabet. Chapter 3 is a tripled acrostic: sixty-six verses, in which each succeeding group of three verses begins with the next of the twenty-two letters. There are some minor variations, with occasional verses being slightly longer than the rest, and some letters—especially the Hebrew *ain* and *pe*—being transposed. It is a clever literary form, though of course it is lost in translation, and it beautifully fits the emotions of lamentation being described (see Bible Dictionary, "Lamentations, Book of"). For a sample of the grief and pathos portrayed in Lamentations, read especially 1:1–2, 8; 2:11, 15; 3:48 (compare Mormon 6:16–20 and Moses 7:28, 37–38); 4:4–6; and 5:7 (compare Jeremiah 31:29–30).

The book of Lamentations is made up of five laments. Other Old Testament books contain laments (the Psalms for example), but this is the only book consisting wholly of laments. The focus of these laments is the destruction of Jerusalem in 586 B.C. Thus, religious Jews read *Eikha* on Tisha B'Av—the ninth day of the month of Av—which commemorates the two destructions of Jerusalem and the Temple, first by the Babylonians in 586 B.C. and again in A.D. 70 by the Romans. Some Jews also read Lamentations regularly during Tisha B'Av while sitting on the ground, also a requirement of the commemoration, at the Western or "Wailing" Wall in Jerusalem.

Jeremiah again makes clear that the Babylonian siege armies were human agents of divine judgment and punishment. It was God himself who caused the destruction of Jerusalem and the Temple because of wickedness (1:12–15; 2:1–8, 17, 22; 4:11).

Lamentations 1

"How doth the city sit solitary [deserted] that was once full of people?" (v. 1). With a single word the author captures the shock, wonder, and despair of horrible happenings. Jerusalem's desolation and the people's misery are emphasized. Wholesale devastation of princes, elders, and priests are reflected on. The pick and flower of Jerusalem's population had been dragged off into exile, and the once great and elaborate system of ritual, sacrifice, and worship was now gone.

Lamentations 2

The wholesale slaughter and devastation involved king, prophet, and commoner. Starving mothers descended to the incomprehensible practice of cannibalism (v. 20; also 4:10).

Lamentations 3

Though Jeremiah sorrowed over the calamity, he also proclaimed God's goodness and his trust in him. God is a being of love, faithfulness, and salvation, and there is hope.

Lamentations 4

The once lustrous commodities of Zion were now dulled and the comparable precious sons of Zion, once worth their weight in gold, were now like clay pots. Those killed by the sword were better off than those who died of famine. The Lord's wrath and fierce anger were responsible for the devastation. But on a positive note, the punishment heaped upon the daughters of Zion (Jerusalem and her people) would end.

Lamentations 5

This lament is a plea for the Lord to remember his people, to restore them and return them to himself, to renew them—unless he has utterly and forever rejected them (which he had not).

EZEKIEL

Ezekiel lived in turbulent times. As a youth he likely resided at Jerusalem during Jeremiah's tumultuous ministry. The Assyrian Empire, which had conquered and deported the northern kingdom of Israel in 721 B.C., began to crumble in 612 B.C. when its capital city of Nineveh was devastated by a combined force of Medes and Babylonians. In 609 B.C. King Josiah of the southern kingdom of Judah was killed at Megiddo, overlooking the Jezreel Valley, when Pharaoh Necho II of Egypt marched north to try to prop up Assyria and reassert Egypt's once powerful influence in the region. The kingdom of Judah began to weaken even more. Josiah's son, Jehoahaz, ruled only three months when Pharaoh Necho put another of Josiah's sons, Jehoiakim, on the throne of Judah. In 605 B.C. the rising empire of Babylon defeated the Egyptians at Carchemish and Nebuchadnezzar was installed as king of Babylon. Jehoiakim switched his allegiance to him. According to Daniel 1:1, that same year, the third of Jehoiakim's reign, Nebuchadnezzar came to Jerusalem, besieged it, and inaugurated the first deportation of Judahite citizens.

A short time later, Babylonian and Egyptian armies met again in battle and Jehoiakim took the opportunity to rebel against his overlord. Babylon and Egypt fought to a standoff, but Nebuchadnezzar responded to Jehoiakim's treachery by sending his army against Jerusalem and conquering it in 598 B.C. It is at this point that Nebuchadnezzar exiled ten thousand of Jerusalem's inhabitants to Babylon. These were the strength, the pillars, of Jerusalem society (2 Kings 24:14). Included among them was Ezekiel (as well as Jehoiakim's son, Jehoiachin). They joined those deportees who had been exiled in 605 B.C. Ezekiel was undoubtedly a very young man at this time.

In exile Ezekiel received his call to be a prophet (Ezekiel 1:1–3). Because he was from a priestly family, he ministered to his fellow exiles as a prophet-priest. He was married (Ezekiel 24:15–18), and lived a relatively free life along with his fellow exiles (akin to house-arrest). As a priest, once associated with the Temple but now cut off from it, his prophetic message had much to do with the Temple and its rituals (see, for example, Ezekiel 8–11; 40–48). Like Jeremiah, he sometimes acted out his message using symbolic images. Ezekiel's influence upon the exiles was significant, and greatly affected their thinking.

Ezekiel knew great personal sadness. While in exile, being informed by the Lord that Jerusalem was under attack again and would be completely devastated this time (Ezekiel 24:1–14), he was told that his wife would die. Just as the delight of Israel's eyes, the Temple, would be gone, so the delight of his eyes, his wife, would be taken. But he was told not to mourn publicly for his wife so that the people would know they should not mourn for Jerusalem (24:15–27).

After Jerusalem fell, Ezekiel's message became one of hope—the Lord's people would experience a restoration and enjoy a future redemption. Ezekiel's ministry lasted until at least 574 B.C. He was faithful in all things. The Prophet Joseph Smith said specifically that he was one of the ancients who had made his calling and election sure. The Prophet's statement is especially instructive since it applies to all of us:

"After a person has faith in Christ, repents of his sins, and is baptized for the remission of his sins and receives the Holy Ghost, (by the laying on of hands), which is the first Comforter, then let him continue to humble himself before God, hungering and thirsting after righteousness, and living by every word of God, and the Lord will soon say unto him, Son, thou shalt be exalted. When the Lord has thoroughly proved him, and finds that the man is determined to serve Him at all hazards, then the man will find his calling and his election made sure, then it will be his privilege to receive the other Comforter, which the Lord hath promised the Saints. . . . [W]hen any man obtains this last Comforter, he will have the personage of Jesus Christ to attend him, or appear unto him from time to time, and even He will manifest the Father unto him, and they will take up their abode with him, and the visions of the heavens will be opened unto him, and the Lord will teach him face to face, and he may have a perfect knowledge of the mysteries of the Kingdom of God; and this is the state and place the ancient Saints arrived at when they had such glorious visions—Isaiah, Ezekiel, John upon the Isle of Patmos, St. Paul in the three heavens" (*History of the Church*, 3:380–81).

Ezekiel 1:1–3

Ezekiel probably grew up in or near Jerusalem but was taken captive by the Babylonians in 598 B.C. His name means "God strengthens," similar to the meaning of Hezekiah, "Jehovah strengthens." There has been a question about Ezekiel's reference to the "thirtieth year." Traditional Jewish commentaries say it was the thirtieth year of the jubilee, but they do not say when the last jubilee year had occurred. Thirty years from 625 B.C., the beginning of the reign of Nabopolassar, father of Nebuchadnezzar, gives the date 595 B.C. That would be about the same as the fifth year of Jehoiachin's captivity and would be a reasonable date for the beginning of Ezekiel's ministry.

The river Chebar could have been the Euphrates by its Babylonian name—Naru Kabari. However, some think it was a canal which connected the Euphrates and the Tigris near their confluence.

We do not have record of any other Hebrew prophet called to the prophetic mission while living outside the land of Israel (Daniel also served in Babylon, but his book does not include a record of his call).

Ezekiel, like Jeremiah, was of priestly lineage, though there is no explicit mention of their functioning in Aaronic ordinances.

Ezekiel 1:4–28

Isaiah, Ezekiel, Daniel, Zechariah, and John the Beloved had some unique, apocalyptic visions of future things. President Wilford Woodruff described the purpose of such unusual revelations:

"The Lord does communicate some things of importance to the children of men by means of visions and dreams as well as by the records of divine truth. And what is it all for? It is to teach us

375

a principle. We may never see anything take place exactly as we see it in a dream or a vision, yet it is intended to teach us a principle" (*Discourses of Wilford Woodruff,* 286).

Ezekiel reverently and cautiously described "the likeness as the appearance of a man" who was "upon the likeness of the throne," with a brightness which was "the appearance of the likeness of the glory of the Lord" (vv. 26–28). It is extraordinarily difficult to describe heavenly things with earthly words. Compare his description of a heavenly being in Ezekiel 8:2; and compare all this with Isaiah's vision of the Lord in Isaiah 6.

Ezekiel 2:1–7

While chapter one describes Ezekiel's call to be a prophet, chapter two outlines his specific task, his mission to take the word of the Lord to Israel in exile. And to say to them: "Thus saith the Lord God" (v. 4). Notice the significant phrases of Ezekiel's mission call and commission: "the spirit entered into me when he spake unto me. . . . And he said unto me, Son of man, I send thee to the children of Israel. . . . And thou shalt speak my words unto them." The labels the Lord used to describe Israel to Ezekiel are stark: "a rebellious nation" (v. 3); "impudent children and stiffhearted" (v. 4); "a rebellious house" (v. 5); "scorpions" (v. 6); "most rebellious" (v. 7). But the Lord also reassured his prophet that he should not be afraid of them or their word, nor be dismayed at their appearance.

Read the important footnote 1*a*. In Hebrew, "son of man" is *ben-adam,* and the English equivalent would be "human" (also in Job 25:6; Daniel 8:17; Moses 1:12). The Lord consistently used it as a title for Ezekiel, as if to emphasize that he was the recipient of the Lord's messages directed to man on earth. Jesus was also called "Son of Man" (Matthew 20:28; John 3:13) but in quite a different context. The more complete title for the second member of the Godhead is "Son of Man of Holiness" (Moses 6:57).

Ezekiel 2:8–3:3

The "eating" of the "roll" (scroll) apparently symbolized the prophet's ingesting or internalizing the Lord's message which he was thereafter to transmit to the people. The revelation experience was "sweet" to him. John the Beloved would later have a similar experience (Revelation 10:9–10; D&C 77:14). In ancient Israelite religion, eating or tasting the word of God was a well-known metaphor: "How sweet are thy words unto my taste" (Psalm 119:103). And the Book of Mormon encourages us to "feast upon the words of Christ" (2 Nephi 32:3).

Ezekiel 3:4–27

While Ezekiel was living in exile at Tel Abib (the same name as modern Tel Aviv in Israel, meaning "Spring Hill"), he received a specific charge and responsibility to be a "watchman." The warning came from God. The watchman has a sacred responsibility to watch out for God's children, his family, by passing the warning along to them, even pleading for their attention and awareness to the point of answering for their sins if they are not properly warned. To be free of the blood and sins of one's own generation a watchman must warn (D&C 88:81). Those of us who are being warned may have complete confidence that the word of the duly authorized watchman is the word of the Lord (D&C 1:14, 38).

Chapter 33 further defines the service of a prophet as a watchman. Leaders and parents in the Church today have a similar responsibility: to sound the alarm and warn Church members and children of evil ways, and correct them while young. If leaders and parents sound no warnings, and the members and children die in their wickedness, those leaders and parents are responsible. As President Spencer W. Kimball once indicated, we must continue to warn those for whom we have stewardship, for we are the watchmen (see *Ensign*, Nov. 1975, 7).

"A voice of a great rushing" (v. 12) is reminiscent of several other scripture passages: Isaiah 17:12; Acts 2:2; and Doctrine and Covenants 109:37; 110:3.

Verses 22–27 describe an additional charge Ezekiel received in his third vision of "the glory of the Lord."

Ezekiel 4

Ezekiel used a number of symbolic methods to teach the people (some of them rather unusual). As a contemporary of Jeremiah and Lehi, but living in Babylonia, Ezekiel depicted for the exiles there the fact that the rest of the inhabitants of Jerusalem were also being taken into captivity.

Ezekiel 5:1–9:11

Verses 5:1–5 present another of Ezekiel's symbolic acts, and 5:12 helps explain what the gestures of shaving his head and beard and dividing the hair into three piles represented (tragically, we note that a similar thing happened in the latter days as in ancient times when one-third of the worldwide Jewish population was exterminated in World War II).

Ezekiel's visions of the Holy City, the center of nations, in chapters 5 through 9 describe more of the evils and sins of the Jerusalemites and contain predictions of their downfall. Ezekiel 5:10 sets a gruesome tone overshadowing all that resulted from the siege of Jerusalem—cannibalism. Such horrors can hardly be comprehended by modern minds in the midst of ease and prosperity.

Ezekiel 10

This chapter records the prophet's vision of the departure of the Spirit of the Lord (or the glory of the Lord) from the Jerusalem Temple. The cloud, the power, and the brightness of the Lord's glory, had filled the Temple in times past (compare Exodus 24:15–18; 1 Kings 8:10–11; D&C 84:5), but now at the Temple's destruction the Spirit would depart. We will see in chapter 40 that the Spirit of the Lord would return to fill a new Temple in the distant future. Another colony of Israelites in a faraway land also learned by means of a vision about the destruction of the Holy City (2 Nephi 1:1–4).

Ezekiel 11

Ezekiel saw twenty-five leaders in Jerusalem who were falsely advising the people to carry on with business as usual, despite the fact that their shortsighted counsel would result in even more deaths when the city was besieged.

Once again, however, we see the prophetic pattern: even in the middle of harsh punishments and dispersion, there is still some comforting hope held out to the people of Israel. God himself would continue to be for them "as a little sanctuary in the countries where they shall come." And not only that but "thus saith the Lord God; I will even gather you from the people, and assemble you out of the countries where ye have been scattered, and

I will give you the land of Israel." And even that is not the final blessing; God crowned his merciful promises with "and I will put a new spirit within you" (vv. 16–19). The scattering and gathering of Israel remains a profound and yet-to-be totally fulfilled doctrine in the latter days.

Ezekiel 12

Apparently Ezekiel, ministering from Babylon, dramatized the removal of the people from Jerusalem to put over the point: "I am your sign" (v. 11). Note what the people had been saying about the fulfillment of prophecies—that they "tarried" and failed to come to pass. After all, more than a decade had passed since tens of thousands had been carried away to Babylon, and there was no report of the city or Temple being destroyed yet. Is there not a message also to people in our own day who think prophetic warnings need not be heeded or feared anymore because time goes on and the prophecies never seem to be fulfilled?

Ezekiel 13:1–14:23

Ezekiel complained about false prophets, idolaters, and weak leaders (for example, in 13:3, those who "follow their own spirit, and have seen nothing!"). Because they seduced the Lord's people, violent judgments, symbolized by natural phenomena (v. 11), would sweep them away.

Ezekiel was convinced of the impossibility of saving the people of Israel of his time. Recall Jeremiah's similar experiences and expressions (Jeremiah 14:13–14; 15:1). Even "Moses and Samuel" (Jeremiah 15:1) and "Noah, Daniel, and Job" (Ezekiel 14:14, 16), with all their own personal faithfulness, would not be able to save the people of Israel of that time. The Joseph Smith Translation records an important correction in 14:9: "if the prophet be deceived when he hath spoken a thing, I the Lord have *not* deceived that prophet, and I will stretch out my hand upon him, and will destroy him."

Ezekiel 15

Israel had been expected to be a fruitful vine but because it produced no fruit it must be cut down and serve no other purpose but to provide fuel for the fire (compare Jesus' similar teaching in John 15:5–6, 16).

Ezekiel 16

Consider what Ezekiel meant by saying "Thy birth and thy nativity is of the land of Canaan; thy father was an Amorite [Genesis 15:16], and thy mother an Hittite [Judges 1:26]." Jerusalem possessed an extended pre-Israelite history in the land of Canaan. The Amorites were pre-Israelite, and the Hittites were non-Semitic residents of the region round about Jerusalem, from whom Abraham purchased the burial ground at Hebron for his posterity, the fathers and mothers of the Israelites.

A prophet once again calls up the beautiful image of God's marriage with Israel, his Bride (recall Jeremiah 3:8, 14 and Hosea 2). Later in the chapter (vv. 60–63) a promise is given of future resumption of the everlasting covenant with the righteous of the people.

THE LORD'S RELATIONSHIP WITH HIS HOLY CITY

Following is an outline of Ezekiel 16 depicting the sacred relationship of the Lord to his Holy City. The instructive allegory depicts the Lord as the Husband and Jerusalem as his wife (a city always carries the feminine form).

Early History

1. Unwanted child of parents, Amorites and Hittites: uncleansed, unclothed as an infant (3–4). As an aside (but a valuable one), verse 4 seems to reflect the ancient practice of how newborn infants were cared for: cutting the umbilical cord, washing with water, and rubbing with salt. This has interesting implications for our study of the birth narratives of notable figures in the Bible, including Jesus.
2. Canaanite parents attempted infanticide, leaving her to die by exposure (5).
3. The Lord, the compassionate passerby, took the infant in his arms and cradled her (6).
4. She grew to become a lovely young woman (7).

Time of David and Solomon

1. She married the Lord and had all luxurious gifts lavished on her (8–14).
2. Other lovers started to take notice of her for her renown and beauty (14–15).
3. Jerusalem became a haven for religious diversity and perversity, especially under Solomon; she allowed her eyes to wander, not wanting to be "tied down" to one husband (16–25).

Time of the Empires

1. She paraded around the ancient world as a harlot; other lovers were invited in to know her (26–29).
2. She made new covenants with others, shamelessly abandoning the Lord, trusting in her beauty and relying on things given, rather than on the Giver (30–32).
3. Instead of being paid for service of prostitution, she paid. She paid out vast sums to those who would conquer her (33–34).
4. The Lord is a jealous God, and in the end, would not be mocked and humiliated. He delivered Jerusalem into the hands of her former lovers, now her enemies. The nations she had loved ended up stripping her of all her beautiful ornaments. They eventually destroyed her, causing unspeakable pain and sorrow (35–43).
5. Jerusalem's sins are detailed, showing her worse than the Canaanite peoples that she originally displaced, even worse than Sodom, and worse than Samaria and the whole northern kingdom (44–59).
6. The Lord is forgiving and invited her back to resume her role as faithful wife (60–63).

Ezekiel 17

There are indications of more than one group of exiles and more than one transplantation of the royal line of Judah in this chapter. Cross-references given in note *a* to verse 22 suggest that the Mulekites, the Book of Mormon people of Zarahemla, fulfilled this prophecy.

Compare verses 8–10 with Psalm 80:8–15.

Ezekiel 18

Verses 1–4: This revelation corrected the misunderstanding of a phrase from the Ten Commandments (the Decalogue) about "visiting the iniquity of the fathers upon the children unto the third and fourth generation" (Exodus 20:5). Alcoholism, drug abuse, infidelity, rebellion, and many other sins of the fathers certainly can influence generations of descendants, but the basic doctrine is "the soul that sinneth, it shall die." It is an issue of individual responsibility. God will not impose punishment upon children because of any sins their fathers commit but only for the children's own sins. As Joseph Smith wrote, "We believe that men will be punished for their own sins, and not for Adam's transgression [or their fathers' transgressions, or anyone else's]" (Articles of Faith 1:2).

Verses 5–9: Regardless of what his parents do, if a man does right himself, he will be rewarded with the blessings of eternity.

Verses 10–13: If the son of a righteous man does wrong, the son will not escape punishment because of his righteous father. His sins bring upon himself the consequent punishment. Righteousness is not predicated upon lineage.

Verses 14–18: If the son of a wicked man does right, that son will not be punished because of his wicked father but will be rewarded for his own good deeds.

Verses 19–20: Thus the question "doth not the son bear the iniquity of the father" is plainly answered in the negative. No matter how bad a father is, the son, if he truly desires, can live a righteous life (compare the case of Terah and Abraham: Terah was an idolator and actually tried to take the life of his son, but Abraham diligently sought the blessings of the Patriarchs—of the priesthood and the gospel—and lived a valiant life and is now exalted; see Abraham 1:1–19).

Verses 21–24: If a man lives wickedly for part of his life but later fully repents and lives his covenants, he can receive his full reward. On the other hand, if a man lives righteously but later turns against the ways of God and grievously sins, "all his righteousness that he hath done shall not be mentioned." He will die in his sins and have to suffer for them all until they are paid for.

Verses 25–31: Clearly what a person does is important, but in the end what a person has become is even more important. Or, as a wise soul observed, what lies behind us and what lies before us are tiny matters compared to what lies within us (author unknown). It is well for us to be found at the conclusion of our lives with "a new heart and a new spirit."

Verse 32 answers the question posed in verse 23. God, our Heavenly Father, desires to save all his children and does all he can, within the boundaries of agency, to influence everyone to turn to him and live.

Ezekiel 19:1–23:49

In chapter 19 the prophet uttered a lament and began reviewing the history of the Lord's covenant people and inventoried and illustrated their violent crimes against God and man. The catalog of sins includes bloodshed, idolatry, adultery and incest, violent government, dishonoring parents, oppressing foreigners, desecrating holy things and the Sabbath, lewdness, violation of privacy, bribery, usury (see Bible Dictionary, "Usury"), and extortion.

Chapter 20 records a date on which the elders of Israel in exile came to Ezekiel to question the Lord. Of all the revelations he had given, the fact that Ezekiel recorded the date of this one indicates how much of an impression the experience made upon him. The Lord said he would not be questioned by them! Ezekiel went on to recount Israel's continual rebellion—from the day of their deliverance from Egyptian bondage to Ezekiel's time. However, the prophet also spoke of times of restoration, culminating in the latter days. But his audience still did not comprehend it and accused Ezekiel of speaking "parables" (20:49).

Ezekiel continued by detailing in graphic imagery the destruction that would befall both the righteous and the wicked in Jerusalem (chapter 21). He enumerated the sins found in Jerusalem and the result they would bring.

Rebellious Israel must know that for all this willful sinning they had been taken captive and would continue to suffer. The throne of Israel would be overturned and vacated "until he come whose right it is; and I will give it him" (21:27; see commentary at Genesis 49:8–12). Ezekiel again holds out future hope by promising that in the last days Israel and the covenant would be restored, and the Messiah would reign.

The parable of the two sinful Israelite "sisters," Israel and Judah, daughters of the same mother (united Israel), in chapter 23 is like that in Jeremiah 3:6–14 (and compare Ezekiel 16). First Israel had declined and fallen, then, astonishingly, Judah had followed in her deviant behavior and suffered the same fate. Both sisters (kingdoms) had eagerly adopted the idolatrous practices, the ritual immorality, personal debauchery, pompous modes of dress, and other such detractors from covenant living found among the nations round about—especially from their eventual conquerors, who had morally conquered Israelites even before the military conquests and deportations. Judah's greater sin lay in her failure to learn from Israel's experience and her failure to use the Temple properly and protect it from abuse. The most heinous transgressions involved idolatrous, ritual adultery resulting in illegitimate children, who were then sacrificed to idols.

Ezekiel 24

Ezekiel must have terrified his fellow Jews by portraying the destruction of Jerusalem and its people as a pot boiling and burning up its meat and bones and the pot itself disintegrating. Plus, he was to teach his people not to lament their temporary state of exile by his example of not mourning the sudden death of his beloved wife. The Lord's instructions are poignant: "Son of man, behold, I take away from thee the desire of thine eyes with a stroke: yet neither shalt thou mourn nor weep, neither shall thy tears run down" (v. 16). His similitude was to teach the people suffering in their irretrievable losses that they should not pine away in the past but go forward with faith in the future.

Ezekiel 25–32

In these eight chapters prophetic pronouncements are placed on neighboring nations. The God and Father of all had something to say about the behavior of his children in these other lands, too (compare commentary at Isaiah 13; Amos 9:1–10; Jeremiah 25:1–38; Jeremiah 46–51; and smaller books such as Nahum and Obadiah that address one specific country). (If interested in economic matters, you may read through chapter 27, which is our most detailed description of the ancient world's economy—the various nations and their merchandising.)

Ezekiel 33:1–11

Here are further details about the duty of *watchmen* (compare Ezekiel 3:12–21). The role of watchmen has been described in this last dispensation in Doctrine and Covenants 88:81—it is the duty of all true Saints to warn their neighbors; that is, teach them, care for them, guard them, watch over them. The meaning of verse 8 is sharpened by the counsel of President John Taylor: "If you do not magnify your callings, God will hold you responsible for those whom you might have saved had you done your duty" (*Journal of Discourses*, 20:23).

This section contains a significant call to repent. The late Elder Theodore M. Burton of the Seventy used some of these verses to explain the nature of repentance:

"Just what *is* repentance? Actually it is easier for me to tell you what repentance is *not* than to tell you what repentance *is*.

"My present assignment as a General Authority is to assist the First Presidency. I prepare information for them to use in considering applications to readmit transgressors into the Church and to restore priesthood and/or temple blessings. Many times a bishop will write: 'I feel he has suffered enough!' But suffering is not repentance. Suffering comes from *lack* of complete repentance. A stake president will write: 'I feel he has been punished enough!' But punishment is not repentance. Punishment *follows* disobedience and *precedes* repentance. A husband will write: 'My wife has confessed everything!' But confession is not repentance. Confession is an admission of guilt that occurs *as* repentance begins. A wife will write: 'My husband is filled with remorse!' But remorse is not repentance. Remorse and sorrow continue because a person has *not* yet fully repented. But if suffering, punishment, confession, remorse, and sorrow are not repentance, what *is* repentance?"

Elder Burton explained that repentance is a doctrine discussed with clarity in the Old Testament. *Repentance* is the English word used to translate the Hebrew word *shuv* (pronounced with a "u," as our English words "prove" and "reprove"), which means "to turn, return, or turn back." Elder Burton then quoted Ezekiel:

"'When I say unto the wicked, O wicked man, thou shalt surely die; if thou dost not speak to warn the wicked from his way, that wicked man shall die in his iniquity; but his blood will I require at thine hand.

"'Nevertheless, if thou warn the wicked of his way to [*shuv;* or] turn from it; if he do not [*shuv;* or] turn from his way, he shall die in his iniquity; but thou hast delivered thy soul.

"'Say unto them, As I live, saith the Lord God, I have no pleasure in the death of the wicked; but that the wicked [*shuv;* or] turn from his way and live: [*shuv, shuv!*] turn ye, turn ye from your evil ways; for why will ye die, O house of Israel?' (Ezekiel 33:8–9, 11)

"I know of no kinder, sweeter passage in the Old Testament than those beautiful lines. Can you hear a kind, wise, gentle, loving Father in Heaven pleading with you to [*shuv*] or turn back to him, to leave unhappiness, sorrow, regret, and despair behind and now turn back to your Father's family where you can find happiness, joy, and acceptance among his other children? In the Father's family, you are surrounded with love and affection. That is the message of the Old Testament, and prophet after prophet writes of [*shuv*], which is that turning back to the family of the Lord where you can be received with joy and rejoicing. . . .

"People must somehow be made to realize that the true meaning of repentance is that we do not require people to be punished or to punish themselves, but to change their lives so they can escape eternal punishment. If they have this understanding, it will relieve their anxiety and fears and become a welcome and treasured word in our religious vocabulary" ("Meaning of Repentance," 96–97; see also Ogden, *Before You Get to Heaven,* 52–83).

Ezekiel 33:12–16

Here is further elaboration of the crime and punishment theme of chapters 3 and 18. This question of responsibility for sin must have been a burning issue among the exiles. In the end, it is more important what we *are* than what we *have been.*

Ezekiel 33:17–33

Ezekiel and many fellow exiles were taken out of Jerusalem in 598 B.C., so "the twelfth year of our captivity" was 586 B.C. This is a more detailed account of the news of Jerusalem's fall and of the prophet's reaction to it. The Lord clarifies the reasons for Judah's fall. Note especially that with their mouth the people showed "much love, but their heart goeth after their covetousness" (v. 31). Just as Isaiah had declared, "this people draw near me with their mouth, and with their lips do honour me, but have removed their heart far from me" (Isaiah 29:13). God always warns his children to keep their hearts away from worldly pleasures and lustful desires; the only way to stay the course to eternal life is to place one's heart on God and his ways. "I, the Lord, require the hearts of the children of men" (D&C 64:22).

When Ezekiel announced the final desolation of Judah's homeland, the Lord reassured his prophet in exile: "And when this cometh to pass, (lo, it will come,) then shall they know that a prophet hath been among them" (v. 33).

Ezekiel 34

The shepherds of the people were of course their leaders. The Lord has strong words for them: "Woe be to the shepherds of Israel that do feed themselves! should not the shepherds feed the flocks?" (v. 2). The sheep "were scattered, because there is no shepherd"; they just became food "to all the beasts of the field" (v. 5). But God himself, the Good Shepherd, proclaims, "I [will] seek out my sheep, and will deliver them out of all places where they have been scattered in the cloudy and dark day. And I will bring them out from the people, and gather them from the countries, and will bring them to their own land" (v. 12)—so it is happening in these last days. Our Shepherd and his servants are in the process of gathering all obedient sheep, and establishing them to their promised lands. "And I will set up one shepherd over them, and he shall feed them . . . And I the Lord will be their God" (vv. 23–24).

Ezekiel 35

This prophecy of doom is directed to Edom (Mount Seir, or Idumea) and really belongs to the series of indictments against the neighboring nations (Ezekiel 25–32).

Ezekiel 36

This revelation is a sequel to chapters 33–34, proclaiming again the latter-day gathering of Israel, previewing latter-day Israel making the name of the Lord known to "the heathen," to the "flocks of men." "The enemy" had long enough taken the land for themselves, causing Israel to bear untold derision and shame, and the Lord now promises that the days of opposition and derision will pass. The waste places of Israel will again be fruitful and flourish.

Ezekiel's own people were reminded that they were in exile because they defiled the promised land and profaned the God of the land, who is the Lord. Nevertheless, because of the covenant promises, He will cleanse later generations and, with a "new heart" and a "new spirit," bring them back into the covenant relationship. A new "garden of Eden," a paradisiacal glory, will be established.

Ezekiel 37:1–14

This is one of the most well-known chapters to Latter-day Saints in all of the Old Testament. It begins by discussing the resurrection. Given Ezekiel's closeness to the Lord and his knowledge of the mysteries of the kingdom, it seems only natural that he would mention this doctrine at some point. Resurrection is of course the foundation of the Christian faith, performed by the very God that Ezekiel communed with—Jehovah, who came to earth as Jesus of Nazareth. The prophet's vision of the resurrection is set in the broader context of Israel inheriting their land in the resurrection, which is part of the restoration of all things.

In 1918, at the end of World War I, President Joseph F. Smith was shown a unique vision of a great gathering of the spirits of the just in the spirit world—those who had "offered sacrifice in the similitude of the great sacrifice of the Son of God, and had suffered tribulation in their Redeemer's name" (D&C 138: 13). Among the noble and great ones that he saw was "Ezekiel, who was shown in vision the great valley of dry bones, which were to be clothed upon with flesh, to come forth again in the resurrection of the dead, living souls" (D&C 138:43). Though they are few, the Old Testament does have passages referring specifically to the doctrine of the resurrection (see also Job 19:25–27; Isaiah 25:8; 26:19; Daniel 12:2). In this case, Ezekiel saw the covenant people of Israel coming forth out of their graves to have their spirits clothed once again with physical elements and live on in a

A depiction of a writing board or tablet. "Take thee one stick, and write upon it" (Ezekiel 37:16)

more glorious state. One purpose for which they will be raised up is to fulfill one part of God's covenant with his faithful followers: to receive their land of inheritance.

Ezekiel 37:15–28

Few passages in the Old Testament are so clearly fulfilled in the latter days. The Hebrew word *'etz* is translated in the King James Version of the Bible as "stick." The word literally means "tree, timber, piece of wood, or stick," and may refer to a writing tablet. Babylonian writing tablets of wood have been found hinged together and faced with wax, with writing engraved on them (for examples and illustrations, see Meservy, *Ensign*, Feb. 1987, 4–13). Another possibility is that the word refers to sticks of the kind that ancient scrolls were rolled around.

A modern prophetic phrase in Doctrine and Covenants 27:5 refers to the record of the tribe of Ephraim as the "stick" of Ephraim (see Bible Dictionary, "Judah, Stick of," and "Ephraim, Stick of").

In speaking of the footnotes and other study aids in the LDS edition of the Bible and the 1981 edition of the other standard works of the Church, President Boyd K. Packer explained:

"The stick or record of Judah—the Old Testament and the New Testament—and the stick or record of Ephraim—the Book of Mormon, which is another testament of Jesus Christ—are now woven together in such a way that as you pore over one you are drawn to the other; as you learn from one you are enlightened by the other. They are indeed one in our hands. Ezekiel's prophecy now stands fulfilled" (*Ensign*, Nov. 1982, 53).

For what purposes have these different records come together? To testify of the Lord's covenants in the latter days. Similar to what Ezekiel wrote, Lehi taught his son, Joseph, that the "fruit of thy loins shall write; and the fruit of the loins of Judah shall write; and that which shall be written by the fruit of thy loins, and also that which shall be written by the fruit of the loins of Judah, shall grow together, unto the confounding of false doctrines and laying down of contentions, and establishing peace among the fruit of thy loins, and bringing them to the knowledge of their fathers in the latter days, and also to the knowledge of my covenants, saith the Lord" (2 Nephi 3:12).

Nephi, son of Lehi, adds to our understanding of the purposes for which these records come together from both sides of the world:

"Know ye not that the testimony of two nations is a witness unto you that I am God, that I remember one nation like unto another? Wherefore, I speak the same words unto one nation like unto another. And when the two nations shall run together the testimony of the two nations shall run together also. And I do this that I may prove unto many that I am the same yesterday, today, and forever. . . . For I command all men, both in the east and in the west . . . that they shall write the words which I speak unto them; for out of the books which shall be written I will judge the world" (2 Nephi 29:8–9, 11).

Ezekiel envisioned more than simply bringing together the inscribed "sticks" or writings of Judah and Joseph. Bones come together, scriptures come together, and people come together (Ezekiel 37:21–22). Ezekiel seems to have envisioned what Paul later wrote of: "That in the dispensation of the fulness of times he might gather together in one all things in Christ, both which are in heaven, and which are on earth" (Ephesians 1:10).

Ezekiel 38–39

These are samplings of information about the battle of "Gog, [from] the land of Magog" against the gathered people of Israel in the last days. For the genealogical identity of Magog, Tubal, Meshech, Gomer, Togarmah, etc., see commentary at Genesis 10:1–5. For the geographical location of some of these Japhethitic peoples, see the map at that passage. What Ezekiel here calls the "battle of Gog and Magog" is called by other writers and other scriptures the "battle of Armageddon." This great battle to end this phase of earth's existence will occur just before the millennial reign of Jesus Christ begins. Confusion sometimes results from the fact that another battle of "Gog and Magog" will happen *after* the Millennium, as mentioned in Revelation 20:7–10. We learn more about the premillennial battle of Armageddon from Joel 3; Zechariah 12–14; and Doctrine and Covenants 45.

We can summarize the confusion in naming the future battles in the following way. The various designations of conflicts is clear if the student of the scriptures remembers two things:

1. The battle of Armageddon is *before* the millennial reign of Christ begins, and the battle of Gog and Magog is *after* the millennial reign; and

2. What Ezekiel here describes is actually the pre-millennial battle of Armageddon, though he (and he only) labels it the battle of Gog and Magog. Keeping that one difference in mind resolves any confusion about which is which.

In Ezekiel's vision, "Gog," the chief prince of Meshech and Tubal, leads a massive coalition of world powers, a combination of nations. He invades Israel and seeks to destroy the people of God. This last battle before millennial conditions prevail will take place after the Lord has gathered "the children of Israel from among the heathen" and brought them "into their own land" (Ezekiel 37:21). It will occur "in the latter years" (Ezekiel 38:8), meaning the latter days.

The hordes will invade a land whose inhabitants have gathered or been "brought forth out of the nations," and who, at that time, "dwell safely" in a "land of unwalled villages" (Ezekiel 38:8,

11), unlike ancient times, when all towns and villages in the Holy Land were built within great walls for protection. Gog and all his troops and the many nations that are with him will "be like a cloud to cover the land" (Ezekiel 38:9).

In other words, the enemy will be, "a great company, and a mighty army" (38:15), coming toward the land of Israel from the north. John the Revelator adds that those opposing forces are two hundred thousand thousand strong (Revelation 9:16); that is to say, "two hundred million men of war mass their armaments at Armageddon" (McConkie, *Ensign*, May 1979, 93).

When Gog invades, the fury of the Lord will rise up against the invaders (38:18). The Lord will defend his people, using his own mighty weapons of nature. The great earthquake (the "great shaking") mentioned in Ezekiel 38:19–20 is further described in Joel 3:2, 14–16; Zechariah 14:4–5; Revelation 6:12–14; 11:13; 16:18–20; and Doctrine and Covenants 45:48. In addition, "the mountains shall be thrown down" (Ezekiel 38:20). The Lord will execute judgment against the invaders "with pestilence and with blood" and with "an overflowing rain, and great hailstones, fire, and brimstone" (Ezekiel 38:22). Said he, "Thus will I magnify myself, and sanctify myself; and I will be known in the eyes of many nations, and they shall know that I am the Lord" (Ezekiel 38:23).

The forces of Gog will be destroyed upon the mountains of Israel and then be given to "the ravenous birds of every sort, and to the beasts of the field to be devoured" (Ezekiel 39:4; see also D&C 29:18–21). Burning the vast armaments of the conflict will provide the cities of Israel seven years' worth of fuel (Ezekiel 39:9) and to bury the bodies of the opposing army will take seven months (39:12), after the scavenging birds and animals have done their work. All people will understand that rebelling against the God of Heaven, and disobeying him, brings on the justice of suffering and punishment. Nevertheless, after the events of horror and destruction have run their course, as described by Ezekiel, glorious days of peace and plenty will abound. The Lord will reign on the earth, and all will know that he is in control of all things. "And I will set my glory among the heathen, and all the heathen shall see my judgment that I have executed, and my hand that I have laid upon them. So the house of Israel shall know that I am the Lord their God from that day and forward" (Ezekiel 39:21–22). This is the prophesied time when the Jewish people will be rescued and know that Jesus of Nazareth was and is their Messiah (see D&C 45:48–53).

Ezekiel 40:1–47:12

Certainly more pleasant than previewing the great worldwide wars to end all wars was Ezekiel's privilege to envision the latter-day Temple to be built in Jerusalem and associated events at the time of the Lord's Second Coming. Chapters 40–48 describe the Lord's Temple in the last days and the millennial reign of Christ, as well as the land distribution to the tribes of Israel.

The Prophet Joseph Smith asked the question, What was the object of gathering the Jews, or the people of God in any age of the world? And he gave us the answer: "The main object was to build unto the Lord a house whereby He could reveal unto His people the ordinances of His house and the glories of His kingdom, and teach the people the way of salvation; for there are certain ordinances and principles that, when they are taught and practiced, must be done in a place or house built for that purpose" (*Joseph Smith* [manual], 416).

If you are interested in architectural blueprints, interior decor, or Temple clothing, you may want to examine chapters 40–44 in detail.

Following are a few notes on selected passages.

Ezekiel 40:2–49

Verse 2: Ezekiel was taken in vision to the future land of Israel, to a "high mountain" like other prophets. Compare other visionary and revelatory experiences on top of high mountains: Matthew 17:1; Revelation 21:10; 1 Nephi 11:1; Ether 3:1; Moses 1:1.

Verse 5: Footnote 5c describes the cubit measurement.

Verse 10: This six-chambered gate is similar to gates discovered at the cities of Hazor, Megiddo, and Gezer by archaeologists and date to the time of Solomon (1 Kings 9:15; see photo in commentary at 1 Kings 9:10–28). Anciently the chambers housed guards to protect the city. In the Temple they might be symbolic, or they might house guardians to secure the sanctity of the Temple, keeping profane things out (Ezra 2:62).

Verse 16: Palm trees were found in Solomon's Temple, recreating the environment of the Garden of Eden (1 Kings 6:29–35).

Verse 38: Burnt offerings will be restored, as Oliver Cowdery said, in order "that the sons of Levi may yet offer an offering" (Joseph Smith–History 1:71n; see commentary at Malachi 3:1–4).

Verse 46: Zadok was the first high priest who remained faithful to King David to officiate in Solomon's Temple (1 Kings 2:2–27, 35).

Ezekiel 43:1–5

The Lord will come to his Temple, and his glory will once again fill his House. Some cross-references to this great prophecy are Exodus 40:34–35; 1 Kings 8:10–11; Malachi 3:1 // 3 Nephi 24:1; Revelation 18:1; Doctrine and Covenants 88:7–13; 109:12; 110:3. Verses 2–5 are the apex of chapters 40 through 48.

Ezekiel was caught up by the Spirit like others, including the Savior (JST Matthew 4:5).

Ezekiel 43:6–11

According to his own testimony, the Lord walks in his Temple— "the place of the soles of my feet" (v. 7). Because the Lord is a God of order, all things regarding his Temple are properly ordered and detailed according to his purposes, including all ordinances.

Ezekiel 43:12–27

The holiness of the Temple is set forth; even the grounds surrounding the Temple, "the whole limit," are holy (v. 12). The distinction between the holiness of God's Temple and the rest of the world is an important theme in Ezekiel's book (see 44:2, 9, 23). As verse 18 implies, one purpose of latter-day and millennial Temples is to provide a place to restore all things, even animal sacrifices (see commentary at Ezekiel 40:38).

Ezekiel 44

Verses 1–3: The east gate of this future Temple was to be shut because only the Lord was to enter through it.

Verses 4–9: Aliens or foreigners among the Israelites were to be excluded from the Temple. No unclean thing was to pollute

God's holy House—or else he could not dwell there, just as in our day (D&C 97:15–17).

Verses 10–14: The limited function of Levites is declared.

Verses 15–31: The conduct, duties, and rewards of priests are mentioned. Though not often realized, priests acted as judges from earliest times (Judges 2:16–19; 2 Chronicles 19:8–11). This function now rests with bishops, who are presidents of their ward priests' quorums. Contact with dead persons or animals made one ceremonially or ritually impure and unfit to officiate in the Temple (Leviticus 21:1–3; 7:24).

Ezekiel 45–46

The chapter headnotes provide inspired summaries.

Ezekiel 47:1–10

The opening verses of this chapter prophesy that just before the Second Coming a life-giving, fresh water stream will issue from the Temple—one of the events heralding the return of Jesus Christ. The Prophet Joseph Smith prophesied: "Judah must return, Jerusalem must be rebuilt, and the temple, and water come out from under the temple, and the waters of the Dead Sea be healed . . . and all this must be done before the Son of Man will make His appearance" (*Joseph Smith* [manual], 252). See chapter heading and cross-references in 47:1, footnote *b*.

According to geologists, the great Rift Valley, one of the deepest cracks in the earth's surface, running about 4,000 miles from Syria to Mozambique in southeast Africa, is gradually opening up to form another ocean. The Lord, knowing where the pressure points are in the earth, could cause that to happen much faster than the millions of years the scientists usually surmise it will take. With the waters of the Red Sea flowing northward and filling up the Rift Valley (in the Holy Land called the Jordan Valley and the Arabah), there would be no more Dead Sea nor Sea of Galilee, but there certainly could be fishermen standing at En-Gedi, as verse 10 says, trying to catch "the fish of the great sea, exceeding many."

Waters coming from the Temple is a literal event, but it is also symbolic of the Living Water, Jesus Christ, who heals all things and who is at the center of Temple worship. In addition, the more we attend the Temple the more deeply we are immersed in its life-giving "waters." Thus, the healing of the Dead Sea should also be understood as a type of healing of the whole bitter world.

Ezekiel 47:13–23

The borders of the land of Israel at the time of the Lord's Second Coming are described. An interesting comparison can be made with the former borders given in the law (Numbers 34:1–12). Notice in verse 22 that "strangers" will also live and enjoy an inheritance among the children of Israel in the Holy Land. Recall Isaiah envisioning the same: "For the Lord will have mercy on Jacob, and will yet choose Israel, and set them in their own land: and the strangers shall be joined with them, and they shall cleave to the house of Jacob" (Isaiah 14; see also commentary at Isaiah 14).

Ezekiel 48

The future Holy Land will be divided with portions for all the tribes of Israel—all the covenant people of God—and the Holy City will no longer be called the "City of Peace" (the meaning of *Yerushalayim/Jerusalem*). Instead it will be named, *YHWH shama,* meaning "The Lord is there," because Immanuel ("God with us") will take up residence on this glorified sphere to rule and reign through the great Millennium. Ezekiel's testimony is true: the Lord will surely be there.

DANIEL

In the third year of the reign of King Jehoiakim of Judah, King Nebuchadnezzar of Babylon laid siege to Jerusalem and initiated the first deportation of Jews to Babylon. Daniel was among them. He was likely a teenager when taken away around 605 B.C. from his homeland to be raised in the Babylonian court. He and his friends were wise and faithful young men and rose to positions of prominence and leadership. Daniel, as a Jewish prophet serving in the court of his captors, provided inspired guidance to Babylonian and Persian kings until he was more than eighty years old.

The book of Daniel divides evenly into two major parts: chapters 1–6 contain a collection of favorite stories about the courage and valiance of Daniel and his friends, as well as one of the most important revelations in history; and chapters 7–12 include Daniel's other revelations regarding world-changing events in the next few centuries, through the Persian, Hellenistic (Greek), and early Roman periods (including the ministry of the Savior), as well as Daniel's eschatological visions (Greek, *eschatos*, "of or relating to the end of times, the last days").

Many biblical scholars believe the book of Daniel to be a fictional or semifictional composition written long after the events of which it purports to prophesy had already taken place. One reason for this view is the belief by such scholars that predictive prophecy is simply not possible, not reasonable. Latter-day Saints, however, affirm that such is not only possible but real. Internal evidence also argues against a late composition date for the book. A reasonable date proposed for its completion is around 530 B.C.

Daniel 1:1–7

The siege of Judah by Babylon took certain of "the king's seed, and of the princes" into captivity, including Daniel and his three friends. Babylonians also took many of the vessels of the Temple. The siege took place in the third year of King Jehoiakim's reign, twenty years before the total fall of Jerusalem.

Babylonian officials were looking for young men who were handsome in appearance, "skilful in all wisdom, and cunning in knowledge, and understanding science" (v. 4), in order to prepare them to be successful and loyal administrators for the crown.

The boys were given the best royal court schooling and learned the Babylonian language. Their names were also changed. Daniel means "God is my judge," Hananiah means "Jehovah is gracious," Mishael means "Who is what God is?" and Azariah means "Jehovah is my help." Belteshazzar means "O protect his life"; the meaning of the name Shadrach is obscure, as is that of Meshach; Abednego means "servant of Nego."

Daniel 1:8–21

Israelites restricted their diets and adhered to "kosher" foods (*kosher* meaning "proper" or "acceptable" according to the Law of Moses). You can see why the Babylonian king's food might "defile" the Jewish boys. (Latter-day Saint boys trying to keep the Word of Wisdom in all places and situations might well run into similar problems.) "Pulse" is a King James English word which translates a Hebrew word referring to the common edible legumes such as peas, beans, and lentils—perhaps foods and drinks made of sprouted grains and vegetables.

With this dietary regimen, the countenances of the Jewish boys were fairer and brighter than those of others who went into the Babylonian basic training program. A modern parallel to verse 17 may be the promises given to those willing to obey a latter-day health code: receiving "health in their navel and marrow to their bones; and shall find wisdom and great treasures of knowledge, even hidden treasures; and shall run and not be weary, and shall walk and not faint" (D&C 89:18–20).

Having refused to compromise their principles, the Jewish boys fared well in their final tests.

Verse 21 gives the duration of Daniel's service in the Babylonian court. The first year of Cyrus was 539; thus, 603 to 539 B.C. is sixty-four years!

Daniel 2:1–3

Latter-day Saints have long been aware of a prophecy in the second chapter of Daniel, and somewhat reiterated in the seventh chapter, about the kingdoms of this world that would break down and be replaced ultimately by the kingdom of God. Reference to this great event is found in many scriptures. See, for example, Doctrine and Covenants 65:1–3 and Revelation 11:15. Jesus prayed for it in his exemplary prayer (Matthew 6:10). This is the introduction to the famous dream of Nebuchadnezzar. If Nebuchadnezzar came to the throne about 605 B.C., Daniel would not have been serving in the court long before the king had this dream.

Daniel 2:4–23

Notice the language mentioned in verse 4. In the middle of that verse the text changes from Hebrew language to Aramaic (what the text calls "Syriack"). It returns to Hebrew again in chapter 8. No one knows the reason for this bilingual composition other than the fact that Aramaic was the lingua franca of the Babylonian world.

In verse 5 the phrase "is gone from me" should probably read "is *certain* with me," as the Persian word *azda* ("sure") is used (see footnote 5*a*). In verse 9 the king makes the point that he knows what he dreamed; therefore if the interpreters can tell him the dream he will know that *they* know what they are talking about, and he will know whether or not he can have confidence in their interpretation.

Daniel was confident that he could arrive at an interpretation, so he prepared to resolve the problem and the challenge. The word "secret" in verses 18 and 19 immediately recalls Amos 3:7— the Lord will always reveal his secret unto his servants, the prophets. When Daniel received the solution from the Lord, his natural response was to show gratitude to him. His psalm of praise and thanksgiving is found in verses 20 through 23.

Daniel 2:24–49

When the young prophet was taken before King Nebuchadnezzar and asked if he could recount and interpret the king's dream, Daniel stated that it was "God in heaven [who] revealeth secrets, and maketh known . . . what shall be *in the latter days*" (v. 28; emphasis added). According to President Spencer W. Kimball, Daniel told the king that his dream was "a portrayal of the history of the world" (*Ensign*, May 1976, 8). Daniel taught Nebuchadnezzar that he was the great world power at the time—represented by the head of gold in the dream. But another kingdom would arise and take over world domination. That kingdom, in turn, would fall and be followed by the rise of yet other kingdoms that would replace their predecessors and hold dominion. Such is the march of history. The rise and fall of kingdoms would continue up to a certain point.

In our own time, another prophetic interpreter of Nebuchadnezzar's dream, President Spencer W. Kimball, further refined this portion of Daniel's interpretation with some specific designations of the kingdoms portrayed in the dream: "Cyrus the great, with his Medes and Persians, would be replaced by the Greek or Macedonian kingdom under Philip and Alexander; and that world power would be replaced by the Roman Empire; and Rome would be replaced by a group of nations of Europe represented by the toes of the image" (*Ensign*, May 1976, 8). President Kimball's interpretation is more valuable to us today than even the words recorded in the book of Daniel, for President Kimball's words are a continuation of prophetic interpretation in these latter days— the more complete and detailed meaning of Daniel's prophecy reserved for the people actually affected by the ancient prophecy.

Finally, standing in front of the king, Daniel finished his interpretation of the dream, which contained "the real revelation," as President Kimball called it (*Ensign*, May 1976, 8). This is found in verses 44 and 45.

Members of The Church of Jesus Christ of Latter-day Saints hardly need help understanding what the Lord, through Daniel, was trying to teach about Nebuchadnezzar's dream. There would come a time in the nations of Europe (represented by feet and toes of mixed iron and clay) when God himself would set up a kingdom controlled not by feeble mortal power but by divine authority, one that would never be destroyed. President Kimball testified of this meaning:

"The Church of Jesus Christ of Latter-day Saints was restored in 1830 after numerous revelations from the divine source; and this is the kingdom, set up by the God of heaven, that would never be destroyed nor superseded, and the stone cut out of the mountain without hands that would become a great mountain and would fill the whole earth.

"History unfolded and the world powers came and went after ruling the world for a little season, but in the early nineteenth century the day had come . . . [that] the Church was organized. Small it was, with only six members, compared to the stone cut out of the mountain without hands which would break in pieces other nations and which would roll forth and fill the whole earth. . . . [T]oday the stone rolls forth to fill the earth" (*Ensign*, May 1976, 8–9).

In a revelation to the Prophet Joseph Smith, the Lord indicated that the final kingdom of Nebuchadnezzar's dream would be established in preparation for the Second Coming and Christ's millennial reign.

"The keys of the kingdom of God are committed unto man on the earth, and from thence shall the gospel roll forth unto the ends of the earth, as the stone which is cut out of the mountain without hands shall roll forth, until it has filled the whole earth.

"Yea, a voice crying—Prepare ye the way of the Lord, prepare ye the supper of the Lamb, make ready for the Bridegroom" (D&C 65:2–3).

The message of this latter-day revelation begins with the same proclamation found in Isaiah 40:3 and Malachi 3:1: "Prepare ye the way of the Lord, make his paths straight" (D&C 65:1). In ancient times, heralds ran before the coming processional of a king or dignitary, clearing stones and other obstacles from the pathway and preparing and warning the people of the dignitary's coming. In our day, the latter days, living prophets fill this role. They are saying, in effect, Jesus Christ is coming, and "the gospel of Jesus Christ is destined to fill the Earth, as the stone in Nebuchadnezzar's dream. . . . The Church will fill the Earth before the end of the Millennium" (Smith and Sjodhl, *Doctrine and Covenants Commentary*, 398).

The Church will fill the earth before the *end* of the Millennium. It will not fill the earth *before* the Millennium begins. The beginning of the Millennium will not be the end of the unfolding of the great kingdom described by Daniel. Practically speaking, The Church of Jesus Christ of Latter-day Saints does not fill every corner of the whole earth in the early years of the Millennium. Other religious beliefs persist on the earth. President Joseph Fielding Smith wrote:

"When the reign of Jesus Christ comes during the millennium, only those who have lived the telestial law will be removed. It is recorded in the Bible and other standard works of the Church that the earth will be cleansed of all its corruption and wickedness. Those who have lived virtuous lives, who have been honest in their dealings with their fellow man and have endeavored to do good to the best of their understanding, shall remain" (*Answers to Gospel Questions*, 1:108).

"The Lord has never taken any course that would deprive any person of his free agency. Even during the millennium that privilege will be granted them. . . .

"It will make a great difference when Satan will have his power taken away during that period, but the inhabitants of the earth will still have their agency. We are taught that during that thousand years, men will not be compelled to believe. . . . The Lord will not take away from them their right to believe as they will. However, if they persist in their unbelief under the conditions which will prevail, they will be condemned. Before that period is over all will have received the truth" (*Answers to Gospel Questions*, 5:141–43).

NEBUCHADNEZZAR'S DREAM AND ITS FULFILLMENT AT A GLANCE

Following are a few points of Nebuchadnezzar's dream and its interpretation:

Verse 28: Daniel wanted the king to know the source of his dream; Daniel's understanding came not from within himself but from God, and he so declared it to the king. Daniel also wanted the king to know the time of his dream's fulfillment.

Verse 32: The generally acknowledged historical interpretation is that the head represented the Babylonian Empire (605–539 B.C.); the breast and arms, the Medo-Persian Empire (539–331 B.C.); the belly and thighs, the Macedonian-Greek Empire (331–161 B.C.).

Verse 33: The legs and feet represented the Roman Empire (161 B.C. to A.D. 395), which divided into the east, with its capital at Constantinople (ending in 1453 with the conquests of Ottoman Turks), and the west, with its capital at Rome (ending in 1806 with Francis II of Austria, the last ruler of the Holy Roman Empire).

Verse 34: In the year A.D. 1830 the Lord himself, without human hands, initiated the restoration of his kingdom on the earth.

Verse 35: A modern prophet envisioned the fulfillment of this dream: "The keys of the kingdom of God are committed unto man on the earth, and from thence shall the gospel roll forth unto the ends of the earth, as the stone which is cut out of the mountain without hands shall roll forth, until it has filled the whole earth" (D&C 65:2).

Verse 44: A kingdom is set up which shall never be destroyed, which is immensely comforting to know (see also D&C 138:44). The Prophet Joseph Smith said: "I calculate to be one of the instruments of setting up the kingdom of Daniel by the word of the Lord, and I intend to lay a foundation that will revolutionize the whole world" (*Joseph Smith* [manual], 512).

Verse 47: Two heathen kings, Nebuchadnezzar and Darius, saw the power of God (4:37; 6:26–27). They recognized it but did not accept it and live by it ("These are they who are honorable men of the earth, who were blinded by the craftiness of men"; D&C 76:75).

Daniel 3

King Nebuchadnezzar set up a huge statue of gold (undoubtedly gold plated) at Dura—a location not precisely known since the word is a noun meaning "walled enclosure." All people were expected, upon penalty of death, to worship it. It may have been a representation of the god Nabu, patron deity of Nebuchadnezzar, whose name incorporates the name of that god.

The three Jewish boys believed in and lived a true principle, and they would suffer even unto death to maintain it (compare Abraham 1:11). They refused to compromise their principles even when the heat was on! Their trust and confidence is dramatically expressed in verse 17. They knew God *could* deliver them, but they did not know if God *would* deliver them—whatever happened, they refused to compromise their high standard of worship. This account depicts why they did not die in the furnace; comparable situations recorded in Helaman 5:23 and 3 Nephi 28:19–22 clearly suggest that these faithful young men were transfigured. Even Nebuchadnezzar could discern that the heavenly Being in the furnace with the boys looked like "a son of the gods" (as the Aramaic literally translates), whom we know as the Son of God. The monarch overturned his own decree and astonishingly made a new decree to protect the young Hebrew men and their God and even promoted the young men.

Daniel 4

This chapter is a personal declaration by Nebuchadnezzar that describes how he gained a testimony of the true God. When Daniel was told about the king's new dream he was reluctant to divulge its meaning because it was a warning from "the most High" that the king would fall from his high status, power, and dominion. The dream did, however, provide a way to escape the inevitable if the king would repent and become obedient to the most High God and merciful to His children.

When the required repentance had not occurred within twelve months and the king vaunted his honor and majesty, his fall began. He suffered for "seven times," likely seven years, until he acknowledged that "the most High ruleth in the kingdom of men, and giveth it to whomsoever he will" (v. 32).

According to this account, Nebuchadnezzar's mind was restored as he conceded that the King of heaven was indeed the true God, who held dominion over all, and he testified that God's works are true and his ways are just. The monarch of Babylon then regained his position of majesty.

Daniel 5:1–30

This chapter relates an incident several generations after Nebuchadnezzar's time. That greatest king of Babylon died around 561 B.C., and then some minor kings reigned, including Evil-merodach, who is mentioned in 2 Kings 25:27. Nabonidus then reigned, along with his coregent Belshazzar (not to be confused with Belteshazzar, which was Daniel's Babylonian name (Daniel 1:7). The reference to "father" in verses 2 and 18 must therefore mean "ancestor."

The drunken debauchery and revelry described in verses 1–4 is well documented in other ancient cultures by respected historians and ancient chroniclers. It even became a practice in some cultures to devote dining rooms and halls to gods of wine and debauched behavior, which actually influenced the remnants of Judaism in the Holy Land.

"Fingers of a man's hand" (v. 5) have been seen on another occasion, too (Ether 3:6). Verses 12 and 14 present a noble characterization of Daniel. When Nabonidus retired to Arabia early in his reign (for some form of religious seclusion), his son Belshazzar governed the kingdom on behalf of his father and was killed when the Persians took the city in 539 B.C. That is why Daniel could be made *third* in the kingdom (v. 16). There were still some living who knew about Daniel's abilities to interpret dreams and decipher heavenly messages, even this new "handwriting on the wall." (We now use that phrase to likewise refer to something that is inevitably scheduled for the future, something that is sure to happen.) Anyone could have read the three Aramaic words, but Daniel interpreted them by the power of God. The message was abrupt and terminal: Belshazzar's reign was over; the "Medes and Persians" were about to take over (under Cyrus, who had united the Medes and the Persians and was in the process of creating a vast, new empire). In fact, that very night Belshazzar lost his kingdom and his life (v. 30).

Daniel 5:31

This verse should actually be the first verse of chapter 6, as it is in the Hebrew Bible (written here in Aramaic). It refers to another time, under another ruler, at least two generations later than verse 30.

Daniel 6

This story unfolds much later than the previous episode of chapter 5, during the reign of Darius (ca. 520 B.C.). Daniel now served as a chief prince and president of the great Persian Empire, over one hundred and twenty princes (having served in similar positions in the Babylonian and early Persian administrations). Verses 3 and 4 again give a positive characterization of Daniel, who "was preferred above the presidents and princes" (the Aramaic reflexive form actually means he "distinguished himself" above the others) because an excellent spirit was in him.

Daniel constantly remained faithful and continued his lifelong habit of prayer to the God of Israel in defiance of a treacherous royal decree. His practice of kneeling "in his chamber toward Jerusalem" and praying three times a day (v. 10) is reflected in Psalm 55:17: "Evening, and morning, and at noon, will I pray, and cry aloud: and he shall hear my voice." Moreover, Daniel's circumstance of facing Jerusalem (actually toward the Temple) was anticipated, perhaps even prophesied, by the author of Chronicles much earlier when he described the dedication of Solomon's Temple at Jerusalem:

"If they sin against thee, (for there is no man which sinneth not,) and thou be angry with them, and deliver them over before their enemies, and they carry them away captives unto a land far off or near;

"Yet if they bethink themselves in the land whither they are carried captive, and turn and pray unto thee in the land of their captivity, saying, We have sinned, we have done amiss, and have dealt wickedly;

"If they return to thee with all their heart and with all their soul in the land of their captivity, whither they have carried them captives, and pray toward their land, which thou gavest unto their fathers, and toward the city which thou hast chosen, and toward the house which I have built for thy name:

"Then hear thou from the heavens, even from thy dwelling place, their prayer and their supplications, and maintain their

Daniel in the den of lions. "My God hath sent his angel, and hath shut the lions' mouths, that they have not hurt me" (Daniel 6:22)

cause, and forgive thy people which have sinned against thee" (2 Chronicles 6:36–39).

Daniel was subsequently accused and cast into a den of lions. Since the episode is set in the reign of Darius, Daniel must have been already an old man in his eighties! He was, as always, quite unwilling to compromise his religious principles in the face of any peril to his life. Because Daniel "believed in his God" (v. 23) and was faithful in all things before him, God "sent his angel" (compare Acts 12:11; 3 Nephi 28:22) and "shut the lions' mouths" that "no manner of hurt was found upon him" (vv. 22–23).

Daniel 7

Chronologically, chapter 7 precedes chapter 5. This vision is related to the prophecy on kingdoms recorded in chapter 2. In chapter 7 we learn that Daniel had visions pass through his mind in the form of a dream. Four beasts represented secular kingdoms of the earth. The first, like a lion with eagle's wings, is the neo-Babylonian empire. The rest of verse 4 may symbolize the destruction of the empire. The second beast (v. 5), was like a bear, representing the Persian empire, and the three ribs in its mouth representing its principle conquests: Lydia (546 B.C.), Babylon (539 B.C.), and Egypt (525 B.C.). The third beast (v. 6) symbolized the swift conquests of Alexander the Great (336–323 B.C.), with the "four heads" representing Alexander's generals who divided up the kingdom among themselves after Alexander's death. The fourth beast (v. 7) stood for the Roman empire, surpassing all its predecessors. The ten horns seem to correspond to the ten toes of Daniel 2:41–42, representing ten states or political entities that arose on the foundation of the Roman empire. Whatever the specifics of the interpretation, all kingdoms ultimately give way to the kingdom of God.

Verses 9–14 refer to the great future priesthood and preparatory conference at Adam-ondi-Ahman in northern Missouri, where father Adam and numerous holders of priesthood keys will report to the Lord Jesus Christ (see D&C 116). Then "the saints of the most High" will be given the kingdom to possess it forever and ever (vv. 18, 27; see also D&C 103:7). This, essentially, is also the concluding message of John's apocalyptic vision, where the Messiah reigns, along with God the Father, in the celestial kingdom, on a celestialized earth (Revelation 19–22).

Daniel 8

This chapter also precedes chapter 5, and, again, expands on the vision of chapter 2. The year (v. 1) is about 552 B.C., and Daniel was in the palace at Shushan (v. 2) in Persia. Consider the following interpretations: the "he goat" (v. 5) represents Alexander the Great; the ram with two horns (v. 6) represents the Persians and Medes—remember that the term "horn" in scripture often signifies power; Alexander's empire was broken up (v. 8). These interpretations are stated in verses 20–21. Those who do not believe in prophecy assume that this book was written later, in the second century before Christ, after all these events have happened and thus are a historical report. There may actually be dual meaning in these symbols and their interpretation; see the end of verse 17.

Angels are mentioned in about half of the books of the Old Testament, but this is the first one mentioned by name. Gabriel, known in mortality as Noah, came to explain these images; in the next chapter we will see that this same Gabriel revealed to Daniel a great prophecy about the coming Messiah (for notes on the ministry and appearances of Gabriel over three millennia, see commentary at Genesis 9:28–29). Gabriel is an Elias, a forerunner, meaning he fulfills the priesthood office or role of an Elias (D&C 27:6–7), and visits mortals to communicate future events about the Messiah.

Daniel 9

This is Daniel's only chapter that concerns his fellow Jews in captivity. It is a prayer for their release and return, dating from about 521 B.C. (v. 1). In verse 2 we learn that the exiles had with them some writings of previous prophets.

Verses 21–27: As evidenced by the repeated mention of the topic "Jesus Christ, Prophecies about" in the footnotes, this message from Gabriel clearly foreshadows and prophesies that after the restoration of the Jews to their land, at a mysteriously calculated time, involving the number seven, the promised Messiah would come, and he would die for the people—although the idea of Messiah being "cut off" was a very un-Jewish idea. He would be killed by "the people of the prince that shall come" and those same people would "destroy the city and the sanctuary"—all of which was literally fulfilled by Titus and his Roman legionaries destroying Jerusalem and the Temple in A.D. 70. In that year, because of the cumulative abominations that had occurred, the Temple Mount was made desolate and the Romans caused "the sacrifice and the oblation to cease," though the Messiah's sacrifice and offering of his own life more than three decades earlier had actually marked the fulfillment of the law of blood sacrifice practiced for centuries by Israelites at that holy Temple site.

Daniel 10

Cyrus, king of Persia, conquered the Babylonian empire in 539 B.C. He became a great benefactor of the Jewish people, allowing them to return to Jerusalem to rebuild their capital city and the Temple (see "Important Historical Background," page 411).

The third year after Cyrus's conquest, about the year 536 B.C., Daniel was in his eighties. Somewhere along the Tigris River

Daniel received a remarkable revelation concerning the future. He had been mourning and fasting for three weeks. Compare the circumstances of Daniel's vision with the experiences of others:

- Description of the Lord (vv. 5–6): Ezekiel 1:26–28; Luke 9:29; Revelation 1:13–15; D&C 110:2–3; Joseph Smith–History 1:17 and compare verse 32
- Only Daniel saw the vision (v. 7): Acts 9:7.
- Daniel was left with no strength (v. 8): 1 Nephi 1:7; JS–H 1:20.
- Daniel was laid out on the ground (v. 9): JS–H 1:20.
- "Fear not" (v. 12): Matthew 17:6–7; Luke 1:12–13; 2:9–10; JS–H 1:32.
- The Lord came in answer to prayers: Mosiah 27:14; D&C 98:1–2.
- Adam appeared (v. 13): D&C 27:11.
- Daniel could not speak (v. 15): Luke 1:20–22; Mosiah 27:19.

Daniel 11

This chapter continues the revelation given to Daniel and describes conflicts during the intertestamental period which were also types of things to come in the last days. Following is the traditional historical interpretation:

Verse 2: four Persian kings: Ahasuerus/Xerxes, Artaxerxes, Darius II, Darius III

Verse 3: a mighty king: Alexander the Great, 333 B.C.

Verse 4: when he shall stand up—or, at his death (323 B.C.)

Verse 4: his kingdom would be broken: divided among Antigonus, Seleucus, and Ptolemy

Verse 5: king of the south: Ptolemy

Verse 6: join themselves together: form an alliance

Verse 6: king's daughter of the south: Antiochus II marries Berenice, daughter of Ptolemy II in 252 B.C.

Verse 7: Ptolemy invades Syria—the Laodicean War, 245 B.C.

Verse 9: Seleucus attacks Egypt, 240 B.C.

Verse 10: Antiochus invades Egypt, 219 B.C.

Verse 11: Ptolemy invades Syria, the Battle of Raphia, 217 B.C.

Verses 13–16: Syria defeats Egypt and controls Judea—the Battle of Panias, 198 B.C.

Verses 18–20: the commander of Roman forces stands up to Antiochus IV at Alexandria—the Battle of Magnesia, 190 B.C.

Verses 21–35: events involving Antiochus IV Epiphanes

Verse 35: Antiochus IV and his army desecrate the Lord's Temple (see also 1 Maccabees 1:54, 59)

Verses 36–45: Antiochus was a type of a terrible anti-Christ to come.

Daniel 12

Troubled times are foreseen in the last days. Verse 2 contains one of the Old Testament's few testimonies of the Resurrection (see also Job 19:25–27; Isaiah 25:8; 26:19; Ezekiel 37:1–14).

Verse 4: Daniel's visions are to be sealed up until the end of time; knowledge will increase in that day (see also Habakkuk 2:14; D&C 128:19). At the end of verse 6 we see that Daniel wondered the same thing most of us wonder: *When* will all these things take place? *When* will the end of the world be? Jesus' apostles would later ask the same question on the Mount of Olives: "Tell us, *when* shall these things be?" (Matthew 24:3). The Lord gave Daniel an answer, but Daniel didn't understand what it meant: "I heard, but I understood not" (v. 8). Over the ages many people have tried to decipher the curious numbers in the final verses of Daniel and have drawn a host of speculative conclusions. However, if the prophet himself didn't understand the meaning of the words and numbers, is that not a lesson or caution to us? The Lord said (v. 9), "Go thy way, Daniel: for the words are closed up and sealed till the time of the end," and later in verse 12, he adds what we might construe as a final word of caution: "Blessed is he that waiteth."

IMPORTANT HISTORICAL BACKGROUND

Though the Babylonian Empire was mighty, it was short-lived. Compared to its predecessor, Assyria, and its successor, Persia (each of which endured for more than two centuries) the new Babylonian Empire rose to greatness, left its heavy mark on ancient Near Eastern history, especially Jewish history, and then was swept into oblivion—all in the short space of seventy years. Babylon's strength and evil grandeur became proverbial in later scripture, a symbol of the wicked. She is called the apostate, the whore of all the earth, the mother of harlots (a foil or contrast to Zion, representing the righteous—see 1 Peter 5:13; Revelation 14:8; 17:5; D&C 1:16; 35:11; 64:24; 86:3). In Doctrine and Covenants 133:14 the Lord warns the Latter-day Saints: "Go ye out from among the nations, even from Babylon, from the midst of wickedness, which is spiritual Babylon." And in our modern hymns we still sing of Babylon as the representative of darkness in the earth: "O Babylon, O Babylon, we bid thee farewell," and "Babylon the great is falling; God shall all her towers o'erthrow" (*Hymns,* nos. 319, 7).

Many see in the words of the prophets to Israel and Judah only a message of doom, despair, and destruction. A closer examination of the prophetic books, however, reveals that the prophets almost universally held out a message of hope to the Lord's people—their teachings anticipate a day of restoration, reinstatement, and redemption.

Just as Jeremiah prophesied, the exile to Babylon was to endure only a generation or two: "For thus saith the Lord, That after seventy years be accomplished at Babylon I will visit you, and perform my good word toward you, in causing you to return to this place" (Jeremiah 29:10; compare Daniel 9:2).

Cyrus united the Medes and the Persians to form what became the greatest empire ever known to that point in the history of the ancient Near East (see Bible Map 7). The two kingdoms, Media in the north and Persia in the south, together occupied the million square miles of today's Iranian plateau. The core of the Persian homeland extended from the Tigris Valley on the west, Persian Gulf on the south, Indus Valley on the east, and Armenian mountains and Caspian Sea on the north. The dominions of the Persian Empire eventually extended from the Indus Valley in the east to Ethiopia in the southwest and Macedonia in the northwest (Esther 1:1). The Persian Empire was among the first to issue gold coinage. The Persians also operated a postal system and constructed a network of state highways. Important capitals or chief cities of the empire were Ecbatana

The Cyrus Cylinder, on display at the British Museum, London. "Thus saith Cyrus king of Persia, The Lord God of heaven hath given me all the kingdoms of the earth; and he hath charged me to build him an house at Jerusalem, which is in Judah" (Ezra 1:2)

(Achmetha in Ezra 6:2), Pasargadae, Persepolis, and Susa. The last-mentioned city, Susa, was the capital of the region called Elam. It was called *Shushan* in the Bible and was the setting for some of the greatest of the concluding historical and religious accounts in the Old Testament:

Daniel 8:2—"I saw in a vision; and it came to pass, when I saw, that I was at *Shushan* in the palace, which is in the province of Elam . . ."

Esther 1:2—"That in those days, when the king Ahasuerus sat on the throne of his kingdom, which was in *Shushan* the palace . . ."

Nehemiah 1:1—"The words of Nehemiah . . . in the twentieth year, as I was in *Shushan* the palace . . ."

Unlike their predecessors, the early Persian rulers were benefi-cent and humane, allowing local autonomy and freedom of religion. Cyrus himself was possibly a Zoroastrian but apparently a religious eclectic, adopting the gods of various conquered peoples and trying to appease them. We have seen that Isaiah foretold the rise of the Persian Empire under Cyrus two centuries before the dramatic events actually occurred, and the prophet called Cyrus the Lord's anointed, a type of the Messiah, foreordained to sponsor the great Return of the Jews (Isaiah 44:28; 45:1).

Cyrus established 127 *satrapies* (provinces or states; see Esther 1:1) throughout the empire, and his chief prince or president was

Daniel, the Hebrew prophet. Cyrus encouraged the Jews to return to their homeland and rebuild their capital city and Temple, as prophesied, and even placed some of the wealth of the empire in their hands to accomplish those tasks. Perhaps Daniel had some influence on that decision.

The Cyrus Cylinder, dating to 536 B.C., is a nine-inch-long, baked clay cylinder with cuneiform inscription corroborating the biblical account that Cyrus permitted captives to return to their respective countries and rebuild their temples. Few events in all of ancient Near Eastern history can parallel in importance the events that Cyrus set in motion.

HAGGAI

Haggai was a prophet called to minister to the exiles who had returned to their own land after the Babylonian Captivity ended in 538 B.C. His was a message both of encouragement and chastisement. His small book tells of the efforts of this old prophet to arouse the people again to rebuild the Temple after all the obstructions to their work suffered since their return (from about 535 to 520 B.C.). His is the second shortest book in the Old Testament, after Obadiah.

Haggai seems to be one of those who remembered the former Temple that Solomon had originally built (Haggai 2:3). If indeed true, he was an old man in the return to Judah. The Temple had been destroyed sixty-six years before his efforts here, which are dated in the "second year of Darius." Darius Hystaspes reigned 521–486 B.C. (see Bible Appendix, "Chronology"). The name *Haggai* means "my festivals" or "my holy days," which describes the prophet as one concerned with the sacred worship and ceremonies of the Temple.

Chapter 1 reports Haggai's appeal to build the Temple and the people's response. Chapter 2 tells of his comparison of the former Temple with the first attempts at reconstruction. He urged better work and promised great glory to come. It also speaks of the coming of the Messiah, called therein "the desire of all nations" (2:7), and links the Messiah with this Second Temple.

Haggai 1

Since Darius Hystaspes reigned from 521 to 486 B.C., this revelation would have been received in the autumn (the sixth month then would have been Elul) of 520 B.C. Verse 1 gives several names. Zerubbabel, the governor, was the grandson of Jehoiachin, a former king of Judah who was taken to Babylon as a boy and later elevated to the position of king in prison there (2 Kings 24:15; Jeremiah 52:31–33). Zerubbabel ("seed of Babylon") led the return of the first group from Babylon about nineteen years before this revelation (Ezra 2:2). For a glimpse of Haggai in the historical books, see Ezra 4:24–5:2; 6:14. Joshua, whose name is rendered Jeshua in the books of Ezra and Nehemiah, was the son of the last high priest, Josedech, who was taken to Babylon (the father's name is rendered Jehozadak in 1 Chronicles 6:15).

Haggai used a number of questions to get his message across. The first emphasized priorities: "Is this a time for you returning exiles to be living in your paneled houses (King James Version, "cieled houses") while the House of the Lord remains a ruin?" (paraphrase of verse 4). The building of the Temple was delayed partly because the people had so much work to do to build their own dwellings again. First they had to clear the interminable rubble of Jerusalem as it had lain for seventy years. But it was delayed mostly because they had so much opposition and harassment by the Samaritans, who had volunteered to help build the Temple but turned bitter when they were rebuffed, according to Ezra 4:1–4. Because of the Gentile origins and the apostate, false religion of the Samaritans (2 Kings 17:24–41), the returning Jews were commanded not to mix or associate with them.

Haggai and his contemporary, the prophet Zechariah, were called to expedite the work of the Temple when Darius renewed Cyrus's decree that the returning exiles could rebuild God's holy House. Not only did the Lord command the people to consider their errant ways and their misguided priorities—"mine house that is waste [while] ye run every man unto his own house"—but he told them that it was because of their neglect that the heavens were withholding their dew and the earth its crops (vv. 9–10). Haggai's revelation motivated the people to get to work. They trusted his assessment and his promises.

Haggai 2:1–5

It must have been discouraging for those who had known the previous Temple to look upon the mass of ruins, but the prophetic message came through loud and clear. It is the same message all discouraged people need to hear and heed. It is the same message modern prophets and apostles have prescribed as a remedy for our economic, social, and spiritual ills: Pray and then get off our knees and go to work! (see Hinckley, *New Era,* July 2000, 7; "In Memoriam," *New Era,* May 1994).

The people were told to be strong and get rid of their fear. Indeed, fear is the enemy of faith and righteousness.

Haggai 2:6–19

The prophet issued a powerful prophecy on the ultimate destiny and future glory of the Second Temple (as well as other future Temples) by foretelling both the first and the second coming of the Messiah. All nations would be shaken and "the desire of all nations [the Messiah] shall come" and "fill this house with glory." The "glory of this latter house" would be greater than its former glory, and in his House the Lord would give peace. This prophecy was obviously fulfilled when Jesus Christ came to the Jerusalem Temple during his mortal ministry and taught daily in the Temple (see Matthew 21:23; 26:55; Mark 12:35–40; 14:49; Luke 19:45–48; John 7:28; 10:23). But it will also be fulfilled again during the Millennium when another Temple will be in Jerusalem and Christ, the Prince of Peace, will reign personally from that holy city (Isaiah 2:3).

Haggai also reminded the people of the need for purity when associating with the Temple. He promised blessings to those who carefully considered the ways of the Lord from that day on.

A revelation on the ultimate destiny and glory of a future Temple evidently motivated them to work. Verse 9 is a simple but powerful statement on what a Temple brings. The people were to cleanse themselves, and not expect work on holy things to cleanse them; then they would be blessed and the holy place would not be defiled.

Haggai 2:20–23

Haggai, the prophet, received a revelation for Zerubbabel, the governor. Although Zerubbabel was of the royal line himself, this revelation defined his role as a type of the ultimate King of the royal line of David, the coming Messiah. Compare Matthew 1:12–13 and Luke 3:27 for mention of Zerubbabel in the genealogy of

Jesus. The Lord declared Zerubbabel to be as his signet ring—a guarantee that his promises would be fulfilled. Anciently, a signet or signet ring was applied to seals on documents and to documents themselves. It functioned as a signature, a pledge that guaranteed the authenticity of a message.

ZECHARIAH

Zechariah was both a prophet and priest, like Jeremiah (1:1) and Ezekiel (1:3). He was born in Babylonia during the exile and was among the first group to return to Judah in 538 B.C. under the leadership of Zerubbabel and Joshua. Zechariah was a contemporary of Haggai, also called to minister to the returning exiles. Both prophets chastised the people and encouraged them to finish rebuilding the Temple. Zechariah also described the glorious future that the Lord's people will enjoy, but not before they will have endured yet another period of difficulty at the hands of their enemies. Yet the Lord will ensure their ultimate triumph. He will personally defend Jerusalem during the last great battle of history before his millennial reign.

Zechariah was the author of the book bearing his name. It contains appeals to the exiles to "remember the Lord," which is the meaning of the prophet's name, *Zachar-Yah*. Chapters 1–8 of Zechariah record eight visions of restoration that emphasize God's relationships with the people, the city, and the Temple. Chapters 9–14 are replete with what must have been mysterious symbolism for many, though for Latter-day Saints they are full of messianic prophecies, culminating in pivotal future events in chapters 12–14 dealing with the way the Messiah-Savior will make the Holy Land finally holy (events that are reiterated and elucidated in D&C 45:48–53).

Zechariah 1

This revelation to Zechariah came only about two months after Haggai's revelation, in October or November of 520 B.C. Zechariah urged the people to be different from their forefathers, whom the prophets warned in vain to turn away from their evil doings. Rather, Zechariah encouraged his people to turn to the Lord immediately.

Though the vision of the horses told in verses 7–17 is obscure to us, the central purpose of it is clear in verses 16–17: God caused Jerusalem to be reestablished, and Zion would be comforted with a house of the Lord in it once again. That, of course, applies to that day, before the Messiah would come, and it applies to the days when the Messiah comes a second time.

Zechariah 1:7–17 constitutes the first of eight visions seen by the prophet (reported in chapters 1–6) and bears some resemblance to an apocalyptic vision later seen by the apostle John. In John's Revelation, the red horse symbolizes battle and bloodshed (6:4) while the white horse symbolizes victory and peace (6:2). Perhaps the speckled horse of Zechariah 1:8 signifies an unsettled period, the aftermath of confusion.

Zechariah 2

The prophet reported his vision of Jerusalem's restoration and his guided tour of the future provided by angels. In the latter days, greater Jerusalem would be as a town without walls, with a great multitude of inhabitants. Anciently, walls were for fortification and protection, but in a yet future day the Lord "will be unto her [Jerusalem] a wall of fire" (v. 5). In other words the Lord would be Jerusalem's Protector. The Lord's words and works have dual significance: In the last days he will "choose Jerusalem again"; the future Zion will again be delivered from Babylon, the wicked world, and millennial Jerusalem will be a safe and glorious place with the Lord dwelling there (see footnotes under 10a; also Zechariah 12:6; 3 Nephi 20:29, 33; Ether 13:5). It is a challenge for many nations to accept Jerusalem today as the capital of the small nation of Israel. However, her prophetic destiny is to become a capital of the whole *world*. In the end, the Lord will govern from there.

Zechariah 3

You may see in this highly symbolic vision of Joshua, the high priest at that time (called Jeshua in Ezra and Nehemiah; see Ezra 5:2), a prophecy of the purification of Israel. It involved the changing of filthy garments (of the Exile) into the clean garments (of the Return, which was a return to their land and return to their

God). But this vision also foreshadows the first and second comings of the Messiah, the "Branch" (see commentary at Isaiah 11:1, 10). The Branch would bring redemption in the meridian of time and peace in the Millennium. Joshua thus symbolizes Christ. As verse 2 indicates, whenever the Lord is revealed, Satan is likewise revealed. But in the end the Lord will rebuke Satan. At the Second Coming, telestial-level iniquity will be removed from the earth and throughout the Millennium this sphere will enjoy an honorable and valiant existence (see commentary at Daniel 2:24–49).

Recall that the name *Jesus* is the English spelling of the Latin form of the Greek form of the Hebrew name *Yeshua,* which means "salvation."

Zechariah 4

Very much like Nephi's experience with an angel who guided his vision (1 Nephi 11:14–1 Nephi 14:20), Zechariah had a continuation of his previous revelation with the angel as his guide. Like Amos, Nephi, and Ezekiel, Zechariah envisioned objects and wondered what they were, what they meant. In this vision the prophet saw a candlestick, actually a *menorah* (a seven-branched lamp like the one used in the Tabernacle and in the former Temple), and two olive trees by it. The two olive trees represent two "anointed ones," two prophets in Jerusalem at the time of Armageddon. We learn more about them from the three passages listed in footnote 14*a* and in the commentary at Isaiah 40:1–2 and 51:19–20.

Verse 6 teaches an important principle through which Jerusalem and the Temple were built up then and will be again in the future: "not by might, nor by power, but by my spirit, saith the Lord of hosts."

In verses 6–10 we are told that Zerubbabel will finish rebuilding the Jerusalem Temple even though obstacles were placed before him. In verse 10 of the Joseph Smith Translation of this passage the phrase "the eyes of the Lord" is changed to "the *servants* of the Lord." In verse 11 the "two olive trees" represent two anointed servants that fulfill the Lord's purposes, Zerubbabel and Joshua.

Zechariah 5

As his revelation continued Zechariah envisioned a huge scroll, fifteen by thirty feet, featuring a long list of sins that must be cleansed. He saw other scenes, including a basket (King James Version, "ephah"—an eight-gallon container) lifted up between earth and heaven, symbolizing the removal of sinfulness back in Babylon, which in turn represents the wicked world, and the Lord's grace in removing all sin.

Zechariah 6

It will be interesting to see what these images of chariots and horses and crowns turn out to mean. The prophet also saw "The BRANCH" (details about Him are found in commentary at Isaiah 11:1, 10) and others who will be charged with building the House of the Lord: "And they that are far off shall come and build in the temple of the Lord" (v. 15; or, as the Revised Standard Version of the Bible words it: "And those who are far off shall come and help to build the temple of the Lord"; or, as in the New American Bible: "And they who are from afar shall come and build the temple of the Lord.") Such holy construction can happen only *if* "ye will diligently obey the voice of the Lord your God."

Elder Bruce R. McConkie interpreted in this way the part of Zechariah's vision found in verse 15:

"Who are those 'that are far off' who shall come to Jerusalem to build the house of the Lord? Surely they are the Jews who have been scattered afar. By what power and under whose authorization shall the work be done? There is only one place under the whole heavens where the keys of temple building are found. There is only one people who know how to build temples and what to do in them when they are completed. That people is the Latter-day Saints. The temple in Jerusalem will not be built by Jews who have assembled there for political purposes as at present. It will not be built by a people who know nothing whatever about the sealing ordinances and their application to the living and the dead. . . . But it will be built by Jews who have come unto Christ . . . and who have learned anew about temples because they know that Elijah did come, not to sit in a vacant chair at some Jewish feast of the Passover, but to the Kirtland Temple on April 3, 1836, to Joseph Smith and Oliver Cowdery. The temple in Jerusalem will be built by The Church of Jesus Christ of Latter-day Saints. 'They that are far off,' they that come from an American Zion, they who have a temple in Salt Lake City will come to Jerusalem to build there another holy house in the Jerusalem portion of 'the mountains of the Lord's house.' (D&C 133:13.)" (*Millennial Messiah*, 279–80).

Zechariah 7

Certain commemorative fasts that had been observed—not with wholeness of heart, and not with commensurate righteous actions—were deemed unnecessary. Fasting as part of true worship, following guidelines from the Lord and his prophets, was proper (see further in commentary at Isaiah 58). Even more important is to be just, merciful, compassionate, assisting the widows, the fatherless, the poor, and in doing good all the days of our lives.

Zechariah 8

The prophet received a series of ten declarations from the Lord, each introduced by "Thus saith the Lord." A word-picture is painted of prosperity and peace for the inhabitants of Jerusalem, the holy mountain of the Lord, in both the immediate and distant future. Verses 4–5 portray the security in the city, evidenced by old men and women walking the streets and young boys and girls playing in the streets. "I will save my people" (v. 7) has double meaning. The Lord would (and did) deliver his people from exile, bondage, and dispersion. But the Lord would (and did) save his people from the greatest calamities of sin, suffering, sorrow, and death.

"They shall be my people, and I will be their God, in truth and in righteousness" (v. 8) is the Lord's constant desire. But it has not yet been achieved in the modern nation of Israel, since it is by and large a secular state, with many of its people professing no religiosity at all. When they are obedient to the God of their land, He says "so will I save you, and ye shall be a blessing: fear not . . . be strong" (v. 13).

Even now many people (pilgrims and tourists) from the nations of the earth come to seek the Lord and pray before him in Jerusalem, but in the future many more will come as they hear that "God is with you" (vv. 22–23).

Zechariah 9

Verses 1–8: A burden of destruction is pronounced on Syria, Lebanon/Phoenicia, and Philistia. This description of the Lord's destruction of Israel's traditional enemies is probably to be taken symbolically to point us to his eternal power to subdue all enemies under his feet (see D&C 58:22; see also commentary at Amos 5:1–27).

Verses 9–17: Zechariah pointedly predicted the first coming of the Messiah, with his triumphal entry into Jerusalem (compare verse 9 with Matthew 21:4–5 and John 12:14–15). He also prophesied that the blood of the covenant, the Savior's atoning sacrifice, will liberate the dead from spirit prison (v. 11 and footnotes).

Zechariah 10

The Lord will always care for his people. He will give rain when asked in righteousness (he controls the elements). Because of false shepherds, the Lord had to punish "the goats" of Israel for a time in exile, but the remnant of Judah had returned (see commentary at Isaiah 7:3; Isaiah 7:21–25; Isaiah 9). Out of Judah would come the Cornerstone, even He of the "nail" in a sure place (v. 4 and footnotes; see also Isaiah 22:23). These are two of the Messiah's name-titles.

Verses 6–12 focus on the missions of Judah and Joseph in the last days, when they will be strengthened, saved, and restored. Ephraim, Joseph's birthright son, had been scattered among the people for the Lord's purposes, but eventually they will be gathered out of "Egypt" and "Assyria" and established in their lands of inheritance.

Zechariah 11

In figurative language employing images of nature, the Lord speaks of Judah's leaders and future events. In verses 3–6 Zechariah indicates that the Jewish people's own shepherds will sell them as slaves to outsiders. This prophetic description was again fulfilled in A.D. 70 when the Romans destroyed the Jewish nation, Jerusalem, and the Temple, and took a remnant of the Jewish people to other parts of the Roman empire in fetters as slaves.

In verses 7–9 Zechariah puts himself in the place of a shepherd, a type or foreshadowing of the messianic Shepherd to come. The Good Shepherd will remove all unfit leaders, represented by "three shepherds" in verse 8. At a certain point, the Good

Shepherd will withdraw his attentive watch-care, and individuals (in Judah) will eat one another's flesh (v. 9). This was actually fulfilled again in A.D. 70 when some turned to cannibalism during the Roman siege of Jerusalem, according to the first-century historian, Josephus. See also Lamentations 4:10 which describes the horrors of the Babylonian siege of Jerusalem.

In the middle of a prophecy regarding some "bad shepherds" Zechariah inserts a prophecy identified by New Testament writers as a reference to the exact amount of money, the price of a slave, received by Judas Iscariot to betray his Master (see vv. 12–13, with footnotes and cross-references). The word "potter" that appears twice in verse 13 in Hebrew is actually the word "treasury," which is apparently the very place Judas had cast those thirty pieces of silver in the Temple. Zechariah must have envisioned that tragic scene.

Zechariah 12–14

These three chapters contain valuable details about the rise of Jerusalem in the last days, the Battle of Armageddon and associated events, and the Second Coming. They should be read in connection with Ezekiel 38–39. Read carefully the sequence of events, along with the commentary.

Zechariah 12

As foreseen by ancient prophets and attested by the Lord and his latter-day prophets, "Jerusalem shall be inhabited again in her own place, even in Jerusalem" (v. 6), and the Jews, children of Judah, would play a key role in accomplishing the rebuilding of the Holy City. In 1832, more than half a century before the World Zionist Congresses convened, the Lord taught Joseph Smith that "in the last days, at the time of the restoration" Jews will have "gathered and . . . built the city of Jerusalem in the land of their fathers" (D&C 77:15), and in 1836 the Prophet Joseph Smith included the following words in his dedicatory prayer of the Kirtland Temple in Ohio: "have mercy upon the children of Jacob, that Jerusalem, from this hour, may begin to be redeemed . . . and the children of Judah may begin to return to the lands which thou didst give to Abraham, their father" (D&C 109:62, 64). Elder Orson Hyde made one of the longest, most perilous journeys in modern Church history to the land of Palestine in 1841 and dedicated that ancient land "for the gathering together of Judah's scattered remnants, according to the predictions of the holy Prophets—for the building up of Jerusalem again after it has been trodden down by the Gentiles so long, and for rearing a Temple in honor of Thy name" (Smith, *History of the Church*, 4:456). In 1843 the Prophet Joseph Smith prophesied of the last days and the second coming of the Messiah in these remarkable words: "Judah must return, Jerusalem must be rebuilt, and the temple. . . . It will take some time to rebuild the walls of the city and the temple, etc.; and all this must be done before the Son of Man will make His appearance" (*History of the Church*, 5:337). Then in 1845 Brigham Young and the Quorum of the Twelve Apostles issued a proclamation to the world wherein they boldly testified "that the Jews among all nations are hereby commanded, in the name of the Messiah, to prepare, to return to Jerusalem in Palestine; and to rebuild that city and temple unto the Lord: And also to organize and establish their own political government, under their own rulers, judges, and governors in that country" (Clark, *Messages of the First Presidency*, 1:254; see also Galbraith, Ogden, and Skinner, *Jerusalem*, 349–64).

It is one of the miracles of modern history that the city of Jerusalem—though hanging by a thread of local inhabitants through long centuries of violent political upheavals and changes of cultures and politics—has revived and flourished into a great and influential city looking toward the glories of the Millennium. Are not verses 2–3 an accurate description of the status of Jerusalem in our day? Through the latter half of the twentieth century and the early part of the twenty-first century, has Jerusalem not become a "cup of trembling" and "a burdensome stone for all people"? And the Lord does not seem to be concerned about the odds: "though all the people of the earth be gathered together against it," he will defend the city where anciently he chose to put his name. For the sake of the oath and covenant he made with his people, he will protect and preserve Jerusalem. The holy city will not be captured and destroyed, as has been its frequent fate in the past, but any attackers will be annihilated:

"And it shall come to pass in that day, that I will seek to

destroy all the nations that come against Jerusalem" (v. 9). Though this verse has in mind all the wars of the latter days that have or will involve Jerusalem, it especially applies to the last great battle at the end of mortal history—Armageddon.

Verse 10 of chapter 12 and verse 6 of chapter 13 combine to present one of the most poignant scenes in all of history, which will occur at the Second Coming: "the house of David" and "the inhabitants of Jerusalem" will "look upon me whom they have pierced, and they shall mourn." "And one shall say . . . What are these wounds in thine hands? Then shall he answer, Those with which I was wounded in the house of my friends." Can there be any mistaking who is spoken of in these verses? This will be a moving meeting between the martyred Redeemer, the one "pierced" and "wounded" and "the house of [his] friends," his own people, the Jews. Read Doctrine and Covenants 45:51–53 for further definition and description of who is involved in this emotional encounter.

Zechariah 13

"In that day there shall be a fountain [a baptismal place] opened to the house of David and to the inhabitants of Jerusalem for sin and for uncleanness" (v. 1). That is to say, after the final battle of Armageddon is finished, and the Savior has appeared, Jews will be convinced and converted to Righteousness (a name-title of Jesus Christ), and a place of true immersion will be available for washing away sin and uncleanness. Mistaken faith and modern idolatry will diminish, but some people will still reject the true prophets and prophecy, and understandably so, for many false prophets will be "ashamed" to acknowledge their failure to know the truth and deny their own priestcraft.

For a fulfillment of the prophecy in verse 7 about the sheep being scattered (during the arrest, trials, and crucifixion of Jesus), see Matthew 26:31.

"The third part" who are spared destruction during the great Battle of Armageddon will be refined as silver and tried as gold and will seek the Lord (for further insight into the process of being purified through the "refiner's fire" see commentary at Isaiah 48:10).

Zechariah 14

"I will gather all nations against Jerusalem to battle," in the conflict called Armageddon, which will likely be fought on many fronts but which centers, as usual throughout history, at Jerusalem. As the wealth of the world is spent for weapons of war, the Jews will make their defensive stand at Jerusalem (vv. 2, 14).

The Lord will get personally involved in the battle, and as his feet touch onto the Mount of Olives (D&C 45:47–53 and 133:20), a major earthquake will strike the city and the mount will divide—part northward and part southward, leaving a great east-west valley; and the Lord God will come with "all the saints" (Hebrew, *k'doshim,* "holy ones"). Living waters will flow out from Jerusalem east and west, toward the "former sea" (Dead Sea) and toward the "hinder sea" (Mediterranean Sea). Compare Ezekiel's vision of water coming out of the Temple and healing the Dead Sea (see commentary at Ezekiel 47:1–10). Then the Lord, "whose right it is" (Genesis 49:10*c;* Ezekiel 21:27; D&C 58:22), will reign as King over all the earth. All earthly potentates will give way to the King of kings, and the grand acclamation will be fulfilled: "The kingdoms of this world are become the kingdom of our Lord, and of his Christ; and he shall reign for ever and ever" (JST Revelation 11:15).

At that point, finally, "Jerusalem shall be safely inhabited" (v. 11). Compare the fate of the persecutors of Jerusalem spoken of in verse 12 with Doctrine and Covenants 29:18–19. It almost sounds like the effects of atomic fallout and radiation.

At long last, there will be a holy people in the Holy City, in the Holy Land, epitomized by the fact that even the bells on horses and the pots in the House of the Lord will be sacred in that day. "And they also of the tribe of Judah, after their pain, shall be sanctified in holiness before the Lord, to dwell in his presence day and night, forever and ever" (D&C 133:35).

"There shall be no more the Canaanite" (v. 21) is a metaphorical way of saying that in that future day, there will be no more unconsecrated people, for all who remain will have had the opportunity to become true members of the Lord's kingdom.

ESTHER

It is not known who wrote the book of Esther, but the author was an advocate of the Jewish people and Jewish nationalism during the Persian period of their history, and it seems likely that the book was composed during that period.

The book of Esther has been the subject of much criticism as well as much commendation. There are more differing versions of it, more Targums (Aramaic translations) of it, and more midrashes (rabbinic expositions) on it than on any other book in the Bible. Yet it is the only Old Testament book not found among the Dead Sea Scrolls—likely because it is the only biblical book that does not mention God (though with the doctrine of fasting and the hints of prayer found therein, understanding of God's involvement among humankind seems to be implied).

Chapter 1 gives the background and sets the stage for Esther's great opportunity. Chapter 2 tells how she actually became a queen in Persia and how her guardian also gained favorable status. Chapter 3 introduces Haman, the villain, and the plot moves toward a crisis. Queen Esther faces a quandary and rises to meet the challenge in chapter 4. The narrative then becomes more complicated as Esther's plan and Haman's plot progress simultaneously; Esther makes her move in time (chapters 5 and 6). Finally, in chapter 7, the villain Haman is destroyed. Chapters 8–10 show how the Jews gained a victory over those who would have destroyed them. According to tradition, this is how the festival of Purim (literally, "lots") originated.

Thus, the author's main purpose is to describe the origins of the festival of Purim and its relation to the survival of the Jewish people in Persia. Esther 9:17–22 suggests that the festival was already being observed by the time the book was written. Some authorities believe that it may have been composed shortly before Ezra returned to Jerusalem in 458 B.C. and also before the Persian Empire was conquered by Greece in 331 B.C.

Whatever its date of composition, it presents powerful lessons for the Lord's covenant people in modern times. One righteous person can make a difference in a wicked world, or against overwhelming odds. Each of us in the latter days must take seriously the principle embedded in the profound question: "who knoweth [but what] thou art come to the kingdom for such a time as this?" (Esther 4:14). Fasting for others does make a difference. And we must do all we can to further the Lord's purposes and then trust in God—even if we perish in the attempt (4:16).

Esther 1:1–9

At the very beginning of this story, King Ahasuerus is introduced, with all the pomp and circumstances of his reign and all the royal luxury of his feasts and receptions. His royal court was located at Shushan (Susa), 150 miles north of the Persian Gulf. His name is an English transliteration of the Hebrew version of the Persian name; to try to transliterate the Persian directly into English would yield something like *Khshayarsha*, while the English transcription of the Greek version of the name is Xerxes. According to the Persian king lists, this would have been Xerxes I, the son of Darius (d. 486 B.C.), who reigned from 486 to 465 B.C. (see Bible Appendix, "Chronology"). King Darius had given his empire, and the Jews within it, an era of peace and relative stability. But he was defeated by the Greeks at the battle of Marathon (490 B.C.). His son Xerxes then waged a series of exhaustive battles of revenge in which he was defeated at Salamis (480 B.C.), and Plataea (479 B.C.), and inaugurated a slow but steady decline of Persia. In the book of Esther he appears to be a vain egotist, showing off "the riches of his glorious kingdom" for one hundred and eighty days, culminating in a royal feast.

Esther 1:10–22

Queen Vashti had her own standards and declined to obey the wishes of the king, who was "merry with wine" and wanted to parade her beauty before the royal guests. A crisis ensued, for the other royal husbands saw in her action a bad example and harmful precedent that might lead to a rebellion of all wives against their lords—and would surely lead to much contempt and wrath. They insisted that Vashti be punished. Accordingly, every province of the empire received the proclamation that Vashti was banished and all wives were to be obedient to their husbands—"great and small."

Esther 2:1–7

Though the text says that when the anger of the king "was appeased" (v. 1), it is probably really saying, "when he sobered up." Such are the consequences of drunkenness. Because of the resultant vacancy, a contest was instituted to find a replacement. Mordecai is introduced in the story, along with his cousin and ward, Esther. Esther's Hebrew name is *Hadassah,* meaning "myrtle," which is a hardy ground cover plant that bears a five-petal blossom like a little blue star. *Esther* is in turn derived from a Persian word for "star." An eminent international Jewish women's organization for compassionate service is called Hadassah, whose influential good works include the operation of Jerusalem's Hadassah Hospital.

Mordecai, Esther's guardian after her parents' death, was apparently a great-grandson of a man taken into Babylonian captivity from Judah over a century before, in the time of Judah's king Jehoiachin (or Jeconiah). These people and their compatriots were among the Jewish people who had not returned to Judah in the days of Zerubbabel.

It is historically true that a large segment of Jewish populace continued to inhabit this former Babylonian area for many centuries after this period. That these were not very religious Jewish people has been suggested, but this assertion is hardly justifiable, in spite of the lack of specific mention of God in the book of Esther. Indeed, very important religious contributions came from the Jewish communities of "Babylon" for many centuries, including the Babylonian Talmud.

Esther 2:8–20

Esther won the contest and became queen. All of this took place apparently right after Xerxes's defeat by the Greeks, in the battle of Plataea in 479 B.C.

Mordecai kept vigil outside the courtyard to try to make sure that all continued to be well with her. It is mentioned from time to time that Mordecai's and Esther's Jewish identity was kept secret.

Esther 2:21–23

It is very plausible that a plot against the king could arise in his own household and be discovered and exposed by one standing by, as Mordecai does. This sort of thing has happened hundreds of times in as many kingdoms. The deed redounds to Mordecai's benefit later in the story.

Esther 3

Enter Haman, the villain. When Haman became chief courtier, or prime minister of the empire, there was not necessarily anything personal in Mordecai's refusal to bow to him; bowing down to anyone or anything was a worshipful act and was generally forbidden by the first two of the Ten Commandments. Haman's rage, however, knew no bounds; he was ready to pay ten thousand talents—equivalent to millions of dollars—for a license to destroy "a certain people," namely, all the Jews. As verse 9 implies, part of Haman's plan included the confiscation of the wealth of the Jews. Such programs have often been part of official governmental plans to persecute Jews at various times in history. It is amazing that the king approved such a vast and clandestine project without inquiry as to its victims. The doom of all Jews throughout all the provinces, presumably even in the land of Judah, was set for the thirteenth of Adar. The fact that the lot fell in the future allowed time to prepare. Apparently the "casting of lots" spoken of was a process of determining which day would be most propitious for the success of Haman's project. Many ancient cultures had "lucky days" and "unlucky days," and it was considered important to choose the right day for any proposed activity. The word *Pur*, borrowed perhaps from the Assyrian language with the meaning "lot," explains the origin of the name and festival of Purim.

Esther 4

The Jewish people of the empire suffered deep shock when the terrible news was spread. A double burden fell upon Esther: first the saddening news of the proclamation of death for her people; then the challenge to risk death herself to try to avert the general calamity.

One of the hints of religiousness in the major characters of this story is given in Mordecai's meaningful statement to Esther, "who knoweth whether thou art come to the kingdom for such a time as this?" (v. 14). An overseeing providence and a purpose are implied, even though God is not explicitly mentioned in the story.

There is also evidence of the religious background of these people in their fasting on Esther's behalf for three days. Certainly Esther's moral courage is evident in her resignation to her fate and her willingness to sacrifice herself, if necessary, for her people, saying "if I perish, I perish" (v. 16). The historian Josephus wrote that Esther made supplication to God after the manner of her people. We may conclude that she exhibited great faith in a time of great jeopardy.

Esther 5

Esther took advantage of her first reception with the king to enhance her good standing with him and bring about a strategic announcement of her request. Notice her approach, step by step: she fasted and prayed; she dressed nicely; she didn't criticize, fight, dictate, or cry; she invited the king to dinner; she served him; she let *him* make the decision. She meant to further her cause by including Haman in the invitation to a *second* banquet.

The writer of this account portrayed well the sequence of episodes leading to the climax. Someone reading this narrative for the first time may begin to suspect at this point that Haman's vainglorious enjoyment of his status, coupled with his anticipation and preparation for gratification of his anger and greed, may ironically return evil upon his own head. And note the exorbitant height of the gallows—seventy-five feet!

Esther 6

With a talent for telling the little details that make the story come alive, the author relates how the king called for the records. He had someone read to him because he could not sleep (sleeplessness as a result of the united fast?); the servant happened to read of Mordecai's lifesaving service to the king, rendered at the time of the plot on the king's life.

It was also ironic that the king asked Haman for a suggestion as to how to honor a certain deserving man. Haman didn't know it was Mordecai for whom he was suggesting honors; he had actually come to get permission to hang Mordecai.

And so Haman, who had hoped to bring honor to himself and hang Mordecai, had the frustration and humiliation of honoring Mordecai instead. Haman's own wife had ominously predicted that a dire fate would befall him if his opponent was "of the seed of the Jews." Incidentally, the Septuagint adds at the end of verse 13, "for the living God is with him."

Esther 7

Then came the crisis: the second banquet was held and the queen announced her request for her life and the life of her people. The king can scarcely contain himself when he realizes what Haman's request had entailed (recall what had been asked and granted, in 3:4–11). Haman inadvertently added insult to injury when he stood to ask the queen for mercy. He appears to have intended to assault her, and there was no chance for mercy left for him.

Esther 8

The task of saving the rest of the Jews after Esther and Mordecai had been saved and elevated in the realm was complicated, because any edict which had been issued in the king's name could not be revoked. Esther and Mordecai had to devise a way to give the Jews authority to defend their lives against those who would try to obey that first edict of death on the thirteenth day of Adar.

Note the phenomenon regarding the "conversion" of many people to Judaism as they saw the growing power of the Jews in the realm (v. 17; see also 9:27).

Esther 9:1–16

The carnage that ensued was not, as some commentators have said, a show of bloodthirsty vengeance by the Jews. Under the circumstances it was the result of an inevitable conflict; some who were sympathetic with Haman and antagonistic to the Jews would follow the first edict; on the other hand, those among the officers, deputies, etc., who knew of the vindicating order and of the trend to favor the Jews, would fight in their behalf.

The slaughter was terrible everywhere, even in the palace; it was complete in the house of Haman. His ten sons were hanged on the gallows. They apparently shared guilt with their father. The word "prey" in verse 16 should be understood to mean "spoil" as in verse 10.

Esther 9:17–32

According to this story, the festival of Purim originated with the change of the day when the "lot" had determined the destruction of the Jews to a day of salvation and joy—with an additional day allowed to make the elimination of enemies complete and the rest from fear and strife secure.

Esther 10

The account ends with a brief summation concerning the relationship of Mordecai to the king and the people.

ESTHER: A TYPE OF CHRIST

After a search throughout the whole kingdom, Esther was chosen as queen to replace Vashti. Her beauty was unsurpassed, and she won the favor of everyone, including King Ahasuerus (Esther 2:2–18). But Esther had a secret. She had not told anyone in the government that she was Jewish and the adopted daughter of Mordecai, an older cousin who had raised her after her parents died (Esther 2:20).

This set the stage for the coming crisis, for against righteous Esther and Mordecai was Haman, one of the nobles of the realm who had been elevated by the king to the position of chief minister (Esther 3:1). It is not hard to see in Haman a symbolic representation of Satan. All who passed by Haman bowed to him and did obeisance because of his high position—all except Mordecai. He refused because, as he said, he was a Jew (Esther 3:2–4). Such deference to government leaders was not forbidden by Jewish law, but nonbiblical texts suggest a detail omitted in the biblical record: "Haman claimed divine honors for himself" (*Interpreter's Bible,* 3:848). From this point on, Haman was filled with wrath (again, a representation of Satan) and "sought to destroy all the Jews that were throughout the whole kingdom of Ahasuerus, even the people of Mordecai" (Esther 3:6).

Haman anticipated the most propitious day to propose to the king a pogrom, or systematic destruction of the Jews. Haman had an official decree drawn up and issued to the provincial governors to "destroy, to kill, and to cause to perish, all Jews, both young and old, little children and women, in one day," and take the spoils of the people (Esther 3:13). Again, we can see the parallel with the adversary, who makes war with the Saints of God to destroy them and encompasses them round about (D&C 76:29). Then "the king and Haman sat down to drink; but the city Shushan was perplexed" (Esther 3:15), meaning that the capital city was thrown into consternation over the ominous decree. These were dark days indeed.

When Mordecai learned all that had been done, he tore his clothing, put on sackcloth and ashes, and mourned with the Jews. More important, Mordecai sent a request to queen Esther, asking her to go to the king and make supplication on behalf of the Jewish people, entreating him to reverse the decree of destruction. Esther was to act as a mediator and savior. Esther responded by reminding Mordecai that, by law, anyone who appeared before the king without invitation could be put to death—and she had not been called to attend the king for thirty days. Mordecai wisely counseled Esther that just because she was in the palace did not mean she would escape the fate of all the other Jews of the realm (Esther 4:4–13). In fact, if she kept silent, said Mordecai, relief and deliverance would surely arise from another quarter. But just maybe, by refusing to act, Esther would be missing out on her foreordained mission. Perhaps Esther herself had been raised up by God for precisely that very moment, for the specific purpose of bringing deliverance to an entire people.

In that comment is the great lesson that applies to each one of us at our particular moment in the history of the kingdom of God. Each of us must seriously consider Mordecai's question: "And who knoweth whether thou art come to the kingdom for such a time as this?" (Esther 4:14).

Esther answered Mordecai in true heroic fashion, in a way that bespoke her great spiritual maturity, power, and faith that are her legacy: "Go, gather together all the Jews that are present in Shushan, and fast ye for me, and neither eat nor drink three days, night or day: I also and my maidens will fast likewise; and so will I go in unto the king, which is not according to the law: and if I perish, I perish" (Esther 4:16).

Her statement reflects the same ultimate commitment to follow God's will that Jesus possessed and uttered in his gravest hour of peril and challenge (see Matthew 26:39; Mark 14:36; Luke 22:42; D&C 19:18–19). Her response foreshadowed and prefigured the Savior's attitude and actions by several hundred years.

Because of Esther, an entire people were delivered from destruction. Because of Esther, mercy was instituted and justice accomplished. Because of Esther, the despised became the honored. Because of Esther, the will of God was accomplished. In all of these things, Esther acted as the anointed of the Lord and acted as *the* Anointed One acted almost five hundred years later. Esther's accomplishment mirrored the effects of the Atonement, whose saving and redeeming consequences are both temporal and eternal. What has been said of Esther is, in reality, the most significant truth about Jesus: Esther's elevation became the only hope for an imperiled people. Indeed, Jesus Christ is our only hope and our only deliverance.

Esther is still honored today. The deliverance of the Jewish people resulting from Esther's saving actions is celebrated every year during the festival of Purim. According to the Bible, this holiday derives its name from the non-Hebrew word for the "lots" (*purim*) that were cast by Haman to determine the destruction of the Jewish people (Esther 9:24–27). More than that, Esther's Hebrew name, Hadassah (Esther 2:7), has been given to Jewish relief agencies and hospitals around the world whose purpose is to relieve and rescue those in need.

EZRA

The earliest manuscripts of the Hebrew Bible (what we call the Old Testament) combined Ezra and Nehemiah and treated them as one book. The oldest manuscripts of the Septuagint did as well. Josephus and the Talmud speak of Ezra but not of a separate composition called Nehemiah. The early church father Origen (ca. A.D. 185–253) was the first writer to treat them as separate books.

The book of Ezra may be dated to around 440 B.C. Ezra was a priest and scribe living among the exiles in the former territory of Babylon who had not returned to the Holy Land. In 458 B.C. he received permission from the Persian government to return to Jerusalem, lead any exiles who chose to accompany him, bestow upon the Jews there certain rights and privileges, and "teach in Israel statutes and judgments" (Ezra 7:10). He was also commissioned to appoint magistrates and judges.

The first six chapters of Ezra preserve the history of events some eighty years prior to Ezra's return and include a list of the first mass exodus from Babylon back to the land of Judah. Chapters 7–10 relate to Ezra's own time.

Ezra 1–2 records the edict of Cyrus permitting the return and the response of some Jews in what had been Babylon. Some who didn't want to go back contributed to help those who did. Ezra 3–4 tells how those who returned gathered in their desolated former homeland and began work. Neighboring Samaritans offered help, but upon being rebuffed by the Jews (because they were, from the biblical point of view, just another group of apostate pagans), they began to harass and impair the work instead. Chapters 5–6 indicate that the prophets Haggai and Zechariah urged the resumption of Temple construction. Samaritan opposition resulted in a search of royal Persian records, and the former enabling edict was confirmed. The work was resumed; it was finished on the third of Adar, 515 B.C., which was, as prophesied, seventy years after the Babylonians destroyed Solomon's Temple. According to chapters 7–8, Ezra was commissioned some years later to go up to Jerusalem. He led a company there and conducted a vigorous reform in the marriage practices of the people (Ezra 9–10). His Hebrew name means "help," which indeed he was.

Ezra 1:1–4 (2 Chronicles 36:22–23)

This account is an immediate continuation of 2 Chronicles 36:22–23. Some scholars believe that the author/compiler of Ezra was also the author of 1 and 2 Chronicles. The edict of Cyrus permitting exiles to return fulfilled the prophecy of Jeremiah and also prophecies of Isaiah (Jeremiah 25:11–12; 29:10; Isaiah 44:28; 45:1–4; 13–14). The date is the first year Cyrus ruled over former Babylon, 538 B.C. Josephus wrote that when Cyrus read Isaiah's prophecies "and admired the divine power, an earnest desire and ambition seized upon him to fulfil what was so written" (*Antiquities of the Jews*, bk. 11, chap. 1, paras. 1–2; see commentary at Isaiah 45:1).

Cyrus's edict of liberation is preserved in the book of Ezra in two versions. One (Ezra 1:2–4) is written in Hebrew, the ancient language of Israel and Judah. The other version (Ezra 6:3–5) is written in Aramaic, the diplomatic language of the Persian Empire, which gradually became the common tongue of the Jewish people during the post-Exilic period.

Ezra 1:5–11

Some of the Jewish leaders and people responded favorably to return, and many gifts were brought forward by others who preferred to stay in Persian-ruled Babylon. The Persian government returned the sacred vessels of the Jerusalem Temple. The "prince of Judah," called Sheshbazzar here, is generally considered to be "Zerubbabel" later; compare references to him and his work in 3:8 and 5:16.

Ezra 2

The census of the various groups who returned from exile is not quite the same as the totals found in Nehemiah 7:7–73, or in the apocryphal work 1 Esdras 5:7ff. Such numerical differences are common in ancient documents, and are difficult to resolve. The totals were 42,360 people; 7,337 servants; and 200 singers (Ezra 2:64–65). Probably the majority did not return from their lands of exile.

The "province" mentioned in verse 1 is Judah; it is translated in 5:6 as "district" from Aramaic. Jeshua, in verse 2 is the Aramaic form of Joshua and means, "the Lord saves." The names in verses 3–20 are families. But in verses 21–35 the names are a series of villages and towns. The "children of Bethlehem" (v. 21) may well have been the ancestors of Jesus. Four clans of priests returned, some 4,289, representing one-tenth of the returnees. The "porters," literally "gatekeepers," are mentioned sixteen times in Ezra and Nehemiah and nineteen times in Chronicles. Their primary function was to tend the doors and gates of the Temple (1 Chronicles 9:17–27). It seems natural that Ezra, being himself a priest, would be highly interested in those associated with the rebuilt Temple.

Ezra 3

Under the leadership of Jeshua, the Levitical high priest, and Zerubbabel, the prince and governor, reconstruction began. They started with the very heart of Israel's religious facilities, the altar, on the site where the Temple formerly had stood. It was made ready for the sacrifices of the week of Sukkot (Feast of Tabernacles) and for other high holy days in the seventh month of the ritual year.

The situation of the returnees was precarious. The people who lived around them were always potential opponents and sometimes active adversaries. Though the foundation of the Temple had not been laid, contributions were begun, and contracts were once more made with the men of craft and commerce in Tyre and Sidon, whose predecessors had supplied craftsmen and materials for Solomon's Temple.

After the foundations of the Temple had been laid, the people

440

rejoiced. However, the voices raised in the celebration were mixed; some rejoiced in the renewal, but many of the very old priests and Levites who remembered the First Temple lamented still the loss of the glorious House of the Lord that had been there before. However, Haggai had prophesied that the people should be strong and take courage—for the Lord would shake the nations and the glory of this latter house would outshine the former (Haggai 2:4–9). Levites and priests were organized in an orderly fashion for work and for worship.

Ezra 4:1–6

The mixed peoples of Samaria, who were by now called Samaritans, were descendants of Assyrian colonists who had replaced the people of the ten tribes and had intermixed with a few remnants of Israel. These mixed peoples wanted to help build the Temple of the Lord (recall their "faith" in 2 Kings 17:33). When the people of Judah rebuffed them, they turned against the Judahites and harassed them all the days of Cyrus, Ahasuerus, Artaxerxes, and Darius I. In spite of this opposition, the Jews found ways to continue the work intermittently (see Bible Appendix, "Chronology").

Ezra 4:7–24

As the foundations of the city and its walls continued to be reconstructed, the opposing forces suggested to the Persian government that they peruse the records of Jerusalem's stormy history to see what a troublemaker that city had been for empires of the past. When the review was concluded, a restraining order was issued. The Temple building would not be resumed for fifteen years.

Incidentally, Ezra 4:8 to 6:18 are in the Aramaic language in the Masoretic Text, with Hebrew before and after this segment. It is not really known why. Other Aramaic texts are Genesis 31:47; Jeremiah 10:11; and Daniel 2:4b–7:28.

Ezra 5

After the reign of Cyrus's son, Cambyses II (529–521 B.C.), Darius (also called Hystaspes and Darius the Great) took control of the empire. He reigned from 522 to 486 B.C.

Chapters 5–6 record that during Darius's administration, the

Second Temple was completed and dedicated under the direction of Zerubbabel, the governor, and with the encouragement of two prophets in the streets of Jerusalem, Haggai and Zechariah.

A letter described the Temple construction and the Jews' reasons for it. The letter invited a search to determine if Cyrus had really ordered it.

Ezra 6

When the record of Cyrus's decree was found, and the Jews' claims were verified, certain Persian officials must have rued their attempt to interfere in the projects of Judah. When the decree of Cyrus was found, Darius honored and implemented it, giving orders to help and not hinder the project to completion.

With the help of those who would otherwise have hindered, and with the added impetus given by the prophets (mentioned again in verse 14), the Temple was completed, and a feast of dedication was celebrated. It is traditionally dated the third of Adar, in the sixth year of Darius I, or 515 B.C.

Since Adar is the last month of the religious year, the celebration of the Passover and the Feast of the Unleavened Bread followed soon after the dedication, from the fourteenth to the twenty-first of Aviv.

Ezra 7

Almost sixty years later, about 458 B.C., Ezra himself entered the scene. He was the descendant ("son") of Seraiah, who died at the capture of Jerusalem (some 130 years before), as told in 2 Kings 25:18–21. He was further genealogically identified as a descendant of Zadok and of Aaron and was a priest as well as an able scribe. Zadok was one of two high priests during the later reign of King Saul and the reign of King David. He remained faithful to David after the rebellion of Adonijah (1 Kings 1:8, 26).

Ezra's purposes were admirable: "For Ezra had prepared his heart to seek the law of the Lord, and to do it, and to teach in Israel statutes and judgments" (v. 10). Nehemiah 8:5, 8 adds a third task to Ezra's outlined work: to interpret and apply the law. Ezra served as a model for future scribes in Judaism, who believed that their threefold task was the same as that of Ezra, the "ready scribe." Thus, their task also included (1) to seek or study and understand the Lord's law as found in scripture, (2) to teach the law of the Lord, and (3) to interpret and apply the law to the peoples' situations. The rabbis from 200 B.C. to A.D. 100 traced the development of their responsibilities directly to Ezra.

Artaxerxes I reigned from 465 to 424 B.C., and during his reign both Ezra and Nehemiah received appointments from the Persian government to carry out religious and political tasks in Yehud (as the Persians called Judah). The prophet Malachi also ministered during this period.

Ezra initiated more mass migrations of Jews back to their homeland. Numerous Jews joined the perilous caravans to help restore the dignity of their former land and society. Though tens of thousands returned, still many of the wealthy and influential Jews remained in Babylon. Jewish communities and academies flourished there for centuries, and accumulated, among other things, the voluminous legacy of the Babylonian Talmud, with its seemingly endless treatment of rabbinic legal and religious polemics and formulations.

The remarkably generous commission of Ezra from Artaxerxes gave him sizeable contributions and assistance, as well as significant authority to organize the priestly teachers and judges of the land, and to demand fidelity to the law. Ezra thanked the Lord and gathered up a company to go up to Jerusalem.

Ezra 8

This is a census of those who went with Ezra. Aware of the need of services of the Levites, Ezra recruited some of them also, as well as descendants of the old Temple servants, called "Nethinim."

Ezra's faith in God's providence and his testimony to the king about the power of the Lord God made it inappropriate for him to ask for protection by the Persian arm of flesh; therefore he called his group to fast and pray before they set out on the fifteen-hundred-mile journey. Then he organized the company and sanctified those who were to be responsible to take care of the treasures dedicated for the Temple. With everything prepared, they set out and traveled in safety.

They arrived, rested, weighed in the treasures (which they

had "weighed out" as they left the Babylonian area), delivered the king's messages, and in other ways promoted the welfare of the people and the house of God.

Ezra is characterized as a conscientious, firm but fair-minded, and effective leader in these accounts as well as in the later accounts in the book of Nehemiah.

Ezra 9

The news that some priests, leaders, and people had intermarried with some of the non-Israelite peoples of the land caused Ezra genuine concern—even shame. The principle that worried Ezra was that the laws of Moses could so soon again be broken; the lessons of history had not been heeded. This particular type of breach was a vital one, because intermarriage with other cultures led to neglect of, and apostasy from, Israel's religion. Tough measures were necessary at the beginning of these rigorous reforms. The Lord's purpose in calling a consecrated, covenant "seed" was, and is, to provide exemplars and messengers to the families of all nations, so that "all that will hear may hear" (D&C 1:11; Genesis 12:3; Abraham 2:9–11). Ezra's concerns about intermarriage in his day translate into a genuine concern over those who marry outside the Temple and, hence, outside the covenant in our day. The blessings of Temple marriage and family life within the Abrahamic covenant are incomparable (see the strong statements of latter-day leaders regarding marriage in the covenant in the commentary at Genesis 6:1–2).

Ezra's prayer had its proper effect upon his Israelite hearers: he recognized the grace and patience of God in contrast to the infidelity, carelessness, and rebelliousness of Israel.

Ezra 10

A spokesman for those who had transgressed the laws proposed that time be given them to repent and separate themselves according to the law. Ezra sponsored a pledge that they do so, and all agreed to it. Verses 18–44 present a roster of those of the priestly families who were guilty.

NEHEMIAH

The book of Nehemiah continues the account begun in the book of Ezra about the return of the Jews from Babylon. Nehemiah 1–7 tells how this Jewish cupbearer (a sort of minister or chamberlain) to Artaxerxes I was commissioned to go to Jerusalem, where he organized the people who had returned and began to rebuild the city walls. Nehemiah is not called a priest or a prophet; he served as a governor—apparently in the same capacity as Zerubbabel the previous century. Chapters 8–10 record an important event in biblical history: the gathering, reading, and discussing of the books of the Law before the people. It is possible that this was the beginning also of the oral translations (*Targums*) of the Bible into the Aramaic language, if they had not begun earlier in Babylon in the sixth century before Christ. Chapters 11 and 12:1–26 review the rosters of people who had returned to Jerusalem. The remainder of chapter 12 tells of the completion of the wall and of its dedication. Perpetual support for the priesthood was provided for. In chapter 13 we learn that after a period back in Persia, Nehemiah returned again to visit Jerusalem and complete his work. The name Nehemiah means "the Lord comforts," and indeed through the efforts of Nehemiah a new generation of returning exiles was comforted. He possessed the ability to motivate others to important activity (see Bible Dictionary, "Nehemiah").

Nehemiah 1

Here, in what seems to be Nehemiah's own personal memoirs, he is introduced as a Jew in Persia in a favored position, a cup-bearer to Artaxerxes (v. 11) in the twentieth year of his reign at Shushan (Susa), "in the palace." The year would be about 445 B.C. News had reached Nehemiah that his compatriots in Jerusalem and the provinces round about were living in poor conditions and that their protective walls and gates had been partly destroyed.

Nehemiah, who was evidently a good example of a righteous layman among the Jews, prayed that the Lord would forgive Israel's many failings and help them in Jerusalem; he asked also that he might be favored by Artaxerxes to be allowed to go to Jerusalem and help them. Fasting and praying became significant practices during the exile (compare verse 4 and Ezra 8:23).

Nehemiah is characterized as sensitive, spiritual, and humble. All through this period of history there is repeated evidence that Jews gained influence and authority in high places because they humbly sought the Lord's guidance (compare Ezra 7:10, 27; 8:21; Esther 4:16; Daniel 2:16–19, 20–23; 6:10; and 9:3–4). Nehemiah was a royal cupbearer (v. 11); that is, one who tested the king's food and drink to be sure it was not poisoned—a trusted official!

Nehemiah 2:1–10

More characterization of Nehemiah: he was an honest, genuine person, without guile or phoniness. When he presented himself before the king he was sad and couldn't hide it. Before turning to the king he uttered a short prayer "to the God of heaven" (2:4). His prayer was answered, and his petitions to Artaxerxes for permission to go to Jerusalem, and for authorization to supervise some reconstruction work there were granted. Later we will see that he was actually appointed to be governor of Judah (5:14).

Nehemiah 2:11–20

Nehemiah described his inspection of Jerusalem's walls at night. He included the names of various gates and landmarks known at the time. See the footnotes to verses 13 and 14. The king's pool is probably the Siloam Pool (see 3:15 and John 9:7). Nehemiah's ability to motivate others resulted in the beginning of efforts to rebuild the city's walls and gates. He also bore his testimony regarding God's help in his life.

Sanballat, a Babylonian name meaning "Sin [the moon deity] has given life," was governor of Samaria under Persian rule. His name is known in a letter from a Jewish community in Elephantine, Egypt, where he is explicitly called "the governor of Samaria" (see 4:2). He was the "chief political opponent in [Yehud, or Judah] of

Nehemiah's efforts . . . to rebuild the walls of postexilic Jerusalem
. . . The bitter opposition of Sanballat to Nehemiah's work was
based presumably on the threat to the control of Judah enjoyed by
Samaria to a greater or lesser degree ever since the fall of Jerusalem
in 586 B.C. to Babylon. Nehemiah's uncompromising refusal to let
his opponent's machinations deter him from his purpose to fortify
Jerusalem . . . is the measure of Nehemiah's own political ability"
(*Interpreter's Dictionary of the Bible*, 4:210).

Along with commendable foresight, Nehemiah certainly
showed capacity for strategy, for gaining cooperation, and for
meeting opposition. He was a practical but knowledgeable
administrator.

Nehemiah 3

This detailed chapter contains one of our most valuable physical descriptions of Old Testament Jerusalem. See any good Bible
atlas for a cartographic depiction of the Jerusalem of Nehemiah's
time; also Galbraith, Ogden, and Skinner, *Jerusalem*, 124–27.

After his inspection tour of the city walls (chapter 2), it appears that Nehemiah's system of parceling out portions of the
wall-building project to various leaders and their groups made for
orderly and rapid progress in the work. It was only fitting that
Eliashib, the high priest, and his fellow priests, should be among
the first to go to work and rebuild the Sheep Gate (perhaps an
entrance to the Temple complex), thus setting an example for
others to follow. Tekoa, residence of a group of workers (v. 5),
was also hometown of the prophet Amos. Portions of the Broad
Wall (v. 8) have been uncovered by archaeologists working in the
Jewish Quarter of Jerusalem's Old City (see photo in commentary
at 2 Kings 18:1–8).

Nehemiah 4

Neither the threatening, the scoffing, the plotting, nor the
suppressed rage of Sanballat and company in Samaria hindered
the work. Nehemiah countered with prayer, planned defenses, and
persistent encouragement which gained the people's respect and
support. Notice the means he used to rally and motivate them
in verse 14 (and compare Alma 46:12 and 58:12—sounds like
Nehemiah's "title of liberty").

This is practical religion: praying and setting a watch (vv. 9, 22), and working with one hand and holding a weapon in the other (v. 17). Compare the scene in Kirtland, Ohio, during the fall and winter of 1833–34, with mobs threatening to tear down the walls of the Temple, and men posted to protect the walls laid during the day: "'Our enemies were raging and threatening destruction upon us,' Heber C. Kimball declared. He added that for weeks some men did not remove their working clothes and slept with their rifles in their arms" (Backman, *Heavens Resound,* 155).

This sounds exactly like Nehemiah's circumstance: "So neither I, nor my brethren, nor my servants, nor the men of the guard which followed me, none of us put off our clothes" (Nehemiah 4:23).

Nehemiah 5

Nehemiah also had internal problems to solve. The common people had worked on the wall and sacrificed time and means for it, and because of the scarcity of goods had become debtors to the richer and more powerful and were thus getting into bondage. Nehemiah by word and example met and solved this problem satisfactorily. The prayers of Nehemiah, written by him as little "asides," give interesting reflections of his personality and spirit.

Again, verse 14 records the fact that Nehemiah was officially made governor of the Persian province of Yehud (Judah), the same position that Zerubbabel had occupied during the previous century. Although history shows that "it is the nature and disposition of almost all men, as soon as they get a little authority . . . they will immediately begin to exercise unrighteous dominion" (D&C 121:39), yet during Nehemiah's twelve-year administration (445–433 B.C.), he refused to overstep his prerogatives as ruler or to be a burden on the people by taxing them for his own sustenance. Instead, he labored with his people, a sign of noble humility. Compare King Benjamin three centuries later in the Book of Mormon (see Mosiah 2:14).

Nehemiah 6

The Samaritan, Ammonite, and Arab opposition mounted. Enemies tried to get rid of Nehemiah by calling him to negotiations in another part of the land (an assassination plot; v. 2), by false accusations (or "blackmail"; vv. 6–7), and by intimidation (v. 10). Notice Nehemiah's magnanimous replies in verses 3, 8, 11. He says, for example, "I am doing a great work, so that I cannot come down" (v. 3). Once again he shows himself a wise and spiritual man (see Uchtdorf, *Ensign,* May 2009, 61). Mainly because of their leader's determination, the people of Judah finished the important security wall around Jerusalem in just fifty-two days. Even their enemies were forced to admit God's hand was in its completion (v. 16).

Nehemiah 7

With the wall-building project complete, Nehemiah organized the inhabitants genealogically into the old patriarchal organization and set his own brother and a civil leader over the "watches" of the city, controlling the opening and closing of the gates (vv. 1–5).

In verses 6–60 the genealogical family-groups, the professional groups, and certain area-identified groups of returnees are all listed and tallied (compare Ezra 2). Some of the people and even some of the priests had difficulty in proving their lineage and were restricted from full privileges until a priest having the Urim and Thummim should arise (who could determine their worthiness). The "Tirshatha" herein mentioned would be the governor, apparently Nehemiah himself (recall 5:14, and see 8:9; 10:1). The word *Tirshatha* means something like "his Excellency."

On the uses of the Urim and Thummim by bearers of the Aaronic Priesthood in ancient times, see Topical Guide and Bible Dictionary, "Urim and Thummim"; see also Ogden and Skinner, *Book of Mormon,* 1:378–79.)

In verses 66–73, the totals of the immigrant groups, plus some of the major contributors to the building projects are listed. The Tirshatha (Nehemiah) was generous and exemplary.

Nehemiah 8:1–8

A grand assembly was once again called (as in Samuel's day) for the reading of the Law, as Moses had commanded they should do periodically. Ezra was the priestly leader.

Tradition says that Ezra gathered up all the sacred writings—the Torah, the Prophets, and the other writings. The Talmud even asserts that those books which were missing, he rewrote. Whether or not that is true, it is quite certain that this was a period of collection, standardization, and canonization of the great Hebrew scriptures, our Old Testament, that have come down to us.

This is also likely the time of the beginning of oral translation of the scriptures from the literary Hebrew into the common language of the people. For some it would have entailed paraphrasing the literature in the vernacular; for some it would have required translation into the spoken Aramaic that was becoming the *lingua franca* of the Near East at the time. This would be the beginning of the *Targums* (Hebrew, *Targumim,* "translations"). Oral portions of the Targumim were permitted; written portions were later permitted, and finally whole translations appear to have been sanctioned but not until the early centuries after Christ.

Nehemiah 8:9–18

The people heard the reading of the Law and the Prophets with mixed feelings. They mourned because of their past failings and transgressions, and yet they rejoiced that they might at last draw near to the Lord again.

The reading and interpreting continued for a week and a day, during the Feast of Tabernacles, or Sukkot. Apparently some of the ordinances and worship procedures began to be put into practice as they were relearned. They celebrated their own exodus from Babylon, as their ancestors' exodus from Egypt.

The people built booths on their own rooftops, in their own courtyards, and in the courtyard of the Temple, just as their forefathers had built tabernacles in the wilderness but with greater intensity and celebration—"for since the days of Jeshua [Joshua] the son of Nun unto that day had not the children of Israel done so. And there was very great gladness" (8:17). Sukkot, or Feast of Tabernacles, is still celebrated this way in certain quarters of the Jewish world.

Nehemiah 9

This chapter tells us that some of the ceremonial holy days were resumed. Most have been carried on ever since that time among the Jews. Yom Kippur and Sukkot occur in the same month, as does *Simkhat Torah,* which means "joy of the Torah."

Simkhat Torah seems to be the holy day referred to in these verses (see Bible Dictionary, "Fasts"; "Feasts").

On the twenty-fourth day, perhaps October 30, 445 B.C., a day of scripture reading, confession, repentance, and prayer was held—much like the purpose of the Day of Atonement as stipulated in the Law of Moses. All the Israelites gathered together, wearing sackcloth and having dust on their heads to signify humility. They stood while the Levites cried out with loud voices to praise God. Verses 6–36 constitute the public prayer they offered—much of it recounting the great deeds done by God for Israel, beginning with Abraham. After the public prayer, eighty-four leaders created a written binding agreement, a covenant, to live as God desired and their own history demanded. Coincidentally, the ninth chapters of Ezra, Nehemiah, and Daniel are all devoted to describing confessions of the nation's sinful behavior and petitions for God's forgiveness.

According to the Septuagint, this was Ezra's prayer for the Jewish leaders, reviewing the history of Israel, making confession, expressing thanksgiving, offering supplication and resolution for reforms, and ending with vows or covenants.

Nehemiah 10

Verses 1–27 list the signatories who affixed their seals to the covenants.

The rest of the chapter describes the oath and covenant which all the people made, on pain of a curse if they should break it, including the following specific promises: not to marry out of the covenant (v. 30), not to buy and sell on the Sabbath (v. 31), to pay all tithes and offerings and perform Temple worship and service (vv. 32–39).

Nehemiah 11

Because the people who lived in Jerusalem were too few to defend it effectively in case of attack (recall Nehemiah 7:4), the people gathered together to cast lots to determine who would live there, so that one tenth of the people would be in "the holy city" at all times. Everyone appreciated those who were willing to go there voluntarily! The people of Judah and Benjamin constituted most of its inhabitants, along with priests and Levites—Temple maintenance workers, ordinance workers, singers, servants, and others.

Nehemiah 12

A census list is given in verses 1–26 of the priests who returned from Babylon with Zerubbabel.

Verses 27–43 tell of the festive assembly for the dedication of the city wall and the sanctification or cleansing of all the people. The organization of the concourses of priests and the proceedings are described in detail. Apparently there were many sacrifices, much feasting, singing, and rejoicing—sufficient that it could be heard some distance away.

Verses 44–47 describe the assignments for priests, Levites, porters, singers, etc. The organization to receive and take care of offerings and distribute them to these groups is indicated.

Nehemiah 13

This chapter describes Nehemiah's final reforms. It appears that after the wall was furnished but before the dedication services just described, Nehemiah had returned to Persia for a time. Upon his return for the dedication, he found some of the people and even some priests violating their covenants. Eliashib the priest had allowed one of Nehemiah's old enemies, Tobiah the Ammonite (see 2:19), to take up residence right in the Temple complex. The Levites' portion had not been given to them, and the Sabbath was being broken. Nehemiah boldly and fearlessly expelled the intruder, rectified the injustice to the Levites, and dealt with those desecrating the Sabbath.

Nehemiah also found that once more there had been improper intermarrying of Jews with outsiders, and children were being brought up speaking the languages of their mothers, unable to speak the Hebrew language. Recalling again for them the laws of Moses on such matters, he corrected abuses of the Law and even removed some violators. Nehemiah prayed for God's approval of his efforts. "Remember me, O my God, for good" (v. 31) are Nehemiah's last recorded words and reemphasize a major theme running throughout his book—prayers for divine assistance and remembrance.

MALACHI

The Hebrew word *Malachi* means "my messenger," and it may be a title rather than the name of the individual who wrote the book. The term occurs in 3:1, and both prophets and priests were called messengers of the Lord (2:7). In addition, the Septuagint translates Malachi in 1:1 not as "my messenger" but "his messenger." The identity of the author of Malachi remains uncertain; however, because some of the same sins are denounced in both Nehemiah and Malachi, it has been suggested that the two leaders were contemporaries. Most scholars argue for Malachi being the last writer and last prophet of the Old Testament. Perhaps he wrote after 433 B.C., the date of Nehemiah's return to Persia and subsequent journey back to Jerusalem.

Though relatively short, the book of Malachi contains several quintessential themes: a call to honor priesthood functions and not neglect or pervert prescribed religious actions; a warning against heathen marriages; a rebuke and reminder about honest tithes and offerings; the second coming of the Lord; the importance of the Temple and the role of the prophet Elijah, and the importance of the sealing power he restored for the benefit of God's holy ones for time and for all eternity (see Bible Dictionary, "Malachi"; *Encyclopedia of Mormonism*, "Malachi, Prophecies of").

Malachi 1:1

Although no date for the prophecies of Malachi is given, his times are reflected in the writings of Ezra and Nehemiah. Malachi certainly came after the Temple had been rebuilt. It was a time when some abuses had again appeared. According to scholarship and tradition, Malachi was the last of the prophets. You may be surprised to learn that "the Talmud declares that with the death of Haggai, Zechariah and Malachi the Holy Spirit departed from Israel" (Cashdan, *Twelve Prophets,* 254).

One can appreciate the burden it must have been for Malachi to bear prophetic responsibilities in his era, just as his predecessors had born theirs. After starts and stops, the exiles had finally finished rebuilding the Temple at the prophetic urging and prodding of Haggai and Zechariah, and under the political leadership of Zerubbabel the governor. In 458 B.C. Ezra, priest and "ready scribe" of the Lord, strengthened the Jewish community in Jerusalem demographically when he brought with him thousands more of the former exiles. He strengthened the Jews spiritually by preaching repentance and inaugurating reforms. A few years later Nehemiah, cupbearer to the Persian king, was allowed to go back to Jerusalem, his ancestral home. He was appointed governor there, reestablished reforms, and preached repentance for breaking the Sabbath and nonpayment of tithes and offerings, among other things. In 433 B.C. Nehemiah returned to Persia for a time and when he arrived back in Jerusalem he found the people had fallen back into sinful ways; the priesthood was being treated lightly, the Sabbath was being broken, and tithes and offerings were not paid. These are the circumstances that Malachi continued to encounter, the same problems. How frustrating it must have been for Malachi to preach repentance but observe continual backsliding.

Malachi 1:2–14

Malachi's main mode of teaching was asking questions and then giving inspired answers (compare Alma 5). Over the centuries God was not pleased with his people's rituals of worship. In order to receive promised blessings, he expected and commanded strict obedience to all his laws, covenants, and ordinances, and the people's obedience had to be sincere and full-hearted or else it was hypocritical and unacceptable. In Malachi's day sacred ordinances and priesthood functions were being corrupted and "polluted" (v. 7). Blind, lame, and sick animals (v. 8) were simply not acceptable as sacrifices, and the people knew it (Deuteronomy 15:21). The best animals were to be offered to God, with the right attitude (Moroni 7:14). Verse 10 should rather be translated as a wish: "Oh that there were even one among you that would shut the doors, that ye might not kindle fire on mine altar in vain. I have no pleasure in you, saith the Lord of hosts, neither will I accept an offering at your hand." Their worship of God had become a "weariness," and "contemptible."

Malachi 2:1–17

Malachi 2:1–9 continues instructions to and condemnation of the priests. Priesthood leaders and workers were supposed to be reverent and dedicated in the performance of their duties, but instead they had corrupted their behavior and their rituals and had lost their reputation "before all the people."

In verse 10 we have perhaps the plainest pronouncement of an indispensable doctrine in the Old Testament: we all have one Father, even God, and we, as his children, are brothers and sisters. Why then would we "deal treacherously" with one another?

Verses 11–17 preach against mixed marriages and divorce. They teach essential doctrine: the covenant man of God, holding his priesthood worthily, must be committed and faithful to God, and not profane his holiness by marrying "the daughter of a strange god" through idolatry and adultery. Again, mixed marriages—marriages out of the covenant—were forbidden because they negate the blessings of eternity; they cancel out the grand purposes of God for his children: bringing about not only their immortality but also their "eternal lives," the "continuation of the seeds forever and ever" (D&C 132:19–24).

With a clear concept of God's noble objectives for his children, verses 13–16 decry the evils of divorce. Compare Jacob 2:31–35 in the Book of Mormon. The people may have had similar problems on both sides of the earth during the same time period.

Verse 15 is somewhat obscure in English, but the sense of it is this: "And did not he [God] make one flesh? . . . And why one? That he might seek a godly seed. Therefore take heed to your spirit, and let none deal treacherously with the wife of his youth." On the loving concern of Heavenly Father for his children, compare Deuteronomy 32:6, 18; Isaiah 63:16; 64:8; and Jeremiah

31:1–3. Again, God's work and glory is helping his children become as he is: immortal and exalted—the latter requiring exact obedience to the laws of the highest degree of the celestial kingdom. And one of those exalting laws is valiance in celestial marriage. Verse 16, then, understandably has God bluntly exclaiming that he hates divorce.

Verse 17 is something of a restatement of Isaiah 5:20. The Lord is tired of those who use clever words to argue that evil is good. Malachi's environment is also ours today.

Malachi 3:1–4 (3 Nephi 24:1–4)

The words of chapters 3 and 4 of Malachi were also given by the Savior to his disciples in Book of Mormon lands (3 Nephi 24 and 25; see also Ogden and Skinner, *Book of Mormon*, 2:211–19). Since the people in the Americas had no record of Malachi (the plates of brass were taken out of Jerusalem almost two hundred years before Malachi lived), God wanted those disciples to have that prophet's teachings also. In fact, prophecies of Malachi are found in all of the standard works.

As we have seen, a prophet's name or title often has something to do with his message. Just as *Malachi* in Hebrew means literally "my messenger," the Lord would send into the world a messenger, or a covenant, a standard, an ensign to prepare the way before him. We may see a composite fulfillment of this great prophecy in the coming of John the Baptist, Elijah, and others, in the ministry of Joseph Smith, and in the gospel itself (D&C 45:9). Orson Pratt and Sidney Rigdon, for example, were told in these latter days that they were preparing the way of the Lord, just as John had done (D&C 34:6; 35:4). Jesus Christ, of course, was the "messenger of the covenant," spoken of by Malachi, in whom we certainly delight. Along with verses 1–4, read also Doctrine and Covenants 84:31–34 and 128:24.

"The Lord, whom ye seek, shall suddenly come to his temple" (v. 1). Here is another unequivocal sign of the Lord's coming: he will come to his Temple (see also D&C 36:8; 42:36; 133:2). But which Temple? He did come to the Kirtland Temple, but he will come again—to the House of the Lord in the New Jerusalem and in the Old Jerusalem. See details about the fulfillment of this prophecy, especially commentary from Elder Bruce R. McConkie, at Isaiah 2:1–2.

"Who may abide the day of his coming? and who shall stand when he appeareth?" This parallel couplet contains a significant question about the Second Coming. Who will be able to survive that day when the harvest will have been gathered and the field will be burned? In that day all telestial people and things will be removed from this planet, and the earth will shift up to a terrestrial or paradisiacal condition. There will be a great cleansing. The Lord and his tens of thousands of holy ones are compared metaphorically to "a refiner's fire, and like fuller's soap." Fire and soap are two well-known cleansing agents. Those who are clean will abide the day of cleansing. See more about the refiner's fire in commentary at Isaiah 48:10. A fuller, who usually had his workshop near a spring or some other water source, worked with his soap to clean cloth, ridding it of all stains to make it white.

The sons of Levi will yet offer unto the Lord an offering in righteousness (v. 3). Does that mean that blood sacrifices of animals will be reinstituted? We do know that the sacrificial shedding of the blood of animals, symbolic of the great sacrifice involving the shedding of the Savior's blood, was part of the proper worship of God since the beginning. The practice will be resumed, but for how long? The Prophet Joseph Smith wrote:

"These sacrifices, as well as every ordinance belonging to the Priesthood, will, when the Temple of the Lord shall be built, and the sons of Levi be purified, be fully restored and attended to in all their powers, ramifications, and blessings. This ever did and ever will exist when the powers of the Melchisedic [sic] Priesthood are sufficiently manifest; else how can the restitution of all things spoken of by the holy Prophets be brought to pass? It is not to be understood that the law of Moses will be established again with all its rites and variety of ceremonies; this has never been spoken of by the Prophets; but those things which existed prior to Moses' day, namely, sacrifice, will be continued" (*History of the Church*, 4:211–12).

Elaborating further on this principle of sacrifice, President Joseph Fielding Smith wrote that "blood sacrifices will be performed long enough to complete the fulness of the restoration in this dispensation. Afterwards sacrifice will be of some other character" (*Doctrines of Salvation*, 3:94).

From Joseph Smith's epistle, canonized as Doctrine and Covenants 128, we read a summary statement which includes an additional aspect of the fulfillment of Malachi's prophecy of the Second Coming: "Behold, the great day of the Lord is at hand; and who can abide the day of his coming, and who can stand when he appeareth? For he is like a refiner's fire, and like fuller's soap; and he shall sit as a refiner and purifier of silver, and he shall purify the sons of Levi, and purge them as gold and silver, that they may offer unto the Lord an offering in righteousness. Let us, therefore, as a church and a people, and as Latter-day Saints, offer unto the Lord an offering in righteousness; and let us present in his holy temple, when it is finished, a book containing the records of our dead, which shall be worthy of all acceptance" (D&C 128:24).

Malachi 3:5–12 (3 Nephi 24:7–12)

These eight verses constitute one of the greatest discourses on the law of tithes and offerings ever given. If we hold back our tithes and offerings, Malachi wrote, we are robbing God. In another sense, we are also robbing ourselves. We are cheating ourselves out of enormous blessings. The payment of tithes and offerings is as indispensable to our salvation as repentance and baptism and other principles and ordinances. This commandment to give of what we have and share what we are to help build God's kingdom has specific promises associated with it.

One of our former students at Brigham Young University, wrote that Malachi's tithing sermon is oft-quoted but sometimes misunderstood. Perhaps some in the latter days consider it to be the formula for materialistic prosperity. In their view, it is money that drops through the open windows of heaven. The main message of Malachi's treatise is to notify us that tithing is only a small portion of what the Lord possesses. We are given a small stewardship and then tested to see if we will give back to him what is already his or rob God through embezzlement. As with all commandments, the Lord promises blessings. However, when the Lord opens the windows of heaven, many possible blessings may pour out of them. Adversity is a blessing! It streams forth from those windows and can strengthen the obedient. When the scripture tells us that "there shall not be room enough to receive it," (v. 10) perhaps we imagine large homes packed with luxuries. "That description brings to mind the 'great and spacious building' in Lehi's dream of the tree of life. When I hear the expression, 'there shall not be room enough to receive it,' I like to picture my heart so full of love, charity, and peace that my spiritual cup runneth over" (Litchko).

Opening the windows of heaven means revelation, and great revelation—coming to know the Father and the Son—is available to us in the holy Temple. But those who wish to enter there must show obedience by paying a full tithing. How could persons be willing to enter into the laws of sacrifice and consecration if they can't even pay a full tithing? Sacrifice indeed brings forth the blessings of heaven. So while you may think you are giving up something to God, he actually enriches you with more than you have given. The word sacrifice derives from the Latin *sacre*, meaning "holy" or "sanctified." When we sacrifice something it is not so much a deprivation as a sanctification. Is the payment of tithing a *loss* of the ten percent or is it a consecration, a sanctification of the ten percent?

The Lord also promises that he will "rebuke the devourer" for our sakes (v. 11), or, as our idiom renders it: He will keep the wolf from our door.

Malachi 3:13–18 (3 Nephi 24:13–18)

The people were saying that it was vain to serve God—while the wicked prospered, only the righteous seemed to suffer. But the reward of the righteous is sure. All will eventually be rewarded who have kept the commandments.

The Lord remonstrates: A Book of Remembrance is being kept, and the ones who have "thought upon [my] name" (v. 16) will be included in it, "and they shall be mine . . . in that day when I make up my jewels" (v. 17). The word "jewels" in Hebrew is *segulla*, and it is the exact same term elsewhere translated as "peculiar" (as in "peculiar people"—Deuteronomy 14:2). *Segulla* means "valued property" or "special treasure." Indeed, the Saints or holy ones of God are his jewels, his valued property or treasure. When he comes to reign, they, his jewels or special property, will be with him. In this dispensation, the Lord declared that those whom he would count his jewels will have been tried and chastened, even as Abraham (D&C 101:3–5). Chastening is of two types: corrective and instructive. Thus, all of the Lord's people will be chastened at some point.

Malachi 4:1–6 (3 Nephi 25:1–6)

Chapter 4 in the Hebrew text is simply a continuation of chapter 3. There is no division into two chapters. Our chapter 4 verse 1 warns that at the Lord's second coming the world will be burned. "This is speaking after the manner of the Lord" (D&C 64:24), for fire is symbolic of God's glory. When the Lord and all his holy ones come to earth at his coming in glory, those people and things that cannot stand his glory will be burned up: "I will burn them up," says the Lord (D&C 64:24).

A series of scriptural passages sheds further light on the burning or fire that will destroy the world at his coming and change it to a loftier sphere (italics are added):

"*The Lord will come with fire,* and with his chariots like a whirlwind, to render his anger with fury, and his rebuke with flames of fire" (Isaiah 66:15).

"The inhabitants thereof are consumed away and utterly destroyed *by the brightness of my coming*" (D&C 5:19).

"All the proud and they that do wickedly shall be as stubble; and *I will burn them up* . . . For I will reveal myself from heaven *with power and great glory* . . . [in] the day of *my coming in a pillar of fire . . . in glory even as I am*" (D&C 29:9, 11–12).

"All flesh shall see me together. And *every corruptible thing . . . shall be consumed;* and also that of element *shall melt with fervent heat*" (D&C 101:23–25).

"The presence of the Lord shall be as the melting fire that burneth" (D&C 133:41).

"The day cometh that shall burn as an oven, and all the proud, yea, and all that do wickedly shall burn as stubble; for *they that come shall burn them,* saith the Lord" (Joseph Smith–History 1:37;

see also Zephaniah 3:8; Ezekiel 1:27; 2 Thessalonians 1:7–8; 2:8; D&C 43:32; 45:57; 63:34; 130:7).

Notice who will be burned at the Second Coming: "all the proud, yea, and all that do wickedly." The Lord singles out one particular sin—pride—and lumps all the rest of the sins of humanity into the generic "all that do wickedly." It is obvious that the Lord hates pride (Proverbs 6:16–17). He knows how that one sin is the basis for, and can lead to, so many other sins. Pride is the great distracter and obstructer to all spiritual progress.

Those who cannot abide the day of burning will be left with "neither root nor branch," meaning that they will have in the eternal worlds neither ancestry nor posterity—no eternal family connections. They are unworthy of the sealing ordinances of the holy priesthood.

In this dispensation, the Lord has declared that there is a way to escape the burning, the Lord's wrath, at the Second Coming. It is the payment of tithes previously discussed by Malachi: "Behold, now it is called today until the coming of the Son of Man, and verily it is a day of sacrifice, and a day for the tithing of my people; for he that is tithed shall not be burned at his coming" (D&C 64:23).

In verse 2, using language reminiscent of Isaiah 60:1 and 19, Malachi indicates that the Lord is like the glory of the sun and the light of righteousness, who will rise and bring healing to others. Luke similarly testified that Jesus Christ is that rising sun of righteousness and power (see Luke 1:78–79). Thus, Malachi foreshadows the Atonement and Resurrection. "Calves of the stall" symbolize young, vibrant creations of God, free from mortal challenges and frailties.

The righteous in the millennial day will enjoy healing and salvation from the Son of Righteousness (3 Nephi 25:2). One of the Father's name-titles is Righteousness; therefore the Savior is the Son of Righteousness. The Son's rising with "healing in his wings" refers to the "power in his extremities, the power that came from his having had nails driven through his hands and feet. In short, the Son of Righteousness came with the power of the Atonement" (McConkie, Millet, and Top, *Doctrinal Commentary*, 4:165). The children of the righteous, says Doctrine and Covenants 45:58,

461

"shall grow up without sin unto salvation." The phrase "calves of the stall" suggests that they receive special care.

It is appropriate that Moses and Elijah, the two who epitomize the Law and the Prophets, should be mentioned together in the final verses of the Old Testament record (vv. 4–5). These two outstanding messengers of God operated in three different dispensations: as mortals, as translated beings (in Jesus' day on the Mount of Transfiguration), and as resurrected beings (in Joseph Smith's day in the Kirtland Temple). Moses restored in the meridian of time, and again in the fulness of times, the keys of the gathering of Israel; Elijah restored in both dispensations the keys of the sealing power—Moses' keys for gathering the living to Christ and Elijah's keys for gathering the dead to Christ. That takes care of everyone.

Joseph Smith taught more about Malachi 4:5–6, the last two verses in Malachi's writings and the concluding verses in our Old Testament, than any other passage of scripture. There is something of utmost importance contained in them.

It is written in everyone's Bible—whether Jewish or Christian—that Elijah the prophet would return before the coming of the Lord. Though many people, especially observant Jews, still maintain expectant tradition of his coming and even prepare a place setting for him at the annual Passover service, the Latter-day Saints are the only people in the world who believe he has actually come, just as prophesied. But Elijah did not come to a Jewish home or synagogue but to the House of the Lord in Kirtland, Ohio, on April 3, 1836, the very occasion of the Passover celebration that year (see Smith, *Doctrines of Salvation*, 2:100–101).

And what did Elijah return to earth to accomplish? The grand and glorious purpose is stated in a single sentence: He came to "turn the heart of the fathers to the children, and the heart of the children to their fathers." The Prophet Joseph Smith later elaborated on the word *turn*, expanding it to mean also "bind" or "seal" (*Joseph Smith* [manual], 472). The spirit and purpose of Elijah and those sealing powers is to promote the labor of love we call genealogy (from the Greek, meaning the study of race or family) and family history—researching and preparing the basic and necessary data on every child of Heavenly Father, in order to perform the saving ordinances: baptism, confirmation, priesthood ordination, marriage, and sealing of man and woman to each other and children to their parents. "For we without them cannot be made perfect; neither can they without us be made perfect" (D&C 128:18). Marriage and family life are the very reasons this earth was created, and the only way "that the earth might answer the end of its creation" (D&C 49:16). We all need the welding links of family units, else the earth would be smitten, cursed, and utterly wasted at the Savior's coming (D&C 110:14–16; Joseph Smith–History 1:36–39).

During Moroni's many hours of instructional interviews with Joseph Smith, "respecting what the Lord was going to do, and how and in what manner his kingdom was to be conducted in the last days" (Joseph Smith–History 1:54), the ancient Nephite prophet quoted the first sentence of Malachi's last verse in this way: "And he shall plant in the hearts of the children the promises made to the fathers, and the hearts of the children shall turn to their fathers" (Joseph Smith–History 1:39). The promises made to the fathers (Adam, Enoch, Noah, Melchizedek, Abraham, Isaac, Jacob, and so on) include the great blessings of the covenant: the gospel of Jesus Christ and its associated principles and ordinances, the receiving of which, and the living of which, seals upon the obedient the blessings of exaltation in celestial glory with the Father, the Son, and the Holy Ghost. All these things are available to men, women, and children—and their ancestors—in the holy Temples of the Lord. Our most ardent desire will be to have the great covenant promises and blessings for ourselves and our progenitors and our posterity.

At the end of our Old Testament are the capitalized words "THE END OF THE PROPHETS." This is the end of the prophets only in the sense of it being the end of the division of the Hebrew Bible known as "The Prophets" (see "The Organization of this Commentary" at the beginning of volume 1). This is also the end of the Old Covenant or Old Testament record; therefore it is the end of that collection of scripture that includes the long line of prophets from Adam to Malachi. The next recorded prophet who would minister in the Holy Land would be a forerunner of the Messiah himself, the prophet who is known in the English New Testament as John the Baptist.

John the Baptist was the last legal administrator of the Aaronic Priesthood, holding the keys of that priesthood. Jesus Christ restored the keys and authority of the Melchizedek Priesthood (JST John 1:28), the priesthood that had operated from Adam to Moses but that had been taken away from the populace in general at the time of Moses (D&C 84:19–28). Although all the prophets had the Melchizedek Priesthood (*Teachings of the Prophet Joseph Smith*, 181), the Aaronic Priesthood was the order that generally operated during much of the Old Testament period we have been studying. But with the coming of the true and living Messiah, a new day would dawn; which is why all the prophets gave him witness (Acts 10:43).

SOURCES

Aharoni, Yohanan. *The Land of the Bible: A Historical Geography.* Translated by A. F. Rainey. London: Burns & Oates, 1974.

Anderson, Hugh. "The Book of Job." In *The Interpreter's One-Volume Commentary on the Bible.* Edited by Charles M. Laymon. Nashville and New York: Abingdon Press, 1971.

Backman, Milton V., Jr. *The Heavens Resound: A History of the Latter-day Saints in Ohio.* Salt Lake City: Deseret Book, 1983.

Ballard, M. Russell. "Great Shall Be the Peace of Thy Children." *Ensign,* Apr. 1994, 59–61.

Ballard, Melvin J. "Classic Discourses from the General Authorities: The Sacramental Covenant." *New Era,* Jan. 1976, 7–11. Reprint, *Improvement Era,* Oct. 1919, 1025–32.

Barkay, Gabriel. *Jerusalem Post Magazine,* 18 July 1986, 10–12.

Benson, Ezra Taft. "Fourteen Fundamentals in Following the Prophet." *Liahona [Tambuli],* June 1981; available online at lds.org. Or *1980 Devotional Speeches of the Year,* 26–30. Provo, Utah: BYU Press, 1981.

———. *The Teachings of Ezra Taft Benson.* Salt Lake City: Bookcraft, 1988.

Bright, John. *A History of Israel.* 4th ed. Philadelphia: Westminster Press, 2000.

Bullinger, E. W. *Figures of Speech Used in the Bible.* Grand Rapids, Mich.: Baker Book House, 1968.

Burton, Theodore M. "The Meaning of Repentance." In *1984–85 Devotional and Fireside Speeches,* 95–101. Provo, Utah: Brigham Young University Press, 1985.

Buttrick, George Arthur, ed. *The Interpreter's Dictionary of the Bible: An Illustrated Encyclopedia.* 5 vols. Nashville: Abingdon Press, 1962.

Byron, Lord. *The Poetical Works of Lord Byron.* London: Oxford University Press, 1909.

Cannon, George Q. *Gospel Truth: Discourses and Writings of George Q. Cannon.* Edited by Jerreld L. Newquist. 2 vols. in 1. Classics in Mormon Literature series. Salt Lake City: Deseret Book, 1987.

Carlyle, Thomas. *On Heroes, Hero-Worship, and the Heroic in History.* New York: Macmillan, 1905.

Cashdan, Eli. *The Twelve Prophets.* Soncino Books of the Bible. Edited by A. Cohen. London: Soncino Press, 1948.

Charles, R. H., ed. *The Apocrypha and Pseudepigrapha of the Old Testament.* 2 vols. London: Oxford University Press, 1976.

Children's Songbook. Salt Lake City: The Church of Jesus Christ of Latter-day Saints, 1989.

Clark, James R., comp. *Messages of the First Presidency of The Church of Jesus Christ of Latter-day Saints.* 6 vols. Salt Lake City: Bookcraft, 1965–75.

Costa, Claudio R. M. "Obedience to the Prophets." *Ensign,* Nov. 2010, 11–13.

"Daniel Webster." *Boston Atlas,* 23 Oct. 1852, 2.

Delitzsch, Franz. *Biblical Commentary on the Prophecies of Isaiah.* 2 vols. Edinburgh: T & T Clark, 1890.

Draper, Richard D. *Opening the Seven Seals—The Visions of John the Revelator.* Salt Lake City: Deseret Book, 1991.

Duncan, Kevin R. "Our Very Survival." *Ensign,* Nov. 2010, 34–36.

Emerson, Ralph Waldo. *Essays of Ralph Waldo Emerson.* Edited by Alfred R. Ferguson and Jean Ferguson Carr. Cambridge, Mass.: Harvard University, Belknap Press, 1987.

Evans, Richard L. "Strength and Struggle . . ." *Improvement Era,* Apr. 1964, 306.

———. *Unto the Hills.* New York: Harper and Brothers Publishers, 1940.

Excavations at Lachish. Tel Aviv: Institute of Archaeology of Tel Aviv University and Israel Exploration Society, 1981.

Galbraith, David B. Unpublished manuscript in possession of D. Kelly Ogden. Used by permission.

Galbraith, David B., D. Kelly Ogden, and Andrew C. Skinner. *Jerusalem, the Eternal City.* Salt Lake City: Deseret Book, 1996.

Goethe, Johann Wolfgang von. *Faust—A Tragedy.* Vol. 1. Translated by Bayard Taylor. Boston: Houghton Mifflin, 1906.

Harvey, Ze'ev. "Jesus in Medieval and Modern Jewish Thought." Israeli government-sponsored seminar on Christ, Galei Zohar Hotel, Israel, Mar. 23–25, 1990. Notes in possession of D. Kelly Ogden.

Hayes, John Haralson, and Stuart A. Irvine. *Isaiah, the Eighth-Century Prophet: His Times and His Preaching.* Nashville: Abingdon Press, 1987.

Herodotus. *The Persian Wars.* Bk. 2. Vol. 117 of Loeb Classical Library series. Translated by A. D. Godley. Cambridge: Harvard University Press, 2004.

Hinckley, Gordon B. "Living in the Fulness of Times." *Ensign,* Nov. 2001, 4–6.

Holladay, William L. *A Concise Hebrew and Aramaic Lexicon of the Old Testament.* Grand Rapids, Mich.: Eerdmans, 1974.

Hunter, Howard W. *The Teachings of Howard W. Hunter.* Edited by Clyde J. Williams. Salt Lake City: Deseret Book, 1997.

Hutchinson, Thomas, ed. *The Complete Poetical Works of Percy Bysshe Shelley.* London: Oxford University Press, 1905.

Hymns of The Church of Jesus Christ of Latter-day Saints. Salt Lake City: The Church of Jesus Christ of Latter-day Saints, 1985.

"In Memoriam: Quiet Example—Elder Marvin J. Ashton, May 6, 1915–Feb. 25, 1994." *New Era,* May 1994; available online at lds.org.

The Interpreter's Bible. 12 vols. New York and Nashville: Abingdon Press, 1954–56.

Jackson, Kent P., ed. *1 Kings to Malachi.* Vol. 4 of Studies in Scripture series. Salt Lake City: Deseret Book, 1993.

Josephus, Flavius. *Antiquities of the Jews.* In *Josephus: Complete Works.* Translated by William Whiston. Grand Rapids, Mich.: Kregel, 1960.

Journal of Discourses. 26 vols. London: Latter-day Saints' Book Depot, 1854–86.

Kimball, Spencer W. *Faith Precedes the Miracle.* Salt Lake City: Deseret Book, 1972.

———. "How Rare a Possession—the Scriptures!" *Ensign,* Sept. 1976, 2–5.

———. *Love versus Lust.* Brigham Young University Speeches of the Year. Provo, Utah, 30 Jan. 1965.

———. *The Miracle of Forgiveness.* Salt Lake City: Deseret Book, 1969.

———. "The Stone Cut without Hands." *Ensign,* May 1976, 4–9.

———. "The Time to Labor Is Now." *Ensign,* Nov. 1975, 4–7.

———. *Tragedy or Destiny?* Salt Lake City: Deseret Book, 1977.

Lachish I (Tell ed Duweir): The Lachish Letters. London: Oxford University Press, 1938.

Lectures on Faith. Salt Lake City: Deseret Book, 1985.

Lee, Harold B. Conference Report, Oct. 1970, 152–53.

———. *The Teachings of Harold B. Lee.* Edited by Clyde J. Williams. Salt Lake City: Bookcraft, 1996.

Lewis, C. S. *Mere Christianity.* New York: HarperCollins, 1952.

Ludlow, Daniel H. *A Companion to Your Study of the Old Testament.* Salt Lake City: Deseret Book, 1981.

Ludlow, Daniel H., ed. *Encyclopedia of Mormonism.* 4 vols. New York: Macmillan, 1992.

Ludlow, Victor L. *Isaiah: Prophet, Seer, and Poet.* Salt Lake City: Deseret Book, 1982.

Lund, Gerald N. "A Prophet for the Fulness of Times." *Ensign,* Jan. 1997, 50–54.

Lundquist, John M. "Temple Symbolism in Isaiah." In *Isaiah and the Prophets—Inspired Voices from the Old Testament.* Vol. 10 of the Religious Studies Monograph series. Brigham Young University, Religious Studies Center, 1984.

McConkie, Bruce R. *Doctrinal New Testament Commentary.* 3 vols. Salt Lake City: Bookcraft, 1965–73.

———. *The Millennial Messiah: The Second Coming of the Son of Man.* Salt Lake City: Deseret Book, 1982.

———. *Mormon Doctrine.* 2d ed. Salt Lake City: Bookcraft, 1966.

———. *The Mortal Messiah: From Bethlehem to Calvary.* 4 vols. Salt Lake City: Deseret Book, 1979–81.

———. *A New Witness for the Articles of Faith.* Salt Lake City: Deseret Book, 1985.

———. *The Promised Messiah: The First Coming of Christ.* Salt Lake City: Deseret Book, 1981.

———. "Stand Independent above All Other Creatures." *Ensign,* May 1979, 92–94.

———. "Ten Keys to Understanding Isaiah." *Ensign,* Oct. 1973, 78–83.

———. "The Testimony of Jesus." *Ensign,* July 1972, 109–10.

McConkie, Joseph Fielding, and Craig J. Ostler. *Revelations of the Restoration.* Salt Lake City: Deseret Book, 2000.

McConkie, Joseph Fielding, and Robert L. Millet. *Doctrinal Commentary on the Book of Mormon.* Vols. 1–3. Salt Lake City: Bookcraft, 1987–91.

McConkie, Joseph Fielding, Robert L. Millet, and Brent L. Top. *Doctrinal Commentary on the Book of Mormon.* Vol. 4. Salt Lake City: Bookcraft, 1992.

Meservy, Keith. "Ezekiel's Sticks and the Gathering of Israel." *Ensign,* Feb. 1987, 4–13.

———. "Isaiah 53: The Richest Prophecy on Christ's Atonement in the Old Testament." In *A Witness of Jesus Christ: The 1989 Sperry Symposium on the Old Testament.* Salt Lake City: Deseret Book, 1990.

Oaks, Dallin H. "Our Strengths Can Become Our Downfall." *Ensign,* Oct. 1994, 11–19.

Ogden, D. Kelly. *Before You Get to Heaven: 8 Mighty Changes God Wants for You.* Salt Lake City: Deseret Book, 2004.

———. *Where Jesus Walked: The Land and Culture of New Testament Times.* Salt Lake City: Deseret Book, 1991.

Ogden, D. Kelly, and Jeffrey R. Chadwick. *The Holy Land—A Geographical, Historical, and Archaeological Guide to the Land of the Bible.* Jerusalem: Jerusalem Center for Near Eastern Studies, 1990.

Ogden, D. Kelly, and David B. Galbraith. "I Have a Question: What are the reasons behind the long-standing conflicts in the Holy Land, and how should Latter-day Saints view such conflicts?" *Ensign,* Sept. 1993, 52–53.

Ogden, D. Kelly, and Andrew C. Skinner. *Acts through Revelation.* Verse by Verse series. Salt Lake City: Deseret Book, 1998.

———. *The Book of Mormon.* 2 vols. Verse by Verse series. Salt Lake City: Deseret Book, 2011.

Old Testament [student manual]. Prepared by the Church Educational System. 2 vols. Salt Lake City: The Church of Jesus Christ of Latter-day Saints, 1980–82.

Packer, Boyd K. "Scriptures." *Ensign,* Nov. 1982, 51–53.

Penrose, Charles W. "The Second Advent." *Millennial Star* 21, no. 37 (10 Sept. 1859): 581–84.

Pratt, Orson. *Orson Pratt's Works on the Doctrines of the Gospel.* Vol. 1. Salt Lake City: Deseret News Press, 1945.

Pritchard, James B., ed. *The Ancient Near East.* 2 vols. Princeton: Princeton University Press, 1958.

Rasmussen, Ellis T. "Zoroastrianism." *Ensign,* Nov. 1971, 32–38.

Revius, Jacobus. "He Bore Our Anguish." Translated by Charles D. Tate Jr. In *BYU Studies* 15, no. 1 (Autumn 1974): 103.

Reynolds, Noel B., and Charles D. Tate, eds. *Book of Mormon Authorship: New Light on Ancient Origins.* Provo, Utah: Religious Studies Center, Brigham Young University, 1982.

Richards, LeGrand. *A Marvelous Work and a Wonder.* Salt Lake City: Deseret Book, 1988.

Scott, Richard G. "Trust in the Lord." *Ensign,* Nov. 1995, 16–18.

Seely, David R. "The Lord Is Our Judge and Our King (Isaiah 18–33)." In Jackson, *1 Kings to Malachi,* 108–27.

———. "The Lord Will Bring Salvation (Isaiah 51–66)." In Jackson, *1 Kings to Malachi,* 146–64.

Seixas, J[oshua]. *A Manual Hebrew Grammar for the Use of Beginners.* 1883. Available online at archive.org.

Shanks, Herschel. "Nahman Avigad, 1905–1992." *Biblical Archaeology Review.* May/June 1992, 48–49.

———, ed. *Understanding the Dead Sea Scrolls.* New York: Random House, 1992.

Shiloh, Yigal. "Excavations at the City of David." In *Qedem 19.* Edited by N. Avigad et al. Jerusalem: Hebrew University of Jerusalem, 1984.

Skinner, Andrew C. *Gethsemane.* Salt Lake City: Deseret Book, 2002.

———. "Two Crucified Men: Insights into the Death of Jesus of Nazareth." In *Bountiful Harvest.* Provo: Neal A. Maxwell Institute for Religious Scholarship, 2011.

Smith, Hyrum M., and Janne M. Sjodahl. *The Doctrine and Covenants Commentary.* Rev. ed. Salt Lake City: Deseret Book, 1978.

Smith, Joseph. *Encyclopedia of Joseph Smith's Teachings.* Edited by Larry E. Dahl and Donald Q. Cannon. Salt Lake City: Deseret Book, 2000.

———. *Joseph Smith* [manual]. Teachings of Presidents of the Church series. Salt Lake City: The Church of Jesus Christ of Latter-day Saints, 2007.

———. *History of the Church of Jesus Christ of Latter-day Saints.* 6 vols. Salt Lake City: Deseret Book, 1973–80.

———. *Teachings of the Prophet Joseph Smith.* Selected by Joseph Fielding Smith. Salt Lake City: Deseret Book, 1977.

Smith, Joseph F. *Gospel Doctrine.* Salt Lake City: Deseret Book, 1986.

———. "A Message to the Soldier Boys of 'Mormondom.'" *Improvement Era,* July 1917, 821–37.

Smith, Joseph Fielding. *Answers to Gospel Questions.* 5 vols. Salt Lake City: Deseret Book, 1957–66.

————. Conference Report, Oct. 1926, 115–18.

————. *Doctrines of Salvation*. Compiled by Bruce R. McConkie. 3 vols. Salt Lake City: Bookcraft, 1954–56.

————. *The Signs of the Times*. Salt Lake City: Deseret Book, 1964.

Smith, Lucy Mack. *History of Joseph Smith by His Mother*. Salt Lake City: Bookcraft, 1958.

Talmage, James E. *Jesus the Christ*. Salt Lake City: Deseret News, 1915.

Trepp, Leo. *A History of the Jewish Experience—Eternal Faith, Eternal People*. New York: Behrman House, 1973.

Uchtdorf, Dieter F. "We Are Doing a Great Work and Cannot Come Down." *Ensign*, May 2009, 59–62.

Uzanne, Octave. "Conversations and Opinions of Victor Hugo: From Unpublished Papers Found at Guernsey." *Scribner's Magazine* 12 (July–Dec. 1892): 570.

Welch, John W., and John F. Hall. *Charting the New Testament*. Provo, Utah: FARMS, 2002.

West, Delno C., and August Kling. *The Libro de las profecias of Christopher Columbus*. Gainesville: University of Florida Press, 1991.

Westermann, Claus. *Isaiah 40–66: A Commentary*. Philadelphia: Westminster Press, 1969.

Woodruff, Wilford. *The Discourses of Wilford Woodruff*. Selected by G. Homer Durham. Salt Lake City: Bookcraft, 1969.

Wright, G. Ernest. *Biblical Archaeology*. Philadelphia: The Westminster Press, 1960.

Yadin, Yigael. *Hazor, the Head of All Those Kingdoms*. London: Oxford University Press, 1972.

Young, Brigham. *Discourses of Brigham Young*. Selected by John A. Widtsoe, 1966.

Young, Edward J. *The Book of Isaiah*. 3 vols. Grand Rapids, Mich.: Eerdmans, 1965–72.

Young, G. Douglas. *Grammar of the Hebrew Language: A New Approach to the Hebrew Language and to Advanced Exegesis Using Hebrew and Romanized Scripts*. Grand Rapids, Mich.: Zondervan, 1951.

INDEX

36–37; Elisha as companion to, 37; appearance of, 43; translation of, 44, 45; coming of, 44–45; as foreshadow and type of Christ, 48–49; involvement of, in politics, 59; return and purpose of, 462

Eliphaz, 116–17, 120, 122

Elisha: as Elijah's companion, 37; heals spring, 46–47; curses youths, 47–48; as foreshadow and type of Christ, 48–49; provides water, 51; blesses widow, 51–52; raises boy from dead, 52; counsels Naaman, 53; floats axe head, 54–55; spares Syrians, 55; foretells reign of Hazael, 56–57; involvement of, in politics, 59; death of, 64

Elohim, 221

Emerson, Ralph Waldo, 273–74

Empathy, 318

En-rogel, 197

Ensign: defined, 195; Joseph Smith as, 218–19; Church as, 219–20; as rallying point, 223; Zion as, 233; and gathering of Israel, 279

Ephraim, 364; stick of, 389–90

"Ephraim shall not envy Judah, and Judah shall not vex Ephraim," 220

Errant leaders, 211

Esau, 338

Eschatology, 237–38

Esther, 431–33, 435–37

Esther (book), 429–30

Ethbaal, 32

'Etz, 389

Evans, Richard L., 132, 358

Everlasting covenant, 238–39

Everlasting Father, 208–9

Evil: distinguishing between good and, 194–95; defined, 267

Exaltation, through trials, 130–32

Exodus, dating, 10

Ezekiel: as prophet under Babylonian exile, 97; ministry of, 374, 375–76; calling and election of, made sure, 374–75; symbolic methods of, 377–78

Ezekiel (book), 373–75

Ezion-geber, 65

Ezra, 442–44, 449–50, 454

Ezra (book), 438–39

Faith: through suffering, 113, 384; through sacrifice, 130; in Lord, 336–37

False prophets, 355, 363, 379

Family, undermining of, 188

Family history, 281–82, 339, 462–63

Famine: caused by Elijah, 33–34; in Samaria, 55–56; spiritual, 146, 194, 246

Fasting: reasons for, 309–10; tips for, 310–11; proper, 423; effectiveness of, 430; for Esther, 433, 436–37; during exile, 446

Fear: Joseph F. Smith on, 241–42; of man, 283; as enemy of faith, 417

"Feast of fat things," 240–41

Feast of Tabernacles, 16, 25, 450

Feet: of Asa, 30; of missionaries, 288

Figs, good and bad, 360

Fire, at Second Coming, 460–61

1 Chronicles (book), 1–2

First Kings (book), 1–2

First Temple: rational for building, 6; construction of, 9–15; dedication of, 15–16, 240, 406–7; cost of, 17; few, if any, Melchizedek Priesthood holders in, 37; money-offerings of, 63; changes to, under Ahaz, 70; items taken from, 95; destruction of, 95–96, 415

Fish, Jonah saved by, 136

Fitches, 245

Flax, 260–61
Flood, 303
Folly, 108
Font(s), in Temples, 13–14
Food poisoning, 80
Foreigners, 306–7, 395
Foreign nations, 369, 384
Foreordination: of Cyrus, 265; of
  Lord's servants, 275; of Joseph
  Smith, 277; of Jeremiah, 344,
  345
Forgiveness, 180, 263
Four, 142
Fulness of times, 156–58, 274, 390,
  462
Future perfect tense verbs, 187–88

Gabriel, 408–9
Galbraith, David B., 327–29
Galgal, 231–32
Garments. *See* Clothing
Gates, of Temple, 393–94
Gathering of Israel: location of,
  158–59; prophecy regarding,
  177, 243, 279, 387; Temples
  and, 182–84, 316, 393; Joseph
  Smith on, 219, 233; Isaiah
  prophesies of, 226; and estab-
  lishment of Zion, 301; Jeremiah
  prophesies of, 351; promise re-
  garding, 356, 360, 366, 378–79,
  387–88; Zechariah prophesies
  concerning, 424
Gedaliah, 96, 368
Gehazi, 54, 56
Gemariah, 93
Genealogy, 281–82, 339, 462–63
Gentiles: conversion of, 226, 238;
  lights to, 275, 277–78; Temple
  ordinances and, 307; Jeremiah
  prophesies against, 369
Gezer, 6
Gibeon, valley of, 245
Gihon Spring, 3, 73–74, 83, 197,
  203
Goat idols, 26

God: presence of, 7; intervention
  of, in human affairs, 22, 253,
  335; protection of, in war, 82;
  power of, 109, 341–42; becoming whole through, 110; Job's
  commentary on, 117–25; Elihu's
  commentary on, 125–27; living
  according to will of, 129–30;
  children of, 134, 455–56; mercy
  of, 148, 152, 179; relationship
  of, with covenant people, 150–
  52, 153, 280, 286–87, 300–303,
  380–81; expectations of, 165;
  Isaiah sees, 174; glory of, 175,
  320; seeking, 204; returning to,
  213; sovereignty of, 222; turning to, 249; those who dwell
  with, 250; greatness of, 257–58;
  name-titles of, 262, 264; ac-
  knowledgement of, 287; sacrifices Son, 298–99; thoughts of,
  305–6; word of, 306, 376–77;
  nature of, 360
Goethe, Johann Wolfgang von, 171
Gog, 391–93. *See also* Armageddon
Gomer, 149, 151–52
Good, distinguishing between evil
  and, 194–95
Government, constitutional, 184
Gozan, 71
Grant, Heber J., 131–32
Grass: humans compared to, 256;
  symbolism of, 283–84

Ha-alma, 199
Habakkuk (book), 334–35
Habor, 71
Hadassah, 431, 437
Haggai (book), 415
Hair, shaving, 201, 378
Halevi, Yehuda, 98
Hallelujah, 222
Haman, 432–36
Hananiah, 362, 398
Hand: stretched out, 210–11; right,
  273